War and Society in Colonial India

Oxford in India Readings

Themes in Indian History

Available in the Series

David Ludden (ed.)	*Agricultural Production and South Asian History* (OIP)
P.J. Marshall (ed.)	*The Eighteenth Century in Indian History: Evolution or Revolution?* (OIP)
Ranbir Chakravarti (ed.)	*Trade in Early India* (OIP)
Aloka Parasher-Sen (ed.)	*Subordinate and Marginal Groups in Early India*
Ian J. Kerr (ed.)	*Railways in Modern India* (OIP)
Jos J. L. Gommans and Dirk H. A. Kolff (eds)	*Warfare and Weaponry in South Asia 1000–1800* (OIP)
Richard Eaton (ed.)	*India's Islamic Traditions, 711–1750* (OIP)
Muzaffar Alam and Sanjay Subrahmanyam (eds)	*The Mughal State 1526–1750* (OIP)
Michael H. Fisher (ed.)	*The Politics of the British Annexation of India 1757–1857* (OIP)
Mushirul Hasan (ed.)	*India's Partition: Process, Strategy and Mobilization* (OIP)
S. Irfan Habib and Dhruv Raina (eds)	*Social History of Science* (forthcoming)

War and Society in Colonial India
1807–1945

edited by
Kaushik Roy

OXFORD
UNIVERSITY PRESS

OXFORD
UNIVERSITY PRESS

YMCA Library Building, Jai Singh Road, New Delhi 110001

Oxford University Press is a department of the University of Oxford. It furthers the University's objective of excellence in research, scholarship, and education by publishing worldwide in

Oxford New York
Auckland Cape Town Dar es Salaam Hong Kong Karachi
Kuala Lumpur Madrid Melbourne Mexico City Nairobi
New Delhi Shanghai Taipei Toronto

With offices in
Argentina Austria Brazil Chile Czech Republic France Greece
Guatemala Hungary Italy Japan Poland Portugal Singapore
South Korea Switzerland Thailand Turkey Ukraine Vietnam

Oxford is a registered trade mark of Oxford University Press
in the UK and in certain other countries

Published in India
by Oxford University Press, New Delhi

First published 2006

ISBN-13: 978-0-19-568149-9
ISBN-10: 0-19-568149-5

Typeset in Goshen 9.5/12
By Jojy Philip, Delhi 110 015
Printed at Sai Printopack Pvt. Ltd., New Delhi 110 020
Published by Oxford University Press
YMCA Library Building, Jai Singh Road, New Delhi 110 001

Contents

Series Note

The series focuses on important themes in Indian history, on those which have long been the subject of interest and debate, or which have acquired importance more recently.

Each volume in the series consists of, first, a detailed Introduction; second, a careful choice of the essays and book-extracts vital to a proper understanding of the theme; and, finally, an Annotated Bibliography.

Using this consistent format, each volume seeks as a whole to critically assess the state of the art on its theme, chart the historiographical shifts that have occurred since the theme emerged, rethink old problems, open up questions which were considered closed, locate the theme within wider historiographical debates, and pose new issues of inquiry by which further work may be made possible.

Preface

The present volume initially started as a sequel to *The British Raj and its Indian Armed Forces: 1857–1939*, edited by late Professor Partha Sarathi Gupta and Anirudh Deshpande, and published by Oxford University Press, New Delhi, in 2002. More than five years ago, a small group of researchers decided to bring out a series on the impact of armies and warfare on colonial Indian state and society. P. S. Gupta agreed to provide leadership to this ambitious project. Unfortunately, he passed away before the first volume saw the light of the day.

However, the response it ultimately received from several historians all over the world encouraged us to proceed with the second volume. Some of the contributors to the first volume have also written essays for the second volume; we have also included new essayists since the aim was to cast the net as wide as possible.The editor regrets being unable to include some notable published articles on account of copyright problems. He thanks all the contributors for making this volume possible.

In 2001, as part of the Themes in Indian History series, a volume on Indian military history titled *Warfare and Weaponry in South Asia: 1000–1800*, edited by Jos J. L. Gommans and Dirk H. A. Kolff was published by Oxford University Press. The present volume centring on the themes of war, state, and colonial society begins with the nineteenth century and carries the story forward to 1945. The principal objective is to analyse the colonial state's armies multidimensionally. The attempt is to integrate traditional military history with broader social and cultural studies. This volume, unlike other volumes in the Themes in Indian History series, has an added advantage—in addition to landmark pieces reprinted, fresh articles provide the reader the latest research on the subject.

Kaushik Roy
Kolkata

Acknowledgements

The editor and publisher would like to thank the following for permission to include these articles in this volume.

Rudrangshu Mukherjee and Manohar Publishers for 'The Sepoy Mutinies Revisited', in Mushirul Hasan and Narayani Gupta (eds), *India's Colonial Encounter: Essays in Memory of Eric Stokes*, New Delhi: Manohar Publishers, 1993; reprint 2004, pp. 193–204.

Stephen P. Cohen for 'The Military Enters Indian Thought', in *The Indian Army: Its Contribution to the Development of a Nation*, Stephen P. Cohen, New Delhi: Oxford University Press, 1990; reprint 1991, pp. 57–87.

Anirudh Deshpande and Nehru Memorial Museum and Library (NMML), New Delhi, for 'Contested Identities and Military Indianization in Colonial India (1900-39)', *Contemporary India*, 1(1), January–March 2002, pp. 99–131. © 2002, NMML.

Lionel Caplan for 'Martial Gurkhas: The Persistence of a British Military Discourse on "Race"', in Peter Robb (ed.), *The Concept of Race in South Asia*, New Delhi: Oxford University Press, 1995, pp. 260–81.

'The Shiver of 1942', originally published in *Studies in History*, 18(1). © 2002, Jawaharlal Nehru University, New Delhi. All rights reserved. Reproduced with the permission of the copyright holders and the publishers, Sage Publications India Pvt. Ltd, New Delhi.

Introduction
Armies, Warfare, and Society in Colonial India

Kaushik Roy

> Again, since Moghul times, the saying that 'He who holds the army holds India', has held true and probably holds true [even] now when India is a Republic.
>
> —Lieutenant General G. N. Molesworth[1]

Rarely do we recognize the importance of armies and warfare in shaping the course of modern Indian history. The Army in India, which included the Sepoy Army commanded by British officers as well as the British units stationed in the Subcontinent, had a dominating presence in the colonial era. Till the 1890s, the Sepoy Army included the Bombay Army, Madras Army, Bengal Army, and the Punjab Frontier Force. The Sepoy Army, or the British-Indian Army, offered the most government employment to the colonized Indians. Annually, the Sepoy Army, or colonial army, enlisted about 15,000 Indians in peacetime.[2] During World War II, about 2.5 million Indians were enlisted in the army. Indeed, the colonial army was the biggest item of expenditure for the colonial regime. About 30 per cent of the British-Indian Empire's revenue went to feed the military establishment in the Subcontinent.[3] Military service moulded the structure and ethos of colonial Indian society. Certain cultural traits that continue to operate in independent India were chiefly the products of rituals and symbols introduced by the Sepoy Army. For instance, the turbaned Sikh and the kukri-wielding Gurkha identities were to a great extent shaped by colonial military service. The Indian armed forces during the World War II and in its immediate aftermath set the pace for decolonization. Mass expansion of the colonial army and rapid Indianization of the officer corps between 1939 and 1945 resulted in the disintegration of the imperial loyalty mechanism. The military legacy of the Raj continues to shape post-colonial polity. Ironically, World War II forced the colonial state to create a quasi-modern military organization which was inherited and which, with certain modifications, has been ably used by the post-colonial state. Nevertheless, colonial India's military history remains relegated to the footnotes of historiography.

The historiography of modern India is characterized by four dominant schools of thought.[4] From the 1970s, the Cambridge School focused on the faction politics of Indian nationalism. The assumption is that the Raj's policies shaped the reactions of the various camps within the national movement. In contrast to the Cambridge School, the Nationalist–Marxist group over-emphasizes the impact of the Gandhian Congress's mass movements in achieving freedom. The decolonization in 1947 is projected as the telos of the history of the 'heroic' Indian independence struggle. This in turn establishes a narrative perspective on preceding Congress mass movements. Then earlier conflicts such as the Non-Cooperation and Civil Disobedience movements are framed as efforts in anticipation of freedom, which found its fulfilment in 1947. From the 1980s, the Subaltern perspective has argued for micro studies of local society. In this paradigm, the agency for historical change remains with the small marginal communities. And in this framework it is not essential that micro studies should always supplement the macro picture. Within Subaltern studies, there has been a shift from analysing the resistance of peasants, workers, and tribes, to the discourse of power–knowledge in the colonial setting. This brings us to the latest intervention in Indian history, that is, the Cultural Studies group. Influenced by post-modernism, they offer a post-colonial critique of the documentation and published literature generated by colonial agencies. They challenge the very role of 'evidence'. For Michel Foucault, power relations lie at the core of production and dissemination of knowledge.[5] Hence, instead of archival research, this group focuses on sophisticated theories and literary criticism. From the 1990s, various new branches of history writing—such as the history of environment, history of medicine, history of science and technology, etc.—have emerged. Despite the presence of numerous scattered studies, military history as a sub-branch of academic history writing is yet to emerge in India.

The present collection of essays (including both the unpublished and some reprints) is an attempt to redress this lacunae. This volume includes six fresh essays based on primary sources, and five landmark reprint pieces that bring into focus the various dimensions of the colonial military infrastructure between 1807 and 1945. Spatially and temporally, these essays cover a wide canvas. Since the role of the Royal Indian Navy and the Royal Indian Air Force were miniscule until 1947, none of the essays in this volume will address exclusively these two services. Again, not much research has been done on the Bombay Army. Apart from that, the essays more or less cover the entirety of India, with special attention to Awadh and Punjab, which were the principal recruiting grounds of the colonial army at various points of its history. Some of the contributors to this volume focus on the principal theatres of deployment of the British-Indian Army—such as North-West Frontier region (presently in Pakistan), Mesopotamia, Burma, Singapore, and Hong Kong. The volume begins with the reorganization initiated after the Vellore Mutiny and ends with the termination of World War II in 1945. The essays are arranged chronologically within broad thematic heads. This collection analyses the complex dialectics between warfare, the British-Indian war machine, and colonial society. The articles not only throw light on the social and cultural dimensions of colonialism, but also assess the nature of the colonial state. Knowledge of the structure of the army clarifies many aspects of the functioning of the Raj. Hence, we categorize these essays as belonging broadly within the 'war, armed forces, and society' approach.

A cross-cultural analysis is attempted to highlight the salient features of the colonial military. The military establishment of British-India was the product of both local forces at the periphery as well as guidance from the metropolitan core. So, what Sanjay Subrahmanyam conceptualizes as 'Connected History' should be useful in studying British-Indian military affairs. One feature of this approach is that the 'history of events' should not be neglected at the cost of structuralist perspectives. Subrahmanyam's greatest contribution is to point out that instead of a structuralist–functionalist approach, event-oriented political interpretation is more fruitful. In fact, the tensions between and perceptions of the antagonists could only be captured, writes Subrahmanyam, 'out of the fine grain of events'. As part of the focus on the history of events, scholars—writes Subrahmanyam—should try to locate crises and turning points rather than the structural complex. Another characteristic of Connected History is the partial focus on the role of contingency.[6] More than two decades ago, Walter Kaegi wrote that military history was part of the broader evenemential history, which should also take into account the role of the individual in history and historical contingencies.[7]

In recent times, the New Imperial History also exhibits some features of Connected History. The New Imperial History emphasizes the connections between empire building at the core and the periphery. The imperial culture is portrayed as the hybrid product of cultural exchanges among the metropole and the colonies.[8] Several concepts of Connected History could be traced further back. For example, the concept of the 'dramatic moment of transformation' was present among the colonial military officers-cum-writers. For them, 1857 was one such crisis point. Instead of a structural crisis, the colonial historiography painted 1857 as an accidental convulsion.[9] Then the colonial army's British officers-turned-historians' principal focus remained on the event-oriented political history.

This introduction is divided into five parts. The first section offers a bird's-eye view of the evolution of military history writing, from British India to independent India. The next three sections attempt to locate the essays within the wider military historiographical landscape. The aim is to throw new light on some of the key issues of colonial warfare, and follow the trajectories of various debates regarding the principal aspects of British-Indian military history. The last section of this Introduction points out possibilities for conducting further research from various perspectives that are not covered by the essays presented in this volume. Let us now see how the colonial military officers viewed their army and wrote about it.

The Sepoy Army in History: From Battle Narratives to the Advent of Social History

Compared to ancient and medieval Indian military history, the database for colonial India's military history appears more solid. This is due to the book-keeping activities of the colonial bureaucracy, as well as a host of unofficial monographs and articles written by the colonial military officers recording their 'glorious' activities in an exotic environment. The memoirs and journals of British officers posted in India chronicle the victories of the White men against innumerable odds in an unfamiliar and picturesque environment, filled with colourful flora, fauna, and 'noble savages'. Such materials found a ready market among the British community in the subcontinent and also the general, educated readers in Britain with an interest in India.

The colonial authors suffered from racial prejudice. They developed an obsession with the mutiny of the Bengal Army sepoys in particular, and the peasants of north India in general during 1857. Their objective was to analyse the causes and lessons of 1857. The colonial writers' description of almost two centuries of British rule in India is characterized by teleological assumptions. To them, it seemed that the Raj's duty was to civilize the 'savages'. The continuous development of India as initiated by the British, the colonial writers assumed, was temporarily suspended by the Mutiny of 1857. The rebellion, in their eyes, was due to the inherent backwardness of the Indians, who were incapable of appreciating the modernizing programmes of the British Raj. In the overarcing framework constructed by the colonial military historians, 1857 was an aberration. Otherwise, in general, argued the colonial authors, the Indians served their White masters with loyalty and honesty.

In the view of the colonial military historians, the Indians—due to their racial incapability and 'capricious' nature—were unable to construct professional military machines and stable state structures. The assumption was that the Indians were neither capable of self-defence nor had been able to organize themselves for self-rule. A modern standing army supported by a centralized bureaucratic state was considered as a 'gift' of the British Raj to the Indians.[10] William Irvine claims that in the pre-British era, Indian military forces were not armies but armed mobs characterized by continuous treacheries on the battlefields.[11] Many modern scholars accept the slightly Whigish nature of British rule and a sort of Diffusionist theory as regards the development of the armed forces. In accordance with the Diffusionist theory in military history, the origins of professional militaries must have one source from which they spread to various parts of the world at different points of time.[12] Influenced by such concepts, several recent works assert that the East India Company laid the foundations of a permanent army in India capable of conducting modern warfare. For S. L. Menezes and Pradeep P. Barua, the 200 years of British domination witnessed the continuous unfolding of a process of military development. The course of military professionalism in colonial India, in their paradigm, reached its culmination during World War II, when ironically British rule entered the twilight zone of its existence.[13]

Most of the British officers-turned-military-historians wrote battle-centric history. The continuous victories of the colonial army against both Indian and foreign enemies was regarded as somewhat inevitable, a sort of 'manifest destiny' on part of the British to rule the subcontinent.[14] The most celebrated of these battle-centric histories is Colonel G. B. Malleson's *The Decisive Battles of India*. A strong utilitarian streak characterizes such work. In 1885, while writing the introduction to his second edition, Malleson reminded his readers:

> When the first edition of this work appeared, two years ago, the dark cloud now threatening our Indian Empire was but a little speck on the horizon, no bigger than a man's hand. The book simply—to use the expression of the critics—told the story of how we had won India. We are now entering upon a period when we shall be called upon to defend the Empire we so greatly gained. Upon this point let there be no mistake in the public mind. Let us at least be honest to our own consciences.[15]

A large number of the colonial officers exhibited Malleson's 'enemy at the gates' syndrome while writing. The works of most of the colonial British officers were a sort of didactic literature. They aimed to provide an exact knowledge of the past which would aid the British rulers to chart their progress through the troublesome future.

The utilitarian aspect is most prominent in the case of small unit histories recording the admirable accomplishments of the 'bands of brothers'. The commanding officers used to write victorious sagas of the different armies[16] and various regiments. The 'glorious saga' of the units' triumphs against all odds, and the increasing technological sophistication of the various branches of military organization was chronicled in order to motivate recruits to emulate the heroic deeds of their predecessors in famous units. Such chronicles did not include the unheroic histories of the regiments, that is, cases of desertion, fragging, mutinies, rape, and retreat. The tradition of gallant regimental histories written by the regimental commanders continues to be encouraged in the post-colonial Indian Army.[17]

The colonial officers' campaign histories portray the Sepoy Army not only as securing India for the British, but also as an instrument of power projection throughout the British Empire. They painted the Sepoy Army as an imperial strategic reserve used for protecting the various parts of British Empire. Brigadier General F. J. Moberly and Colonel R. Evans show how the Indian contingents established British presence in Mesopotamia during World War I.[18]

The multi-volume *Official History of the Indian Armed Forces in the Second World War* under the editorial leadership of Bisheshwar Prasad somewhat continues in the vein of the 'blood and guts' version of colonial historiography. Prasad and his team depict the Indian Army as surpassing all difficulties despite facing a multitude of problems, and going on to win victories in different parts of the world. However, there is a slight distinction to be made here. Unlike the British military officers-turned-historians, Prasad and his followers give most of the credit not to the sahibs but to the *jawans* and their Indian officers. Since Prasad represents the official line, his edited volumes give no space to the voice of dissent, of grievances among the Indian soldiery, who are projected as professional automatons.

At least some Indians before independence wrote about the British-Indian Army from a critical perspective. They were aware of the adverse economic impact of colonialism. They realized that the British-controlled military establishment in India was proving to be a burden on the country's economy. Captain G. V. Modak, in a monograph published in the 1930s, argued for the replacement of British battalions and the British officers with Indian privates and Indian officers. Modak was one of the earliest Indian proponents of Indianization of the Sepoy Army's officer corps. Such a scheme, asserted Modak, would save not only a lot of government money but would also aid in the fact that defence would rest upon the sons of the soil.[19]

Nevertheless, it would be wrong to assume that the amateur colonial historians generated only Drums and Button histories. From the late nineteenth century onwards, some of the British military officials associated with the colonial army started producing ethnographic handbooks. The ethnological studies conducted by the Sepoy Army's officers were somewhat influenced by the works of colonial anthropologists such as H. H. Risley. The production of ethnographical handbooks[20] on the various Indian communities was part of the Raj's policy of 'knowing the Other'. The objective was gathering of data regarding the various communities' social and cultural mores, to aid the British task of governance. These handbooks somewhat bridged the gap between the earlier battle-oriented narrative histories of the Raj's military officers, and the social and cultural histories of the army that began to be written from the late twentieth century onwards.

In recent times, the dominant approach in British-Indian military history writing is Army and Society Studies. The somewhat related

War and Society approach is also dominant when one scans the academic landscape on Western warfare.[21] Probably the rise of social history in the 1980s, both within and outside India, explains the dominance of the Army and Society approach in analysing South Asia's military past. Some scholars have termed it the New Military History of South Asia. There seems to be a parallel with the rise of so-called 'New Social History', associated with the followers of E. P. Thompson in Britain during the 1970s. From the late 1960s in the West, a school started emerging which turned the limelight on the linkages between politics and social relations. This approach later came to be categorized as New Social History.[22] In reality, then, there is little 'new' in the approach of the New Military History. In 1954, Stanislav Andreski first introduced the interpretation that a military organization is shaped by the host society.[23] The focus of this framework is the interaction between various social groups and the military institution. The army is regarded as an institution for the social control of diverse groups. One of the most potent examples of the Army and Society approach, as regards colonial military history, is Seema Alavi's monograph titled *The Sepoys and the Company* (1995). Alavi views the pre-1857 Bengal Army as a vehicle of upward mobility for the *Bhumihars* in *Purab*, the region comprising present day west Bihar and eastern Uttar Pradesh. By providing these communities with enhanced social and economic status in local society, claims Alavi, the colonial state—through the Sepoy Army—was able to co-opt them in establishing its own political dominance.[24] The social reconstruction of the post-1857 Mutiny Sepoy Army has been done ably by David Omissi. In his book, Omissi shows that the British, by modulating their military policy in accordance with the norms of Indian society, were able to mobilize loyal and brave recruits.[25]

Coercion, Discipline, and Dissent in the Sepoy Army

> The Indian soldier has three loyalties: to his home, to his religion, and to his regiment and his officers.
>
> Field Marshal Viscount Slim[26]

Besides recruiting manpower, the colonial army had to manipulate them properly. After all, the Indian recruits had to be trained and motivated to fight Imperial wars. At the core of the army's management techniques for Brown military labourers was the problem of the sepoys' loyalty towards the colonial regime. The colonial army, in the writings of British military officers such as Lieutenant General George MacMunn[27] and Louis Allen,[28] and also in the perspective of most modern scholars, has been categorized as a mercenary force. Both Imperialist historiography[29] and Indian scholarship influenced by liberal Marxism accept that the sepoys and sowars joined the military service for regular wages and pensions. A minority group considers that the sahib–sepoy entente was a complex cultural alliance. For instance, Robert Eric Frykenberg conceives the sepoys' loyalty to the sahibs within the traditional Indian cultural norm of *namak halali*, that is, loyalty to the salt-giver.[30] Frykenberg is somewhat influenced by the anthropologists' argument that peoples belonging to different cultures possess distinct value systems.[31] So the sepoys' loyalty could not be construed as a Western contract system based merely on tangible incentives. Among the contributors of this volume, Kaushik Roy, Sabyasachi Dasgupta, and Saul David consider the sepoys as more or less mercenaries. In contrast, Rudrangshu Mukherjee and Chandar S. Sundaram view the sepoys and sowars of the British-Indian Army as imbued with a sense of nationalism which occasionally went against the imperial logic.

Despite the questionable loyalty of the colonial soldiers, the Raj required Indian military manpower for several reasons. First, the Indian troops were more healthy compared to the White troops for deployment within the Subcontinent. Throughout the first half of the nineteenth century, more than 30 per cent of the European soldiers in India were hospitalized at any given moment.[32] The same imperative forced the Dutch to recruit indigenous soldiers in Indonesia. As early as the seventeenth century, the Dutch found out that the European soldiers were dying too quickly in battling 'Mother Nature' in the Moluccas.[33] Second, Indian soldiers were four times cheaper than White troops.[34] Hence, utilization of colonial manpower for military purpose was a necessity and not a luxury for the imperial powers.

The Sepoy Army was composed of long-service volunteers. The eighteenth-century Prussian Army was also composed of long-service soldiers, but they were conscripts rather than volunteers.[35] Due to the massive demographic resources of India and for political reasons, the colonial polity never resorted to conscription in India. In the mid-nineteenth century, following Prussia's example, the West European armies went for the short-service mass army model of the elder Moltke. However, the Sepoy Army remained wedded to the long-service volunteer-soldier framework. The four essays by Roy-Dasgupta, David, Mukherjee, and Sundaram in this volume focus on the loyalty mechanism of the quasi-mercenary Indian volunteer Army. The dynamics of fidelity and cooperation between the White officers and the Brown soldiers is the theme of these essays. The contributors turn the spotlight on the complex interaction between Indian society, the sepoys, and the Raj's military officers.

The British officers of the colonial regime, and many modern historians too, assumed that the crux of the sepoys' loyalty to the colonial army lay in the shadowy sahib–sepoy relationship.[36] While one group of historians notes that gradual relaxation of the penal system under an incompetent White officer corps resulted in the 1857 Mutiny, another bunch of scholars claim that the increasing autocracy of the sahibs resulted in the collapse of the fragile sahib–sepoy entente. Modern scholars presume that the White officer corps constituted the brain of the army. They argue that the capability of the sahibs to control the sepoys was the barometer of their professionalism. American political scientist, Stephen P. Cohen, in his monograph on the Indian Army, analyses the evolution of professionalism among the officers of the Sepoy Army.[37] A colonial bureaucrat-turned-scholar, Philip Mason portrays the professionalism of the sahibs as the amalgamation of Victorian paternalism and British gallantry.[38] In contrast, Rudrangshu Mukherjee argues that the sahib–sepoy relationship was based on violence inflicted by the racially prejudiced, merciless sahibs on the ill-paid sepoys.[39] From Mason viewing the sahibs as *mai-bap* to the sepoys, to Mukherjee arguing that the British officers were more or less sadists, the pendulum has registered a complete swing. The American historian Lorenzo M. Crowell advances a more balanced view. He comes up with the concept of colonial professionalism. While Cohen, Mason, and Mukherjee concentrate principally on the Bengal Army, Crowell turns the limelight on the Madras Army. Crowell asserts that in the colonial context, the British officers of the pre-1857 Madras Army were quite professional. They were sensitive to the Brown soldiers' linguistic and material needs.[40] And this probably prevented any mutiny in the Madras Army during 1857.

Proponents of Agrarian and Social History dominate the historiography of 1857. The common assumption of these followers of social history is that the social background of the protagonists shaped their deeds. Historians have poured out a lot of ink over the social composition of the Bengal Army. Most scholars agree that the

Bengal Army was composed of the north Indian, land-owning, high castes. The young American historian James W. Hoover provides a useful corrective to the view that the Bengal Army's sepoys came exclusively from the land-owning high castes.[41] The spokespersons of the Agrarian School view the 1857 Mutiny in terms of a massive agrarian uprising: the differential impact of the Company's agrarian programme on north India's rural society is considered the principal factor behind the 1857 uprising. For Eric Stokes, the agrarian uprising was due to the culmination of profound causes (ecology, economic changes, and caste groupings, etc.), while the military uprising was merely a side show, a prelude to the real drama.[42] Nevertheless, C. Bayly accepts that the timing and duration of the 1857 uprising were to a large extent shaped by the military mutinies.[43] Here lies the importance of analysing the origin of military mutinies.

However, both the spokespersons of Agrarian History[44] and Subaltern historiography push the notion that the sepoys were merely peasants in uniform. The concept of a sepoy–peasant continuum continues to dominate works dealing with the social history of the Bengal Army.[45] Mukherjee's essay in this volume, which leans somewhat to the Subaltern history paradigm, pushes this view with admirable dexterity. Influenced by Antonio Gramsci, Mukherjee asserts that the sepoys' rebellious consciousness had much in common with the mentality of the rebel peasants. Followers of the Subaltern approach such as Mukherjee and Tapti Roy accept Thompson's opinion that the downtrodden people's consciousness, shaped by their own experience, influenced the course of history.[46] Thompson's 'working class' becomes 'people' in the Subaltern model. For Tapti Roy, the category 'people' includes both the elites (such as rajas, *thakurs*, and zamindars) as well as the exploited groups (such as the peasants and soldiers) of the colonized society. Since the methodology of Subaltern studies is that of 'bottom-up' history, Tapti Roy in her case study of Bundelkhand during 1857 asserts that it was the 'lower' groups who influenced the actions of the elites of colonial society. In the paradigm of Subaltern history, the 'rebellious' activities of the sepoys and sowars during 1857 converged with the rebellious activities of the 'people'. In other words, the sepoy rebellion is considered part and parcel of the multilayered popular rebellion that swept through British India in 1857.[47]

From the opposite pole, the Organizational History of the army as represented by Roy-Dasgupta, David, and Sundaram's essays in this volume, as well as the work of Maya Gupta on the Vellore Mutiny,[48] challenge this neat notion of amalgamating the ideas and actions of the 'rebel' sepoys with the rebellious peasants. The Organizational approach's focus is on the service conditions within the military establishment. In the framework of Organizational Studies, soldiers rebel when their service conditions deteriorate or when military personnel band together and use pressure tactics to gain more privileges from the military bureaucracy. Roy and Dasgupta's comparative analysis of the Bengal and Madras armies in their joint article shows that repeated mutinies and indiscipline during the first half of the nineteenth century rocked both forces. Roy and Dasgupta agree with MacMunn's view that the withdrawal of efficient British officers away from the regiments to mann the state's bureaucracy, and the centralizing mania of the Company state resulted in the breakdown of loyalty bonds the Bengal sepoys.[49] Roy and Dasgupta assent in part to the nineteenth-century British officers' view that the withdrawal of the summary power of punishment from the hands of the commanding officers encouraged the sepoys to challenge military authority.[50]

However, at least some British officials empathized with the sepoys. Colonel Keith Young, Judge Advocate General of the Bengal Army, in a letter dated 24 March 1857, wrote to Colonel H. B. Henderson: 'So far as we know yet, the whole business has been caused by an idea that got into the men's heads that pig's and cow's fat was used in the preparation of the cartridges for the Enfield rifles, and I believe that there was some foundation for the report.'[51] Malleson, a colonial historian of the late nineteenth century, claimed that the greased cartridge was not the real issue behind the 1857 uprising.[52] David shows how the sepoys used it as a mere pretext for rebellion. Malleson goes on to say that the mutinies of the Sepoy Army before 1857 were different from the 1857 uprising. The pre-1857 mutinies, according to him, were the product of local and temporary disaffections; but the 1857 Mutiny was the culmination of quasi-patriotic feelings.[53] Mukherjee's essay in this volume shows that a sort of pre-national patriotism was an important motivational force among the rebel sepoys in 1857. As to the debate on whether 1857 was the product of contingent and local factors or the culmination of long-term structural factors, the jury is still out.

It must be noted that there were certain similarities as well as dissimilarities between the various colonial and metropolitan armies. The American-led Filipino Scouts recruited Filipinos, and the new recruits were vouched for by the senior scouts.[54] Similarly, in the Sepoy Army, the senior soldiers stood as guarantors for the good behaviour of raw recruits when the latter were enlisted. Partly due to Benthamite legislation,[55] and partly by way of the imperial attempt to hit the sepoys' sense of honour rather than their bodies,[56] the penal system of the Sepoy Army in the post-1857 era was quite humane when compared to other armies of the late nineteenth century.[57] While runaway slaves and marginal elements joined the colonial African armies,[58] the Sepoy Army recruited men of substance with an inherent sense of honour. Rather than the lash, the imperial attempt was to retain the loyalty of the soldiers with monetary and non-monetary incentives.[59] It is to be noted that British-led African soldiers, unlike the sepoys and the sowars, were denied pensions. Again, corporal punishment was abolished in the King's African Rifles only after World War II.[60] In contrast, corporal punishment in the Sepoy Army was on its way out during the second half of the nineteenth century. Roy-Dasgupta's essay refers to the debate regarding corporal punishment in the Company's armies before 1857.

The point is that despite the colonial officers' emphasis on the honour and justice of the White men serving in India, the British soldiers serving in the subcontinent also proved troublesome for the military authorities. Two years after the 'Sepoy Mutiny' of 1857, the Raj experienced the White Mutiny. Like the *Purbiyas*, the high caste recruited from Purab, of the Bengal Army, the clerks and artisans of Britain also joined the Company's White regiments for upward mobility. Peter Stanley shows that educated personnel among the Bengal Europeans provided leadership to the White mutineers.[61] Again, the hypothesis equating pecuniary gains with the motivation of 'mercenary' soldiery as typically colonial is problematic. Rather than nationalism, the Tommies also fought for monetary rewards. Raffi Gregorian's article and Richard Holmes' quasi popular monograph shows that in the nineteenth century, when the British troops were dissatisfied with financial rewards, they did not hesitate to revolt.[62] So, whether it was White, Brown, or Black personnel, mutinies or disobedience and their connection with service conditions was inherent in all military organizations.

After 1857, the contradiction between the professional grievances of the sepoys and their loyalty again emerged during World War II. That British racial discrimination of the Indian soldiers resulted in the scattering of seeds of disloyalty among the sepoys during the 1940–1 campaign in South-East Asia is accepted by Louis Allen.[63]

Memoirs of the Indian officers also point to the colour bar that operated in wartime Malaysia.[64] Furthermore, inadequate training was responsible for the poor performance of the Indian divisions in South-East Asia during the opening stages of World War II. Thus, the morale of the jawans was poor.[65] In one of his essays, Sundaram points out that the Brown soldiers and the Brown commissioned officers were in a state of transformation as well. They were influenced by English ideals of fairness, equality, and democracy.[66] Sundaram's piece in this volume portrays the dissent and the emergence of nationalism among Brown soldiers and officers in 1940–1. And the memoirs of participants tend to support his position. For instance, Indar Jit Rikhye, who served in the 6th Lancers during World War II, points to political consciousness among the Indian officer corps.[67]

Military Culture and Society

The assumption common to proponents of the War and Society perspective is that armies are mirror images of their host societies. American political scientist Stephen Peter Rosen, operating within the War and Society approach, applies the *longue duree* perspective. He views armies in India from the Vedic age to the nuclear age as products of caste fragmentation in Indian society.[68] A similar approach (though somewhat restricted in time frame) is that of Dutch historian Dirk Kolff, depicting the Indian armies between 1450 and 1850 as social formations shaped by demographic pressure. Kolff claims that it was the culture of military service that shaped society by influencing caste formations.[69] It is interesting to note that both Rosen's and Kolff's models isolate a key determinant shaping Indian history. For Rosen, it is the unchangeable caste system; in Kolff's framework, the crucial determinant was the vast demographic resource of India. In the eyes of the two historians, these key determinants have been raised to the status of a Braudelian key determinant —geography. In Braudelian framework, geography is the principal driver behind historical forces.

Caste and race, assumed colonial ethnographers, were the principal ingredients of Indian history, and had divided Indian society hopelessly. The new scholarly term for 'race' seems to be 'ethnicity' which was introduced into academic discourse by American political sociologists. For Rosen, Indian society is characterized by caste divisiveness. Hence, the colonial army remained an agglomeration of various castes. In somewhat similar tune, DeWitt C. Ellinwood and Cynthia H. Enloe, following the Historical–Sociological approach, argue that Indian society is ethnically fragmented. Ethnic identity is the product of primordial attachments resulting from religion, culture, language, and political influence. So the Sepoy Army, assert Ellinwood and Enloe, reflected ethnic imbalances.[70] For Rosen, divisions in the host society were automatically reflected in the army. Unlike Rosen, Enloe gives space to the programmes of the power elites. For Enloe, the degree and nature of ethnic imbalances in the armies were to an extent shaped by the politicians in power.[71] In an article Omissi notes that the ethnic make-up of the colonial army was not only shaped by the policies of the politicians and the generals, but also by the attitudes of the ethnic communities of the Subcontinent. Only those ethnic groups who calculated that they would gain from military service joined the army. So the ethnic make-up of the colonial forces was the result of a fusion of the policies of colonial strategists and the dispositions of the various ethnic groups.[72] In a plural social set-up (in an ethnically heterogeneous society), ethnicity has enormous social and political importance. In a way, ethnic policies are the products of political manipulations as well as 'natural' divisions within a society.[73] The presence of ethnic communities with distinct characteristics, and jostling for power within the military bureaucracy, reminds one of Namierite factions. This is because the advocates of ethnicity accept that ethnic identities are closely related to interest-group orientations.[74] For political sociologists, ethnic politics paves the way for political socialization and subsequent mobilization.[75] The persistence of ethnic groups which are leftovers from the pre-colonial state system even in modern armies[76] somewhat challenges the Modernization theory.

A group of scholars within the War and Society framework view the army as a modernizing agency which transformed the peasant recruits into progressive individuals. This group could be categorized as the Modernization School. The Modernization theory became popular with American political scientists during the 1960s.[77] Ellinwood and S. D. Pradhan widen the analytical frame of the Modernization theory, and claim that mobilization for global warfare not only modified the social relationship and mentality of the soldiers, but also transformed colonial society as a whole.[78] Ellinwood, in an essay written in the 1970s, argues that military service during the World War I transformed the rustic Punjabis into modern men.[79]

The Modernization theorists occasionally view the army as modernizing the state apparatus and culture of the marginal groups such as women, lower castes, and untouchables. Carol Hills and Daniel C. Silverman write that the Indian National Army of Subhas Chandra Bose functioned as a catalyst, modernizing those Hindu Tamil women of South-East Asia who joined the Azad Hind Fauj's Rani of Jhansi Regiment between 1943–5.[80] In Cohen's view, during emergencies the colonial army functioned as an instrument of modernization for the low castes.[81]

In recent times, the idea of the positive impact of military service on wider social formations has been challenged. One scholar who has studied twentieth-century colonial African soldiers critiques the interpretation that the army functions as an instrument of social change.[82] The rise of Cultural Studies, or New Cultural History, with its focus on mass/popular culture and concern with the daily lives of common people, challenges the Modernization theory. The Cultural Studies approach emphasizes the assumptions, perceptions, expectations, and values of the common man. The agenda of Cultural Studies highlights the day-to-day activities of ordinary people, which were previously regarded as trivial.[83] To an extent, Cultural Studies has been influenced by Thompson's assumption that ordinary people shape history through their everyday experience.[84] It is essential to note that the colonial British officers, while writing the military handbooks in their attempt to study the various races and castes of India, collected data on the marriage patterns, dietary habits, occupational activities, etc., of the various groups they targetted for recruitment.[85] So one can establish a tenuous connection between the proponents of contemporary Cultural Studies and the colonial ethnographers of the Sepoy Army.

Cultural Studies, being a part of the post-colonial critique of academics' existing methodologies is linked to Edward Said's deconstruction of the imperial construct of 'Orientalism'. The binary division between the imperial 'Self' and the colonized 'Other', as put forward in Said's thought-provoking book *Orientalism* (1978),[86] has largely influenced those who have undertaken a cultural analysis of the colonial military. Rather than ethnicity, some scholars argue that the construction of the late-eighteenth century sepoys was due to an amalgam of British views of the 'Orient' with India's social and cultural reality. One such historian is Channa Wickremesekera.[87] Another Indian historian, Premansu Kumar Bandopadhyay views the early-nineteenth century Bengal sepoy as a symbol of north India's high-caste society burdened by a lot of the cultural baggage associated with Hinduism.[88] The continuous dialectics between Indian society and culture, and British military organization, as Vivien Ashima Kaul shows, continued even in the late nineteenth century. In fact, the Westernized military system absorbed various Indian customs in the process of its intrusion into indigenous society.[89]

Wherever the Sepoy Army operated, it left behind a host of cultural paraphernalia. The imperial construct of certain indigenous soldiers as belonging to the 'martial races' was probably the most ambitious cultural–anthropological project undertaken by the Raj in the late nineteenth century. Naturally, the Martial Race theory attracted many scholars.[90] British officers were at the forefront of acquisition and dissemination of knowledge, both about India's animate and inanimate objects. In the mid-nineteenth century, Douglas M. Peers shows, how the British, while constructing the Sepoy Army, introduced the category of 'race', which replaced the category of 'caste', hitherto used for interpreting colonial society.[91] If one replaces the word 'nation' with 'race' in Benedict Anderson's frame, then the 'martial races' could be categorized as 'imagined communities'. The so-called martial communities of the Raj were also cultural artefacts.[92] Lionel Caplan, an anthropologist somewhat inspired by Said, rightly claims that the British military officers' writings about the 'martial races' was a sort of Orientalist project, and the resultant discourse involved power equations between the colonizers and the colonized. Through the special exercise of power, the Oriental 'Other', that is, the inferiors, were transformed into a cherished pet, that is, the childlike soldiers of the Raj. Nevertheless, writes Caplan, unlike the Orientalists' argument, the British officers did not always stress the 'Otherness' of the Gurkhas. At times, the British military writings highlighted the elements of 'Self' present in the Gurkhas.[93] Kate Teltscher says that, contrary to Said's concept of Orientalism, British writings about Indians were contradictory, competing, as well as fragmentary.[94] All these attributes could be applied to the case of the Martial Race ideology, which was neither monolithic nor coherent. While Barua and Mary Des Chene analyse the foreign elements that went into the making of the Martial Race doctrine,[95] Philip Constable scrutinizes the indigenous elements embedded in this theory in the context of west India.[96] Ellinwood, in one of his essays, claims that the Martial Race theory was a concoction of

British ideas on race and India's social distinctions.[97] In contrast, Roy has seen the evolution of the Martial Race theory as mostly the product of a factional struggle within the army.[98]

Martial identities are backed up by traditions. The Functionalist approach adopted by a group of scholars asserts that traditions were manufactured by institutions controlled by politicians.[99] In one article, John Keegan narrates how regimental genealogies and culture were invented by the Western military institutions through a complex amalgam of dress and public rituals.[100] Roy, in one of his articles, shows how the imported British regimental organization selected, appropriated, and invented certain social and cultural mores of Indian society for constructing the martial identities of Sikhs and Gurkhas.[101]

Ellinwood's essay in this volume shows the parallel flowering of the Martial Race theory and a sort of indigenous martial–manly concept among the Rajputs of Rajasthan. Ellinwood's essay is an exercise in the History of Ideas. He compares and contrasts the intellectual climate of the British-Indian Army's White officer corps with the mentality and ethos of Rajput society. The Rajput 'martial' culture was symbolized by an officer of the Sepoy Army named Amar Singh. Ellinwood, S. I. Rudolph, and L. I. Rudolph use the concept of liminality to explain Amar Singh's views as presented in his diary. The theory of liminality is borrowed from the works of sociologist Victor Turner. In the view of the Rudolphs and Ellinwood, Amar Singh interacted both with the Western culture represented by the White officer corps of the Sepoy Army as well as the Rajput culture as typified by the thakurs. Amar Singh accepted and rejected elements from both these cultures. He was thus in a 'liminal' state and engaged in a dialogue while facing these contradictory cultures simultaneously.[102] How far the elite Rajput military ethos could be considered a counter-culture to the British-Indian military-sponsored Martial Race theory remains open to question. Interestingly, Ellinwood's article in this volume shows several similarities between the British-sponsored Martial Race theory, and the Rajput ideas of manliness and a soldiering ethos.

New Imperial History highlights British imperialism as a cultural phenomenon which moulded the colonial societies' cultural ethos. This perspective attempts to evolve a socio-cultural approach involving cross-disciplinary works on popular culture, children's literature, media studies, art history, religion, and sports history. The emphasis remains on migration and race.[103] An example of New Imperial

History is Thomas R. Metcalf's essay, in which he claims that the British Empire in Afro-Asia sustained the global network of migration, with India at the centre. The Sikh community and the Martial Race ideology spread from India to South-East Asia and along the eastern coast of Africa. Metcalf, in what could be categorized as a sort of Connected History, shows how the Martial Race theory exported from India shaped the social composition of the security service of Hong Kong, Perak, etc.[104]

The feminists operating within the paradigm of New Imperial History throw light on new dimensions of the colonial army's ideologies. For the feminists, the Martial Race discourse was also an expression of racial super-masculinity. Heather Streets argues that the Martial Race discourse developed in response to the challenge posed by feminists and nationalists in Britain and in India during the late nineteenth century. The feminists in Britain emphasized drunkenness, prostitution, and poor health in the army. In opposition, the Martial Race doctrine portrayed the Gurkhas, Sikhs, and Highlanders as loyal, obedient, healthy, and masculine soldiers with a strong streak of morality. It is to be noted that the nationalists of Ireland and India who were challenging British imperialism were regarded as ungrateful, child-like, and feminine. The language of the 'martial races', continues Streets, was a discursive tool. It appealed to the racial and gendered language for political purposes.[105] Caplan, in his piece in this volume, shows that not only the inhabitants of particular regions, but also those very regions, were categorized as martial. The British officers believed in the Gurkhas being hill-bred, hence martial, people. By contrast, the Hindus from the north Indian plains were categorized as effeminate. So in the eyes of the British officers, while the Gangetic plains represented feminine characteristics, the Himalayas of Nepal stood for masculinity. Ellinwood notes the inter-relationship between gender and race in Rajput-generated martial culture in his essay in this volume. One could make a case that most armies apply their own concept of 'martialness' to the elite units; and such concepts of martiality always stress hyper-masculinity.[106]

The influence of racial prejudice and the Martial Race ideology on the imperial policy towards Indianization of the colonial army's officer corps continues to divide historians. While one group of historians, following the Whig methodology, claims that the British were following a consistent policy of Indianization of the Sepoy Army's officer corps from the very beginning, others challenge this notion. According to Barua, the structuring principle of the history of British rule was the master narrative of controlled devolution of power to the Indians under imperial guidance.[107] This grand narrative becomes an exercise in teleological thinking. In opposition, somewhat influenced by the nationalist historiography, P. S. Gupta, Chandar S. Sundaram, Gautam Sharma, and Anirudh Deshpande view the Martial Race theory purely in instrumental terms. The British were unwilling to open the officer corps to the Indians. Even a minority group of British officials, shows Sundaram, failed to overcome the opposition of the 'official mind of imperialism' to induct the traditional 'martial' groups as commissioned officers in the late nineteenth century. But due to the pressure of Indian nationalism, the imperialists were forced to give limited concessions from the 1920s. Then the imperial attempt was to confine Indianization to the 'martial races', who were supposed to be more loyal and brave than the university-educated, urban, middle-class babus infected with the 'virus' of nationalism.[108] William Gutteridge's article[109] and Cohen's essay in this volume take something of a middle-of-the-road view: Cohen argues that the complex process of Indianization was shaped by a traditional militarism in Indian society and an instrumental gradualism of the imperialists, somewhat instigated by the Moderate Indian nationalists.

From Small War to World War

The world during the first half of the twentieth century witnessed two global wars which modern scholars categorize as examples of 'total war'.[110] The two World Wars resulted in expansion of state powers and 'forced' industrialization in at least some countries. For the Army in India also, this era marked a shift from colonial policing, which involved waging 'Small Wars', to participation in the mass, industrialized World Wars. And this transition had economic, political, and strictly technical ramifications on the armed forces, on the administrative apparatus, and on Indian society. So any attempt to study the impact of the World Wars on the British-Indian army demands that attention be focused on the colonial state.

The state-centric approach is gaining credence slowly. Both Peers and Tan Tai Yong categorize the colonial state as a quasi-garrison state. American political scientist Harold Lasswell first introduced the Garrison State model. Following Alfred Vagts' concept of militarism, Douglas Peers writes that military issues remain dominant within the Garrison State. Peers' monograph assesses the financial and military resources of the Company state before the 1857 Mutiny. Somewhat influenced by John Brewer's fiscal–military state model, Peers and C. A. Bayly claim that the Company state was also a military–fiscal sponge in the colonial setting.[111] In an article, Peers shows how the fiscal system of the East India Company was able to sustain the British-Indian war machine during the Burma War I by extracting resources from trade and land revenue.[112]

Besides money, the conduction of war demanded personnel. Mobilizing military manpower also involved diplomatic maneuverings. Purushottam Banskota and Mary Des Chene chart the complex tripolar relationship between the British Raj in India, the Sepoy Army, and the semi-independent kingdom of Nepal for recruiting the Gurkhas.[113] Even for procuring manpower from within British India, the authorities had to tackle a web of intricate relationships. The 'home front', especially in the strategic province of Punjab, remained quiet during and after World War I, but registered unrest in the immediate aftermath of World War II. Yong, by comparing and contrasting the colonial state's policies and the differential effects of the two World Wars, attempts to answer this problem. The colonial state started tapping the military manpower of Punjab from the 1840s.[114] Yong studies the impact of manpower mobilization during World War I and in the inter-war era on colonial Punjab. He paints a picture of cooperation between the civilian and military administrations, and the emergence of a militarized bureaucracy in wartime Punjab.[115] The civil-military consensus which the British had nurtured in Punjab begun to unravel, writes Yong, due to the pressure of World War II. The Raj's policies of food requisition, rationing, and price controls alienated Punjab's landed military families.[116]

Even in the nineteenth century, argues Roy, for feeding and maintaining the Sepoy Army, the colonial state had to expand its administrative infrastructure and penetrate into the agrarian sector.[117] Crowell shows that during the first half of the nineteenth century, for supplying the Madras Army in the field, the colonial polity fused Western bureaucratic institutions with traditional Indian elements such as bazaars etc.[118] So the colonial state evolved as a burgeoning hybrid. The expansion of the colonial polity reached its apogee during World War II. The military manpower base of the colonial state widened due to the massive expansion of the British-Indian Army between 1939 and 1945. The colonial state seemed to be a powerful mobilizing agent. The debate about whether the colonial state was a weak state or a strong state continues. But the reach of the state in recruiting military manpower shows that the colonial polity could not be categorized as a sort of 'limited Raj'.[119] However, Yong asserts that the dependence of the Garrison State on the Punjabi landed elites for mobilizing manpower was an aspect of its weakness.[120]

The colonial state was no Leviathan. Speaking about 'total war', Michael Howard says that mobilization of the maximum amount of military manpower required consensus in the domestic societies of the warring nations. There exists a direct relationship between the broadening of the political basis of the state and the increasing military effectiveness of the forces at the disposal of the polity. Hence, waging of 'total war' required the total participation of entire communities. Howard suggests that 'total war' gave rise to increasing governmental authority geared towards the welfare of the subjects.[121] However, the social, political, and economic structures of colonialism obstructed thorough mobilization of India during the two World Wars.

Despite the predominance of the Marxist historical approach among Indian academics at least till the 1980s, the economic aspects of colonial defence have not been examined properly. Even the most recent survey of colonial India's economic history neglects the impact of armies and of warfare on the Raj's economic policies.[122] An exception is the article by K. N. Reddy, which emphasizes the continuity of defence expenditure from the late-nineteenth century colonial state in peacetime to the post-colonial state.[123] Most of the sepoys were the younger sons of the small peasants. Their pay and pension had a strong impact on the village economies of the recruiting areas. Yet historians studying the peasants and agriculture of colonial India more or less neglect this issue. The impact of colonial defence expenditure on Punjab is a theme that some historians have looked into.

The Marxist scholars believe that high expenditure on the military results in less investment by the government in the spheres of industry, agriculture, and education. The net result is unbalanced growth in some sectors of the military-related industries which in the long run creates underdevelopment and economic chaos. Clive Dewey, in a path-breaking article, shows the positive impact of colonial military expenditure on the colonized.[124] Rajit K. Mazumder elaborates Dewey's thesis in his monograph and in an article. He demonstrates the benefits accruing to Punjabi agrarian society from military spending. The fall out of this military spending was monetization of the agrarian economy and extension of cash-crop cultivation. To sum up, military infrastructure—comprising road–rail networks, cantonments, and canals—established by the colonial state had a multiplier effect on Punjab's economy.[125]

One group of scholars highlights the military dimension of the British state in India and links it with the international political context. They accept that World War II set the pace for decolonization. They could be grouped under the War and Decolonization category. In 1987, German historian Johannes H. Voigt first undertook an analysis of the structure and functioning of the colonial state in wartime. In his book, Voigt investigates India's role within the wider framework of 'total war'. He meshes military, economic, strategic, and political perspectives into a coherent narrative. With remarkable proficiency, he concludes that decolonization, or the freedom struggle, was hastened (if not caused) by India's war effort during World War II.[126] In a similar tone, P. S. Gupta asserts that the pressures of war accelerated Indianization of the colonial state, resulting in the final withdrawal of British power in 1947.[127]

Somewhat inspired by the System theory, one group of historians has studied British-India as part of the imperial system dominated by London. The incapability of the colonial state to demobilize a massive army quickly and efficiently weakened the state in the immediate aftermath of World War II. The problem was aggravated for the colonized states because London was in no position to aid the colonies. This issue has received some scholarly attention.[128] Even before 1939, write John Gallagher, Anil Seal, and Keith Jeffery, India was becoming the soft underbelly of the British imperial system. The strategic and economic importance of India in the British *imperium* was declining.[129] So London was neither willing nor able to aid British-India in case of an emergency. Jeffery asserts that before the outbreak of World War II, London realized that British rule in India was based on consent and not on coercion.[130] To their eyes, it seems that the British-Indian state was a weak one, ready for disintegration if the imperial system faced a global crisis. The linkage between global warfare, demobilization of the commonwealth armies of World War II and the decolonization of South Asia is the theme of Chris Bayly and Tim Harper's *Forgotten Armies*. Bayly and Harper conceive of the British Empire in Asia as a somewhat homogeneous structure. Yet the imperial fabric was fragile, because British imperialism had no popular support base within indigenous societies. The physical and psychological shocks generated by the Japanese invasion in 1942 gave a deathblow to British rule.[131]

As regards India, Indivar Kamtekar's brilliant essay in this volume, 'The Shiver of 1942', shows with a slight counter-factual slant and the fragility of the colonial state in wartime. Kamtekar's powerful essay also seriously challenges the established wisdom regarding modern Indian history. He shows that instead of the so-called powerful Gandhian national movement, as depicted in the writings of Nationalist School, the British were more afraid of the Japanese armies stationed in Burma during 1942. In another article, Kamtekar shows that, compared to the wartime British state, the colonial state was weak vis-à-vis its relationship with the upper segment of Indian society.[132] Kamtekar's essay in this volume emphasizes the dysfunctional role played by rumour in destabilizing the colonial state. And this brings us to the domain of information warfare.

One aspect of the increasing power of a state during the two World Wars was control over information. Britain during the World War I witnessed the reduction of freedom for war correspondents. Both the military and the politicians agreed to introduce an apparatus for controlling wartime information. Besides Britain, France, and Russia also introduced censorship of all information related to military affairs.[133] An analysis of the information policies of the Raj during wartime is undertaken by Sanjoy Bhattacharya and Philip Woods. Both of them agree that the colonial state became more interventionist in wartime to control the channels of mass communications. Bhattacharya writes that British military propaganda during World War II was more sophisticated than being merely misleading information. He says that the groups targeted by the Raj as part of information management remained unaware of the activities of the censor department.[134] Bhattacharya goes on to argue that the very information procured by surveillance apparatus about Indian soldiers' activities and their thinking made the colonial state nervous regarding its fragile hold over the Brown soldiery. Ironically, instead of strengthening the hold of the state, the operation of the surveillance apparatus weakened the 'iron will' of the colonial authorities with respect to 'holding' India.[135] Whatever may be the ultimate result of the information control and propaganda generated by the colonial state, the World War II witnessed the use of new techniques and technologies for conducting propaganda warfare. Woods shows, for instance, the use of films for influencing the mentality of civilians and soldiers.[136]

Though the present volume intends to look at military history from the broader perspective of state and society, we do not want to do away with battles. Peter Paret has rightly warned us of the New Military History's emphasis on 'demilitarized military history'.[137] After all, Von Clausewitz rightly says that armies exist primarily for combat.[138] Following Clausewitz, we do think that it is essential to include military operations and operational doctrines within the ambit of academic military history. However, instead of a purely narrative tradition describing military operations, which is vulgarized within the high towers of academics as Smoke and Shell History, an interpretative approach towards certain selected themes is followed. Raymond Callahan and Tim Moreman turn the limelight on the Army in India's activities in the field of fire. The duty of the Army in India was to guard India against Indians, to protect the frontier and to function as an imperial reserve. While Callahan focuses on the military leadership of the British-Indian Army in Burma during the World War II, Moreman studies the frontier protection role of the Army in India till 1939.

The Indus frontier has shaped Indian history from the dawn of civilization. The Greeks, Scythians, Huns, Mongols, Mughals, and finally the Afghans entered India through the North-West frontier passes. Nonetheless, very few scholars have turned their attention to the frontier question. Even in the British period, the security of the North-West frontier remained a crucial policy question for the Raj. Those scholars who analyse the dialectics between the North-West frontier and the British-Indian Army could be categorized as the Frontier School.[139] While T. R. Moreman and Alan Warren point out the interaction between the state, the army, and the frontier, Charles Allen, in his semi-academic monograph, views the making of frontier policy through the actions of certain leading personalities.[140]

Moreman, in one of his essays, defines frontier warfare as punitive expeditions for protecting the frontier from tribal aggressions. Moreman and Warren highlight the deployment of the army to back up civil administration during tribal unrest. This sort of operation is also categorized as an aid to civil duties. The British policy was either to win over the armed tribes or, at best, to maintain a loose control over them by launching numerous 'butcher and bolt' expeditions to prevent the Russians and later the Axis powers from gaining an upper hand in that strategically-sensitive area.[141]

Frontier warfare was not always a skirmish. Such low-intensity warfare occasionally escalated into hot war of sizeable proportions.

The Tirah campaign of 1897 involved 60,000 tribesmen.[142] The conduct of even such small wars involved sophisticated techniques and innovative tactical ideas. Theorists of the 'small war' lay down several normative principles. Charles Callwell, the late-nineteenth century British theorist, divides the 'small war' into several categories. One type of small war is the 'hill war' in the frontier. Callwell, the 'Liddell-Hart of frontier warfare', writes:

Hill warfare may fairly be said to constitute a special branch of the military art—typical hill warfare, that is to say, such as Anglo-Indian troops have been fitfully employed upon two generations beyond the Indus, culminating in the memorable Tirah campaign .... It is the campaigns of regular troops against hill-men fighting in guerrilla fashion in their own native mountains and in defence of their own homes, campaigns almost the most trying which disciplined soldiers can be called upon to undertake, which creates the conditions of genuine hill warfare and which deserves to be considered as a subject quite apart.[143]

Following Callwell's framework, one of the major frontier war theorists to emerge within the British-Indian Army was G. J. Younghusband. In his book which was published in 1898, Younghusband asserts:

Though the broad strategical principles on which civilized warfare is based throughout the world are the same, yet local conditions so far alter their tactical bearings that methods suitable to the country and the foes to be encountered have had to be gradually evolved in the course of practice. Thus in India the experience gained during decades of constantly recurring frontier expeditions has taught the Indian Army how to modify the broad principles which obtain in Europe to agree with local conditions.[144]

Younghusband continues that in Asiatic warfare, offence remains the best defence.[145] It is interesting to note that Czarist generals engaged in military operations against the Asiatic nomads also developed the doctrine of offence at all costs.[146] Operations on the North-West frontier during 1919–20 involved more than 83,000 soldiers. In light of this, General Andrew Skeen wrote a book titled *Passing it On*.[147] The trio of Callwell, Younghusband, and Skeen argued that frontier warfare is different from conventional operations in Europe, and so it requires a special theory. In an article, Moreman argues that the tactics, training, equipment, and doctrine necessary for conventional operations in Europe were distinct from the skills required for combat against the Pathans of the North-West frontier.[148] Moreman's piece in this volume elaborates on the theoretical as well as tactical challenges faced by the British-Indian Army in its odyssey west of the Indus. However, there is an inherent limitation in such a study of ideas. Historians cannot effectively demonstrate the linkages between ideas and actions on the battlefield.

The post-Civil War American Army, the nineteenth-century British Army, and the Sepoy Army had several similarities. All these organizations lacked a Prussian-style 'general staff' system. The commanders of these forces lacked the capabilities to handle large numbers of soldiers,[149] and these armies were mostly engaged in small wars.[150] Both the British and the Sepoy armies were colonial police forces and were composed of volunteer soldiers.[151] The Sepoy Army's conduct of small wars west of the Indus had certain similarities with the Frontier Wars waged by the American Army in the nineteenth century. The American Army's expedition to Mexico in the first half of the nineteenth century was like the Sepoy Army's expeditions to the North-West frontier, dependent on mules for logistical purposes. Both the Sepoy Army units and the American Army formations, while waging small wars, had to negotiate with the leaders of the tribes, conduct patrols, and so on.[152] In the first decade of the twentieth century, the American Army was deployed in the Philippines, when civil authority collapsed and after restoring 'law and order', it was withdrawn.[153] This pattern repeated itself on the North-West frontier of British-India. It is to be noted that not all the nineteenth-century armies were able to master guerrilla warfare. For instance, the Spanish Army in the last decade of the nineteenth century, failed to cope with the 'hit and run' attacks launched by the insurgents in Cuba.[154] In the first decade of the twentieth century, the German commanders found out to their cost that the techniques of European warfare were almost useless against the Namas, who conducted guerrilla warfare in German Africa.[155] Counter-insurgency operations required special training and tactics.

After 1857, the Indian Army was continuously engaged in imperial policing inside India. A small bunch of historians points out that the colonial army functioned as an essential back-up for the colonial state by continuously dousing the fires generated by various low-intensity threats. Besides the frontier commitment, the British-Indian Army also had to offer aid to civil duties within India against the nationalists and other 'troublesome' groups both during peacetime as well as even when the World Wars were raging. Narayani Gupta, in her article, shows how the fear of uprisings among the subject populace shaped the urban architecture of Delhi in the post-1857 era.[156] In fact, writes Gyanesh Kudaisya, one-third of the British-Indian Army was continuously deployed for imperial policing within

India.[157] In the last days of the Raj, writes Robin Jeffrey, the Army failed in its aid to civil duties in Punjab due to interference by the Indian and Pakistani politicians.[158]

The debate as to whether the frontier commitment and internal security tasks acted as a brake on the upgradation of British-India's military establishment in the age of 'total war' continues. One group of historians argues that the conduct of small wars resulted in demodernization of the military, which in turn had a negative impact on its capacity for waging mobile and amphibious operations within the high technology context of a 'total war'. Brian Bond, in his seminal work, asserts that the British Army's preoccupation with its overseas empire impeded modernization, which in turn had an adverse effect on the army's performance in Continental battles.[159] Christina Goulter asserts that air policing along the North-West frontier had a negative effect on the Royal Air Force.[160]

Moreman's article is this volume shows the limitations of technology in hill warfare west of the Indus. And this sort of war was the principal occupation of the Army in India before the outbreak of World War II. In fact, the 'hill warfare lobby' in the interwar period resisted the entry of new machines. Instead of a capital-intensive army, the experts on frontier war wanted to continue with a manpower-intensive army.[161] In the nineteenth century, military operations by the Sepoy Army in East Africa[162] as well as in South Asia were dependent on an animal-centric logistical infrastructure. Moreman's article in this volume shows that mules rather than lorries remained important in hill warfare till 1939. Probably all these factors impeded the mechanization of the Army in India, which in turn had a disastrous effect on its combat effectiveness during the early phase of World War II.

Though the British-Indian Army failed to develop a tradition of large-scale armoured warfare, its very expertise in hill warfare enabled it to conduct pacification campaigns both in North-East India and Kashmir after India's independence. The post-1947 Indian Army inherited the tradition of waging low-intensity operations from the British era.[163] And even today the Indian Army's principal task remains policing the Subcontinent. Moreman's essay in this volume shows that minimizing collateral damage was a principal feature of frontier warfare as conducted by the Army in India. Minimizing collateral casualties remains a crucial feature of modern peacekeeping operations both within and outside India.[164] It is to be noted that many military officers of independent India got their training on the

North-West frontier. For example, K. V. Krishna Rao served in the Second Mahar Regiment, which in 1944 was deployed in Malakand. In 1981, Rao became the chief of army staff, and in 1993 was appointed governor of Kashmir for dealing with the ongoing insurgency.[165] So the British-Indian Army's involvement in small wars beyond the Indus might appear from the Eurocentric perspective a dead albatross hung around the imperial neck; but for independent India it turned out to be a blessing in disguise.

While one group of scholars asserts that the Indian Army during the two World Wars was mostly an armed constabulary, the other lobby argues that the Sepoy Army was indeed coming of age during the latter period of World War II. The organizational and ideological inadequacies of the British-Indian Army during World War I have been listed by Jeffrey Greenhut.[166] Case studies undertaken by historians to analyse the performance of the colonial army in particular theatres offer the same depressing picture. As regards the Indian Army's performance in Mesopotamia, Edwin Latter writes that the military organization of British India was incapable of fighting attritional campaigns which characterized the Great War.[167] Anirudh Deshpande, in his PhD thesis-turned-monograph, claims that being a conservative organization, the British-Indian Army was unsuited for conducting modern mass warfare. Deshpande locates the Army within the wider ambit of British imperial policies. The Sepoy Army's organization and ideology, argues Deshpande, were incapable of handling the complexities of 'total war'. He goes on to show how the regimental organization of the Sepoy Army, with its focus on recruitment from a particular, narrow social and regional base, prevented the army from emerging as a true national army. Worse, the military authorities were handicapped as to replacing the large number of casualties. And the economic decline of Britain further hamstrung British India when it came to acquiring new weapons.[168]

At the opposite end of the spectrum, F. W. Perry argues that the organizational format of the Raj's military bureaucracy was able to expand the size of the British-Indian Army successfully during the two World Wars.[169] Institutional study of the army is becoming popular in the field of military history. Following the institutional approach, some historians note the transformation of the British-Indian Army from a police force into a combat-effective organization capable of sharing the burdens of the World Wars. S. D. Pradhan argues that despite some defects in the recruiting process, reserves, training, and equipment in 1914, substantial improvements occurred in the combatant and non-combatant branches of the Sepoy Army between 1915 and 1918.[170] Gordon Corrigan applies the institutional approach by meshing organizational mechanism, tactics, and technology in explaining the Sepoy Army's commendable military experience in France during 1914–15.[171] Barua and Daniel P. Marston, in their institutional analysis of the Indian Army during World War II, show that it exhibited a high learning curve vis-a-vis its opponents. They focus on those units which fought in North Africa and on the Burma front, and show that the organizational format of the Army developed with time. By focusing on training and tactics, Barua and Marston claim that the backward British-Indian Army was transformed between 1942 and 1944 into a progressive force capable of conducting 'total war'.[172]

The British officers commanded the Indian military formations. And Indian officers who later served in independent India acquired training under them. So any institutional approach to the colonial military history cannot afford to neglect the uniformed White Man's leadership in the killing zone. There is, of course, a danger in overemphasizing the 'movers and shakers' on the battlefield. Structuralist historians would criticize such an approach as a degenerate form of the 'great men' theory of history or the 'great hero' theory. Paul Kennedy perceptively argues that Whig, Marxist, New Left, and Radical–Liberal historians have a bias for 'profound forces' in history. Long-term forces are cited for explaining inevitable political and social changes. They are a bit uncomfortable with assigning critical importance to individual personalities[173] and their managerial capabilities. Till recently, biographical studies as a genre was looked down upon as somewhat crude and unscientific. Sanjay Subrahmanyam, as part of his agenda of 'Connected History', argues for the revival of 'social biographies' which will throw light on social, cultural, and institutional history.[174] In recent times, parallel biographies have come into fashion. The foremost of US military historians, Dennis Showalter in *Patton and Rommel* follows the dual biography approach in contextualizing these two larger-than-life commanders within the military cultures and the polities they served.[175]

Whether one likes the biographical approach or not, the British commanders cannot be neglected if one is to achieve a balanced understanding of the evolution of colonial India's military system. Officers such as S. P. P. Thorat, J. N. Chaudhuri, K. Thimayya, K. M. Cariappa, Harbakhsh Singh, *et al.*, who occupied the top echelons of the Indian military in the post-colonial era were influenced by the British-Indian Army's operations in South-East Asia. Harbakhsh Singh joined the 5th Battalion of the 11th Sikh Regiment. From Quetta, his unit was transferred to Malaysia. After independence, Singh rose to the rank of lieutenant general in the Indian Army.[176] Thorat was in the twentieth Indian Division, which took part in the Imphal-Kohima Battle of 1944. In 1950, Thorat became India's Chief of General Staff.[177] Hence a critical analysis of top-level generalship in the 14th Army in particular (which Callahan attempts in his essay in this volume) and the British-Indian Army in general is essential in assessing independent India's generalship.

Defining generalship is tricky. Generalship, according to Howard, includes three elements: command, control, and leadership.[178] Geoffrey Evans rightly says that a general must know his men. And through his personality and inspiration, he has to gain their confidence.[179] Stephen Hart claims that a commander has to concern himself with the morale of the troops under him.[180] Gary Sheffield writes that generalship in the last analysis includes both human and managerial elements.[181] Howard uses the term 'urbane normality' to characterize British generalship during World War II. He says that the British generals were brisk, competent, and unromantic.[182] Let us now focus on generalship in wartime Burma.

Even admirers of Major General Orde Wingate, such as Christopher Sykes and John W. Gordon, accept the great military leadership of Bill Slim.[183] Sykes portrays Slim as a bit jealous of Wingate's capabilities, but supporting him somewhat passively. Probably the reality was much worse. Callahan portrays the tension-filled relationship between Wingate and Slim. Slim was a better general than Field Marshal Alexander, whose generalship in Italy is described by a British historian as 'lackadaisical'.[184] G. D. Sheffield categorizes Slim as a persuasive general, that is, possessing the capacity to influence others. In contrast, Monty—says Sheffield—was a dominant one, that is, a general with a forceful personality.[185] Callahan's portrayal of Slim as a great general falls within the tradition established by Ronald Lewin, Geoffrey Evans, *et al.*[186] They categorize Slim as a 'heaven born general'. Lewin describes Slim as a master strategist and the best Allied commander in the South-East Asian theatre.[187] The formidable John Keegan asserts that while Slim was the 'Montgomery of the Far East', Wingate lacked the genius of Lawrence of Arabia.[188] Robert Lyman points out that Slim was a great innovator of military techniques. During the inter-war period, when Slim was a student at the Indian Army Staff College at Quetta, he emphasized the role of aeroplanes in supplying the ground troops.[189] And it was put to good effect in Burma during the later parts of World War II. But the pendulum has swung too far by then. Lyman and Duncan Anderson claim that Slim was a model as regards conducting manoeuvre warfare.[190] Anderson, in an earlier essay, has compared Slim's campaign in central Burma during late 1944 with the achievements of panzer knights such as Heinz Guderian and Erich Von Manstein.[191] Callahan's estimate of Slim is much more balanced. At the opposite pole, Carter Malkasian asserts that Slim's 1944–5 Burma campaign was a classic example of attritional warfare.[192]

Jointness (necessary for conducting manoeuvre operations) of adequate degree was absent among the top command aechelons of the British Army. Nigel de Lee shows that during the Scandinavian campaign of 1940, a lot of the time and energy of the commanders was spent in acrimonious confrontations among themselves. Callahan shows these fractious tendencies operating between the British Army and Indian Army commanders in North Africa and in the South-East Asia Command.[193] To sum up, during World War II, the British Army failed to emerge as an effective instrument for manoeuvre warfare. The British military leadership was capable of an attritional approach characterized by set-piece battles conducted with massed firepower and superior resources.[194] Slim, with all his qualities, falls within this paradigm. And the post-1947 Indian Army exhibits lack of jointness at the operational level, and is surely not a master of deep mobile penetration like the Soviet, German, and Israeli armies.

Avenues for Future Research

Deconstruction is most welcome; but before one indulges in it, there is a need for 'construction' of various aspects of colonial military history based on primary data. Much more research is required in highlighting several aspects which remain in the dark. Was there any jingoism in the Indian populace before the two World Wars? There is a fine study which shows that the Britons before 1914 believed that war was inevitable. And at least some groups in Britain believed that war had a positive impact on society.[195] We have no knowledge about the degree to which Indian society was conditioned to accept military activity as desirable. Whether a pacific ideology held sway or whether militaristic ideas were dominant in general among the common people is yet to be ascertained. It is not clear whether the ideals of military service were rampant only among the 'martial' groups. Rather than government documents, an analysis of fiction and newspapers will yield more results on such a topic.

It took time and money to transform a peasant recruit into a veteran soldier of the Raj. Moreover the 'precious' soldiers had to be protected against the 'diseased and poisonous' climate of the Orient. So the nineteenth century witnessed the genesis of medical care for the Army in India. The point to be noted is that several volumes of the *Official History of the Indian Armed Forces in the Second World War*, edited by Prasad, focuses on the linkages between operational efficiency and military medicine. For instance, the volume by E. K. K. Pillai narrates the medical infrastructure which supported the Indian Army in Iran, Syria, East and North Africa, and Italy.[196] Several scholars are now turning their attention to reconstructing the medical history of the Raj's military. It is part of the recent trend of historians focusing on the connections between disease and the conduct of imperial warfare. To give one example, Kenneth F. Kiple and Kriemhild Conee Ornelas point to links between troop deployment and disease in the eighteenth-century Caribbean.[197] This approach is indeed part of a wider discourse of historians analysing imperial attitudes towards race and disease in tropical climates.[198] For some authors, medicine played a crucial role in giving rise to modern warfare. Modernization is equated with increasing bureaucratization at all levels. Modern medical practice, by regimenting and regulating human lives, attempts to construct a rational society, which witnesses the elaboration of bureaucratic technologies for knowing and controlling the minds and bodies of human beings. The net result is the depersonalizing of individuals.[199] In *Medicine and Victory*, the connections between the battlefield victories of the Allied armies in World War II and the increasing use of modern medical facilities is shown by Mark Harrison. Public health became a technique in the hands of the authorities for winning the hearts and minds of soldiers.[200] Harrison, in one of his articles analyses the link between disease and disobedience among Indian soldiers during World War I.[201] This shift is part of a wider inclination of the historians studying public health and hygiene of colonial India as constituents of the functional mechanism of the Raj. Sumit Guha, in an article, studies the relationship between environmental sanitation, public health, and the medical state of the Army in India during the late nineteenth century.[202] In *Climate and Constitutions*,

Harrison analyses the changing imperial attitude towards races and diseases in India, and the proliferation of British rule.[203] The links between morality, increasing state control, and venereal disease is highlighted by Arnold P. Kaminsky in one of his articles.[204] David Arnold analyses the introduction of Western medical culture in colonial India as a colonizing process, which was contested by the colonized.[205]

Though the 'War and Culture' approach is a novelty as far as India's colonial military history is concerned, such an approach is quite common as regards European military history. In such a paradigm, the combat effectiveness of a particular army depends on its surrounding cultural matrix. V. D. Hanson asserts that the lethality of Western armies over non-Western armies throughout history has been due to the cultural institutions and practices of Europe which can be traced back to Classical Greece.[206] However some scholars, following the Culturalist approach, have indeed challenged this assumption about an unique military culture of the 'West'.[207]

Hitherto, scholars have studied the evolution of racial–ethnic cultural policies of the colonial military as being completely detached from the army's job of killing its opponents. A recent study links attitudes to race and ethnicity inherent in the British-Indian military culture with the events of war. The links between the ethnic 'Self' and images of the 'Other', that is the enemy, writes Tarak Barkawi, is shaped by the exigencies of particular campaigns. He asserts that as far as the Sepoy Army was concerned, ethnic identities provided the basis for the group solidarity required on the battlefield. This was necessary, since nationalism was absent among the Indian soldiers. The military organization's policy of incorporating, shaping, and conditioning ethnic identities was related to the harsh requirements of the battlefield. To conclude, ethnic pride generated racial arrogance associated with concepts of warrior masculinity, which in turn were shaped by barbaric wartime experiences.[208] Barkawi is obviously influenced by Craig M. Cameron's *American Samurai*, which brings out the dialectical relationship between myth, imagination, and the behaviour of soldiers, and the dynamics of land warfare. The soldiers' cultural and social myth and imagination were responses to battlefield threats. The abstract images and assumptions of soldiers about their enemies resulted in the barbarization of warfare. The imaginary construction of the Japanese 'Other' was shaped, claims Cameron, by the Americans' cultural perceptions and attitudes. He points out to the racial–cultural assumptions of the American marines who perceived the Japanese as pests. Such ideas and imaginations were manipulated by the military organization for stirring up hatred among the soldiers vis-à-vis their enemies,[209] which in turn motivated the soldiers to fight and die.

This in turn brings us to the terrain of the battlefield experiences of the sepoys, both at individual and collective levels. In recent times, with the aid of psychology, historians of biographical studies are beginning to probe the human psyche more deeply. History concerns human beings both as individuals and as an aggregate, acting and reacting to both personal and impersonal forces. Maurice Matloff claims that psychological insights allow the portrayal of the past to be more enriched and humanized.[210] Robert Pois and Philip Langer follow psycho-historical methods in assessing the leadership capabilities of some of the European and American military leaders.[211]

It is high time that we rescue the nameless and faceless sepoys and sowars from obscurity. The battle behaviour of ordinary Indian soldiers remains a mystery. Thanks to John Keegan's *The Face of Battle*,[212] the common soldiers' experience of combat has emerged as a powerful trend within Western military historiography.[213] The shock waves resulting from Keegan's mindboggling work has affected scholarship on ancient Greek military history[214] and, to an extent, naval history.[215] The behaviours displayed by soldiers on the killing field are analysed both through sociological theories and psychological approaches. Tony Ashworth portrays the social dynamics of the trench culture of British soldiers in France during 1914–18. Ashworth goes on to show how informal social relationships among soldiers within an army as well between two opposing armies gave rise to a counter-culture of war which opposed the formal bureaucratic rules of warfare as charted out by the respective high commands.[216]

Historians must try to recover the sepoy as an agency on the battlefield between 1857 and 1945. The interaction between ideology and combat motivation of the sepoys is a virgin area of study. Rajat Kanta Ray portrays the rebel sepoys of 1857 as desperadoes who fought for their dharma.[217] Unfortunately, the sepoys and sowars, being illiterate, have left us with no memoirs. The same problem exists as regards colonial African soldiers.[218] For the period before 1857, we have to depend on Subedar Sitaram's autobiography.[219] However, its authenticity could be questioned. There is also a memoir by a Bengali clerk associated with the Bengal Irregular Cavalry during the 1857 Mutiny.[220] Some glimpses of the soldiers' mentality could be pieced together from the petitions they submitted to the high command. Numerous such petitions are preserved in the Military Department Proceedings at National Archives of India, New Delhi.

The database becomes a bit brighter for the twentieth century. The Indian soldiers, when deployed in France during World War I, wrote letters back home which the censor department preserved. This enables historians to reconstruct the voice of the private soldier, as refracted through the lens of the censor department.[221] About the Indian officers, we have a voluminous diary kept by one Amar Singh, who was one of the earliest Indian commissioned officers. While the Rudolphs have analysed Amar Singh's diary as the product of an ethnologist operating in the liminal zones of Western military culture and chivalrous Rajput society;[222] Ellinwood in his latest monograph stresses Amar Singh's military experience.[223] A Gurkha who rose from the ranks to become an officer wrote a memoir, and it too has been published.[224] Two Bengali medical officers left memoirs noting their experiences in Mesopotamia and in the Middle East during the two World Wars.[225] As to non-combatants, we have the memoirs of an Indian Christian named John Baptist Crasta, who worked in the army's supply department and claimed to have been tortured by Indian National Army personnel.[226] Such memoir materials enable historians to peep into the mentality of the soldiers. For instance, while Crasta did not feel any inkling of nationalism, a junior naval officer belonging to the Royal Indian Navy who witnessed the naval uprising of 1946 felt the pangs of nationalism within the inner recess of his heart.[227] For World War II, we have a host of memoirs and also some private papers of the Indian officers (especially those who fought in the Indian National Army), but not by any privates.[228] Besides the memoirs, for the World War II period we also have fortnightly newspapers for the Army in India, such as the *Fauji Akhbar*. Overall, on the basis of these materials, a Keeganian approach reconstructing the Indian soldiers' experience in encountering the 'face of battle' is probably difficult to attempt, if not impossible. An example is John Latimer's *Burma*, which tries to paint the Burma campaign through the eyes of the soldiers.[229]

We know very little about the type of weapons used by the combatants and the way they were manufactured. After Daniel Headrick's classic *Tools of Empire*,[230] the history of military technology in colonial India has failed to take off. In Headrick's approach, technology is equated with hardware. A broader definition of technology in the context of military history, which includes the applications of science in the conduct of war, would be more fruitful. The study of military technology, writes John F. Votaw, must comprise ideas, techniques, equipment, and their applications.[231] As regards Western military historiography, Jeffrey J. Clarke writes that instead of 'nuts and bolts' work on military hardware, it is necessary to look at the interplay between history and technology.[232] But as for the colonial military, even 'nuts and bolts' histories are lacking. Ordnance factories constituted the Raj's fourth arm of defence. Roy, in an article, studies the evolution of ordnance factories in nineteenth-century British India.[233] Future scholars of the British Indian military history ought to analyse the interrelationship between tactics, technology (mines, machine guns, and tanks), and the changing nature of the battlefield. In the final analysis, studying military history without battles is like eating fish curry without a piece of fish in it. Again, 'total war' probably did have some impact on the colonial state's nascent industrial sector. Future studies ought to analyse how far World War II initiated 'limited industrialization' within the colonial framework in the Subcontinent.

This volume opens up a window for analysing the complex nature of the colonial state and society. The colonial polity was not a nightwatchman state. At the same time, it was not a totalitarian state of the type which existed in Hitler's Germany or Stalin's Russia. The military activities of the colonial state show how dynamic and vigorous the state apparatus was when it came to core issues. The essays not only help us to understand the past better, but also function as signposts to interpreting the present and the near future. While the Indian Army's tactical deployments for counter-insurgency duties in north-east India, Punjab, and Kashmir are to an extent shaped by its pre-1947 experiences on the North-West frontier, its present training for conventional warfare is partly the product of fighting in Burma during 1944–5. The continuation of the colonial army's regimental infrastructure both in the Indian and Pakistani armies illustrates the transference of cultural ceremonials and rituals from colonial to post-colonial societies. In fact, the colonial heritage to a large extent continues to mould independent India's Army. Herein lies the importance of this volume.

NOTES

1. G. N. Molesworth, *Curfew on Olympus*, Bombay: 1965, p. 221.
2. DeWitt C. Ellinwood, 'Ethnicity in a Colonial Asian Army: British Policy, War and the Indian Army, 1914–18', in DeWitt C. Ellinwood and Cynthia H. Enloe (eds), *Ethnicity and the Military in Asia*, New Brunswick/London, 1981, p. 97.
3. T. A. Heathcote, *The Military in British India: The Development of British Land Forces in South Asia, 1600–1947*, Manchester/New York: 1995, p. 241.
4 For a short survey of Indian historiography see Thomas R. Metcalf, 'Introduction', in Thomas Metcalf, *Forging the Raj: Essays on British India in the Heyday of Empire*, New Delhi: 2005, pp. 2–21.
5. Michel Foucault, *Politics, Philosophy, Culture: Interviews and Other Writings, 1977–84*, tr. by Alan Sheridan *et al.*, edited with an Introduction by Lawrence D. Kritzman, 1988; reprint, New York/London: 1990, pp. 38–9.
6. Sanjay Subrahmanyam, *Explorations in Connected History: Mughals and Franks*, New Delhi: 2005, pp. 15, 25, 42, 69.
7. Walter Emil Kaegi Jr., 'The Crisis in Military Historiography', *Armed Forces and Society*, 7(2), 1981, p. 313.
8. Heather Streets, *Martial Races: The Military, Race and Masculinity in British Imperial Culture, 1857–1914*, Manchester/New York: 2004.
9. S. B. Chaudhuri, *English Historical Writings on the Indian Mutiny: 1857–59*, Calcutta: 1979, p. 281.
10. George MacMunn, *The Armies of India*, 1911; reprint, New Delhi: 1991; Major Dirom, *A Narrative of the Campaign in India which Terminated the War with Tipu Sultan in 1792*, 1793; reprint, New Delhi: 1997.
11. William Irvine, *The Army of the Indian Moghuls: Its Organization and Administration*; reprint, New Delhi: 1994.
12. The Diffusionist theory is originally much used by the practitioners of history of technology. See Donald Cardwell, *The Fontana History of Technology*, London: 1994, p. 506. The Diffusionist School of military history asserts that the origin of professional standing army could be traced back to Classical Greece. They trace a linear evolution of Western warfare through Rome and Charlemagne's Europe down to modern times. In their framework, the Western military tradition spread to various parts of the world at different times with varying effectiveness. See Geoffrey Parker (ed.), *The Cambridge Illustrated History of Warfare: The Triumph of the West*, Cambridge: 1995.
13. S. L. Menezes, *Fidelity and Honour: The Indian Army from the Seventeenth to the Twenty-First Century*, New Delhi: 1993; Pradeep P. Barua, *The State at War in South Asia*, Lincoln/London: 2005.
14. See for instance Charles Gough and Arthur D. Innes, *The Sikhs and the*

Sikh Wars: The Rise, Conquest and Annexation of the Punjab State; reprint, Delhi: 1986.

15. G. B. Malleson, *The Decisive Battles of India from 1746 to 1849 inclusive*, 1883; reprint, Jaipur: 1986, p. v.
16. F. G. Cardew, *A Sketch of the Services of the Bengal Native Army to the Year 1895*, 1903; reprint, New Delhi: 1971.
17. Geoffrey Betham and H. V. R. Geary, *The Golden Galley: The Story of the Second Punjab Regiment, 1762–1947*; reprint, New Delhi: 1975; Chandra B. Khanduri, *The History of the First Gorkha Rifles: The Malaun Regiment*, vol. 3, *1947–1990*, New Delhi: 1992; Rufus Simon, *Their Formative Years: History of the Corps of Electrical and Mechanical Engineers*, vol. 1, New Delhi: 1977.
18. F. J. Moberly, *History of the Great War based on Official Documents: The Campaign in Mesopotamia, 1914–18*, vol. 1, London: 1923; R. Evans, *A Brief Outline of the Campaign in Mesopotamia: 1914–18*, 1926; reprint, London: 1935.
19. G. V. Modak, *Indian Defence Problem*, Poona: 1933.
20. For example, H. W. Bellew, *The Races of Afghanistan being a Brief Account of the Principal Nations Inhabiting that Country*, 1880; reprint, New Delhi: 2004; A. H. Bingley, *Handbook on Rajputs*, 1899; reprint, New Delhi: 1999.
21. See for instance John Rich and Graham Shipley (eds), *War and Society in the Greek World*, 1993; reprint, London/New York: 1995; Frank Tallett, *War and Society in Early Modern Europe: 1495–1715*, 1992; reprint, London/New York: 1997; Brian Bond, *War and Society in Europe: 1870–1970*, 1984; reprint, Phoenix Mill, Thrupp: 1998. One could go on adding to this list.
22. Geoff Eley, 'Edward Thompson, Social History and Political Culture: The Making of a Working Class Public, 1780–1850', in Keith McClelland and Harvey J. Kaye (eds), *E. P. Thompson: Critical Perspectives*, Cambridge: 1990, p. 13.
23. Stanislav Andreski, *Military Organization and Society*, London: 1954.
24. Seema Alavi, 'The Makings of Company Power: James Skinner in the Ceded and Conquered Provinces, 1802-40', *Indian Economic and Social History Review* (henceforth *IESHR*), 30(4), 1993, pp. 437–66; Seema Alavi, *The Sepoys and the Company: Tradition and Transition in Northern India, 1770–1830*, Delhi: 1995.
25. David Omissi, *The Sepoy and the Raj: The Indian Army, 1860–1940*, Houndmills, Basingstoke: 1994.
26. Field Marshal Viscount Slim, *Defeat into Victory*, 1956; reprint, Dehra Dun: 1981, pp. 43–4.
27. George MacMunn, *The Indian Mutiny in Perspective*, London: 1931, p. 11.
28. Louis Allen views the Indian Army during World War II as a mercenary force. Louis Allen, 'The Campaigns in Asia and the Pacific', in John

Gooch (ed.), *Decisive Campaigns of the Second World War*, London: 1990, p. 169.

29. One representative of Imperialist historiography is Denis Judd. See his *The Lion and the Tiger: The Rise and Fall of the British Raj*, New Delhi: 2004, p. 154.
30. Robert Eric Frykenberg, 'Conflicting Norms and Political Integration in South India: The Case of Vellore Mutiny', *Indo-British Review*, 13(1), 1987, p. 52.
31. For the anthropologists' notion see Renato Rosaldo, 'Celebrating Thompson's Heroes: Social Analysis in History and Anthropology', in McClelland and Kaye (eds), *E. P. Thompson*, p. 119.
32. Douglas M. Peers, 'Imperial Vice: Sex, Drink and the Health of British Troops in North India Cantonments, 1800–1858', in David Killingray and David Omissi (eds), *Guardians of Empire: The Armed Forces of the Colonial Powers c. 1700–1964*, Manchester/New York: 1999, p. 34.
33. Jaap de Moor, 'The Recruitment of Indonesian Soldiers for the Dutch Colonial Army, c. 1700–1950', in Killingray and Omissi (eds), *Guardians of Empire*, p. 54.
34. Henry Mead, *The Sepoy Revolt*, 1857; reprint, Delhi: 1986, p. 2.
35. Willerd R. Fann, 'On the Infantryman's Age in Eighteenth Century Prussia', *Military Affairs*, 41(3–4), 1977, pp. 165–70.
36. For the literature on sahib-sepoy entente, see Kaushik Roy, 'The Historiography of the Colonial Indian Army', *Studies in History*, New Series, 12(2), 1996, pp. 255–71.
37. Stephen P. Cohen, *The Indian Army: Its Contribution to the Development of a Nation*, 1971; reprint, New Delhi: 1991.
38. Philip Mason, *A Matter of Honour: An Account of the Indian Army, Its Officers and Men*, 1974; reprint, Dehra Dun: 1988. To be fair to Mason, he also notes the importance of economic incentives in generating loyalty bonds between the sepoys and the sahibs. See, Philip Mason, 'Introduction', in George Otto Trevelyan, *Cawnpore*, 1865; reprint, New Delhi: 1992, pp. 2-3.
39. Rudrangshu Mukherjee, *Awadh in Revolt: 1857–58: A Study of Popular Resistance*, New Delhi: 1984, p. 72.
40. Lorenzo M. Crowell, 'Military Professionalism in a Colonial Context: The Madras Army, circa 1832', *Modern Asian Studies* (henceforth *MAS*), vol. 24, 1990, pp. 249–72.
41. James W. Hoover, 'The Recruitment of the Bengal Army: Beyond the Myth of the Zemindar's Son', *Indo-British Review*, 21(2), 1996, pp. 144–56.
42. C. A. Bayly, 'Editor's Concluding Note: Eric Stokes and the Uprising of 1857', in Eric Stokes, *The Peasant Armed: The Indian Revolt of 1857*, edited by C. A. Bayly, Oxford: 1986, pp. 230–1; Eric Stokes, 'Rural Revolt in the Great Rebellion of 1857 in India: A Study of the Saharanpur

and Muzaffarnagar Districts', *Historical Journal*, 12(4), 1969, pp. 606–26.

43. C. A. Bayly, 'Two Colonial Revolts: The Java War, 1825–30, and the Indian "Mutiny" of 1857–59', in C. A. Bayly and D. H. A. Kolff (eds), *Two Colonial Empires: Comparative Essays on the History of India and Indonesia in the Nineteenth Century*, Dordrecht/Lancaster: 1986, p. 128.
44. C. A. Bayly, 'Introduction', in Stokes, *The Peasant Armed*, p. 14.
45. Stephen Peter Rosen, *Societies and Military Power: India and its Armies*, New Delhi: 1996, pp. 180–96; Dirk H. A. Kolff, *Naukar, Rajput and Sepoy: The Ethnohistory of the Military Labour Market in Hindustan, 1450–1850*, Cambridge: 1990, pp. 182–99.
46. William H. Sewell, Jr., 'How Classes are Made: Critical Reflections on E. P. Thompson's Theory of Working Class Formation', in McClellannd and Kaye (eds), *E. P. Thompson*, pp. 52–6.
47. Tapti Roy, 'Visions of the Rebels: A Study of 1857 in Bundelkhand', *MAS*, 27(1), 1993, pp. 205–28; Tapti Roy, *The Politics of a Popular Uprising: Bundelkhand in 1857*, New Delhi: 1994.
48. Maya Gupta, *Lord William Bentinck in Madras and the Vellore Mutiny, 1803–7*, New Delhi: 1986.
49. MacMunn, *Indian Mutiny*, p. 15.
50. One such officer was Keith Young. See Henry W. Norman and Keith Young, *Delhi 1857*, 1902; reprint, Delhi: 2001, p. 7.
51. Norman and Young, *Delhi 1857*, p. 3.
52. G. B. Malleson, *The Indian Mutiny of 1857*, 1891; reprint, Delhi: 1988, p. v.
53. Malleson, *Indian Mutiny*, p. 7.
54. Brian McAllister Linn, 'Cerebrus' Dilemma: The US Army and Internal Security in the Pacific, 1902-40', in Killingray and Omissi (eds), *Guardians of Empire*, p. 118.
55. Eric Stokes has stressed the role of J. Bentham, James Mill, and broadly Utilitarian philosophy in influencing the legal system in colonial India. Eric Stokes, *The English Utilitarian and India*, 1959; reprint, Delhi: 1982.
56. Douglas M. Peers, 'Sepoys, Soldiers and the Lash: Race, Caste and Army Discipline in India, 1820–50', *Journal of Imperial and Commonwealth History* (henceforth *JICH*), 23(2), 1995, pp. 212–47.
57. Kaushik Roy, 'Coercion through Leniency: British Manipulation of the Courts-Martial System in the Post-Mutiny Indian Army, 1859–1913', *Journal of Military History* (hereafter *JMH*), vol. 65, 2001, pp. 937–64. Roy, 'Spare the Rod, Spoil the Soldier? Crime and Punishment in the Army of India, 1860–1913', *Journal of the Society for Army Historical Research* (henceforth *JSAHR*), 84(337), 2006, pp. 9–33.
58. David Killingray, 'Gender Issues and African Colonial Armies', in Killingray and Omissi (eds), *Guardians of Empire*, p. 222.

59. Kaushik Roy, 'Logistics and the Construction of Loyalty: The Welfare Mechanism in the Indian Army, 1859–1913', in P. S. Gupta and Anirudh Deshpande (eds), *The British Raj and its Indian Armed Forces: 1857–1939*, New Delhi: 2002, pp. 98–124.
60. Timothy Parsons, 'All *Askaris* are Family Men: Sex, Domesticity and Discipline in the King's African Rifles, 1902–1964', in Killingray and Omissi (eds), *Guardians of Empire*, pp. 170, 172.
61. Peter Stanley, '"Dear Comrades": Barrack Room Culture and the "White Mutiny" of 1859–60', *Indo-British Review*, 21(2), 1996, pp. 165–75; Peter Stanley, *White Mutiny: British Military Culture in India, 1825–75*, London: 1998.
62. Raffi Gregorian, 'Unfit for Service: British Law and Looting in India in the Mid-Nineteenth Century', *South Asia*, 13(1), 1990, pp. 63–84; Richard Holmes, *Sahib: The British Soldier in India, 1750–1914*, London: 2005.
63. Allen, 'Campaigns in Asia and the Pacific', in Gooch (ed.), *Decisive Campaigns*, p. 169.
64. Harbakhsh Singh, *In the Line of Duty: A Soldier Remembers*, New Delhi: 2000, pp. 92–3.
65. Louis Allen, *Burma: The Longest War, 1942–45*, 1984; reprint, London/New York: 2002, pp. 27–9, 33.
66. Chandar S. Sundaram, 'Soldier Disaffection and the Creation of the Indian National Army', *Indo-British Review*, 18(1), 1990, pp. 155–62.
67. Indar Jit Rikhye, *Trumpets and Tumults: The Memoirs of a Peacekeeper*, New Delhi: 2002, pp. 62-3.
68. Rosen, *Societies and Military Power*.
69. Kolff, *Naukar, Rajput and Sepoy*.
70. DeWitt C. Ellinwood and Cynthia H. Enloe, 'Preface', in Ellinwood and Enloe (eds), *Ethnicity and the Military in Asia*.
71. Cynthia H. Enloe, 'Ethnicity in the Evolution of Asia's Armed Bureaucracies', in Enloe and Ellinwood (eds), *Ethnicity and the Military in Asia*, pp. 2–14.
72. David Omissi, '"Martial Races": Ethnicity and Security in Colonial India, 1858–1939', *War and Society*, 9(1), 1991, pp. 2–27.
73. Zakaria Haji Ahmad, 'The Bayonet and the Truncheon: Army/Police Relations in Malaysia', in Ellinwood and Enloe (eds), *Ethnicity and the Military in Asia*, pp. 209–10.
74. Lanny Bruce Fields, 'Ethnicity in Tso Tsung-T'ang's Armies: The Campaigns in North West China, 1867–80', in Ellinwood and Enloe (eds), *Ethnicity and the Military in Asia*, pp. 55, 74.
75. William R. Heaton, 'The Chinese People's Liberation Army and Minority Nationalities', in Ellinwood and Enloe (eds), *Ethnicity and the Military in Asia*, p. 177.
76. Constance M. Wilson, 'Burmese-Karen Warfare, 1840–50: A Thai View', in Ellinwood and Enloe (eds), *Ethnicity and the Military in Asia*, p. 19.

77. For a discussion on these aspects see Jonathan R. Adelman, 'The Formative Influence of the Civil Wars: Societal Roles of the Soviet and Chinese Armies', *Armed Forces and Society*, 5(1), 1978, pp. 93–116.
78. Dewitt C. Ellinwood and S. D. Pradhan, 'Introduction', in Ellinwood and Pradhan, *India and World War I*, New Delhi: 1978, pp. 2–18.
79. DeWitt C. Ellinwood, 'An Historical Study of the Punjabi Soldier in World War I', in Harbans Singh and N. Gerald Barrier (eds), *Punjab Past and Present: Essays in Honour of Dr. Ganda Singh*, Patiala, 1976, pp. 337–62.
80. Carol Hills and Daniel C. Silverman, 'Nationalism and Feminism in Late Colonial India: The Rani of Jhansi Regiment, 1943–45', *MAS*, 27(4), 1993, pp. 742–60.
81. Stephen P. Cohen, 'The Untouchable Soldier: Caste, Politics, and the Indian Army', *Journal of Asian Studies* (hereafter *JAS*), 28(3), 1969, pp. 453–68.
82. Frank Furedi, 'The Demobilized African Soldier and the Blow to White Prestige', in Killingray and Omissi (eds), *Guardians of Empire*, pp. 179–97.
83. John A. Lynn, *Battle: A History of Combat and Culture from Ancient Greece to Modern America*, Boulder, Colorado: 2003, pp. xix, xxi.
84. Keith McClelland, 'Introduction', in McClelland and Kaye (eds), *E.P. Thompson*, p. 3.
85. Eden Vansittart, *Gurkhas: Handbooks on the Indian Army compiled under the Orders of the Government of India*, 1906; reprint, New Delhi: 1991, pp. 48–64; C. J. Morris, *The Gurkhas: An Ethnology*, 1933; reprint, New Delhi: 1993, pp. 38–53.
86. Edward W. Said, *Orientalism: Western Conceptions of the Orient*, 1978; reprint, New Delhi: 2001.
87. Channa Wickremesekera, *'Best Black Troops in the World': British Perceptions and the Making of the Sepoy, 1746–1805*, New Delhi: 2002.
88. Premansu Kumar Bandopadhyay, *Tulsi Leaves and the Ganges Water: The Slogan of the First Sepoy Mutiny at Barrackpore, 1824*, Kolkata: 2003.
89. Vivien Ashima Kaul, ' "Sepoys" Links with Society: A Study of the Bengal Army, 1858–95', in Gupta and Deshpande (eds), *British Raj and its Indian Armed Forces*, pp. 125–78.
90. For an exhaustive analysis of the literature on the 'martial race' theory, see Kaushik Roy, 'Beyond the Martial Race Theory: A Historiographical Assessment of Recruitment in the British-Indian Army', *Calcutta Historical Review*, vols 21–2 combined (1999–2000), pp. 139–54.
91. Douglas M. Peers, '"The Habitual Nobility of Being": British Officers and the Social Construction of the Bengal Army in the Early Nineteenth Century', *MAS*, 25(3), 1991, pp. 566, 569; Peers, 'Colonial

Knowledge and the Military in India, 1780–1860', *JICH*, 33(2), 2005, pp. 157–80.

92. Benedict Anderson, *Imagined Communities: Reflections on the Origin and Spread of Nationalism*, 1983; reprint, London/New York: 1987, pp. 13, 15–16.
93. Lionel Caplan, *Warrior Gentleman: 'Gurkhas' in Western Imagination*, Providence/Oxford: 1995, pp. 1, 3; Lionel Caplan, '"Bravest of the Brave": Representations of "The Gurkhas" in British Military Writings', *MAS*, 25(3), 1991, pp. 572–97.
94. Kate Teltscher, *India Inscribed: European and British Writing on India, 1600–1800*, New Delhi: 1995, pp. 2, 6.
95. Pradeep P. Barua, 'Inventing Race: The British and India's Martial Races', *Historian*, 58(1), 1995, pp. 107–16; Mary Des Chene, 'Military Ethnology in British India', *South Asia Research*, 19(2), 1999, pp. 122–35.
96. Philip Constable, 'The Marginalization of a Dalit Martial Race in Late Nineteenth and Early Twentieth Century Western India', *JAS*, 60(2), 2001, pp. 439–78.
97. Ellinwood, 'Ethnicity in a Colonial Asian Army', in Ellinwood and Enloe (eds), *Ethnicity and the Military in Asia*, p. 92.
98. Kaushik Roy, 'Recruitment Doctrines of the Colonial Indian Army: 1859–1913', *IESHR*, 34(3), 1997, pp. 322–54.
99. Eric Hobsbawm and Terence Ranger (eds), *The Invention of Tradition*, 1983; reprint, Cambridge: 1995.
100. John Keegan, 'Inventing Military Traditions', in Chris Wrigley (ed.), *Warfare, Diplomacy and Politics: Essays in Honour of A.J.P. Taylor*, London: 1986, pp. 58–79.
101. Kaushik Roy, 'The Construction of Regiments in the Indian Army: 1859–1913', *War in History*, 8(2), 2001, pp. 127–48.
102. Susanne Hoeber Rudolph and Lloyd I. Rudolph, 'Becoming a Diarist: Amar Singh's Construction of an Indian Personal Document', *IESHR*, 25(2), 1988, pp. 113–32.
103. Streets, *Martial Races*, p. viii.
104. Thomas R. Metcalf, 'Sikh Recruitment for Colonial Military and Police Forces, 1874–1914', in Metcalf, *Forging the Raj*, pp. 250–81.
105. Streets, *Martial Races*, pp. 157–8, 167, 178.
106. Craig M. Cameron in *American Samurai: Myth, Imagination and the Conduct of Battle in the First Marine Division, 1942–51*, Cambridge: 1994, pp. 49–88, shows how masculine ideal is integral to the ideology of creating marines, the elite within the American armed services.
107. Pradeep P. Barua, *The Army Officer Corps and Military Modernization in Later Colonial India*, Hull: 1999.
108. P. S. Gupta, 'The Army, Politics and Constitutional Change in India, 1919–39', in P. S. Gupta, *Power, Politics and the People: Studies in British Imperialism and Indian Nationalism*, New Delhi: 2001,

pp. 219–39; Gautam Sharma, *Nationalization of the Indian Army: 1885–1947*, Bombay: 1996; C. S. Sundaram, 'Preventing "Idleness": The Maharaja of Cooch Behar's Proposal for Officer Commissions in the British Army for the Sons of Indian Princes and Gentleman, 1897–98', *South Asia*, 18(1), 1995, pp. 115–30.

109. William Gutteridge, 'The Indianization of the Indian Army: 1918–45', *Race*, 4(2), 1963, pp. 39–48.
110. For the debate how total World War II was, see Roger Chickering and Stig Forster, 'Are We there Yet? World War II and the Theory of Total War', in Chickering, Forster and Bernd Greiner (eds), *A World at Total War: Global Conflict and the Politics of Destruction, 1937–45*, Cambridge: 2005, pp. 2–16.
111. Douglas M. Peers, *Between Mars and Mammon: Colonial Armies and the Garrison State in Early Nineteenth Century India*, London/New York: 1995; Peers, 'Between Mars and Mammon; The East India Company and Efforts to Reform its Army, 1796–1832', *The Historical Journal*, 33(2), 1990, pp. 385–401; C. A. Bayly, 'The British Military-Fiscal State and Indigenous Resistance: India, 1750–1820', in C. A. Bayly, *Origins of Nationality in South Asia: Patriotism and Ethical Government in the Making of Modern India*, New Delhi: 1998, pp. 238–75. For the genesis and operation of the fiscal-military machine in Britain during the early modern era see John Brewer, *The Sinews of Power: War, Money and the English State, 1688–1783*, London: 1989.
112. Douglas M. Peers, 'War and Public Finance in Early Nineteenth Century British India: The First Burma War', *International History Review*, 11(4), 1989, pp. 628–47.
113. Purushottam Banskota, *The Gurkha Connection: A History of the Gurkha Recruitment in the British Indian Army*, New Delhi: 1994; Mary Des Chene, 'Soldiers, Sovereignty and Silences: Gorkhas as Diplomatic Currency', *South Asia Bulletin*, 13(1–2), 1993, pp. 67–80.
114. Tan Tai Yong, 'Sepoys and the Colonial State: Punjab and the Military Base of the Indian Army, 1849–1900', in Gupta and Deshpande (eds), *British Raj and its Indian Armed Forces*, pp. 7–44.
115. Tan Tai Yong, 'Maintaining the Military Districts: Civil-Military Integration and District Soldiers Boards in the Punjab, 1919–39', *MAS*, 28(4), 1994, pp. 833–74; Tan Tai Yong, 'An Imperial Home Front: Punjab and the First World War', *JMH*, 64(2), 2000, pp. 372–410.
116. Tan Tai Yong, 'Mobilization, Militarization and "Mal-Contentment": Punjab and the Second World War', *South Asia: Journal of South Asian Studies*, new series, 25(2), 2002, pp. 137–51.
117. Kaushik Roy, 'Feeding the Leviathan: Supplying the British-Indian Army, 1859–1913', *JSAHR*, 80(322), 2002, pp. 144–61.
118. Lorenzo M. Crowell, 'Logistics in the Madras Army *circa* 1830', *War and Society*, 10(2), 1992, pp. 2–33.
119. Anand A. Yang, after a micro-study of rural structure of a particular

region has reached the conclusion about the limited reach of the colonial regime in his monograph titled *The Limited Raj: Agrarian Relations in Colonial India, Saran District, 1793–1920*, New Delhi: 1989.

120. Tan Tai Yong, *The Garrison State: The Military, Government and Society in Colonial Punjab, 1849–1947*, New Delhi: 2005.
121. Michael Howard, 'Total War in the Twentieth Century: Participation and Consensus in the Second World War', in Brian Bond and Ian Roy (eds), *War and Society: A Yearbook of Military History*, New York: 1975, pp. 218, 224.
122. Tirthankar Roy, *The Economic History of India: 1857–1947*, New Delhi: 2000.
123. K. N. Reddy, 'Indian Defence Expenditure: 1872-1967', *IESHR*, vol. 7, 1970, pp. 467–88.
124. Clive Dewey, 'Some Consequences of Military Expenditure in British India: The Case of Upper Sind Sagar Doab, 1849–1947', in Clive Dewey (ed.), *Arrested Development in India: The Historical Dimension*, New Delhi: 1988, pp. 93–169.
125. Rajit K. Mazumder, *The Indian Army and the Making of Punjab*, New Delhi: 2003; Rajit K. Mazumder, 'Military Imperatives and the Expansion of Agriculture in Colonial Punjab', *International Journal of Punjab Studies*, 8(2), 2001, pp. 157–85.
126. Johannes H. Voigt, *India in the Second World War*, New Delhi: 1987.
127. P. S. Gupta, 'Imperial Strategy and the Transfer of Power, 1939–51'; 'India in Commonwealth Defence, 1947–56', in Gupta, *Power, Politics and the People*, pp. 240–322.
128. For instance, Ronald Spector, 'The Royal Indian Navy Strike of 1946: A Study of Cohesion and Disintegration in Colonial Armed Forces', *Armed Forces and Society*, 7(2), 1981, pp. 272–83; Anirudh Deshpande, 'Hopes and Disillusionment: Recruitment, Demobilization and the Emergence of Discontent in the Indian Armed Forces after the Second World War', *IESHR*, vol. 33, 1996, pp. 175–207.
129. John Gallagher and Anil Seal, 'Britain and India between the Wars', *MAS*, 15(3), 1981, pp. 387–414; Keith Jeffery, 'The Eastern Arc of Empire: A Strategic View, 1850–1950', *Journal of Strategic Studies* (henceforth *JSS*), 5(4), 1982, pp. 532–45.
130. Keith Jeffery, '"An English Barrack in the Oriental Seas"? India in the Aftermath of the First World War', *MAS*, 15(3), 1981, pp. 369–86.
131. C. A. Bayly and Tim Harper, *Forgotten Armies: The Fall of British Asia, 1942–45*, London: 2004.
132. Indivar Kamtekar, 'A Different War Dance: State and Class in India, 1939–45', *Past and Present*, no. 176, August 2002, pp. 187–221.
133. Philip Towle, 'The Debate on Wartime Censorship in Britain', in Bond and Roy (eds), *War and Society*, pp. 103–12.

134. Sanjoy Bhattacharya, 'British Military Information Management Techniques and the South Asian Soldier: Eastern India during the Second World War', *MAS*, 34(2), 2000, pp. 483–510.
135. Sanjoy Bhattacharya, *Propaganda and Information in Eastern India 1939–45: A Necessary Weapon of War*, Richmond, Surrey: 2001.
136. Philip Woods, '"Chappatis by Parachute": The Use of Newsreels in British Propaganda in India in the Second World War', *South Asia*, 23(2), 2000, pp. 89–109.
137. Peter Paret, *Understanding War: Essays on Clausewitz and the History of Military Power*, Princeton: 1992, p. 219.
138. Carl Von Clausewitz, *On War*, ed. and tr. by Michael Howard and Peter Paret, 1976; reprint, Princeton: 1989, pp. 80, 99.
139. Two examples of this School are T.R. Moreman's, *The Army in India and the Development of Frontier Warfare: 1849–1947*, Houndmills, Basingstoke: 1998; and Alan Warren's, *Waziristan: The Faqir of Ipi and the Indian Army, The North West Frontier Revolt of 1936–37*, Karachi: 2000.
140. Charles Allen, *Soldier Sahibs: The Men who made the North West Frontier*, London: 2000.
141. T. R. Moreman, 'The Arms Trade and the North-West Frontier Pathan Tribes, 1890–1914', *JICH*, 22(2), 1994, pp. 187–216; T. R. Moreman, '"Small Wars" and "Imperial Policing": The British Army and the Theory and Practice of Colonial Warfare in the British Empire, 1919–39', *JSS*, 19(4), 1996, pp. 105–6; Alan Warren, '"Bullocks Treading down Wasps"?: The British Indian Army in Waziristan in the 1930s', *South Asia*, 19(2), 1996, pp. 35–56.
142. Philip Warner, *Auchinleck: The Lonely Soldier*, 1981; reprint, London: 2001, p. 266.
143. Colonel C. E. Callwell, *Small Wars: A Tactical Textbook for Imperial Soldiers*, 1896; reprint, London: 1990, p. 286.
144. G. J. Younghusband, *Indian Frontier Warfare*, 1898; reprint, New Delhi: 1985, pp. 2–3.
145. Younghusband, *Indian Frontier Warfare*, p. 4.
146. V. J. Parry and M. E. Yapp, 'Introduction', in Parry and Yapp (eds), *War, Technology and Society in the Middle East*, London: 1975, p. 19.
147. General Andrew Skeen, *Passing it On: Short Talks on Tribal Fighting on the North West Frontier of India*, 1932; reprint, New Delhi: 1965, Preface to 4th Edition.
148. Tim Moreman, '"Watch and Ward": The Army in India and the North West Frontier, 1920–39', in Killingray and Omissi (eds), *Guardians of Empire*, pp. 148, 151.
149. Ronald J. Barr, 'High Command in the United States: The Emergence of a Modern System, 1898–1920', in G. D. Sheffield (ed.), *Leadership and Command: The Anglo-American Military Experience Since 1861*, London/Washington: 1997, p. 57.

150. For the British and American armies, see Sheffield, 'Introduction', in Sheffield (ed.), *Leadership and Command*, p. 12.
151. J. M. Bourne, 'British Generals in the First World War', in Sheffield (ed.), *Leadership and Command*, p. 94.
152. Joseph G. Dawson III, '"Zealous for Annexation": Volunteer Soldiering, Military Government, and the Service of Colonel Alexander Doniphan in the Mexican-American War', *JSS*, 19(4), 1996, pp. 13, 15.
153. Linn, 'Cerebrus' Dilemma', in Killingray and Omissi (eds), *Guardians of Empire*, pp. 117–18.
154. Joseph Smith, 'The Spanish-American War: Land Battles in Cuba, 1895–98', *JSS*, 19(4), 1996, pp. 38–40.
155. Kirsten Zirkel, 'Military Power in German Colonial Policy: The *Schutztruppen* and their Leaders in East and South-West Africa, 1888–1918', in Killingray and Omissi (eds), *Guardians of Empire*, pp. 100–101.
156. Narayani Gupta, 'Military Security and Urban Development: A Case Study of Delhi, 1857–1912', *MAS*, 5(1), 1971, pp. 62–77.
157. Gyanesh Kudaisya, '"In Aid of Civil Power": The Colonial Army in Northern India, *c.* 1919–42', *JICH*, 32(1), 2004, pp. 42–68.
158. Robin Jeffrey, 'The Punjab Boundary Force and the Problem of Order, August 1947', *MAS*, 8(4), 1974, pp. 492–520.
159. Brian Bond, *British Military Policy between the Two World Wars*, Oxford: 1980, pp. 7–8.
160. Christina Goulter, 'Sir Arthur Harris: Different Perspectives', in Gary Sheffield and Geoffrey Till (eds), *The Challenges of High Command: The British Experience*, Houndmills, Basingstoke: 2003, p. 127.
161. Bond, *British Military Policy*, p. 105.
162. Ian F. W. Beckett, 'Command in the Late Victorian Army', in Sheffield (ed.), *Leadership and Command*, p. 38.
163. Kaushik Roy, 'Goliath against David: Militaries against the Militias', *Contemporary India*, 1(1), 2002, pp. 138–42.
164. J. J. A. Wallace, 'Maneuver Theory in Operations other than War', *JSS*, 19(4), 1996, p. 224.
165. K.V. Krishna Rao, *In the Service of the Nation: Reminiscences*, New Delhi: 2001, pp. 392–544.
166. Jeffrey Greenhut, 'The Imperial Reserve: The Indian Corps on the Western Front, 1914–15', *JICH*, 12(1), 1983, pp. 54–73.
167. Edwin Latter, 'The Indian Army in Mesopotamia, 1914–18', Part II, *JSAHR*, LXXII(291), 1994, pp. 160–79.
168. Anirudh Deshpande, *British Military Policy in India, 1900–1945: Colonial Constraints and Declining Power*, New Delhi: 2005.
169. F. W. Perry, *The Commonwealth Armies: Manpower and Organization in two World Wars*, Manchester: 1988, pp. 82–123.
170. S. D. Pradhan, 'Indian Army and the First World War', in Ellinwood and Pradhan (eds), *India and World War I*, pp. 49–67; Pradhan,

'Organization of the Indian Army on the eve of the Outbreak of the First World War', *Journal of the United Service Institution of India*, 102(426), 1972, pp. 62–78.

171. Gordon Corrigan, *Sepoys in the Trenches: The Indian Corps on the Western Front, 1914–15*, Staplehurst, Kent: 1999.
172. Pradeep P. Barua, 'Strategies and Doctrines of Imperial Defence: Britain and India, 1919–45', *JICH*, 25(2), 1997, pp. 240–66; Daniel P. Marston, *Phoenix from the Ashes: The Indian Army in 3urma Campaign*, Westport, Conecticut/London: 2003.
173. Paul Kennedy, 'A.J.P. Taylor and "Profound Forces" in History', in Wrigley (ed.), *Warfare, Diplomacy and Politics*, p. 15.
174. Subrahmanyam, *Mughals and Franks*, p. 72.
175. Dennis Showalter, *Patton and Rommel: Men of War in the Twentieth Century*, New York: 2005.
176. Singh, *In the Line of Duty*.
177. S. P. P. Thorat, *From Reveille to Retreat*, New Delhi: 1986, pp. 53–5, 115.
178. Michael Howard, 'Leadership in the British Army in the Second World War: Some Personal Observations', in Sheffield (ed.), *Leadership and Command*, p. 117.
179. Geoffrey Evans, *Slim as Military Commander*, 1969; reprint, Dehra Dun: 1977, p. 15.
180. Stephen Hart, 'Montgomery, Morale, Casualty Conservation and "Colossal Cracks": 21st Army Group's Operational Technique in North West Europe', *JSS*, 19(4), 1996, p. 139.
181. Gary Sheffield, 'The Challenges of High Command in the Twentieth Century', in Sheffield and Geoffrey Till (eds), *Challenges of High Command*, pp. 3, 7.
182. Howard, 'Leadership in the British Army', in Sheffield (ed.), *Leadership and Command*, pp. 118–19.
183. Christopher Sykes, *Orde Wingate*, London: 1959, p. 543. A positive image of Wingate also emerges from David Rooney, 'Command and Leadership in the Chindit Campaigns', in Sheffield (ed.), *Leadership and Command*, pp. 142–56. See also John W. Gordon, 'Major-General Orde Wingate', in John Keegan (ed.), *Churchill's Generals*, 1991; reprint, London: 1993, pp. 277–97.
184. Brian Holden Reid, 'The Italian Campaign, 1943–45: A Reappraisal of Allied Generalship', in Gooch (ed.), *Decisive Campaigns*, p. 149.
185. G. D. Sheffield, 'Introduction: Command, Leadership and the Anglo-American Experience', in Sheffield (ed.), *Leadership and Command*, p. 10.
186. Ronald Lewin, *Slim: The Standardbearer*, 1976; reprint, London: 1978; Evans, *Slim*.
187. Lewin, *Slim*, pp. 192, 196.
188. John Keegan, 'Introduction', in Keegan (ed.), *Churchill's Generals*, pp. 13–14.

189. Robert Lyman, 'The Art of Maneuver at the Operational Level of War: Lieutenant-General W.J. Slim and Fourteenth Army, 1944–45', in Sheffield and Till (eds), *Challenges of High Command*, p. 91.
190. Duncan Anderson, 'The Very Model of a Modern Maneuverist General: William Slim and the Exercise of High Command in Burma'; Lyman, 'Art of Maneuver at the Operational Level of War', in Sheffield and Till (eds), *Challenges of High Command*, pp. 73–87, 88–112.
191. Duncan Anderson, 'Field-Marshal Lord Slim', in Keegan (ed.), *Churchill's Generals*, p. 319.
192. Carter Malkasian, *A History of Modern Wars of Attrition*, Westport, Connecticut: 2002, pp. 92–117.
193. Nigel de Lee, 'Scandinavian Disaster: Allied Failure in Norway in 1940', in Sheffield and Till (eds), *Challenges of High Command*, pp. 59–60.
194. John Kiszely, 'The British Army and Approaches to Warfare since 1945', *JSS*, 19(4), 1996, pp. 179–87; Reid, 'The Italian Campaign', in Gooch (ed.), *Decisive Campaigns*, p. 152.
195. John Gooch, 'Attitudes to War in Late Victorian and Edwardian England', in Bond and Roy (eds), *War and Society*, pp. 88–102.
196. *Official History of the Indian Armed Forces in the Second World War 1939–45*, E. K. K. Pillai (ed.), B. L. Raina, Director Bisheshwar Prasad (series eds), , *The Campaigns in the Western Theatre*, New Delhi: 1958.
197. Kenneth F. Kiple and Kriemhild Conee Ornelas, 'Race, War and Tropical Medicine in the Eighteenth Century Caribbean', in David Arnold (ed.), *Warm Climates and Western Medicine: The Emergence of Tropical Medicine, 1500–1900*, Amsterdam: 1996, pp. 65–79.
198. Warwick Anderson, 'Race and Acclimatization in Colonial Medicine: Disease, Race and Empire', *Bulletin of the History of Medicine*, 70(1), 1996, pp. 62–7.
199. Roger Cooter and Steve Sturdy, 'Introduction', in Cooter, Sturdy and Mark Harrison (eds), *War, Medicine and Modernity*, Phoenix Mill, Thrupp: 1998, pp. 2–21; Mark Harrison, 'Medicine and the Management of Modern Warfare', *History of Science*, Part 4, 34(106), 1996, pp. 379–410.
200. Mark Harrison, *Medicine and Victory: British Military Medicine in the Second World War*, Oxford: 2004.
201. Mark Harrison, 'Disease, Discipline and Dissent: The Indian Army in France and England, 1914–15', in Mark Harrison, Roger Cooter and Steve Sturdy (eds), *Medicine and Modern Warfare*, Amsterdam: 1999, pp. 185–203.
202. Sumit Guha, 'Nutrition, Sanitation, Hygiene, and the Likelihood of Death: The British Army in India c. 1870–1920', *Population Studies*, vol. 47, 1993, pp. 385–401.
203. Mark Harrison, *Climates and Constitutions: Health, Race, Environment and British Imperialism in India, 1600–1850*, New Delhi: 1999.

204. Arnold P. Kaminsky, 'Morality Legislation and British Troops in Late Nineteenth Century India', *Military Affairs*, 43(2), 1979, pp. 78–83.
205. David Arnold, *Colonizing the Body: State Medicine and Epidemic Disease in Nineteenth Century India*, New Delhi: 1993.
206. Victor Davis Hanson, *Carnage and Culture: Landmark Battles in the Rise of Western Power*, New York: 2001.
207. Lynn, *Battle*.
208. Tarak Barkawi, 'Peoples, Homelands, and Wars? Ethnicity, the Military, and Battle among British Imperial Forces in the War against Japan', *Comparative Studies in Society and History*, 46(1), 2004, pp. 134–63.
209. Cameron, *American Samurai*, pp. 2–20.
210. Maurice Matloff, 'The Nature of History', in John E. Jessup, Jr. and Robert W. Coakley (eds), *A Guide to the Study and Use of Military History*, Washington D.C.: 1982, pp. 5, 7.
211. Robert Pois and Philip Langer, *Command Failure in War: Psychology and Leadership*, Bloomington: 2004.
212. John Keegan, *The Face of Battle: A Study of Agincourt, Waterloo and the Somme*, 1976; reprint, Harmondsworth, Middlesex: 1978.
213. One example is Christopher Duffy, *The Military Experience in the Age of Reason*, London: 1987.
214. See the essays in Victor Davis Hanson (ed.), *Hoplites: The Classical Greek Battle Experience*, 1991; reprint, London/New York: 1993.
215. Felipe Fernandez-Armesto, *The Spanish Armada: The Experience of War in 1588*, 1988; reprint, Oxford: 1989.
216. Tony Ashworth, *Trench Warfare 1914–18: The Live and Let Live System*, 1980; reprint, London: 2000.
217. Rajat Kanta Ray, 'Race, Religion and Realm: The Political Theory of "The Reigning Indian Crusade", 1857', in Mushirul Hasan and Narayani Gupta (eds), *India's Colonial Encounter: Essays in Honour of Eric Stokes*, New Delhi: 1993, pp. 156–66.
218. Killingray, 'Gender Issues', in Killingray and Omissi (eds), *Guardians of Empire*, p. 223.
219. *From Sepoy to Subedar, being the Life and Adventures of Subedar Sita Ram, a Native Officer of the Bengal Army, Written and Related by Him*, tr. by Lieutenant-Colonel Norgate, 1873; reprint, ed. by James Lunt, London: 1970.
220. Durgadas Bandopadhyay, *Amar Jivancharit* [*My Life* in Bengali], 1924; reprint, Calcutta: 1985.
221. *Indian Voices of the Great War: Soldiers' Letters, 1914–18*, selected and introduced by David Omissi, Houndmills, Basingstoke: 1999; Susan Vankosi, 'Letters Home, 1915–16: Punjabi Soldiers Reflect on War and Life in Europe and their Meanings for Home and Self', *International Journal of Punjab Studies*, vol. 2, 1995, pp. 43–63.
222. *Reversing the Gaze: Amar Singh's Diary, A Colonial Subject's Narrative of Imperial India*, edited with Commentary by Susanne Hoeber

Rudolph and Lloyd I. Rudolph with Mohan Singh Kanota, New Delhi: 2000.

223. DeWitt C. Ellinwood, Jr., *Between Two Worlds: A Rajput Officer in the Indian Army, 1905–21*, Lanham, Maryland: 2005.
224. *Rifleman to Colonel: Memoirs of Gajendra Malla 9th Gorkha Rifles*, compiled by Tony Mains and Elizabeth Talbot Rice, New Delhi: 1999.
225. *Kalyan Pradip, being the Memoir of Captain Kalyan Kumar Mukhopadhyay, IMS* (in Bengali), Calcutta: 1928; Satyen Basu, *A Doctor in the Army*, Calcutta: 1960.
226. Richard Crasta (ed.), *Eaten by the Japanese: The Memoir of an Unknown Indian Prisoner of War John Baptist Crasta*, with an Introduction and two essays by, 1998; reprint, Bangalore: 1999.
227. Percy S. Gourgey, *The Indian Naval Revolt of 1946*, Hyderabad, 1996.
228. For instance, Rikhye, *Trumpets and Tumults* and Field Marshall Cariappa Papers at National Archives of India, New Delhi.
229. John Latimer, *Burma: The Forgotten War*, 2004; reprint, London: 2005.
230. Daniel R. Headrick, *The Tools of Empire: Technology and European Imperialism in the Nineteenth Century*, New York: 1981.
231. John F. Votaw, 'An Approach to the Study of Military History', in Jessup, Jr. and Coakley (eds), *Study and Use of Military History*, p. 48.
232. Jeffrey J. Clarke, 'World Military History, 1786–1945', in Jessup, Jr. and Coakley (eds), *Study and Use of Military History*, p. 119.
233. Kaushik Roy, 'Equipping Leviathan: Ordnance Factories of British India: 1859–1913', *War in History*, 10(4), 2003, pp. 398–423.

Section I

Coercion, Discipline, and Dissent in the Sepoy Armies

1

Discipline and Disobedience in the Bengal and Madras Armies, 1807–56

Kaushik Roy and Sabyasachi Dasgupta

This article attempts to investigate questions of loyalty and dissent among the Indian soldiery of the Bengal and the Madras armies between 1807 and 1856. Links between the evolution of a corporate identity in the sepoys and their sense of loyalty are investigated. While the Bengal Army retained strong links with civilian society, the Madras Army, after initial setbacks, had by the 1820s evolved a corporate identity of its own and was relatively isolated from its host society. The term 'corporate identity' means the construction of a distinctive sepoy mentality, overriding the soldiers' primordial loyalty. To an extent, corporate identity is related to the notion of professionalism. Military professionalism, writes John F. Votaw, is an attitude or state of mind distinguishing the expert from the amateur. The military professional is an expert in the management of violence and has a sense of responsibility to the state.[1] This essay examines how strong the corporate identity was and how much the sepoys identified with the values, fears, and prejudices imbibed from civilian society.

In 1806, the Madras Army faced a formidable challenge in the form of the Vellore Mutiny. The mutiny was sparked off by the refusal of Indian troops stationed at Vellore, in May 1806, to wear the new turbans issued to them.[2] The first signs of dissent surfaced over the publication of an army order by the commander-in-chief of the Madras Army on 13 March 1806, forbidding the wearing of caste marks and ornaments during parade.[3] In reaction to the Vellore Mutiny, the Madras government rescinded the order.[4]

This essay attempts to examine the Madras Army in the aftermath of the Vellore Mutiny in comparison with the Bengal Army. By the 1820s, the colonial authorities could claim that the Madras Army was an effective and professional fighting force that could be relied upon to put down Indian rebellions. For example, the Madras Army in 1832 put down a rebellion in Vishakapatnam district. This, Lorenzo M. Crowell says, was only one of the many routine punitive expeditions the Madras military personnel were engaged in. Crowell ascribes a high degree of professionalism to the British officers and the Viceroy's Commissioned Officers (VCOs, i.e., Indian officers) of the Madras Army of the 1830s.[5] Douglas Peers turns the focus on the Bengal Army. He argues that the Bengal Army was characterized by the sepoys' sense of primordial exclusivity and the lack of authority of the British officers in the management of their regiments. Peers also says that the internal cohesiveness of these regiments was further entrenched by the tendency of the sepoys to extend their contracts beyond the initial time of three years. With a slow turnover of personnel and with the army being dependent for recruitment on the sepoys themselves, Peers argues that a sense of continuity and corporateness evolved. The Bengal sepoys constituted an extended military family from which the officers, both British and Indian, were being increasingly excluded. This indigenous high-caste identity was further strengthened by the system of accommodation. Instead of living in the barracks where, Peers feels, military socialization would have been accelerated, the sepoys arranged for their own accommodation by establishing their own hearths and messing arrangements.[6]

The present study partially agrees with Peers. Undoubtedly recruitment in the Bengal Army, with its marked high-caste bias and the manner of residence prevalent among the 'native' soldiers, must have led to a strong sense of ethnic identity based on primordial ties of caste and clan. However, if one were to take Samuel Huntington's description of a corporate identity, the personnel of a fighting force could be described as having developed a corporate identity when they had a sense of organic unity and considered themselves as a group apart from laymen. The soldier's collective sense of identity, according to Huntington, has its origin in the lengthy training and discipline necessary for professional competence, the common bond of military experience, and the sharing of a unique social responsibility.[7] While service in the army no doubt exposed the sepoys to army discipline and training, the recruitment policy of the Bengal

Army ensured that they would not consider themselves a group completely apart from common people. Judging by Huntington's index, the Bengal sepoys could not be said to possess a corporate identity. However, army life and discipline must have moulded their mentality to an extent. The sepoys were by no means peasants in uniform. While the sepoys had strong links with civilian society, they often came into conflict with the peasantry and the traditional elite. It would be more correct to say that the Bengal sepoy had a dichotomous mentality.

Social Construction of the Bengal and Madras Armies

Despite an initial bias for recruiting men of high-caste origin, the Madras Army, by the third decade of the nineteenth century, was composed mainly of Muslims, middle-caste Hindus, some low castes, and only a few high castes.[8] For instance, the 1st Infantry Regiment, which could be taken as a microcosm of the Madras infantry, in 1824 was composed of 45 per cent Muslims, 25.6 per cent Telingas, 14.5 per cent Tamils, 5 per cent low castes, and 9.2 per cent high castes. While most of the high castes came from Hindustan, (Purab, that is, west Bihar, eastern and southern Awadh/Oudh, especially the Bhojpur region) the other communities came from Karnataka, Mysore, and Andhra Pradesh.[9] Peers ascribes this preference for middle- and low-caste soldiers to the fact that military service was not the preserve of high-caste communities in south India.[10] Then too, the Bengal Army monopolized the better sorts of higher-caste recruits from north India, leaving second-grade recruits for the Madras Army.[11] However, we feel that the induction of low- and middle-caste recruits on part of the Madras Army was not entirely due to the non-availability of high-caste soldiers. There were deeper ideological underpinnings involved. Probably this decision to recruit low-caste recruits was intended to isolate the Indian contingent of the Madras Army from local attachments and sensibilities. General Harris, one of the main proponents of low-caste recruitment, noted that the lack of religious prejudices and local attachments, among others, as qualities of the low-caste recruits.[12] The objective clearly was to foster a corporate identity in the belief that an army possessing an identity separate from the linguistically and religiously divisive host society would be a disciplined and professional army.[13] Though the Vellore Mutiny in 1806 was a temporary setback in the creation of a corporate identity, the Madras Army persisted in its efforts to create a distinct identity in the sepoys.[14] It was also decided not to interfere with the religious customs of Indian soldiers, since the Vellore Mutiny had proved that even low-caste recruits were not totally devoid of caste and religious consciousness.[15]

In contrast, the recruitment policy of the Bengal Army had a pronounced high-caste bias right from the very outset. Warren Hastings laid the foundation of high-caste recruitment in the Bengal Army.[16] The Bengal Army recruited mainly from Awadh and Bihar. High-caste recruits from these areas were supposed to be loyal, obedient, faithful, and ideal soldier material. The British officials praised the deference of the Bengal sepoy for constituted authority. According to them, in the families from which the Bengal Army drew its recruits, it was unthinkable for a son to utter a disrespectful word to his parents.[17] In the eyes of the East India Company's officers, high-caste sepoys were supposed to be morally and physically a finer race in comparison with low-caste troops of the other presidencies.[18]

The general mode of recruitment was to order the sepoys and Indian officers leaving home on *furlough* (paid leave) to bring back recruits from their village.[19] In exceptional circumstances, recruiting parties were sent to Bihar and Awadh.[20] A closed-shop system originated, where ties of clan, caste, and residence ensured intimate interrelationships among the sepoys and Indian officers. As a result of this high-caste preponderance, caste became a major factor in the functioning of the Bengal Army. Convinced of the immutability of caste sentiments among its predominantly high-caste recruits, caste feeling and prejudices came to be tolerated and at times even encouraged in the Bengal Army. For instance, the Bengal sepoys refused to strike the gong at the quarter guard, fearing a loss of status. Men called *ghante pandays* were maintained and paid for the job.[21] Taking into consideration the high-caste sentiments regarding sea voyages, overseas service was voluntary until 1856, when a general order made overseas service beyond the territories of the Company compulsory.[22]

Though the two armies differed in their recruitment policies, there were certain common issues confronting these two forces which had a bearing on discipline. In the initial years the Company, guided by stereotypes that the Asiatic sepoys favoured despotic rule, sought to develop an authoritarian structure over the sepoys. John Malcolm, in his observations on the Madras Army, expressed the opinion that the sepoys were attached to their European officers.[23] In a similar vein, Governor of the Madras Presidency William Bentinck in the post-Vellore Mutiny era, stressed the importance of commanding officers in maintaining discipline among the sepoys. Bentinck claimed: 'It is understood that a popular commanding officer can do with his men mostly what he pleases.'[24] Bentinck continued that the inhabitants of this country do not comprehend the new system of government which had reduced the power of the commanding officers. A democratic sort of government was not suited for India because Indians were accustomed to despotic and arbitrary rulers. Bentinck argued that the sepoys were accustomed to look up to their British officers as all-powerful despots. So the sepoys were confused when the government reduced the power of the officers.[25]

The colonial government was also guided by the assumption that the sepoy was a mercenary soldier who could not be expected to have any sort of national loyalty while serving under British leadership. Therefore loyalty was sought to be generated by developing a strong personal bond between the sepoy and the White officer. An officer of the Madras Army, in his survey of the Maratha and Pindari campaigns in 1817 and 1818 respectively, had this to say about the native soldier: 'They serve us to make money'.[26] Henry Russell, deposing before the Select Committee during 1831–2, opined that the military force was the sole and exclusive basis on which the foundations of British rule in India lay. That military force was composed mainly of troops of whose fidelity he was doubtful. Russell commented:

> They are foreigners and mercenaries, they are attached to a government that pays them well and treats them kindly and they will generally follow wherever their officers will lead them, but we have no hold upon them through either national honour or national prejudices, and cannot expect from them what we do from English soldiers fighting for English objects. They are peculiarly susceptible of being practiced upon and may be induced by our own mismanagement or by the artifices of designing persons.[27]

Guided by such stereotypes, the colonial government followed a policy of paternalism vis-à-vis the sepoys of the three presidency armies. By paternalism, we mean the colonial government's programme of portraying the British officer as a type of stern but fair father figure, quick to reward and quick to punish. He would be a strict person, yet merciful and kind. Brave and meritorious deeds of the sepoys were to be rewarded promptly, while the officer would come down with a heavy hand on alleged misdemeanours. As part of the Company's attempt to project the European officer as a severe father figure, the British officers were vested with a lot of arbitrary powers.

The paternal officer was supposed to socialize with the sepoys off duty. In the words of Lieutenant Colonel Greenhill:

> When I entered the service in 1795 and joined a corps in 1796, most of the corps were in single corps stations. Few of the companies were at head quarters, most of them detached. The commanding officer then had unlimited powers. The men looked up to him accordingly with great respect and never thought he could do wrong, many abuses were practised by him, but they were not thought wrong. I do not advocate these abuses, he had the power to make and the power to break, and he promoted Native commissioned and non-commissioned officers as he himself pleased and always agreeable to seniority. He felt the strongest interest in their welfare, and treated them with the greatest kindness, though often with a great deal of violence, they saw no person superior to him, superior mentality could not interfere, they respected him accordingly.[28]

Autobiographical accounts by the British officers and Indian soldiers take us to a world where the former played the role of a benevolent despot. While the British officer, as mentioned before, came down heavily on perceived misdemeanours, he also buttressed his toughness by mixing with the sepoys off duty, attending their religious festivals, going out on hunting missions, and so on. For instance, the autobiography of Sitaram Panday, a subedar of the pre-1857 Bengal Army, offers an interesting insight into the dynamics which determined the functioning of the Company's Bengal infantry regiments until the first half of the nineteenth century. Sitaram came from a high-caste family of moderate means from a village in Awadh. He joined the Bengal Army as a sepoy in 1812. After his retirement in the 1860s Sitaram, at the behest of a colonel under whom he once served, wrote an autobiography. In the autobiography he throws an interesting light on the nature of sahib–sepoy interactions. Sitaram was in awe of the 'masculine and heroic' regimental captain. The fact that he used to wrestle with the sepoys, a traditional Indian recreation, and beat them at it seemed to have especially endeared the captain to the sepoys.[29] The European officers, during the early decades of the nineteenth century, were also prepared to attend nautches and often entered into liaisons with Indian women. Reminiscing about his early days in the Bengal Army, Sitaram says:

> Most of our officers had Indian women living with them and these had great influence in the regiment. They always pretended to have more influence than probably was the case, in order that they might be bribed to ask the sahibs for favours on our behalf. The sepoys themselves were sometimes instrumental in persuading the officers to take their female relations into their service.[30]

Instances of European officers showing respect to the sepoys' cultural sensibilities could also be found in the reminiscences of European officers. H. Bevan, a Madras Army officer who joined the service in 1812, affirms in his memoirs that the custom of the British officers contributing to Indian religious festivals, though condemned by many on conscientious grounds, was rendered essential by the dictates of political expediency.[31]

The Company during the closing years of the eighteenth century introduced some radical organizational changes, which had a long-term impact on the paternal relationship between the European officers and the sepoys. The year 1796 saw some far-reaching reforms. These reforms robbed of the commanding officers much of their erstwhile power by formalizing regimental organization. Promotions had to be based on seniority and were to be published in the regimental orders. The articles of war were ordered to be published in Persian and Devnagari characters. Only the commanding officer of a regiment was authorized to approve a new recruit, grant leave of absence to an Indian soldier, and to dismiss an invalid sepoy. Further, the Indian soldiers could only be dismissed for disciplinary reasons through a general court martial and the reasons for dismissal had to be recorded in the regimental orders.[32] Thus the colonial government was keen to eliminate the arbitrary powers of European officers. Also by depriving him of his financial power and privileges, the government divested the British officer of his halo and aura. The European officer was now in no position to awe the sepoy with his power, of which arbitrariness and a luxurious lifestyle had been a vital part. From now on, things were to be more bureaucratized. The only way an officer could hope to inspire awe and personal loyalty among the sepoys was by showing personal valour on the battleground.

The European officers also suffered from the ill effects of slow promotions. It took six years to become a lieutenant, 21 years to become a captain, 30 years to become a major, 39 years to become a lieutenant colonel, and 52 years to reach the rank of colonel. Such excruciatingly slow promotions naturally wore out the zeal and patience of European officers. Promotions were totally dependent on deaths and retirement. It was in no way dependent on the professional calibre of the young officers. The Company's officers also suffered in comparison to the King's officers. A man rose faster to the rank of lieutenant colonel in the British Army's regiments posted in India, compared to in the Company's armies.[33] The European officers of the Company's armies also suffered from other bad service conditions. While furlough with pay for a period of three years was allowed, very few availed of it as most officers were unable to meet the expense of travel to Britain. Some did not go home in the hope that they would secure lucrative staff appointments. Many officers also suffered so much from the weather in India that they were reluctant to come back from their holiday in England.[34]

Faced with unsatisfactory service conditions, the British officers sought solace in staff appointments, especially in the civilian spheres of the administration. In 1834, the Bengal Army had 257 officers, the Madras Army had 166 officers, while the Bombay Army had 121 on such appointments.[35] In 1851, the Bengal Army had 581 officers on civil appointments. The corresponding figures for the Madras and Bombay armies' officers were 244 and 207 respectively.[36] This in turn weakened the sepoys' familiarity with the sahibs, which resulted in fragile personal loyalty bonds.

Philip Mason says that, along with organizational changes, there occurred attitudinal changes which cast their shadow on the sahib–sepoy relationship. Mason says it was a gradual transformation and was less dramatic than supposed. One of the reasons, Mason writes, was the newfound arrogance which the British had acquired as a result of a series of victories culminating in the Third Anglo-Maratha War (1817–18). Then too, the advent of British women and missionaries brought about a sea change. The shortening of 'distance' between Europe and India also led to a change in outlook and in the recreational habits of the European officers. The practices of European officers smoking the hookah or attending nautches, says Mason, became more and more uncommon. While instances of European officers cohabiting with Indian women were common till the turn of the century, this practice was increasingly frowned upon under pressure from White women and evangelical sources. Hence the European male's contact with Indian women became progressively less.[37]

Dismayed by the apparent indifference and insensitivity of most European officers, many colonial officials were scathing in their criticism of the new generation of military officers. Officials such as Charles Napier, John Jacob, and William Sleeman were critical of the new breed of officers. Brigadier General Jacob said, 'All vital power, all good feeling, all personal attachment, all binding force of reason and moral sense had been eradicated from our native army. The outward appearance, the showy form, the mechanical discipline was greatly improved, but the ties, which formerly bound the sepoy to his English officer, were completely destroyed.'[38] Jacob commented on the inadequacy of the young subalterns in commanding regiments. He said that these young subalterns had to rely on the old Indian officers and in general were not interested in regimental matters. Their objective was to get a profitable staff posting as soon as possible.[39] Young officers were also accused of not attending to regimental duties. Subalterns spent much of their time making merry, the bar and the billiard room being their major attractions. In the words of Sleeman, 'They exhibited little interest in their regimental duties and turned instead to beer and billiards and their clubs. In the process they were alienated from their men and listened to them with impatience.'[40]

Disquiet over deterioration in the relationship between the European officers and the sepoys was also expressed in some of the depositions before the Select Committees set up periodically to take stock of Company rule in India on the basis of information given by both civil and military officials. Lieutenant Colonel Greenhill of the Madras Army, deposing before the Select Committee of 1831–2, said that the Madras sepoys were not as respectful and obedient to their officers as before. He ascribed it to the fact that they were no longer dependent on the British officers, since authority was now divided between the top bureaucrats of the Company and the commanding officers of the regiments. Greenhill also complained of excessive interference on the part of superior authorities, which had the effect of weakening discipline.[41] In similar vein, General George Pollock, deposing before the Select Committee in 1852–3, was highly critical of the way European officers interacted with the sepoys. Pollock was critical of the fact that European officers no longer attended the religious ceremonies of the sepoys and, consequently, the sepoys were not as fond of their officers as was previously the case.[42] Henry Lawrence, in the minutes dated a few days after the mutiny at Meerut in 1857, lamented that the European officers, particularly of the regular infantry regiments, did not mix with their men. Consequently, they were unable to gauge their sentiments and therefore could not sympathize with them in everyday life. Lawrence called for a reorganization of the Indian regular regiments. The British officers to these regiments should be carefully selected, said Lawrence, since the European officers posted with Indian regiments had the tendency to try to get staff appointments, failing which they became discontented.[43] In fact, interaction between the sepoys and the officers was acrimonious at times. A general order in 1832 lamented the widespread practice among Europeans and VCOs of hitting the sepoys. The Commander-in-Chief warned that in future any officer committing such abuses would be severely punished.[44]

Against this backdrop, let us examine the questions of discipline, dissent, and loyalty in the colonial armies: we will ask whether the relative isolation of the Madras Army from Indian society made it more disciplined and loyal vis-à-vis the Bengal Army, despite the overall deterioration of the British officer corps in both the armies of the Company.

Discipline and Dissent in the Bengal and Madras Armies

Cases of day-to-day dissent were comparatively rare in the Bengal Army compared to the Madras Army. By day-to-day dissent, we mean instances where a single individual chooses to defy authority. If court martial records may be taken as an index, it would seem that compared to the Madras Army, cases of day-to-day dissent in the Bengal Army were infrequent. Court martial records indicate that day-to-day cases of indiscipline were rare and the average rate in the pre-1857 Mutiny years was 1.5 cases per year. The years 1834 and 1835, saw a slight increase in the murder rate in the Bengal Army. There were 11 instances of murder committed by the sepoys of the Bengal Army in 1834 and 1835, in comparison with only 10 in the preceding 10 years. For crimes such as theft, disgraceful conduct, and desertion, the average was not higher than in the preceding decade. For instance, six Indian soldiers had been convicted for mutinous conduct between 1825 and 1833. Between 1834 and 1835, only one Indian soldier was convicted for the same reason. Three Indian soldiers deserted between 1834 and 1835, whereas the preceding 10 years had seen 16 desertions. The number of thefts during 1834–5 was six; the same rate as in the preceding 10 years. Probably the slight increase in indiscipline between 1834–5 was due to the abolition of corporal punishment.[45]

In 1834, corporal punishment for Indian soldiers was abolished. It was ordered that any regimental or brigade court martial could sentence a soldier of the Indian Army to dismissal from service for any offence for which the punishment was formerly flogging. However, a sentence of dismissal could not be implemented unless confirmed by the general officer or any other officer commanding the division.[46] The abolition of the lash sparked a lively debate and provoked conflicting opinions. Supporters of the lash argued that it was an effective weapon for maintaining discipline. However, the gist of the matter was that the lash was always sparingly used on sepoys of the Bengal Army, compared to the armies of other presidencies. Table 1.1 illustrates this fact. Thus we see the 'native' regiments in the Madras Army were flogged about seven times more frequently as the regiments of the Bengal Army. Peers argues that the preponderance of high-caste sepoys in the Bengal Army was the reason for the lash being sparingly used. As evidence, he cites the opinion of British officers, who were convinced that the use of the lash on Bengal sepoys was counter-productive. These officers felt that to strike a man in India was considered an act of great dishonour, and the higher the caste, the greater the degradation. Peers says that the preferred punishment for sepoys in the Bengal Army was dishonourable discharge. Dismissal was seen as a punishment directly affecting a caste-ridden army. In cases of the Bengal Army's sepoys being flogged, flogging was followed by immediate dismissal. Peers says that dismissal of the flogged sepoys was bound with questions of status. For one, it meant ignominy and reflected the British belief that flogging the high-caste sepoy would destroy his pride and confidence. Peers quotes Bentinck, who considered discharge to be so severe a punishment as to make the application of corporal punishment unnecessary.[47]

TABLE 1.1: LASHING IN THE BENGAL AND MADRAS ARMIES: 1829–34

	Strength of the armies	*Lashes inflicted yearly (average)*	*Lashes inflicted per regiment (average)*
Bengal Army	59,264	8,062	145
Madras Army	42,111	40,285	948

Source: Report of H. M. Commissioners for Enquiring into the System of Military Punishments in the Army, *Parliamentary Papers*, vol. 22, 1836, p. 285.

While the high-caste orientation of the Bengal Army may have been, to some extent, a determining factor in the lash being sparingly used, we feel that the very low incidence of serious crimes among the sepoys of the Bengal Army was an equally compelling factor behind the sparing use of the lash. In the wake of the abolition of the lash, the Bengal Army did not exhibit any of the characteristics which supporters of the lash had feared. Though there were some cases of sepoys defying their European officers, the frequency of such cases did not increase. In the initial days of the existence of sepoy armies, the Company relied on the vast discretionary powers of the commanding officers apart from the institution of court martial. Consequent to the reorganization of 1796, the Company increasingly relied on the mechanism of the court martial, to awe and intimidate the 'native' soldiery, as well as on the distribution of welfare measures to win over the Brown sword-arm of the Raj.

Some examples of individual indisciplinary activities of the sepoys and the response of the court martial are given below. Fateh Khan, a sepoy of the 66th Bengal Infantry Regiment, was accused before a court martial at Karnal on 20 June 1839 of having threatened to shoot his superior officer, a lieutenant named Thomas Riddel, who was also acting as adjutant. The court charged Khan with refusal to lay down his musket when ordered to do so. Fateh Khan was found guilty on both counts and was sentenced to imprisonment with hard labour for two years.[48] In another case, Busarut Khan, a sepoy in the 1st Grenadier Company of the Calcutta Native Militia, was charged with direct disobedience of orders in going to his commanding officer's quarters at Alipur on 1 August 1839. Busarut Khan repeatedly asked for discharge from service though warned by the commanding officer not to do so. Busarut Khan was also accused of refusing the punishment drill awarded to him for former misconduct. The court found him guilty on both counts and sentenced him to imprisonment with hard labour for six months.[49]

As far as the Madras Army was concerned, cases of outright defiance on the part of sepoys towards Indian and European officers were not infrequent. To cite certain instances, Jemadar Ramaswamy of the 26th Madras Infantry Regiment was accused of drunkenness while on guard at the Cutchery at Coimbatore on 15 August 1829. He was also charged with having abused the Indian non-commissioned officers and privates of the detachment. The court found him guilty on both counts and dismissed him from service.[50] Defiance was not just directed towards Indian officers; there were instances of European officers being defied too. Gopal Naik, a private in the 25th Madras Infantry Regiment, was accused of having abused his British commanding officer. The court martial which sat on 4 July 1837 at Vellore further alleged that on being asked to behave by Havildar Copeh of his company, he reiterated in an insolent and contemptuous voice: 'I am not afraid—now what can you do to me? You can only get me discharged.' The court found him guilty on both counts and dismissed him from service.[51] An examination of the sentences handed out in the above cases makes it clear that the colonial government took cases of defiance towards both European and Indian officers quite seriously. While all armies view challenges to the established hierarchy very seriously, it must remembered that in the Company's colonial armies, the Indian personnel were officered by an elite corps of foreign officers. Therefore questions of loyalty and dissent were sensitive issues in the colonial context, and the military authorities tended to clamp down on issues of defiance towards the officer corps with an iron hand.

The practice of court martial was also used to make an example out of deserters. The colonial government was especially severe on soldiers who deserted while on the field or during the course of a campaign. An indication of the seriousness with which desertion was viewed can be gauged from the fact that a soldier deserting on duty was liable to be sentenced to corporal punishment, exile, or even death. An examination of certain court martial cases involving desertion would help to illuminate this point. Abdul Singh, a sepoy of the 25th Madras Infantry Regiment, was sentenced to death on the charge of desertion on 10 December 1814 in Nagpur.[52] Havildar Husain Khan of the 2nd Madras Light Cavalry Regiment was charged with desertion in the face of the enemy on 26 July 1818. The court ordered that the Havildar be shot to death. [53]

Desertion was a problem in the Bengal Army, especially when its units were deployed in the lower provinces of the Bengal Presidency. The climate was unsuitable for the upcountry sepoys, the pay lower, and the food different.[54] Bedanput Das, a sepoy of the Second Grenadier Company, Calcutta Native Militia, was accused of desertion by a court martial assembled at Barrackpore on 5 August 1839. He was found guilty and sentenced to imprisonment with hard labour for a term of seven months.[55] A look at the court martial records would, however, indicate that the desertion rate was normally not more than 1.5 to 2 sepoys per year. It was a very low rate indeed. For instance, the number of desertions in the Bengal Army between 1825 and 1835 was 19.[56] In contrast to the Bengal sepoys, the Madras sepoys' families moved with the regiments. Consequently, the Madras sepoys' need for furlough was much less. Cases of desertion from the Madras Army were indeed very rare.[57]

Apart from cases of outright defiance and desertion, the problem of drunkenness was another concern for the colonial authorities. For example, a court martial held at Masulipatnam on 24 January 1831 charged Fakir Muhammad, subedar of the 4th Golundaz Battalion of the Madras Army, of appearing drunk at his commanding officer's quarters. The court found him guilty and dismissed him from service.[58] The problem was serious enough to warrant a public proclamation by the commander-in-chief of the Madras Army in 1831, where he lamented the progressive increase of the degrading and demoralizing vice of drunkenness among the Madras Army personnel. What the commander-in-chief found especially galling was that, while in other armies the problem of drunkenness was usually confined to the lower ranks, it was to the contrary in the Madras Army. Even socially respectable and high-ranking Indian officers could not evade its influence.[59] In contrast, drunkenness was hardly in vogue among the sepoys of the Bengal Army. One hardly comes across instances of the VCOs or sepoys of the Bengal Army being punished for what would be often termed as 'drunken misbehaviour'. There were just two isolated instances of Indian officers of the Bengal Army being tried and dismissed for misconduct while drunk in 1827 at Kanpur.[60]

Thus we see that the institution of court martial was used as a tool to discipline the Indian soldiery. And this institution was quite successful in maintaining order among the sepoys. However, certain changes within the British officer corps prepared the way for mutinies. Changes in the style of command, that is, the transition from paternalism to a more impersonal style of command, paved the way for large-scale collective indiscipline in the long run.

Concerned over the supposed deterioration in the relationship between the European officer and the sepoy, the colonial authorities sought to win the attachment of the sepoy by providing him with more privileges. Therefore, a spate of welfare measures was announced. In 1837, the Order of Merit for distinguished service in action was instituted for Indian soldiers. In accordance with this scheme, distinguished soldiers got enhanced pay. The First Class Order of Merit was reserved for subedars and resaldars in the irregular cavalry, who were to get an allowance of two rupees a day each in addition to their regimental allowances or pensions. The order ensured that Indian soldiers were officially mentioned for meritorious service.[61] The government also announced enhanced rates of pension in 1837. The pension rates are given in Table 1.2. Colonial officials placed great value on the system of pension as a mechanism for securing loyalty, since they were convinced that the pension was a novel scheme which no Indian ruler before the advent of the East India Company, had attempted. According to Viscount Gough (Commander-in-Chief of India, 1843–9), the pension was one of the greatest assets in the hands of the Company. Gough says that the poor, wounded soldiers of the erstwhile Sikh state frequently used to come up to him and point out the great distinction between the soldiers of the Company and those of the Sikh state.[62]

TABLE 1.2: PENSION IN THE COLONIAL ARMIES

Rank	*After 15 years of service*	*After 40 years of service*
Subedar	Rs 25	Rs 40
Jemadar	Rs 12	Rs 20
Havildar	Rs 7	Rs 12
Naik	Rs 7	Rs 12
Sepoy	Rs 4	Rs 7

Source: General Order by the Commander-in-Chief, 1 February 1837, Military Department, National Archives of India, New Delhi.

In the Madras Army, to acquire and retain the loyalty of Indian officers and men, the authorities allowed them certain benefits. Upon every new posting, the unit received a 'hutting allowance' for constructing huts. In addition, Indian officers were rewarded for meritorious services by extra pension, grants of land, carriage allowances, the right to move in palanquins, and so on. With a view to winning over the serving Indian soldiers, every regiment maintained about 70 male children of retired or serving sepoys. Upon attainment of the required age, these boys were drafted into the army.[63] It is to be remembered that the Madras government, recognizing the need to foster a greater interaction between Indian sepoys and European officers in the aftermath of the Vellore Mutiny, revived the practice of attaching the male progeny of sepoys as orderlies to the young European officers of the Madras Army.[64]

Despite strident criticism by colonial officials and historians of the colonial army, a perusal of court martial records indicates that day-to-day cases of dissent did not increase in the Bengal Army with the transition to a more impersonal style of command, a process which had started in the early decades of the nineteenth century. However, this is not to say the transition did not bring any problems in its wake. The new generation of European officers interacted on a more impersonal basis. A consequence of this aloofness was that the British officers often failed to master the native languages. Both the Madras and Bengal armies were plagued by this lack of knowledge of Indian languages among the European officers. Crowell, commenting on the attempts of the Madras Army to make its British officers proficient in Indian languages, says that the effectiveness of the language study programme was difficult, if not impossible, to judge. In all probability, Crowell says, the vernacular languages study programme for British officers of the Madras Army was not as effective as it should have been, but was effective enough for the British to exercise and maintain control over the sepoys, which was the basic objective of their language studies.[65] One could say that the language study programme of the Madras Army was partly successful. The results of a language examination conducted by the Madras Army in 1833 revealed that only six officers had passed, whereas the great majority fell short of the prescribed standard. Eight officers had failed outright. A general order in 1833 laid down that officers with inadequate knowledge of the Indian languages should be denied staff appointments.[66] Actually, the military authorities held the carrot of lucrative staff appointments before the sahibs in order to encourage them to learn the vernaculars seriously. As a result, the situation improved during the 1840s. The percentage of European officers in the Madras Army passing language examinations showed an upward trend. The results of an Indian language examination for British officers in the Madras Army held in September 1844 recorded a marked improvement in their performances. Among 50 officers, there were no failures, while some of the officers were marked as having made creditable progress.[67] The results of the Indian languages examination conducted for the British officers in the Madras Army for the months of March, April, and May 1853 presented a perceptively improved proficiency in 'native' languages on the part of the British officers. There were no failures; six of the officers were granted *munshi* allowances as a mark of appreciation, making them eligible for the post of interpreter; several others were judged as having made creditable progress.[68]

Passing examinations, however, did not guarantee that the British officers could converse freely with the sepoys in their own language. The British officers in the Bengal Army were often incompetent as far as conversing with the troops or reading of letters and articles of war in the Indian languages were concerned. Following the example of the Madras Army, the Bengal Army also initiated compulsory examinations in the Indian languages, specifying that no officer would be considered for staff appointments unless he had adequate knowledge of Indian languages. The general order of 9 June 1837 made the knowledge of Indian vernacular languages an indispensable qualification for staff appointments.[69] However, there was a basic problem with the order. It in effect meant that officers would be tempted to learn Indian languages with the sole aim of securing plum staff appointments, where knowledge of Indian languages was not very essential as compared to leading sepoy regiments. In effect, any benefit the Company might have accrued from officers having a better knowledge of Indian languages was negated by making it a stepping stone for securing staff promotions.

Due to the above reforms initiated by the Company state, dissent in the day-to-day functioning of the Bengal and Madras armies was within manageable limits. Interestingly, the Madras Army, in spite of being relatively detached from its host society, had a marginally inferior record than the Bengal Army as far as instances of dissent in the day-to-day functioning of the army was concerned. Large-scale collective disobedience occurred in situations where time-tested conventions had been flouted, or a conflict had arisen between the sepoy's sense of duty and his religious beliefs. In such cases, the situation could rapidly snowball into a major crisis. Such a situation arose among the Indian troops of the Bengal Army (especially the 47th Infantry Regiment) stationed at Barrackpur in 1824.

Anxiety over the apparent lack of communication between the European officers and the sepoys was often perceived as a central cause whenever large-scale disturbances broke out. Extremely revealing are the depositions of Brigadier Page. He commented on the unpopularity of Lieutenant Cartwright, the commanding officer at Barrackpur during the mutiny. Cartwright lacked the art of gaining esteem, and had an unhappy disposition. Page said:

> On parade he managed ill, got angry ... and another source of dissatisfaction was that all the old officers being removed and none being present who could suppose to be acquainted with the men and their little grievances, hopes and complaints. The men finding themselves deprived of their officers and having little or no confidence in their juvenile successors naturally felt disheartened and this saddled on to other subjects of complaints led them on gradually to a state of mutiny.[70]

In the case of the Barrackpur Mutiny, depositions before the enquiry committee seemed to indicate that the surly deposition of the commanding officer, Cartwright, was a major contributory factor. Brigadier Page, deposing before the committee, commented that Cartwright had the habit of making the corps parade for an unusually long time in the sun. The fact remains that Cartwright was a new officer with the regiment and had not had time to gain the confidence of the sepoys. In all fairness, it must be said that Cartwright did make attempts to communicate directly with the sepoys. He did try to convince the government to provide at least 10 bullocks per company for use by the sepoys. He also informed the Indian officers that they should not expect the use of any of these bullocks as their pay was sufficient to enable them to arrange for their own carriages. He was also willing to make an advance of cash out of his own private funds.[71] In spite of his attempts, Cartwright's efforts came to naught probably because he was new to the regiment and did not have enough opportunities to establish a rapport with the sepoys. Thus the importance of dialogue and negotiation was again underscored. A popular and trusted officer might have managed to make the sepoys accept unpleasant decisions, thereby avoiding a mutinous situation.

If the conduct of the White officers was unsatisfactory, the role of the Indian officers was intriguing, to say the least. The VCOs made no effort to check the growing discontent among the Bengal troops stationed at Barrackpur. At best, the officers were indifferent; at worst, they were accomplices in crime. The colonial authorities seem to be of the opinion that the Indian soldiers had no great attachment in general to the Company's service. Captain Balmain, explaining the causes of this lack of attachment before the Select Committee, said that in an army of 2–3 lakh men, no 'native' could rise above the rank of subedar-major, which was equal to that of the European sergeant-major.[72] Likewise, the enquiry committee for the Barrackpur Mutiny affirmed that the absence of promotions was an issue seriously felt and dwelt upon by the Indian officers.[73] Sitaram, for instance, was critical of the fact that he had been promoted at an age when it was difficult for him to perform military duties.[74] John Jacob, writing in the 1850s, termed the 'native' commissioned officers as imbeciles on account of their old age. He was of the opinion that most of the Indian officers should have been pensioned long ago, but instead, under the present system of seniority-based promotion, the old officers cut a ridiculous figure.[75]

However, the promotion prospects for Indian soldiers in the Bengal Army were not as bleak as portrayed by many European officers. There were instances where Indian soldiers serving in the Bengal Army were promoted out of turn due to conspicuous bravery displayed on the field of battle. For instance, Havildar Singh of the 26th Bengal Infantry Regiment was promoted to the rank of jemadar on 31 March 1833 on account of calmness and gallantry displayed in battle.[76] Thus, promotion on the basis of merit, disregarding seniority as a criterion, was not unknown in the Bengal Army. In fact, prior to the Barrackpore Mutiny, the sepoys of the 62nd Infantry Regiment were reportedly upset by out of turn promotions being awarded to undeserving sepoys. Apparently a sepoy named Muhammad Khan was made a naik, superseding 27 other sepoys.[77] While this particular promotion might have been a case of favouritism, the point was that promotion by selection was not unknown in the Bengal Army.

The Bengal Army also rewarded sepoys for meritorious service by awarding them enhanced rates of pension. For example, a Muslim subedar of the 26th Bengal Infantry Regiment was granted an increased pension of Rs 25 per month in recognition of gallantry in battle and exemplary conduct on all occasions. While on one hand the Indian officer might have suffered from a lack of importance in this new era of impersonal relationships, the colonial government sought to counter a possible sense of frustration by rewarding them for meritorious service and announcing several welfare schemes in the 1830s. Thus one would say that merit was recognized and rewarded in the Bengal Army. While undoubtedly a significant section of the 'native' officers must have been old, the poor quality of Indian officers in the Bengal Army might have been a trifle exaggerated. As mentioned before, there were officers who displayed conspicuous bravery on the battlefield and were rewarded with promotions and special pensions on retirement. And the Indian officers were not all 'old imbeciles'. Contrary to general perception, the Indian officers of the Artillery and Sapper Corps in the Bengal Army provided excellent leadership to the mutineers during the 1857 Mutiny.[78]

As a group, the Indian officers of the Bengal Army often behaved in an ambivalent manner. Sitaram, describing his experience before a court martial, seemed to believe that the Indian commissioned officers presiding over his trial pronounced him guilty solely because the colonel commanding the regiment desired it so.[79] If one were to deduce from this incident, it would seem that the VCOs were often eager to be in the good books of their European superior officers, even if it meant committing an injustice against fellow Indian soldiers. However, the tenuous alliance between the Indian officers and their European superiors easily snapped under stress and strain. In a crisis, the European officer could afford to rely on his Indian subordinate only at his own peril. The Indian officers were often accused of failing to bring to the notice of their superior British officers signs of discontent in the regiment.[80] This fact was reaffirmed during the mutiny at Sind.

After the conquest of Sind in May 1843, the Company decided to garrison this province with Bengal troops though the conquest had been achieved with Bombay troops. The Commander-in-Chief sent the 4th, 34th, 64th, and 69th infantry regiments of the Bengal Army then stationed near the Sind frontier.[81] The sepoys of the Bengal Army were unwilling to proceed to Sind. The 64th Infantry Regiment sent a petition to the Adjutant General of the Bengal Army in October 1843. The petition stated that the regiment had recently served in Kabul and it was extremely unfair that it was being ordered to go to Sukkur in Sind after only a seven-month stay at Ludhiana. The petition also threatened the colonel and certain Indian officers of their regiment of serious consequences if the order to go to Sind was enforced. Another grouse of the petitioners was that the havildar of their regiment had been promoted improperly by superseding many senior candidates and they had not received six months pay ever since the current colonel had been appointed to their regiment. The petition further alleged that Subedar Durga Prasad had undue influence upon the colonel and, in addition, they had not had any peace ever since Adjutant Flyer had joined. The petitioners requested the government to investigate all these grievances and asked for the removal of these officers while themselves expressing a desire to be discharged from service. An enquiry revealed that nightly meetings were being held in the sepoy lines of the 64th Regiment. No enquiry was however made regarding the validity of the grievances stated by the petitioners. The sepoys of the 64th Regiment remained steadfast in their refusal to march to Sukkur. As retribution, the regiment was ordered to march to Barrackpore, where they were to expect further disciplinary action. The government decided to punish this unit by stopping all promotions and furlough for the Indian officers. Further, the sepoys were not to be allowed to obtain their discharge.[82]

The sepoys continued to be in a mutinous mood and stated to Major General Hunter that Lieutenant Colonel Mosley and Captain Bard had deceived them with promises of *batta* (extra money for campaigning in areas far from the regiments' recruiting grounds) to the tune of Rs 12 per month. Instead of that amount, the sepoys had been paid at the rate of Rs 8 per month. Finally, on 20 June 1844, the sepoys seemed tired and ready to submit. Hunter, on asking one man from each company to state their grievances, realized that Mosley and Bard had misled the sepoys with promises of extra pay if they agreed to march to Sind.[83] On 25 June 1844, the regiment was marched from Shikarpur to Sukkur in Sind. About 39 personnel were tried by a general court martial. Mosley was also brought before a European court martial. The court sentenced six of the sepoys to be immediately executed; another seven were awarded hard imprisonment with labour; others were given prison sentences ranging from 7 to 14 years. Only one sepoy was acquitted. As for Mosley, he was cashiered and relieved of his duties.[84]

As with the Bengal Army, the Madras Army too witnessed large-scale disturbances. In October 1843, the 6th Light Cavalry Regiment of the Madras Army was ordered to proceed from Kampti to a field duty assignment. On termination of field duty, they were supposed to move down to Arcot.[85] Instead, the regiment was then ordered to occupy the post of Jabbalpur. This declaration occasioned considerable discontent in the regiment. To add to their dissatisfaction, an order was promulgated to the effect that field batta had been erroneously promised to them and therefore their batta would be withdrawn with immediate effect.[86] Finally, mutiny broke out on 8 December 1843, when sowars of the 6th Light Cavalry Regiment refused to obey the command of their commanding officer, Major Edmund Litchfield, to assemble for parade. Refusing to serve under Litchfield, the sepoys drew up petitions against him and submitted them to the brigadier on inspection, one Louis Wentworth Watson, at the parade.[87] In the enquiry that followed, the blame was laid squarely on the Indian officers for instigating the revolt, although there was no definite proof against them. The enquiry report commented that it was quite inconceivable that the Indian officers did not notice any discontent considering the fact that the order cancelling extra pay had been talked of openly in the regiment for quite some time. Although the Indian officers were but a short distance away from the men, they claimed that they had not heard the mutinous rumblings of the sepoys.[88] To set an example, the commanding officer summarily discharged several Indian commissioned and non-commissioned officers. Severely censuring the VCOs, the commanding officer commented that in future Indian officers would run the risk of inviting severe punishment in the event of remaining passive spectators in the face of mutiny. Citing as an example the recent summary dismissals of Indian officers, the commander-in-chief made it clear that Indian officers were in future expected to report any misconduct on the part of the sepoys. Considering the close social and psychological links between the Indian officers and the sowars, it was hardly probable, argued the Madras Army's top brass, that Indian officers would be ignorant of the intentions and feelings of the sowars.[89] The colonial authorities placed the blame squarely on the VCOs of the regiment. They were categorized as old and stupid and unable to hold their own against the men, unless supported by their commanding officer. Apparently, they were so intimidated by the sowars that they did not dare to report mutinous activities going on among the rank and file.[90]

Thus it seems that while Indian officers would side with their European superiors in punishing individual instances of indiscipline or dissent, they could not be relied upon in cases of mass discontent. Indian officers on such occasions gave tacit approval by not reporting the activities of the rebellious sepoys and sowars. At times they even took the lead in fomenting discontent.

Thus one could say that the command structure of the Bengal and Madras armies was just adequate in maintaining day-to-day discipline. In spite of a change in the style of leadership and the consequent pitfalls, the ill effects of a more impersonal style of leadership were offset by the reliability of the 'native' officers in matters of the day-to-day running of the army. The VCOs presided over the court martial apparatus and did not hesitate to award harsh punishments to Indian soldiers though the ultimate authority lay with the British officers. As already seen, the Indian officers were more than willing to collude with the sahibs in punishing errant sepoys and sowars. In cases of mass discontent, though, the Indian officers could not be relied upon. In spite of adopting some welfare mechanisms, the Madras Army's disciplinary record, as already indicated, was hardly better than that of the Bengal Army. As in the Bengal Army, Indian officers sided with the European officers in punishing individual cases of dissent and indiscipline on the part of the sepoys and sowars, but were mute spectators in cases of collective indiscipline.

Conclusion

The disciplinary records of the Madras Army show that isolation from society was no guarantee against discontent or rebellion in an army. If discipline was considered an index for professionalism in an army, then the Madras Army, in spite of its relative isolation from society, was hardly more professional than the Bengal Army, which had very strong links with society. An army having a corporate identity, while relatively immune to the stress and strain of civil society, can have problems arising from organizational deficiencies. Mutiny might occur over discontent resulting from inadequate pay, lack of facilities, broken promises, etc. While it is true that the Madras Army, unlike the Bengal Army, stayed loyal during 1857, this may have been due to the fact that the rumours about cow and pig fat being used in making cartridge papers originated in north India. By the time the rumours reached south India, they might have become diffused. While the rumours had caught the Bengal Army unawares, the Madras Army had more time to cope with these rumours and to take the necessary steps. Another important fact that may have gone in favour of the Madras Army was the negligible amount of high-caste soldiers in the rank.

Both the armies were however quasi-mercenary forces commanded by a foreign group of officers, who had established their sway by force. Consequently, the question of national loyalty did not arise. Loyalty in a quasi-mercenary army could only mean loyalty towards commanding officers who, by exhibiting dynamic leadership, sought to win allegiance. The British initially tried to ensure personal loyalty by encouraging a very personal and heroic style of leadership. With the transition to an impersonal style of leadership, both the armies suffered to an extent, especially in times of crisis caused by contractual violations, flouting of long-standing traditions, and so on. Consequently, in mutiny-like situations where the sepoys and sowars were trying violently to assert their rights and privileges, both the armies were extremely vulnerable and mutinies were often marked by a total collapse of the command mechanism. While the Indian officers sided with European officers in maintaining day-to-day discipline, they could not be relied upon in times of acute or mass discontent. Then the European officers were left helpless spectators.

Notes

1. John F. Votaw, 'An Approach to the Study of Military History', in John E. Jessup, Jr. and Robert W. Coakley (eds), *A Guide to the Study and Use of Military History*, Washington DC: 1982, p. 48. Votaw is speaking of professionalism of the officer corps.
2. Captain Moore, Court of Enquiry into the Vellore Mutiny, Minutes of Evidence, Foreign (Secret), 1806, National Archives of India, New Delhi (henceforth NAI).
3. General Orders by the Commander-in-Chief of Madras Army, 13 March 1806, Tamil Nadu State Archives, Chennai (hereafter TNSA).
4. Ibid., 22 August 1806, TNSA.

5. Lorenzo M. Crowell, 'Military in a Colonial Context: The Madras Army, circa 1832', *Modern Asian Studies* (henceforth *MAS*), 24(2), 1990, pp. 249, 255–70.
6. Douglas Peers, 'The Habitual Nobility of Being: British Officers and the Social Construction of the Bengal Army in the Early Nineteenth Century', *MAS*, 25(3), 1991, pp. 551–2.
7. Samuel Huntington, *The Soldier and the State: The Theory and Politics of Civil-Military Relations*, Cambridge, Massachusetts: 1957, p. 10. It is to be noted that Huntington's focus remains the officer corps.
8. Henry Russell, Select Committee for Indian Affairs, 1831–32, Minutes of Evidence, vol. 13, p. 567, West Bengal State Archives, Kolkata (henceforth WBSA).
9. Henry Dodwell, *Sepoy Recruitment in the Old Madras Army*, Calcutta, 1922, Appendix, p. i.
10. Peers, 'Habitual Nobility of Being', pp. 551–2.
11. Kaushik Roy in 'Recruitment Doctrines of the Colonial Indian Army, 1859–1913', *Indian Economic and Social History Review*, 34(3), 1997, pp. 345–6, argues that a lobby existed in the pre-1857 Madras Army, which pursued an open-door policy of recruitment. General Harris was one of the prominent proponents of the open-door policy of recruitment. Roy suggests that in the pre-1857 Madras Army, the open-door policy won against the selective enlistment school due to certain factors. One of the reasons was that since Awadh and Bihar were under the jurisdiction of the Bengal Presidency, the Bengal Army had the first choice of Brahmin and Rajput recruits in these areas. As a result, the Bengal Army acquired the better variety of Purbiya recruits, leaving the second-grade high-caste personnal for the Madras Army. So the Madras Army decided to go for the non-high-caste men.
12. W. J. Wilson, *History of the Madras Army*, vol. 3, Madras: 1883, p.151.
13. Stephen P. Rosen, *Societies and Military Power: India and its Armies*, New Delhi: 1996, pp. 162–96. For Rosen, the Madras Army was more separated from Indian society than the Bengal Army.
14. General Orders by the commander-in-chief of Madras Army, 22 August 1806, TNSA.
15. Maya Gupta, *Lord William Bentinck in Madras and the Vellore Mutiny, 1803–7*, New Delhi: 1986, pp. 209–15. Gupta also counts the on inadequate service conditions of the Madras sepoys and harsh treatment by the officers as reasons behind the Vellore uprising.
16. Channa Wickremesekera, *'Best Black Troops in the World': British Perceptions and the Making of the Sepoy, 1746–1805*, New Delhi: 2002, p. 161.
17. Report of the Court of Enquiry into the Barrackpore Mutiny, 1824, Military Miscellaneous, vol. 11, p. 479, NAI.
18. Russell, Select Committee for Indian Affairs, 1831–2, Minutes of Evidence, vol. 13, p. 567.

19. One important break the East India Company achieved as far as recruiting was concerned was that it stopped the practice of recruiting matchlock men under their own jobber-commander, or jemadar, who would join directly as an officer, a practice prevalent in the princely Indian armies. In the Company's armies, the Indian officers rose from the ranks. Dirk Kolff, *Naukar, Rajput and Sepoy: The Ethnohistory of the Military Labour Market in Hindustan, 1450–1850*, Cambridge: 1990, p. 178.
20. Major General Jasper Nicolls, Select Committee for Indian Affairs, 1831–2, Minutes of Evidence, vol. 13, p. 113, WBSA.
21. Brigadier John Jacob, *A Few Remarks on the Bengal Army and Furlough Regulations with a View to their Improvement*, London: 1855, p. 38.
22. Field Marshal Roberts, *Forty-One Years in India: From Subaltern to Commander-in-Chief in India*, vol. 1, London: 1897, p. 256.
23. John Malcolm, *Observations on the Disturbances in the Madras Army*, London: 1812, p. 9.
24. William Bentinck, Foreign Secret, minute of 1 November 1806, NAI.
25. William Bentinck, Secret Sundry volumes on the Vellore Mutiny, minute of 10 September 1806, para 2c, p. 81, NAI.
26. An anonymous officer, *Summary of the Maratha and Pindari Campaign during 1817, 1818 and 1819 under the Directions of The Marquess of Hastings*, London: 1820, pp. 298–9.
27. Russell, Select Committee for Indian Affairs, 1831–2, Minutes of Evidence, p. 262.
28. Lieutenant Colonel Greenhill, Select Committee for Indian Affairs 1831–2, vol. 11, Minute of Evidence, p. 388, WBSA.
29. *From Sepoy to Subedar being the Life and Adventure of Subedar Sita Ram, a Native Officer of the Bengal Army, Written and Related by Himself*, James Lunt (ed.), 1873; reprint, London: 1988, p. 23.
30. Ibid., p. 24.
31. Major H. Bevan, *Thirty Years in India, or A Soldier's Reminiscences 1808–1838*, London: 1839, p. 83; Philip Mason, *A Matter of Honour: An Account of the Indian Army, Its Officers and Men*, 1974; reprint, Dehra Dun: 1988, pp. 185–6.
32. Amiya Barat, *The Bengal Native Infantry: Its Organization and Discipline*, Calcutta: 1962, p. 65.
33. Major of the Bombay Army, Select Committee for Indian Affairs, 1831–2, vol. 11, Minutes of Evidence, p. 573.
34. Jasper Nicolls, Select Committee for Indian Affairs, 1831–2, vol. 11, Minutes of Evidence, p. 15.
35. Philip Melville, Select Committee for Indian Affairs, 1852–3, vol. 14, Minutes of Evidence, Appendix 4, p. 350, Nehru Memorial Museum and Library, New Delhi (henceforth NMML).
36. Ibid.

37. Mason, *A Matter of Honour*, pp. 174–5.
38. Jacob, *A Few Remarks on the Bengal Army*, p. 36
39. Ibid., p. 50.
40. W. Sleeman, *Rambles and Recollections of an Indian Official*; reprint, Madras: 1995, p. 321.
41. Lieutenant Colonel Greenhill, Select Committee for Indian Affairs, 1831–2, vol. 11, p. 388.
42. G. Pollock, Select Committee for Indian Affairs, 1852–3, vol. 14, Minutes of Evidence, p. 35, NMML.
43. Lieutenant General J. McLeod Innes, *Sir Henry Lawrence: The Pacificator*, Oxford: 1898, p. 151.
44. General Orders by the commander-in-chief of Madras Army, 4 July 1832, p. 275, NAI.
45. William Hough, *Simplification of Her Majesty and the Honourable East India Company Mutiny Acts and Articles of War*, Calcutta: 1846, p. 3.
46. General Orders by the governor general, Fort William, 24 October 1834, NAI.
47. Douglas Peers, 'Sepoys, Soldiers and the Lash: Race, Caste and Army Discipline in India, 1820–50', *Journal of Imperial and Commonwealth History*, 23(2), 1995, pp. 229–30.
48. General Orders by the commander-in-chief, Fort William, 1 July 1839, NAI.
49. Ibid., 1 August 1839.
50. Ibid., 1 September 1829, NAI.
51. Ibid., 1 July 1837, NAI.
52. William Hough, *A Casebook of European and Native Court Martials Held from the Year 1801–1821*, Calcutta: 1821, p. 124.
53. Ibid., p. 123.
54. Report of the Court of Enquiry into the Barrackpore Mutiny, 1824, Military Miscellaneous, vol. 11, p. 510, NAI.
55. General Orders by the commander-in-chief, Fort William, 1 July 1839, NAI.
56. Hough, *Simplification of Her Majesty and the Honourable East India Company Mutiny Acts and Articles of War*, p. 55.
57. Jasper Nicolls, Select Committee for Indian Affairs, 1831–2, vol. 13, Minutes of Evidence, p. 258.
58. General Orders by the commander-in-chief, the Madras Army, 5 February 1831, NAI.
59. Ibid., 5 June 1831, NAI.
60. Hough, *Simplification of Her Majesty and the Honourable East India Company Mutiny Acts and Articles of War*, p. 55.
61. General Order by the commander-in-chief, 5 March 1837, NAI.
62 Lieutenant General Viscount Gough, Select Committee for Indian Affairs, 1852–3, vol. 14, Minutes of Evidence, p. 524.

63. Russell, Select Committee for Indian Affairs 1831–2, Evidence, vol. 13, p. 258, WBSA.
64. General Orders by the commander-in-chief, Madras Army, 1 September 1806, TNSA.
65. Crowell, 'Military Professionalism in a Colonial Context: The Madras Army, circa 1832', p. 249.
66. General Orders by the commander-in-chief, Madras Army, 10 July 1833, NAI.
67. Ibid., 30 September 1844, NAI.
68. Ibid., 31 May 1853, NAI. Munshi allowance was extra money given to the European officers for having Indians who would aid the former to master the vernacular.
69. Ibid., 9 June 1837, NAI.
70. Brigadier Page, Minutes of Evidence, Court of Enquiry into the Barrackpore Mutiny, 1824, Military Miscellaneous, p. 388, NAI.
71. Ibid., p. 45.
72. Captain Balmain, Select Committee for Indian Affairs 1831–2, Minutes of Evidence, vol. 13, p. 156.
73. Court of Enquiry into the Barrackpore Mutiny, p. 75.
74. Sitaram, *From Sepoy to Subedar*, p. 75.
75. Jacob, *A Few Remarks on the Bengal Army*, p. 34.
76. General Orders by the commander-in-chief, Fort William, 31 March 1833, NAI.
77. Evidence of Captain Enfield, Court of Enquiry into the Barrackpore Mutiny, 1824, p. 151.
78. G. Clerk, Peel Commission for Reorganization of the Indian Army, Minute of Evidence, 24 August 1858, p. 83, NAI.
79. Sitaram, *From Sepoy to Subedar*, p. 74.
80. Military Proceedings, Fort William, 1845, p. 4070, NAI.
81. General Order by the commander-in-chief, Fort William, 15 September 1843, NAI.
82. Barat, *Bengal Native Infantry*, pp. 238–9.
83. Foreign Secret Consultations, 17 August 1844, no. 102, NAI.
84. Barat, *Bengal Native Infantry*, p. 248.
85. General Orders of the commander-in chief, Madras Presidency, 24 March 1844, pp. 418–19, TNSA.
86. Ibid.
87. Ibid., p. 420.
88. Ibid., p. 421.
89. Ibid., p. 422.
90. Ibid., pp. 418–19.

2

Greased Cartridges and the Great Mutiny of 1857

A Pretext to Rebel or the Final Straw?

Saul David

As every schoolchild knows, the Great Mutiny of 1857 came about because the Indian troops of the Bengal Army refused to bite cartridges greased with cow and pig fat: the former unacceptable to Hindu sepoys and the latter abhorrent to Muslims. Of course historians have shown the underlying causes to be far more complex. Yet certain unresolved questions remain: were the prime motives for mutiny really the preservation of caste and religion, or were grievances particular to the Bengal Army more to blame? Did the sepoys act of their own volition, or was there an element of manipulation both from within and outside the military?

This article is an attempt to reinstate the military dimension of the mutiny. There has been a trend among recent scholars—such as S. B. Chaudhuri, Eric Stokes, C. Bayly, Rudrangshu Mukherjee, and Tapti Roy[1]—to view the Mutiny as a reflection of what was happening in Indian society. The sepoys were an integral part of peasant society, they argue, and were therefore susceptible to the same social, economic, and religious pressures that affected civilians. Seen in this light, the Mutiny was little more than a precursor to a general revolt by disaffected elements of the 'native' population. Yet by taking this approach, there is a tendency to lose sight of the fact that the Mutiny was, first and foremost, a military uprising and that without it, the civil rebellion would almost certainly not have taken place.

All armies have grievances relating to conditions of service, particularly pay, promotion, and relations with officers. What sets a colonial force such as the Bengal Army apart is that it was a volunteer mercenary force officered by men of a different race and religion. Its loyalty to its paymasters, therefore, was entirely dependent upon the incentives for service outweighing the disincentives. By 1857, this was no longer the case—mainly because the number and seriousness of the sepoys' grievances were increasing, while the Bengal Army's control over its soldiers was weakening.

I

It is almost impossible to identify with any degree of certainty the exact reason why almost three-quarters of the regular Bengal Army chose to mutiny in 1857.[2] Most historians have pinpointed the fear of an enforced conversion to Christianity as the primary motive. They cite a series of laws and trends that appeared to undermine traditional customs and beliefs—such as the legalization of widows' marriages, the establishment of group messing in jails, the passing of the General Service Enlistment Order, and the upsurge of missionary activity—and argue that the introduction of Enfield cartridges greased with cow and pig fat was the last straw. But a detailed study of the so-called 'cartridge question' can lead to a quite different conclusion.

All the East India Company's weapons were ordered directly from British manufacturers by its Military Store Department in London. These arms were similar to those supplied to the British Army by the Board of Ordnance, thus enabling both Company and British troops in India to use the same ammunition. In 1840, in line with the British Army, the Company switched from flintlock to percussion small arms. The muzzle-loading muskets retained the same 'Brown Bess' design that had been in use since the eighteenth century, but with their flints replaced by percussion caps. The first Company troops to use percussion arms in action were the sepoys of the 2nd Madras Infantry Regiment at the storming of Chin-kiang Fu in China in July 1842. Over the next decade or so, nearly 4,60,000 percussion muskets, carbines, and pistols were despatched to India. But the procurement of these smooth-bore firearms ceased in June 1851, when the British government decided to equip its troops with the revolutionary Minie rifle.[3]

Rifles had been used by the British and East India Company armies for skirmishing and sniping since the early nineteenth century. But their accuracy had been more than offset by a slow rate of loading, a seemingly inevitable consequence of the need for the ball or bullet to have a loose fit during loading and a tight fit in the rifling grooves on being fired. This conundrum was solved in the 1840s by two French officers: the first, Delvigne, developed an elongated bullet with a hollow base which expanded when fired; and then Captain Minie improved the design by adding a cup in the cavity to assist uniform expansion. Though both men wanted the concept to be called the 'Delvigne-Minie', it came to be known by the latter's name alone. The first such weapon chosen by the Board of Ordnance for the British Army was the Pattern 1851 Rifled Musket, otherwise known as the Minie rifle. But it was never generally issued because the British government's Committee on Small Arms decided in 1852 that the Minie's .702 bore was too large. The Pattern 1853 Rifled Musket, or Enfield rifle, with a .577 bore was eventually chosen instead.[4]

Though the East India Company was promised 30,000 new Enfield rifles by the Board of Ordnance in 1854, it did not receive any for two years. This was partly because the government factory at Enfield was neither large nor modern enough to meet the demand; and partly because Britain's entry into the Crimean War in 1854 meant that Lord Raglan's expeditionary force was given priority. The war also enabled the British government to corner the small-arms market and extinguish unwelcome competition by forcing the Court of Directors in March 1856 to cede control of its arms procurement to the new War Department (which had replaced the Board of Ordnance in February 1855).[5] The first consignment of 1500 Enfield rifles finally reached the Bengal Presidency in the spring of 1856. They were earmarked for the Bengal Army, but the Indian government agreed to assign them to Her Majesty's 60th Rifles on the grounds that their existing rifles were unservicable and should be replaced immediately.[6] By the outbreak of the Mutiny in 1857, the Bengal Presidency had received just over 12,000 Enfields. But the only regiment in possession of these weapons was Her Majesty's 60th Rifles (it had received 1040). The remainders were in the arsenals at Fort William (4395), Allahabad (3000), Ferozepore (3000), Delhi (41), the Artillery Depot of Instruction at Meerut (525), and the musketry depots at Dum Dum, Sialkot, and Ambala.[7]

It was not the rifles themselves, however, but their ammunition that was to prove so controversial. Cartridges for most muzzle-loading percussion firearms of this period took the form of a tube of paper that contained a ball (lead tin alloy) and enough powder for a single shot. The approved method of loading such a cartridge was to bite the top off to allow the powder to be poured down the barrel. The rest of the cartridge, including the ball, would then be forced down the barrel with the ramrod. Both the existing percussion musket and the Enfield rifle used this type of ammunition. But the crucial difference between the two was that the Enfield rifle's grooved bore required the bottom two-thirds of its cartridge to be greased to facilitate loading.[8] Another rifle, the two-grooved Brunswick model, had been used by the 60th Rifles and rifle companies in some Bengal Infantry regiments since the early 1840s. Its ammunition consisted of a powder cartridge and a separate ball covered with a 'patch' of fine cloth smeared with beeswax and coconut oil, and was therefore considered to be inoffensive to both Hindus and Muslims. This was not the case with the substance used to grease the new Enfield cartridges.

In 1853, when the first Enfield cartridges were sent to India to test their reaction to the climate, General Gomm warned the Secretary to the Military Board that unless it be known that the grease employed in these cartridges is not of a nature to offend or interfere with the prejudices of caste, it will be expedient not to issue them for test to the Indian corps. As it happened, the grease contained an element of tallow (animal fat) which may well have come from either cows or pigs. But the Military Board chose to ignore Gomm's counsel and the ammunition was tested over a period of some months by being carried in the pouches of sepoy guards at Fort William, Kanpur, and Rangoon. No objection to these cartridges was raised either by the sepoys themselves or by the committees of European officers set up to report on them.[9] The tests confirmed that the grease could stand up to the Indian climate and the consignment was returned to England in 1855. A year later, following hard on the heels of the first batch of Enfield rifles came a shipment of greased cartridges and bullet moulds.[10] Thereafter the Bengal Army's Ordnance Department began to manufacture its own cartridges at its Fort William, Meerut, and Dum Dum arsenals. The grease used for the rifle patch—a mixture of wax and oil—was discounted because its lubricating properties disappeared when cartridges were bundled. Instead the same combination preferred by the Royal Woolwich Arsenal—five parts tallow, five parts stearine, and one part wax—was used.[11] But the Department made the fatal, and unforgiveable, error of not specifying what type of tallow was to be used.[12]

The 60th Rifles received their full complement of 1040 Enfield rifles on 1 January 1857.[13] At around the same time, Bengal infantry regiments began to send detachments of seven men (one European officer, one 'native' officer, and five non-commissioned officers and sepoys) for instruction in the care and handling of the new weapon at the Musketry Depots at Dum Dum near Calcutta, Ambala in the Cis-Sutlej States, and Sialkot in the Punjab.[14] But not a greased cartridge had been issued, nor a practice shot fired, by the time a rumour began to circulate among the sepoys at the Dum Dum depot in late January 1857 that the grease for the new cartridge was offensive to both Hindus and Muslims, and that this was part of a systematic plot by government to convert all Indians to Christianity. The origin of the rumour was a conversation between a high-caste sepoy of the 2nd Bengal Infantry Regiment and a low-caste *khalasi* (labourer) from the Dum Dum magazine. According to a report by Captain Wright, commandant of the Rifle Instruction Depot, a sepoy had rejected the khalasi's request to drink from his *lota* (vessel) because he did not know his caste, to which the khalasi replied: 'You will soon lose your caste, as ere long you will have to bite cartridges covered with the fat of pigs and cows.'[15]

Wright's report was submitted to the station authorities on 23 January 1857 by Major J. Bontein, commanding the Musketry Depot, who also gave details of a parade held the evening before at which two-thirds of the Indian personnel of the depot (including all the Indian officers) had stated their objection to the grease applied to the new cartridges and a request for wax and oil to be used instead. Both letters were then forwarded to Major General J. B. Hearsey, commanding the Presidency Division, who sent them on to Colonel Birch, the Military Secretary to the Government of India, with the comment that the khalasi's claim was no doubt totally groundless, but so suspiciously disposed were the sepoys that the only remedy was to allow them to grease the cartridges themselves with materials from the bazaar.[16] The Government of India, ever conscious of religious issues, was swift to react. On 27 January 1857, having consulted Colonel Abbott (Inspector General of Ordnance), Birch ordered that all cartridges at the Depots of Instruction (including the Artillery Depot at Meerut) were to be issued free from grease and that the sepoys were to be allowed to apply, with their own hands, whatever mixture for the purpose they may prefer. Abbott, however, was quick to inform Colonel Chester, the adjutant general, who was upcountry with the Commander-in-Chief General Anson, that such a solution would answer well enough for practice, but would be impracticable in service because balled cartridges needed to be greased before they were bundled. He therefore suggested the replacement of balled cartridges with balls covered with grease patches and powder-only cartridges.[17]

Abbott also anticipated the government by making inquiries as to the exact composition of the grease used on the cartridges. On 29 January, he reported to Colonel Birch that in line with the instructions received from the Court of Directors, a mixture of tallow and beeswax had been used and that no extraordinary precaution appeared to have been taken to ensure the absence of any objectionable fat. In a separate letter that day, Abbott informed Birch that strict orders would be given for the exclusive use of sheep or goat fat if it was decided that some form of tallow was necessary.[18] It has never been proven beyond doubt that the original grease for the Enfield cartridge contained beef or pork fat. But the circumstantial evidence is compelling. In a letter to the President of the Board of Control on 7 February 1857, Governor General Canning himself stated that the grease grievance had 'turned out to be well founded'.[19] In March 1857, the officer in charge of the Fort William Arsenal testified that no one had bothered to check what type of animal fat was used. At the same tribunal, Abbott admitted that the tallow may well have contained the fat of cows or other animals.[20]

At this stage, therefore, the sepoys stationed at Dum Dum appear to have had a genuine grievance—though not one of them had been, or ever would be, issued with a greased cartridge. Even more perplexing is the claim by Major Bontein that no greased cartridges were ever made at the Dum Dum Magazine because its operatives were still learning the complicated process of manufacture when the rumour began. Nor were any greased cartridges ever sent from the Fort William Arsenal, where they were being made, to the Dum Dum Depot.[21] How, then, did the Dum Dum khalasi discover the truth about the cartridge grease? We can only speculate.

What we do know is that the government moved swiftly to correct its earlier error by halting the production of greased cartridges and authorizing the sepoys to apply their own grease. No sooner had this concession been announced, however, than sepoys from the four regiments of Bengal Infantry at Barrackpore, the great military station 16 miles north of Calcutta and about 30 miles from Dum Dum, were voicing their fears that the paper encasing the new cartridges also contained objectionable fat. These suspicions first arose when ungreased Enfield cartridges and the paper used for making them were shown to a parade of the 2nd Bengal Infantry

Regiment at Barrackpore on 4 February 1857. Similar fears were also expressed during a separate parade of the 34th Bengal Infantry Regiment. At a subsequent court of inquiry, held four days later, witness after witness stated his belief that the paper was objectionable to his caste. One said that the rumour began with khalasis from the Fort William Arsenal; others referred to bazaar gossip. Two witnesses, a sepoy and a havildar major (equivalent to sergeant major), claimed to have experimented with the paper. The former said that it made a fizzing noise when burnt and smelt as if there was grease in it; the latter said that the paper would not dissolve in oil and that this had convinced him there was no grease in it. However, even the havildar major would not bite off the end of an ungreased cartridge because of his anxiety that the other men would object to it.[22] This objection to the cartridge paper was groundless: it contained no grease and certainly no tallow. Suspicions had arisen partly because the British-manufactured paper was slightly thicker than that used to make musket cartridges.[23] But the lack of a genuine reason prompts the speculation that some guiding hand—within or without the regiments—was trying to keep the cartridge controversy alive by switching attention from the grease (which was no longer an issue) to the paper. Canning suspected such a conspiracy and told Vernon Smith that there was a mutinous spirit in the 2nd Bengal Infantry Regiment, or at least part of it, which had 'not been roused by the cartridges alone if at all'.[24]

II

The first serious outbreak of open mutiny occurred during the night of 26/27 February at Baharampur, 110 miles north of Calcutta. The previous afternoon, the men of the 19th Bengal Infantry Regiment had refused to receive their copper caps for firing exercise on the morning of 27 February because they suspected that the paper for the blank practice cartridges contained objectionable grease. These cartridges, it should be stressed, were for their old muskets—not the new Enfield—and were the same type that had been issued to the army for many years. They had, moreover, been made up in the regimental magazine the previous year by the sepoys of the 7th Bengal Infantry Regiment. Lieutenant Colonel Mitchell reminded the Indian officers of these facts and warned them that any sepoy who refused to accept the blank cartridges at the morning parade would be court-martialled. At around 11 p.m., however, the sepoys broke into their bells-of-arms and seized their muskets. Mitchell responded by ordering a detachment of the 11th Irregular Cavalry and some European artillery to cover the mutinous sepoys while he went to speak to them. Four hours later, after much negotiation, Mitchell finally agreed to the Indian officers' suggestion to withdraw the cavalry and guns. The men then lodged their weapons and returned to their lines.[25]

During the subsequent Court of Inquiry, the Indian officers, non-commissioned officers, and sepoys of the 19th Bengal Infantry Regiment sent a petition to General Hearsey to explain their behaviour. They stated that the rumour about the new cartridges containing objectionable fat had been in circulation for more than two months and that they were very much afraid for their religion. Their minds had been temporarily put at ease by Colonel Mitchell's announcement that grease for the new cartridges would be made up in front of the sepoys by the company pay-havildars. But their fears returned when they inspected the blank cartridges at their bells-of-arms on the afternoon of 26 February. 'We perceived them to be of two kinds,' they wrote, 'and one sort appeared to be different from that formerly served out. Hence, we doubted whether these might not be the cartridges which had arrived from Calcutta, as we had made none ourselves, and were convinced that they were greased'. It was for this reason, they claimed, that they refused to accept the firing caps. Colonel Mitchell had angrily responded by threatening to take the regiment to Burma, where they would all die of hardship, if they did not accept the cartridges. This outburst had convinced them that the cartridges were greased. They had seized their arms in fear of their lives amidst shouts that they were about to be attacked by European cavalry and artillery.[26]

The sepoys' objections, therefore, had switched from the grease on the Enfield cartridge, to the paper used for the Enfield cartridge, and finally to the paper on the old musket cartridge. The reference to two different kinds of blank cartridge is explained by the fact that, since the mid-1850s, some of the paper used for musket ammunition had been produced by the Serampore mills near Calcutta. Its paper was of a slightly darker shade than the familiar English product of John Dickinson and Co.[27] Yet it contained no grease, nor was grease ever applied to cartridges for smooth-bore muskets. There is, therefore, no rational explanation for the behaviour of the 19th Bengal Infantry Regiment on the night of 26 February beyond a complete breakdown of trust between the sepoys and their European officers. Colonel

Mitchell had assured them that the cartridges were of the old type and contained no grease, and yet they preferred to believe the wild rumour that the government was planning their forcible conversion to Christianity. It is highly probable that certain members of the regiment were playing upon the fears of their comrades to incite mutiny. These ringleaders were almost certainly behind the false reports that the blank cartridge paper contained grease and that the regiment was about to be attacked during the night of 26/27 February.

By mid-March, the disaffection had spread to the Musketry Depot at Ambala, where detachments from 41st Bengal Infantry Regiments were being instructed in the use of the new Enfield rifle. On the morning of 16 March, as all the Indian detachments were being paraded for drill, Lieutenant Martineau, instructor of musketry, called aside the 'native' officers to express his surprise that the men were still discussing whether or not to use Enfield cartridges despite his assurance that they could apply their own grease. At this point an Indian officer from the 71st Bengal Infantry Regiment stepped forward and stated that the men at the depot were against using any of the new cartridges until they had ascertained that their doing so was not unacceptable to their comrades in their respective corps, for they feared being taunted with loss of caste on return to their regiments. That this was not the generally held opinion, however, is proved by the interjection of a jemadar from the 36th Infantry Regiment, who claimed that the previous speaker knew perfectly well that many of the detachments present entertained no such feelings. The jemadar added that he, along with many others, were ready to use the cartridges. The jemadar continued that he had sufficient confidence in the government. The jemadar further added that those who were refusing to fire the cartridges on the pretext of caste and religion were guilty of mutinous and insubordinate conduct. According to Martineau, the jemadar's sentiments were backed up by the Indian officers of the 10th and 22nd Bengal Infantry Regiments. They loudly denounced the views of the Indian officer from the 71st Regiment.[28] Here then is evidence that not all the Indian soldiers were sufficiently disillusioned with either their European officers or the government to believe, or even claim to believe, that the cartridge question was still a legitimate issue. Those who continued to do so were, in the 36th Regiment's jemadar's opinion, using religion as a pretext.

Nevertheless, the fear of social ostracization was not without foundation. On 19 March, the Commander-in-Chief, General George Anson, arrived in Ambala on a tour of inspection with his escorting unit, the 36th Bengal Infantry Regiment. But when a havildar and a naik from the regiment (part of the detachment doing duty at the Musketry Depot), went to the camp to greet their comrades, they were refused entry to the tents and taunted by one subedar with having become Christians. Martineau was asked to obtain some redress not only by the two aggrieved non-commissioned officers, but also by the Indian officers at the depot, who regarded the insult as intended for all who as good soldiers were obeying the orders of Government by using the new Enfield rifle.[29] He therefore conducted his own inquiry among the depot's detachments and discovered, so he told the assistant adjutant general, the existence of a rumour that the Enfield cartridge had been purposely greased with beef and pork fat 'with the express object of destroying caste', and to convert all the Indian army personnel to Christianity. That so absurd a rumour should meet with ready credence was proof to Martineau that the feeling of 'native' troops was anything but sound. Yet it was generally credited, he added, and panchayats had been formed in all Bengal corps from Calcutta to Peshawar determined to regard as outcastes any men who used the new cartridges.[30]

On 23 March, having been informed of the above developments, General Anson addressed a parade of the Indian officers at the depot. Through the medium of an interpreter, he told them that the rumoured intention of the government to interfere with their caste and religion, or to coerce them or the people of the country in general to do anything which would involve loss of caste, was groundless and false, and that he looked to them to satisfy those under their authority on this point.[31] The response of the 'native' officers, through the medium of Lieutenant Martineau, was that they knew the rumour to be false, but it was universally credited, not only in their regiments, but in their villages and their homes. They would not disobey an order to fire, but they wanted the commander-in-chief to understand the social consequences to themselves, namely loss of caste. Martineau himself could not offer any definitive explanation, yet he was disposed to regard the greased cartridge 'more as the medium than the original cause of this wide spread feeling of distrust that is spreading dissatisfaction to our Rule'.[32] Part of his reason for believing this, he later testified, was because only Hindu sepoys appeared to be genuinely worried by the cartridge question; the Muslim sepoys, on the other hand, simply laughed at it.[33] Anson was of a similar conviction. 'The "Cartridge" question is more a pretext, than reality,' he informed Lord Elphinstone on 29 March, adding: 'The sepoys have been pampered and given way to, and have ... grown insolent beyond bearing.'[34] Yet, he accepted that the Indian officers at Ambala genuinely feared social ostracism, and so ordered the deferment of actual target practice at the three musketry depots until the government had voiced its opinion.[35]

The Supreme Government had meanwhile come to another decision. On 27 March, Canning's general order announced the forthcoming disbandment of the 19th Bengal Infantry Regiment for mutiny. Canning also took the opportunity to assure the Bengal Army that it had ever been the rule of the Government of India to treat the religious feelings of all its servants of every creed with careful respect, and that had the sepoys of the 19th Regiment confided in their government and believed their commanding officer instead of crediting the idle stories with which false and evil-minded men had deceived them, their religious scruples would still have remained inviolate.[36] The 19th Regiment was disbanded at Barrackpore on 31 March, in the presence of four regiments of 'native' infantry, the governor general's bodyguard, and five companies of Her Majesty's 84th Foot sent up from Calcutta and Chinsurah respectively.

Two days earlier, Barrackpore witnessed the first outbreak of mutinous violence when Sepoy Mangal Panday of the 34th Bengal Infantry regiment, armed with a musket and a sword, tried to murder the European Sergeant Major Hewson and Adjutant Lieutenant Baugh. Both received severe sword cuts before Panday, confronted by General Hearsey and his staff, turned his gun upon himself. What was particularly shocking about this incident was the fact that upwards of 400 sepoys watched Panday's unprovoked attack without intervening. Furthermore, the jemadar of the Quarter Guard ignored repeated orders to disarm Panday. And there is even evidence to suggest that some members of the Guard assisted in the attack upon the two Europeans. Hewson, for example, recalled receiving blows from behind by a sepoy's musket. That Hewson and Baugh survived was mainly due to the intervention of sepoy Shaikh Paltu, the only Indian to offer assistance and who was badly wounded in the process.[37]

Panday's intention is unclear, though it would appear to have been a failed attempt to incite the whole regiment to mutiny. 'Come out, you *bhainchutes* [sister-violaters], the Europeans are here', he is said to have shouted on emerging from his hut. 'From biting these cartridges we shall become infidels. Get ready, turn out all of you.'[38] A separate statement by the same witness says that Panday was warning the men that the guns and Europeans had arrived for the purpose of slaughtering them.[39] Hewson recalled him saying: '*Nikul ao, pultun; nikul ao hamara sath*' (Come out, men; come out and join me).[40] According to a report Panday himself admitted that he had recently been taking *bhang* (an infusion of Indian hemp) and opium, and was not aware of what he was doing at the time of the attack.[41] Going by this, it seems likely, therefore, that an intoxicated Panday acted prematurely, before his co-conspirators were ready. Certainly his false references to the approach of Europeans and the loss of religion were repeated in many other mutinies, and they had clearly been decided upon as the best way to win over the waverers. But in the case of the 34th Regiment, there had been no specific dispute over the issue of cartridges (though the men had expressed their suspicions about the paper for the new Enfield cartridge), and the ground was not yet prepared for full-blown mutiny. It was later suggested that the evangelism of the 34th Regiment's commanding officer, Colonel Wheler, was largely to blame for the bad feeling in the regiment. Wheler himself admitted that he had been in the habit of speaking to 'natives of all classes, sepoys and others' on the subject of Christianity 'in the highways, cities, *bazars* and villages', though not in the lines and regimental bazaars.[42] He had, he said, often addressed sepoys of his own and other regiments in the stations where he had been quartered with the aim of converting them to Christianity.[43] Such an officer, Canning told the President of the Board of Control, was not fit to command a regiment.[44] But others supported Wheler. An anonymous letter to the *Friend of India* asked, with reference to a report that Wheler was about to be removed from his command, 'by what law a man who lives as a Christian, and peaceably endeavours to induce others to be Christians like him, is made an offender'.[45] The *Bengal Hurkaru* responded with the comment that the 'least likely way of making Christians of the Natives in this country, is to get turned out of it ourselves'.[46] Lieutenant Martineau later testified that he had never heard any sepoys at Ambala speak complainingly of the efforts of Wheler and missionaries in general to convert Indians to Christianity and did not think 'they cared one bit about it'.[47]

Anson did not believe the disaffection of the Bengal Army could be traced to the preaching of commanding officers because Wheler was an isolated case.[48] The *Bengal Hurkaru* also had no reason to suppose that the prevalence of disaffection and insubordination in the Bengal Army had been caused by the proceedings of proselytizing officers. Yet, it added, what was most likely to cause general disaffection in an army of illiterate natives was the spectacle of a military commander teaching and preaching a foreign religion. In other words, the actions of Wheler and men like him were grist to the mill of those who wished to win away the allegiance of the sepoys from the government.[49]

III

In civil society, many Indians had become increasingly wary of the government's attempts at Anglicization during the previous forty years. In 1813, as part of the twenty-year renewal of the East India Company's Charter, two decisions were taken which were to have far-reaching consequences for Indian language and culture: the Indian government was committed to spending £10,000 a year on education; and the long-standing ban on Christian missionaries was removed. As a result of the first initiative, Anglicizers and Orientalists began a fierce debate as to what kind of education—English or classical Indian—should be funded.[50] The question was finally settled in 1835 when Thomas Babington Macaulay, Law Member to the new Legislative Council of India, penned his *Minutes on Education* which recommended raising up an English-educated middle class 'who may be interpreters between us and the millions whom we govern—a class of persons Indian in colour and blood, but English in tastes, in opinions, in morals, and in intellect'.[51] Already a new Anglicized elite in Calcutta had begun to create institutions to serve its own interests. These were largely educational establishments that taught English language, literature, and Western sciences, and included the Hindu College (1816), the Calcutta School Society (1818), the Sanskrit College (1824), and the Oriental Seminary (1829). They were supplemented by missionary schools that generally taught Indians of all religions and castes gratis, notably Dr Duff's Free Church Mission in Calcutta. But even those Calcutta elites who accepted the necessity of learning English were split between conservatives who wanted to limit the incorporation of foreign culture within Hindu society (such as the members of the Hindu Dharma Sabha) and the cultural radicals who rejected Hindu social norms in favour of English culture and secular rationalism imported from Europe (led by the brilliant young Eurasian Henry Derozio, who supported the abolition of sati in 1829, just two years before his untimely death at the age of 22).[52] The extent to which these cultural developments affected rural communities and military cantonments, however, is open to question. The abolition of sati, for example, caused hardly a ripple among the Indian troops.

The activity of Christian missionaries, however, was potentially more problematical. With the ending of the ban on their activity in 1813, missionaries of all denominations made rapid inroads into Company territory. At first they were required to possess an official licence; but this stipulation was dropped when the Company's Charter was renewed for a further twenty years in 1833. By then, moderate evangelicals were receiving the enthusiastic support of both William Bentinck, the Governor General (1828–35), and Daniel Wilson, the Bishop of Calcutta (1832–58).[53] In 1834, the American Presbyterian Mission established its headquarters at Ludhiana in the Cis-Sutlej States (then part of the Punjab). A year later the Mission acquired a printing press and began to publish tracts, translations of the scriptures, and dictionaries in Punjabi, Urdu, Persian, Hindi, and Kashmiri. After the annexation of the Punjab in 1849, a number of new missions sprang up. A similar process took place at Agra, where the Anglican Church Missionary Society set up a mission, orphanage, and printing press in 1838. By 1846, the major missionary societies had an annual budget of £425,000, nearly half of which was spent by Anglicans and Methodists. The campaign of proselytism in the North-Western Provinces, in particular, provoked a stream of pamphlets, books, journals, and newspapers in defence of the Hindu and Muslim religions from Indian-owned presses in Agra, Delhi, and Meerut. But despite the Christian zeal of a number of governor-generals—including Lord Canning, who made donations to the Calcutta Bible Society, the Serampore College (established by Baptist missionaries), and the Free Church Mission—the actual number of conversions to Christianity in the Bengal Presidency prior to the Mutiny was relatively insignificant. The Anglican Church Missionary Society, for example, had just 19,000 church attendants throughout India by the 1840s, most of them outside Bengal; in Punjab, where the American Presbyterian Mission was active, the total number of converts was fewer than 4000 by the 1880s. In the Madras Presidency, on the other hand, the Tinnevelly district recorded nearly 40,000 Christian converts by 1850, with a further 20,000 in southern Travancore (though the process of conversion had actually been begun by Jesuits in the seventeenth century). They were chiefly untouchables who had little social status to lose. Respectable Hindus in southern India responded in the mid-1840s by forming two organizations: the Vibuthi Sangam (Sacred Ash Society), a shadowy group dedicated to ending Christian conversions; and the Madras-based Sadu Veda Siddhanta Sabha (Society for Spreading the Philosophy of the Four Vedas), which sought the same end by legal means. Both societies were probably behind the spate of attacks on Christian villages that were commonplace in the late 1840s and the 1850s. If anything, therefore, the antagonism towards missionaries was much higher in the Madras Presidency than in Bengal. However, Hindus across India—especially those of the higher castes—were undoubtedly alarmed by the Company's amendment of Hindu law: first, in 1850, to allow Christian converts the right of inheritance; and second, in 1856, to legalize the second marriage of Hindu widows (and thereby legitimize their subsequent offspring).[54]

Perhaps of more relevance to the disaffection of the 19th and 34th Regiments than issues of caste and religion, however, was the fact that both were commanded by relatively unfamiliar officers. Mitchell had been with his regiment for just 18 months, Wheler a few years longer, though he had only returned to take command of the 34th in 1856 after an absence of seven years. Wheler had also been in temporary command of the original 34th Bengal Infantry Regiment when it was disbanded in 1844 for refusing to serve in Sind without extra benefits (see Chapter 1). It may be assumed, therefore, that he was not particularly popular. Furthermore, it was surely no coincidence that both regiments were stationed in Lucknow, the capital of Awadh, when that kingdom was annexed by the East India Company in February 1856 on grounds of 'misgovernance'. Many of their sepoys came from that province (as did a large proportion of sepoys in the Bengal Army as a whole). Not only was the annexation a blow to their 'national' pride, but it also brought an end to the privilege enjoyed by all Company soldiers from Awadh of being able to prosecute their legal cases and petitions through the British Resident. So abused had this privilege become, with some sepoys receiving upto 10 months leave for the sole purpose of prosecuting their claims, that in 1853 the maximum leave was stipulated as only that much time which would enable the applicant to travel to Lucknow, remain there for 10 days, and then return, unless the Resident certified that the man's continued presence was necessary.[55] Yet the privilege remained until annexation, and there is no doubt that its loss, and with it the prestige of serving the Company, was keenly felt. In his letter to Canning of 1 May 1857, Henry Lawrence mentioned that he had received a number of letters attributing the present bad feeling not to regarding the cartridge or any specific question, but to a pretty general dissatisfaction at many recent acts of government which had been skilfully played upon by certain elements. Lawrence gave the example of an Awadh sowar in the Bombay Cavalry who was asked if he liked annexation. 'No', the sowar replied. 'I used to be a great man when I went home; the best in the village rose as I approached; now the lowest puff their pipes in my face.'[56] There were other occasions when the annexation of Awadh was cited as a grievance. Lieutenant De Kantzow of the 9th Infantry Regiment noted that some of his younger sepoys, who had seen the annexation of Awadh with their own eyes (including the auctioning of the king's property), referred to their country as having been 'snatched'.[57] Martineau recalled that dissatisfaction with the annexation of Awadh was occasionally alluded to by sepoys at the Musketry Depot at Ambala.[58] And during the mutiny itself, Captain Thomson of the 53rd Infantry Regiment, one of only four men to survive the Kanpur massacre, was informed by mutinous sepoys that the Company's Raj would cease because of the annexation of Awadh alone.[59]

The upshot of the aborted rising of the 34th Bengal Infantry Regiment was that Mangal Panday and the jemadar of the Guard, Ishwari Panday, were hanged for mutiny on 8 and 21 April respectively. With just 10 exceptions—three Indian officers, three non-commissioned officers, and three sepoys—the remainder of the seven companies present at Barrackpore when the incident took place (the other three companies were on detached duty at Chittagong) were found guilty of passive mutiny and disbanded by order of the governor general on 6 May.[60] The reaction of the 'native' newspaper the *Hindoo Patriot* to the outbreak of disaffection in the Bengal Army was to indicate a cause far deeper than the cartridge question. 'Months before a single cartridge was greased with beef-swet or hogslard,' it commented on 2 April,

> we endeavoured to draw public attention to the unsatisfactory state of feeling in the sepoy army .... There is no want of distinctness or prominence in the symptoms which have already appeared to warn us against the existence of a powder mine in the ranks of the native soldiery that wants but the slightest spark to set in motion gigantic elements of destruction.[61]

IV

In early April 1857, on the advice of Lieutenant Colonel Hogge (the Director of the Artillery School of Instruction at Meerut) and Major

Bontein, the government attempted to remove any remaining objection to the new cartridges by altering the firing drill for both rifles and muskets.[62] Instead of tearing the top of the cartridge with their teeth, sepoys would now do so with their left hand.[63] With this and the other main concession in place (that of allowing sepoys to apply their own grease), Canning authorized the musketry depots to commence firing practice. Any further postponement, he observed, would be viewed by the sepoys' comrades in their regiments as a victory, and the prejudice would take deeper root than ever.[64]

The first live firing at the Ambala Musketry Depot using Enfield cartridges greased by the sepoys with a composition of *ghee* and beeswax took place on 17 April. The Indian troops at the depot had warned Martineau that it would lead to an outbreak of mutiny in the station—which was garrisoned by the 4th Light Cavalry, the 5th and 60th Infantry Regiments, Her Majesty's 9th Lancers, and two troops of the European Bengal Horse Artillery. The increased frequency of arson attacks seemed to confirm this.[65] As early as 26 March an attempt was made to burn down the hut of the Indian officer in the 36th Infantry Regiment, who had been the first to declare his willingness to fire the new cartridge. The fires resumed on 13 April, when the authorities at Ambala received orders to commence firing practice, and continued on into May. The targets included the depot hospital, a barrack in the European lines, an empty bungalow, a European officer's stables, and huts belonging to two high-caste Indian officers and a havildar from the 5th Infantry Regiment who were attached to the depot (and who, according to the commanding officer, had fired the new cartridges without demur and repeatedly assured him that there was nothing objectionable in them).[66] That no one would identify the attackers despite the offer of a large reward, Martineau perceived, was a certain sign of general dissatisfaction and some impending outbreak.[67] However, not all the Indian regiments were outraged by the news from Ambala. When the detachments of the Kanpur regiments returned from Ambala, noted Captain Thomson, they were amicably received and allowed to eat with their own caste although they had been using the Enfield rifle and the suspect cartridges. One Muslim sepoy from Thomson's 53rd Infantry Regiment even brought with him specimens of the cartridges to assure his comrades that no animal fat had been employed in their construction.[68] Jhokun, the servant of Colonel Williams of the 56th Bengal Infantry Regiment, another of the Kanpur units, noted, 'The cartridge question used to be talked about, but it did not engross much attention. The 53rd and 56th infantry regiments showed great lukewarmness until the mutiny actually broke out.'[69] This was probably because the instigators of the eventual mutiny at Kanpur were from the other two regiments: the 2nd Light Cavalry and the 1st Infantry Regiment. The cartridge question, therefore, was only of interest to those who wished to foment mutiny.

At the Dum Dum depot, live firing commenced on 23 April 1857 without any untoward incident. Major Bontein told the assistant adjutant general of the Presidency Division that his orders had been obeyed, which was only to have been expected after the alteration in the method of loading and greasing the cartridges.[70] One of the first to step forward and declare his willingness to fire the new cartridge was Subedar Bholah Upadhya, a Brahmin from the 17th Infantry Regiment. His loyalty was rewarded when his commanding officer, Major Burroughs, recommended him for the post of subedar major (which was vacant) in the regiment, though he was only the second senior subedar. The subedar who was passed over, Bhoondu Sing (an Ahir), would later lead the regiment in mutiny at Azimgarh on 3 June 1857.[71] Before that event took place, the men frequently voiced their suspicions about the new cartridges. Unable to understand their objections in the light of the government's concessions over greasing and loading, Burroughs sought an answer from his shrewdest and most intelligent havildar, Jagannath Tiwary. While refusing to enter into specifics, Tiwary replied, 'From villainy.' But he would say no more.[72]

It is difficult to pinpoint the exact day on which firing practice began at the Sialkot depot. But we do know that on 26 April 1857, the day after an uneasy feeling about the Enfield rifle and cartridge showed itself, Lieutenant Colonel Darwall of the 57th Infantry Regiment at Ferozepur caused a letter to be written to the detached party at the Sialkot Depot to assure them that no greased cartridges were in the regimental magazine, nor would be used. The letter was also read out to the regiment. The men were satisfied, noted Darwall, and nothing further occurred until 286 men deserted when the regiment was disarmed on 14 May.[73] At Sialkot, meanwhile, the sepoys were firing the Enfields without a murmur. After a visit to the depot in early May, John Lawrence informed Canning that the sepoys were pleased with the new musket and quite ready to adopt it, not least because they realized the advantage it would give them in mountain warfare on the North-West frontier.[74]

Within a week, the mutiny proper had began at Meerut. The ostensible cause, as it had been at Baharampur in February 1857, was a refusal to accept blank cartridges for firing practice. The soldiers in question were 90 skirmishers of the 3rd Light Cavalry, made up of the 15 men in each troop to whom carbines were issued, and described by one officer as 'more or less picked men, and quite the elite of the regiment'.[75] On 23 May, these skirmishers were ordered to attend a parade the following morning to practise the new firing drill, wherein the cartridge was torn rather than bitten. That evening, five of the six troop commanders were warned by their men that the skirmishers would not fire the cartridges for fear of getting a bad name. One of these officers informed the adjutant (for transmitting the information to the commanding officer Colonel Carmichael-Smyth) that the men had said that if they fired any kind of cartridge at present, they laid themselves open to imputation from their comrades and other regiments of having fired the objectionable ones.[76] In other words, they did not care whether the cartridges they were being asked to fire were unobjectionable or not; their concern was escaping social ostracization. The warnings were genuine. At the following day's parade, 85 out of the 90 skirmishers refused to accept the three blank cartridges they were offered, despite Carmichael-Smyth's assurance that they were not greased and were the same as they had been using before. According to the Colonel, none of those who refused gave any reason for doing so beyond that they would get a bad name; not one of them urged any scruple of religion. They all said they would take these cartridges if the others did.[77] They numbered 48 Muslims and 37 Hindus. Of the five non-commissioned officers who took the cartridges, three were Muslims and two were Hindus.

At the subsequent court of inquiry, both the Indian quartermaster-havildar and the former acting quartermaster-havildar testified that the blank cartridges involved had been manufactured in the regimental magazine during the previous year. They also confirmed that the paper was the same as that in use for many years, and that there was nothing in the material of the cartridges or the manner in which they had been made up that would be objectionable to either a Hindu or a Muslim. The former acting quartermaster-havildar, one of the five men to accept the cartridges, had even supervised their production.[78] So, too, had Bhuggun, the regimental tindal, who had been making similar cartridges in the regiment for over thirty-three years.[79]

Apart from Carmichael-Smyth, the other witnesses to give evidence to the Court of Inquiry were the senior Muslim and Hindu sowars from each troop, none of whom was involved in the parade. Asked in turn whether they were aware of anything objectionable in the material of the cartridges, most admitted that they knew of nothing and that the cartridges seemed to be of the type always used. And yet, many added, there was a general rumour or suspicion that there was something wrong with them. Only the senior Muslim sowar said that though the cartridges apparently looked like old ones, they had pig fat rubbed over them.[80] The court, made up of seven Indian officers from the two regiments then at Meerut (three from the 3rd Light Cavalry and four from the 20th Infantry Regiment),[81] concluded that that there was no adequate cause for the disobedience in the previous day beyond a vague rumour that the cartridges contained a suspicious material. They, however, were unanimously of the opinion that there was nothing objectionable in the cartridges and that they could be received and used as before without affecting the religious scruple of either a Hindu or a Muslim.[82]

In the opinion of Major G. W. Williams, who later conducted an extensive investigation into the outbreak at Meerut, those cartridges served out to the troopers could not have been confused with the new Enfield cartridge. He concluded the presence of a significant hostile feeling against the government, and a determination to make the worst of the matter by extending the prejudice originally incited by the Enfield cartridges to those of the same kind as had been used for generations past.[83] As a result of the court's findings, Anson agreed with the recommendation by the Judge Advocate General, Colonel Young, that the 85 skirmishers should be charged with collective disobedience before a general court martial.[84] Before the trial could be convened, two similar episodes occurred. First, on 27 April, a squad of Indian artillery recruits at Meerut refused to accept blank cartridges for carbine drill. They were paid up and discharged from service forthwith.[85] Five days later, at Lucknow, the 7th Oudh Irregular Infantry (a local corps under British command) also refused cartridges for musketry practice, alleging they were greased. The officer involved is said to have ordered them to bite the cartridges because he had not received the revised instructions for loading drill. Nevertheless, noted Lieutenant Bonham of the Awadh Artillery, the cartridges were the same as those always in use with the regiment, and being of the ordinary kind, for use with the old smooth-bore musket, they were not greased. All this was fully explained by the officer in charge of the parade, but the men still remained obdurate.[86] The following day, 3 May, it was discovered that men from the

7th Regiment were inciting another regiment at Lucknow to mutiny. Thereupon the Chief Commissioner of Awadh, Henry Lawrence, ordered the disarmament of the 7th Regiment, and during this operation a number of sepoys panicked and deserted. Lawrence's aim was to disband the remaining sepoys and re-enlist those whose innocence could be proved.[87] Canning disagreed, pointing out that only the guilty ones should be discharged.[88] In the event, Lawrence erred on the side of caution by dismissing only 15 sepoys and all the Indian officers bar two; the others were forgiven, though as a precaution only 200 were re-armed.[89] However, Canning's fellow Supreme Council members held very different opinions as to the motive for the 7th Regiment's disobedience. Major General Low and J. P. Grant thought that most of the regiment refused to bite the cartridges because they genuinely feared a loss of caste; whereas Joseph Dorin regarded the biting of the cartridge as an excuse for mutiny on the ground that no new rifles or greased cartridges had been issued to the 7th Regiment.[90]

The court martial of the 85 men of the 3rd Light Cavalry took place over the three days of 6, 7, and 8 May. The court comprised 15 Indian officers: four from the 11th Infantry Regiment (which had arrived in Meerut at the end of April), two from the 3rd Light Cavalry, one from the 20th Infantry Regiment, one from the artillery, and five from the infantry regiments stationed in nearby Delhi (one from the 74th and two each from the 38th and 54th respectively). Havildar Matadeen, the most senior ranking of the accused, tried to excuse his actions by claiming that the night before the parade, Brijmohan Singh, the havildar major's orderly, had boasted that he had fired off two of the new greased cartridges. It was therefore a fear of losing their caste that had caused him and the other men to disobey orders the following day.[91] This accusation is highly suspect. Brijmohan had in fact fired two old blank carbine cartridges using the new loading drill in the presence of his colonel. Why, then, would he lie to his comrades? Palmer has suggested a desire to create mischief.[92] Certainly Brijmohan, a low-caste Hindu who was considered to be Carmichael-Smyth's pet, was unpopular in the regiment and his hut was duly burnt down during the night of 23 April. But presumably that was because he had admitted to firing any cartridge, rather than a greased cartridge which did not exist. The truth is that there was no real justification for refusing the cartridges on 24 April beyond a general determination to stick together in defiance of legitimate authority. Some may have swallowed the canard that their religion and caste really were in danger; others dared not step out of line. But most were probably being manipulated by a hard core of conspirators who had other ends in sight: not least the replacement of the East India Company with a more amenable employer. For Lieutenant Mackenzie of the 3rd Light Cavalry was surely right when he noted that word had been 'passed throughout the Bengal native army to make the cartridge question the test as to which was stronger—the native soldier or the Government'.[93]

By a majority verdict of 14 to 1, all 85 defendants were found guilty and sentenced to 10 years imprisonment with hard labour. The court recommended favourable consideration on the grounds of good character and the fact that the men had been misled by rumours. But the reviewing officer, Major General Hewitt, thought that the latter circumstance aggravated rather than mitigated the crime. He therefore confirmed the majority of the sentences, while halving those of the 11 men who had served less than five years on the basis that they were young and had been led astray by their seniors.[94] The verdict of the court was read out to the prisoners on Saturday, 9 May, at a morning parade attended by the whole Meerut garrison: the 3rd Light Cavalry, the 11th and 20th infantry regiments, Her Majesty's 60th Rifles, Her Majesty's 6th Dragoon Guards (Carabiniers), a troop of European horse artillery, and a battery of European foot artillery. The prisoners were then stripped of their uniforms and shackled in irons. During the hour or so it took to complete the shackling, some men cried out '*bey kussor*' (without fault) and threw their boots away in disgust; others called upon their comrades for assistance while also castigating their colonel, the Indian officers who had composed the court martial, and the government. But however tempted they may have been, the watching Indian troops did nothing, not least because they were being covered by the guns of the European soldiers. With the shackling complete, the prisoners were marched to the jail in Meerut and there handed over to the civil authorities.[95]

It has often been claimed that the bloody rising at Meerut the following day—the start of the mutiny proper—was motivated by a desire to free these prisoners. However, Palmer has shown beyond doubt that the Indian infantry, rather than the cavalry, were the first to rise, and that the plot to mutiny had been maturing for at least a fortnight. The rescue of the prisoners, therefore, was a probably a last-minute addition to the plan.[96] Suffice it to say that the cartridge question—even in its most watered-down form, as seen at Meerut—

was a perfect vehicle for conspirators to turn the rank and file of sepoys against British rule. 'Some scoundrel has seized upon the cartridge question as an opportunity to unite both creeds,' wrote the veterinary surgeon of the 3rd Light Cavalry on 9 May, the day before his death at the hands of mutineers.[97]

A particularly convincing argument for the cartridge question being merely a pretext for mutiny was put forward by Major Marriott, the prosecutor, at the trial of the king of Delhi in March 1858. Neither the Muslims nor the Hindus had any objection to the use of any of the cartridges at Meerut or Delhi, declared Marriott. Rather, the troops were eager to possess the greased cartridges while fighting the Europeans. Marriott also mentioned the fact that not one of the numerous petitions that had been sent to the 'restored' king of Delhi by mutineers during the summer of 1857 made any reference to the cartridge question, though they contained a host of other 'trivial' grievances. Lastly, Marriott made the point that Muslims had no caste nor had they ever claimed a loss of religion by touching pork; many Muslim servants of Europeans, he said, handled pork daily. And to back this up he reminded the court of Martineau's claim that the Muslim sepoys at Ambala had laughed at the cartridge question. Rather, the Muslim soldiers, concluded Marriott, had induced the Hindus to join them by exciting in them the fear of being deprived of their caste.[98] Marriott's additional evidence for this was Mrs Aldwell's claim to have been told by Hindu sepoys, after the battle of Hindun on 30 May 1857, that they greatly regretted what they had done and reproached the Muslims for having decieved them on pretence of their religion, and seemed to doubt greatly whether the English Government had really had any intention of interfering with their caste.[99]

Marriott was trying to prove that the king of Delhi was at the centre of a Muslim conspiracy to overthrow British rule. He was not the only one to blame the Muslims. In mid-May, shortly after the disarmament of Indian troops at Lahore, Donald MacLeod, the judicial commissioner for the Punjab, told Bartle Frere that the cartridges had been used to seduce the credulous, weak, and superstitious, and that he believed the intrigues to be of Muslim origin.[100] A month later, Canning's private secretary confided to the governor of Ceylon that the 'rebellion is now pretty well understood to be a Mahomedan one—and the Cartridge question to have been only a pretext to unite the Hindus with them.'[101] It is probably incorrect to blame the mutiny on the Muslims alone. What is not in doubt is that a sizeable number of sepoy conspirators—Hindu and Muslim alike—were prepared to use the cartridge question to unite opposition to British rule, not because they genuinely feared for their caste and religion, but because they believed they would be better off in the service of a 'native' government. Service under the Indian regimes, the sepoys believed, would provide them with greater pay and career opportunities.[102] Major General Hearsey made just this point in his evidence to the Peel Commission, describing the mutiny as a 'general movement among the soldier class of Hindustan' to 'throw off the dominion of a foreign race, and then to sell their services to the highest native bidder.'[103] Hearsey had no doubt been influenced by a letter from an officer of the 70th Infantry Regiment reporting a comment made to him by a Muslim sepoy that

> when first the report was spread about, it was generally believed by the men, but that subsequently it had been a well understood thing that the cartridge question was merely raised for the sake of exciting the men, with a view of getting the whole army to mutiny and thereby upset the English Government; that they argued, that as we were turned out of Cabool [Kabul in 1842] and had never returned to that place, so, if once we were entirely turned out of India, our rule would cease and we should never return.[104]

Many other officers were similarly unconvinced that the cartridge question—or religion in general—was a genuine cause of mutiny. 'It was all a sham about the cartridges,' wrote a Bengal Artillery officer at the siege of Delhi, 'for they are now firing them against us'.[105] Another Bengal officer on detached duty from his regiment described the cartridge question in July 1857 as a mere farce, adding: 'The mutiny is a well organized and pre-concerted plan for the extermination of the hated English from India.'[106] According to Hervey Greathed, the senior civilian at Delhi during the siege, sepoy deserters invariably cited the cartridge question as the cause of disaffection. However, Greathed considered the real cause to be the growth of a consciousness of power in the army which could only be exercised by mutiny.[107] William Muir, the intelligence chief at Agra to whom these views were divulged, was of a similar opinion:

> The fact is [he informed the Secretary to the Home Department on 19 August 1857] that the sepoys had long been puffed up with conceit that the Imperial fabric rested on their shoulders alone: they had constructed it; they maintained it. This filled them with an arrogant and independent feeling, which led to the constant feeling of grievance when they were not petted and humoured in everything. Here were the elements of disaffection and mutiny. The cartridge was used by the bad designing men of each regiment to inflame the otherwise contented soldiery, and when distrust was once

infused our most solemn disavowals of interference with caste were disbelieved.[108]

In a memorandum for the Supreme Council in 1858, John Lawrence characterized the cartridge question as simply the spark that ignited a combustible mass. What had made the mass combustible, he declared, was the fact that the Sepoy Army had become too powerful. The sepoys were aware that most of the key installations in the country—the fortresses, magazines, and treasuries—were largely under their control. They imagined they could overthrow the British government at will, and replace it with one of their own. It was this sense of their own power, said Lawrence, that had induced them to revolt.[109]

However, arguably the most perspicacious comment on the cartridge question and the causes of the mutiny was provided by Christopher McGuinness, a lowly sergeant in the Bengal Army's Public Works Department, in a letter to his brother-in-law. He wrote:

> For some years past the Bengal sepoy has been changing the tone of his conduct. He was in former years a humble man. He became a pet in all cases where his caste could be brought forward. He was allowed every indulgence. His commanding officer became a mere cypher, without the power to either punish or promote; his officers instead of studying regimental duties were seldom present with their corps, in fact each eagerly sought staff employment from it .... The result of such mis-regulations soon became apparent. The sepoy became self-conceited, impertinent, careless, a grumbler .... From recent information we are led to suppose that an excuse for a general uprising of sepoys in open mutiny was long wanted, and an unfortunate affair of cartridges being made at home for our improved rifle, gave the first spark to the flame.[110]

Conclusion

There is, of course, much evidence that appears to support the theory that the sepoys were motivated by nothing more than a desire to preserve their caste and religion. Some of it is provided by European officers. At the height of the cartridge question, for example, Lieutenant De Kantzow of the 9th Infantry Regiment was asked by some of his Awadh sepoys why, having already endured the loss of their country, they could be expected to stand by and see their caste also contaminated.[111] Having spoken to the Indian officers of the 4th Infantry Regiment in May 1857, Captain Taylor was convinced that they genuinely believed the cartridges were a 'trick injurious to their religion'.[112] Captain Sneyd of the 28th Infantry Regiment, in a letter to his mother of 27 May, noted that the majority of the sepoys liked their officers but were suspicious of the government's designs on their religion.[113]

Other evidence comes from Indian sources. According to Ghulam Abbas, during a stormy interview with the king of Delhi in the Red Fort on 11 May, the Indian officers of the 3rd Light Cavalry justified the mutiny at Meerut on the grounds that they had been required to bite cartridges greased with beef and pork fat.[114] This lie was then repeated in the *Delhi Proclamation*, issued by the rebels between 11 and 15 May 1857, which stated that the governor general had served out cartridges made up with swine and beef fat to deprive the army of their religion.[115] A similar attempt to justify the rebellion on the grounds of religion was made by Nana Sahib's proclamation of 6 July.[116]

Tapti Roy is convinced that such evidence proves the mutiny-rebellion was religiously motivated. 'Let us listen ... to what the soldiers said after they had mutinied,' she writes.

> Without exception, they answered in the idiom of religion. Not only are there official reports on sepoy actions but also letters and proclamations written by the rebels themselves in which they declare their reasons for turning against their masters ... . The widely shared opinion among the British officers that the 'soldiery had a hard religious panic' was substantially corroborated by the language used in the written addresses sent out to mobilize men in the cause of religion. Here the uprising was described not so much as a struggle for political ends as an imperative, a sacred duty, for upholding religion which stood threatened by the British rule.[117]

Much of what Roy says is true. Many officers, sepoys, and rebels did talk in the idiom of religion. The real question is why. The officers were simply repeating the accusations made by their own troops. They may even have wanted to believe that religion was the primary grievance because the alternative—deeper professional grievances—would have reflected badly on them and the service in general. Some of the sepoys (perhaps even the majority) may well have considered their caste and religion to be in danger, however irrational this belief became in relation to the cartridge question itself. However, that in itself shows a complete breakdown of trust between them and their European officers, an intra-service issue. The disintegration of the personal relationship between the sahibs and the sepoys which manifested itself in 1857 was the culmination of a long-term process. For the sepoys, the defence of religion may have provided a personal justification for mutinying about professional grievances. Lastly, there were the conspirators (both within and without the Bengal

Army) and the rebel leaders who jumped onto the bandwagon. These men were bound to set up a cry of 'religion in danger' as the only way to unite both Muslims and Hindus against their British overlords. Their aspirations were the real driving force behind the mutiny. Ahsanullah Khan, the king of Delhi's personal physician, who had much contact with the leading mutineers, wrote later:

> Although the issue of the new cartridges was the ostensible cause of the mutiny, it was not in reality so. Some individuals of the native army had long before been adverse to and dissatisfied with the British Government. They considered that they were treated with severity, and eagerly seized the opportunity of the issue of new cartridges as affording a good pretext for their defection. The wily and intriguing among them made it the fulcrum of their designs to excite the whole army against their rulers, and, mixing therewith a religious element, alienated the minds of the troops from the Government ... [Had] the new cartridges not been issued, they would have made some other pretext to mutiny, because if they had been actuated by religious motives alone, they would have given up service; and if they wished to serve, they would not have mutinied.[118]

NOTES

1. S. B. Chaudhuri, *Civil Rebellion in the Indian Mutinies 1857–1859*, Calcutta: 1957; Eric Stokes, *The Peasant and the Raj: Studies in Agrarian Society and Peasant Rebellion in Colonial India*, Cambridge: 1978, and *The Peasant Armed: The Indian Revolt of 1857*, C. A. Bayly (ed.), Oxford: 1986; C. A. Bayly, *Rulers, Townsmen and Bazaars: North Indian Society in the Age of British Expansion, 1770–1870*, Cambridge: 1983; Rudrangshu Mukherjee, *Awadh in Revolt 1857–58: A Study of Popular Resistance*, New Delhi: 1984, and '"Satan let loose upon the Earth": The Kanpur Massacres in India in the Revolt of 1857', *Past and Present*, no. 128, 1990, pp. 92–116; Tapti Roy, *The Politics of a Popular Uprising: Bundelkhand in 1857*, New Delhi: 1994.
2. Seven out of 10 Bengal Light Cavalry regiments and 54 out of 74 Bengal Native Infantry regiments mutinied or partially mutinied in 1857. These figures do not include the many other regiments that displayed a mutinous disposition before they were disarmed.
3. D. F. Harding, *Smallarms of the East India Company 1600–1856*, vol. 1, London: 1997, pp. 232–3, 239.
4. Ibid., pp. 119–23.
5. Ibid., pp. 123–44.
6. Colonel A. Abbott to Colonel R. J. H. Birch, 7 April 1856 and Birch to Abbott, 25 April 1856, P/43/36, nos 194 and 195 of 25 April 1856, India Military Consultations, Oriental and India Office Collection (hereafter OIOC), British Library, London (henceforth BL).

7. Colonel Chester to Colonel Abbott, 29 April 1857, P/47/18, no. 81 of 19 June 1857, India Military Consultations.
8. Lewis Winant, *Early Percussion Firearms: A History of the Early Percussion Firearms Ignition*, New York: 1959, pp. 255–6.
9. G. B. Malleson (ed.), *Kaye and Malleson's History of the Indian Mutiny*, vol. 1, London: 1888, pp. 379–80.
10. Birch to Abbott, 7 November 1856, P/46/55, no. 24 of 7 November 1856, India Military Consultations.
11. Evidence of Lieutenant M. E. Currie, Commissary of Ordnance, 23 March 1857, *Parliamentary Papers* (hereafter *PP*), House of Commons (hereafter HC), 1857, vol. 30, p. 261; Memorandum by J. G. Bonner, Inspector-General of Stores, 23 March 1857, *PP*, HC, 1857, vol. 30, p. 4.
12. Malleson (ed.), *Kaye and Malleson's History of the Indian Mutiny*, vol. 1, pp. 380–1.
13. J. A. B. Palmer, *The Mutiny Outbreak at Meerut in 1857*, Cambridge: 1966, p. 14.
14. Birch to John Lawrence, 5 February 1857, P/47/5, no. 51 of 6 February 1857, India Military Consultations.
15. Captain J. A. Wright to the Adjutant of the Rifle Instruction Depot, 22 January 1857, in G. W. Forrest (ed.), *Selections from the Letters, Dispatches and other State Papers Preserved in the Military Department of the Government of India, 1857–58* (hereafter *State Papers*), Calcutta: 1893, vol. 1, p. 3.
16. Major J. Bontein to the Station Staff Officer, 23 January 1857 and Hearsey to Major W. A. J. Mayhew, 24 January 1857, in Forrest (ed.) *State Papers*, vol. 1, pp. 1–3.
17. Birch to Major Mayhew, 27 January 1857; Birch to Colonel C. Chester, 27 January 1857 (telegraphic); Abbott to Chester, 28 January 1857, *PP*, HC, 1857, vol. 30, pp. 37–40.
18. Abbott to Birch, 29 January 1857 (two separate letters), *PP*, HC, 1857, vol. 30, pp. 40–1.
19. Canning to Vernon Smith, 7 February 1857, Lyveden Papers, MSS, EUR/F231/4, OIOC.
20. Evidence of Lieutenant Currie and Colonel A. Abbott, 23 March 1857, *PP*, HC, 1857, vol. 30, p. 261.
21. Evidence of Major Bontein, 18 March 1857, *PP*, HC, 1857, vol. 30, p. 259.
22. Proceedings of a Special Court of Inquiry, 6 February 1857, in Forrest (ed.), *State Papers*, vol. 1, pp. 7–13.
23. Evidence of Major Bontein and Lieutenant Currie, 18 March 1857, *PP*, HC, 1857, vol. 30, pp. 259–60.
24. Canning to Vernon Smith, 22 February 1857, Lyveden Papers, MSS EUR/F231/4.
25. Lieutenant Colonel W. St. L. Mitchell to Major A. H. Ross, 27 February 1857, in Forrest (ed.), *State Papers*, vol. 1, p. 41.

26. Forrest (ed.), *State Papers*, vol. 1, pp. 45–7.
27. David Harding, 'Arming the East India Company's Forces', in Alan J. Guy and Peter B. Boyden (eds), *Soldiers of the Raj: The Indian Army, 1600–1947*, London: 1997, p. 145.
28. Captain E. M. Martineau to Sir John Kaye, 20 October 1864, Kaye Mutiny Papers, H725, pp. 1023–4, OIOC.
29. Ibid., pp. 1027–8.
30. Lieutenant Martineau to Captain S. Becher, 20 March 1857, Martineau Letters, MSS, EUR/C571, OIOC.
31. Becher to Colonel Birch, 25 March 1857, no. 335 of 3 April 1857, India Military Consultations.
32. Martineau to Becher, 23 March 1857, Martineau Letters, MSS, EUR/C571.
33. Examination of Captain Martineau, 23 February 1858, *PP*, HC, 1859, vol. 18, p. 210.
34. Anson to Elphinstone, 29 March 1857, Elphinstone Papers, MSS, EUR/F87/Box 11B/18, OIOC.
35. Becher to Colonel Birch, 25 March 1857, India Military Consultations, no. 335 of 3 April 1857, P/47/11, OIOC.
36. Forrest (ed.), *State Papers*, vol. 1, pp. 94–7.
37. Examination of Sergeant Major J. T. Hewson and Lieutenant B. H. Baugh, 6 April 1857, Forrest (ed.), *State Papers*, vol. 1, pp. 117–22.
38. Examination of Havildar (late Sepoy) Shaikh Paltu, 6 April 1857, Forrest (ed.), *State Papers*, vol. 1, p. 124.
39. Examination of Shaikh Paltu, 9 April 1857, Forrest (ed.), *State Papers*, vol. 1, pp. 129–30.
40. Examination of Hewson, Forrest (ed.), *State Papers*, vol. 1, p. 119.
41. Interrogation of Mangal Pandey, 4 April 1857, Forrest (ed.), *State Papers*, vol. 1, p. 108.
42. S. Wheler to the officiating brigadier major, 4 April 1857, *PP*, HC, 1857, vol. 30, p. 202.
43. Wheler to Major Ross, Assistant Adjutant General, Presidency Division, 15 April 1857, *PP*, HC, 1857, vol. 30, p. 205.
44. Canning to Vernon Smith, 9 April 1857, Lyveden Papers, MSS, EUR/F231/5.
45. *Friend of India*, 13 April 1857.
46. *Bengal Hurkaru*, 19 April 1857.
47. Examination of Captain Martineau, 23 February 1858, *PP*, HC, 1859, vol. 18, p. 210.
48. Anson to Lord Elphinstone, 10 May 1857, Elphinstone Papers, MSS, EUR/F87/ Box 6A/no. 4, OIOC.
49. *Bengal Hurkaru*, 28 and 29 May 1857.
50. Kenneth W. Jones, *The New Cambridge History of India: Socio-Religious Reform Movements in British India*, 3(1), Cambridge: 1989, p. 27.

51. Quoted in Eric Stokes, *English Utilitarians in India*, London: 1959, p. 46.
52. Jones, *The New Cambridge History of India*, 3(1), pp. 28–9.
53. Andrew Porter, *The Oxford History of the British Empire: The Nineteenth Century*, vol. 3, Oxford: 1999, p. 231.
54. Jones, *The New Cambridge History of India*, 3(1), pp. 52–3, 87, 156–8; Lawrence James, *Raj: The Making and Unmaking of British India*, London: 1997, pp. 222, 228–9; Michael Maclagan, *Clemency Canning*, London: 1962, pp. 114–15.
55. Colonel Sleeman to C. Allen, 14 October 1852, P/43/61, no. 375 of 5 November 1852, India Military Consultations; General Order by the Governor General, 16 February 1853, Abstract of General Orders from 1848 to 1853, L/MIL/17/2/437, OIOC.
56. G. Anderson and M. Subedar (eds), *The Last Days of the Company: A Source Book of Indian History, 1818–58*, London: 1918, vol. 1, p. 110.
57. Kantzow Papers, vol. 1, p. 5, MSS EUR/Photo/EUR 86, OIOC.
58. Examination of Captain Martineau, 23 February 1858, *PP*, 1859, vol. 18, p. 210.
59. Captain Mowbray Thomson, *The Story of Cawnpore*, London: 1859, p. 194.
60. General Order by the governor general, 4 May 1857, and Major General Hearsey to Colonel Birch, 6 May 1857, Forrest (ed.), *State Papers*, vol. 1, pp. 222–6.
61. *Hindoo Patriot*, 2 April 1857.
62. Lieutenant Colonel Hogge to Colonel Chester, 20 February 1857, *PP*, HC, 1857, vol. 30, p. 68; Bontein to Major Ross, 2 March 1857, in Forrest (ed.), *State Papers*, vol. 1, pp. 36–8.
63. Govornor General in Council to the Court of Directors, 8 April 1857, *PP*, HC, 1857, vol. 30, pp. 5–6.
64. Colonel Birch to Colonel Chester, 3 April 1857, no. 346 of 3 April 1857, P/47/11, India Military Consultations.
65. Examination of Captain Martineau, 23 February 1858, *PP*, 1859, vol. 18, p. 210.
66. Captain E. W. E. Howard to G. C. Barnes, 4 May 1857, *PP*, HC, 1857, vol. 30, p. 443; return by Major F. Maitland, 5th Infantry Regiment, 24 February 1858, *PP*, HC, 1859, vol. 18, p. 44. A jemadar in the 5th Infantry Regiment was charged with inciting the regiment to ostracize these men, but was acquitted by a court martial manned by the Indian officers.
67. Examination of Captain Martineau, 23 February 1858, *PP*, HC, 1859, vol. 18, p. 210.
68. Thomson, *The Story of Cawnpore*, pp. 24–5.
69. Deposition of Jhokun, no. 34, in Forrest (ed.), *State Papers*, vol. 3, Appendix, p. cxcvii.

70. Bontein to Major Ross, 23 April 1857, P/47/15, no. 334 of 15 May 1857, India Military Consultations.
71. Statement by Lieutenant Colonel F. W. Burroughs, 3 June 1857, in S. A. A. Rizvi and M. L. Bhargava (eds), *Freedom Struggle in Uttar Pradesh*, vol. 1, Lucknow: Publications Bureau, 1957), pp. 344–5.
72. Burroughs to Captain I. H. Chamberlain, 23 January 1860, in Rizvi and Bhargava (eds), *Freedom Struggle*, vol. 1, p. 348.
73. Return of the 57th Infantry Regiment by Lieutenant Colonel E. Darwall, 3 March 1858, *PP*, HC, 1859, vol. 18, p. 50.
74. Lawrence to Canning, 4 May 1857, quoted in Malleson (ed.), *Kaye and Malleson's History of the Indian Mutiny*, vol. 1, pp. 427–8.
75. Sir Patrick Cadell, 'The Outbreak of the Indian Mutiny', *Journal of the Society for Army Historical Research*, vol. 33, 1955, p. 119.
76. Captain H. C. Craigie to Lieutenant Melville-Clarke, 23 April 1857, in Forrest (ed.), *State Papers*, vol. 1, pp. 228–9
77. Evidence of Colonel G. M. Carmichael-Smyth, 25 April 1857, in Forrest (ed.), *State Papers*, vol. 1, pp. 230–2.
78. Evidence of Quartermaster-Havildar Thakur Singh and Havildar Prasad Singh, in Forrest (ed.), *State Papers*, vol. 1, pp. 232–3.
79. Evidence of Bhuggun, in Forrest (ed.), *State Papers*, vol. 1, pp. 236–7.
80. Forrest (ed.), *State Papers*, vol. 1, pp. 234–6.
81. The 15th Infantry Regiment had left Meerut for Nasirabad in early April and would soon be replaced by the 11th Infantry Regiment from Mirzapur.
82. Forrest (ed.), *State Papers*, vol. 1, p. 237.
83. Memorandum by Major G. W. Williams, 15 November 1857, in Rizvi and Bhargava (eds), *Freedom Struggle in Uttar Pradesh: Source Material*, vol. 5, pp. 10–11.
84. Memorandum by Colonel K. Young to Colonel Chester and Anson to Chester, 29 April 1857, in Rizvi and Bhargava (eds), *Freedom Struggle*, vol. 5, pp. 237–240.
85. Major J. H. Campbell to Major J. Waterfield, 30 April 1857, in Rizvi and Bhargava (eds), *Freedom Struggle*, vol. 5, pp. 241–2.
86. Colonel John Bonham, *Oude in 1857: Some Memories of the Indian Mutiny*, London: 1928, pp. 20–1.
87. G. Couper to the Secretary to the Government of India, 4 May 1857, Forrest (ed.), *State Papers*, vol. 2, pp. 8–9.
88. Canning's minute of 10 May 1857, *PP*, 1857, vol. 30, p. 248.
89. Lawrence to Canning, 17 May 1857, in Forrest (ed.), *State Papers*, vol. 2, p. 20.
90. Minutes by Dorin and Low, 10 May 1857, and Grant, 11 May 1857, in Forrest (ed.), *State Papers*, vol. 2, pp. 11–16.
91. Palmer, *The Mutiny Outbreak at Meerut*, pp. 65–6.
92. Ibid., p. 60.

93. Colonel A. R. D. Mackenzie, 'The Outbreak at Meerut', a chapter in Colonel E. Vibart, *The Sepoy Mutiny*, London: 1898, p. 216.
94. Palmer, *The Mutiny Outbreak at Meerut*, p. 67.
95. Mackenzie, 'The Outbreak at Meerut', *The Sepoy Mutiny*, pp. 218–19; Veterinary Surgeon John Phillipps, to R. M. Edwards, 9 May 1857, Edwards Papers, National Army Museum (hereafter NAM), London, pp. 7902–8.
96. Palmer, *The Mutiny Outbreak at Meerut*, pp. 129–31.
97. Phillipps to R. M. Edwards, 9 May 1857, Edwards Papers, NAM, pp. 7902–8.
98. Address by Major F. J. Harriott, 9 March 1858, *PP*, HC, 1859, vol. 18, pp. 245, 363.
99. Evidence of Mrs Aldwell, *PP*, HC, 1859, vol. 18, p. 203.
100, MacLeod to Frere, 15 May 1857, Elphinstone Papers, MSS, EUR/F87/Box 6B/8/1, OIOC.
101. George Talbot to Henry Ward, 19 June 1857, Talbot Papers, MSS, EUR/F271/1, OIOC.
102. Saul David, *The Indian Mutiny 1857*, London: 2002, p. 384.
103. *PP*, 1859, vol. 5, Appendix 71, p. 562.
104. Captain Greene to Hearsey, 15 June 1857, *PP*, HC, 1857, vol. 30, p. 503.
105. Second Lieutenant H. Chichester to his mother, 14 June 1857, Chichester Letters, MSS, EUR/Photo EUR. 271, NAM.
106. Captain Pierce to his parents, 12 July 1857, Pierce Letters, Add. MSS 425000, III, BL.
107. Greathed quoted in W. Muir to Brigadier-General Havelock, 12 August 1857, *PP*, HC, 1857–8, XLIV, p. 200.
108. Muir to C. Beadon, 19 August 1857, Rizvi and Bhargava (eds), *Freedom Struggle*, vol. 1, p. 331.
109. Quoted in Sir Richard Temple, *Lord Lawrence*, London, 1889, pp. 127–8.
110. Sergeant McGuiness to Mr Moore, dated 1857, McGuiness Letters, MSS, EUR/Photo EUR 183, OIOC.
111. Kantzow Papers, OIOC, MSS, EUR/Photo/EUR 86, vol. 1, p. 5.
112. Captain Reynell Taylor to Major D. Wilkie, 19 May 1857, Wilkie Correspondence, NAM, 5607–74.
113. Captain H. Sneyd to his mother, 27 May 1857, Sneyd Letters, NAM, 7802–79.
114. Examination of Ghulam Abbas, 29 January 1858, *PP*, HC, 1859, vol. 18, p. 137.
115. Rizvi and Bhargava (eds), *Freedom Struggle*, vol. 1, pp. 438–9.
116. *PP*, HC, 1857–8, XLIV, pp. 112–13.
117. Roy, *The Politics of a Popular Uprising*, p. 51.
118. Supplementary Evidence of Hakim Ahsanullah Khan, *PP*, HC, 1859, vol. 18, p. 267.

3 The Sepoy Mutinies Revisited*

Rudrangshu Mukherjee

The revolt of 1857, or the Indian Mutiny, as it is still conveniently labelled in most of the Western world, was spread over a large area, covering Delhi in the north-west to Bihar in the east, from the foothills of the Himalayas to Jhansi. There were scattered instances of revolt outside this area. Within the area, again, the region north of the River Yamuna right upto Awadh seems to have been the core where the sepoy mutinies were clustered and the rebellion most popular and intense.

This article concentrates, against the current fashion, on the sepoy mutinies: on the *sipahi* and his activities. There are reasons for looking at the sepoy mutinies separately. In the literature on 1857, rich as it is, this is a neglected aspect. In the nineteenth century, in the high noon of British imperialism, when the great narratives of the 'Mutiny' were written, the activities of the sepoys were written about as something disorderly and chaotic: the work of disloyal soldiery. This could give rise to ambiguities. For example, J. W. Kaye called his account *The History of the Sepoy War, 1857–58*. For him, the events of 1857 were nothing more than the work of sepoys, a very small section of the population; yet, he called it a 'war', a term that implies the involvement of a large section of the population and also, more importantly, a degree of planning, coordination, and organization. More recently, Eric Stokes has drawn attention to the military tactics of the sepoys.[1] But for him, the mutinies were, 'the work of a small minority'; the mutinies were the product of 'designing men'; a conspiring few substituted for collective action.[2] In

* First published in Mushirul Hasan and Narayani Gupta (eds), *India's Colonial Encounter: Essays in Memory of Eric Stokes*, New Delhi: Manohar Publishers, 1993; reprint 2004, pp. 193–204.

nationalist historiography, prone as it is to prove that 1857 was much more than a mere mutiny, the tendency is to gloss over the activities of the sepoys. Thus, in the writings of S. B. Chaudhuri, the activities of the sepoys are not discussed; he writes only about the civil rebellions which, to him, were important.[3] This chapter attempts to show that these approaches are flawed: they fundamentally misunderstand the nature of sepoy action, thereby also missing the crucial interconnections between the sepoy mutinies and the popular rebellion.

I have argued elsewhere[4] that a chronological survey of the mutinies suggests a certain pattern. The first outbreak took place on 10 May at Meerut. There the soldiers, having mutinied, sped off towards Delhi. It is significant that between 10 and 14 May there were no mutinies in any of the garrisons of north India. It is only after the sepoys in Delhi had mutinied (11–12 May) that the other garrisons in north India followed suit as if in chain reaction: 20 May Aligarh, 23 May Etwah and Mainpuri, 27 May Etah, 30 May Lucknow, 4 June Kanpur, and so on. There is here a contagion of movement facilitated by the fact that there was a degree of communication between the sepoy lines. Often, such communication could be direct. The 7th Awadh Irregular Infantry, who had refused to take the cartridges in early May, wrote to the 48th Native Infantry (N. I.) that 'they had acted for the faith and awaited the 48th orders'.[5] Men moved from one cantonment to another carrying the message of mutiny: in Kaye's words, these were the 'emissaries of evil'.[6] Sepoys came from Benaras to Lucknow, British officers reported, 'to corrupt the troops'.[7] The sepoy lines in Fyzabad were swarming with mutinous sepoys from neighbouring Azamgarh and Jaunpur.[8] In Salon, the mutiny occurred only when mutineers from Allahabad, Sultanpur, and Partapgarh had come there and 'goaded' the troops in Salon to rise.[9]

Edwards, the magistrate of Budaun, noted that the 10th Native Infantry in Fatehgarh would mutiny depending on the movements of other mutinous corps, with whom they were in daily correspondence.[10] In the context of communication of the message of revolt, the experience of Francois Sisten, a native Christian police inspector in Sitapur, is revealing. He had gone to pay his respects to the joint magistrate of Saharanpur and was dressed and seated like an Indian. A Muslim *tahsildar* of Bijnor entered and asked Sisten where he was from. On hearing that the latter was from Awadh, the tahsildar said, 'What news from Awadh? How does the work progress, brother?' Sisten replied, 'If we have work in Awadh, your highness will know it well.' The tahsildar, interpreting this as caution, said 'Depend upon it, we will succed this time. The direction of the business is in able hands.' People were thus planning and talking of the uprising. In fact, the tahsildar was later to be the chief rebel leader of Bijnor.[11]

There were others instances, too, of communication through non-military sources. The official narrative for Meerut noted that

> one of the many emissaries who were moving about the country, appeared at Meerut in April, ostensibly as a fukeer, riding on an elephant with the follower and having with him horses and native carriages. The frequent visits of the men of the native regiments to him attracted attention and he was ordered through the police to leave the place. He apparently complied, but it is said, he stayed some time in the lines of the 20th N.I.[12]

Lucknow, too, immediately after the annexation of Awadh, was full of religious leaders and self-styled prophets all preaching the destruction of British rule.[13] The outbreak of the mutinies was not chaotic or disorderly. On the contrary, the sipahis showed a remarkable degree of planning and coordination in the way the mutinies were carried out. The mutinies began at a preappointed signal: in Bareilly, Lucknow, and Meerut, the signal was the firing of the evening gun. In Fyzabad, it was the sounding of the bugle at 10 p.m.[14] In Kanpur, the sounding of the bugle was the signal for the massacre to begin at Satichaura Ghat.[15] The execution of the mutiny, in most places, was well planned. In Fyzabad, for example, as the bugle sounded, the troops quickly organized themselves: they stopped the gunners from touching their guns and, under the direction of a *risaldar* (an Indian infantry officer), the English officers of the 22nd and 6th were placed with the Quarter Guard. The sowars patrolled all roads and approaches to the cantonment.[16]

Such instances indicate planning and suggest decision-making bodies which laid down the plan of action. The crucial question is, of course, what were these bodies, and how and when were they formed. Unfortunately, no direct answers to these questions can be provided. But from two events, one can get clues as to how the mutinies came to be so well organized. The first is the experience of Captain Hearsey of the Awadh Military Police. During the mutiny, he had been given protection by his Indian subordinates. The 41st Native Infantry, stationed in the same place, insisted that as they had murdered all their officers, it was necessary for the military police to do the same or deliver Hearsey up as prisoner to the 41st. The Military Police refused to do either and so it was decided to settle the matter by referring it to a panchayat, that is, a collective body composed of native officers drawn from each regiment.[17] Ball, in his *The History of the Indian Mutiny*, noted that panchayats were a nightly occurrence in the Kanpur sepoy lines.[18] There is a suggestion here that matters were decided collectively and, given the character of the sepoy lines, it is not difficult to imagine sepoys sitting together to decide their own future.

The other piece of evidence is a little more vivid. It concerns the Mangal Panday episode. This is one of the better-documented episodes of the Revolt and its origins. The investigations revealed that before Mangal Panday decided to act, there had been midnight meetings in Barrackpore which had been attended by sepoys from different regiments. And, on that fateful afternoon when he opened fire on his officers, none except one of his fellow sepoys, all of whom had gathered around, tried to stop him. The only exception was Sheikh Paltu. In fact, the other sepoys displayed a complicity, for while Mangal Panday drew his sword and slashed and wounded Lieutenant Baugh, an unidentified sepoy hit Sergeant Major Hewson from behind. During his trial, Mangal Panday steadfastly refused, in a remarkable show of solidarity, to name the sepoys who were implicated. He had only one answer: that he had acted on his own. His reiteration of his own responsibility for his own actions can be read as an attempt to shield the reality, which was the exact opposite of an individual acting on his own. The collective aspect was again made evident when sepoys of the 34th, Mangal Panday's regiment, trampled their caps on the ground when they were disarmed: a gesture of protest carried out collectively, which would in a month's time transform itself to more violent and concrete forms.[19]

The sepoys were thus the makers of their own rebellion: they did not undertake to challenge the might of the Company Bahadur in a fit of absent-mindedness. They were conscious agents and their acts were marked by deliberation and planning. This needs emphasis, because all too often in the literature on the subject, their actions are described as 'spontaneous', that is, lacking a coherent programme and plan. As Gramsci wrote, it is only a 'scholastic and academic historico-political outlook which sees as real and worthwhile only such movements of revolt as are one hundred per cent conscious, that is, movements that are governed by plans worked out in advance to the last detail or in line with abstract theory.' Indeed, as Gramsci would have it, '"pure" spontaneity does not exist in history'. The sepoys had a consciousness which was framed, one could say following Gramsci, 'through everyday experience illuminated by "common sense"'.[20] As conscious agents, the sepoys chose to destroy. Direct action, that commonest form of popular protest, informed the sepoys' moment of insurgency. In each and every station, the commencement of the mutiny was marked by extensive arson and plunder. The official narrative from Meerut described the ferocity of the destruction,

> the inveterate animosity with which the work of destruction was carried out ... may be judged of by the fact, that houses built entirely of masonary, with nothing inflammable, except the doors and beams which a considerable height from the ground supported the roof formed of cement, resting on kiln-burnt bricks, were as effectually destroyed as the thatched bungalows. Property, which the miscreants could not carry off, was thrown out and smashed into fragments, evidently pounded to pieces with heavy clubs.[21]

The mutinies were signalled by arson. Kaye noted this:

> What meetings and conspiracies and oath-takings there may have been in the sipahi's quarter ... can only be conjectured; but one form of expression in which the feelings declared themselves, was patent to all. It was written in characters of fire and blazed out of the darkness of the night. From the verandahs of their houses the European officers saw these significant illuminations and knew what they portended.[22]

As W. H. Carey put it, 'And thus the Fire King began to demonstrate an inkling of what was in store for almost every station in the North-Western Provinces.'[23]

The destruction was not indiscriminate. Property owned, used, or lived in by the British were always the first to be attacked. Thus the bungalows in which the Europeans lived, alien to any kind of Indian residence, were always the first to be attacked and burnt. Buildings identified with the British, their institutions, the symbols of their power were invariably destroyed. Thus, in Aligarh, one large indigo factory, the property of an European, went up in flames. Similarly, 'the records of the Suddur Cutcherry and those of four out of eight Tehseels were destroyed.'[24] Invariably, the government offices were the object of rebel wrath. In Etawah, the *kachahri*, the sessions courthouse, the postoffice—all symbols of alien domination—were victims of incendiary attacks.[25] Almost always the records of the tahsil were destroyed in a symbolic rejection of all that a foreign power had enshrined in its records. For the rebel the mark of enmity was unmistakable. The enmity could also be extended through association. Friends of the British became enemies of the sepoys. Thus, the Bengalis who were seen as the next thing to a Christian, were plundered and forced to swear allegiance to the 'native' government. Bholanath Chunder, a Bengali, wrote,

The Bengalis cowered in fear, and awaited within closed doors to have their throats cut. The women raised a dolorous cry at the near prospect of death from massacring their officers, and plundering the Treasury, and letting open the gaol-bird, the sipahis spread through the town to loot the inhabitants. Our friend, as well as his other neighbours, were soon eased of all their valuables, but were spared their lives on promise of allegiance to their (the Native) Government.[26]

To most north Indians, Bengalis at this time were an object of ridicule. As one of them put it, the Bengalis were only good for being attorneys or for teaching Milton and Shakespeare.[27]

By this logic of extension, those that had gained from British rule became targets of rebel fury. Dunlop described vividly one such attack:

many of the prisoners released had enemies in the district, mostly Bunyahs who had brought suits in our courts and the arrival of a period of anarchy was at once seized on by them to wreak a summary revenge on almost all the Bunyah caste. Thus at the village of Bhojpore, the best house, a large brick building with a courtyard in the center and massive wooden portals, belonged to the family of a Mahajun or Bunyah, by name Beharee Lall, who was a four Biswa (or one fifth) sharer of that village; one of the other shareholders, a Jat, was at the time of the outbreak in prison, confined for debt under the Civil court decree at the suit of the Bunyah. He arrived during the light of the 11th at Bhojpore with a few of his fellow prisoners and at daylight the villagers were collected for an attack on the Bunyah house.[28]

What began as an individual vendetta soon transformed itself into an entire village's fury against an oppressor and led to the latter's destruction.

As the above quotations make evident, one of the obvious targets of destruction was the jail. One of the first things the mutineers did was to break open the jails. It appeared to them to be the epitome of domination of an alien legal system. In Meerut, the mutineers rushed to the new jail, 'dug out of the wall the gratings of some of the windows of the ward ... and took their comrades away', and in the jail 'about 300 or 400 sipahees released the convicts'.[29]

Through the previous one hundred years of colonial rule the sepoys had been kicked, flogged, and brutalized: they had seen comrades blown from the mouth of canons. In their own movements against their quondam masters, they replicated that violence on the master's property and on the master's body. 'Troopers and sipahees', the official narrative of the Meerut outbreak noted, 'were plundering, burning and destroying in every direction and savagely hunting to death every European, every Christian, man, woman or child they could find.'[30] Such replication is, of course, not uncommon. George Rude, in his study of the eighteenth-century crowd in Paris and London wrote 'The eighteenth-century crowd ... could hardly fail to be corrupted by the example set them by their social betters. It was an era of brutal floggings, torture of prisoners and public executions.'[31] Again, Richard Cobb, in his study of French popular protest, juxtaposed the violence of the *sans cullottes* with the violence of the ruling class of the *ancien regime.*[32]

The springboard of this violence was the common hatred of all things British. But this hatred itself grew from or was aggravated by two interrelated factors. I have discussed already the contagion of the mutiny in its spread from one sepoy line to another. A similar transmission was noticeable in the rumours that circulated in north India in the summer of 1857. There were rumours about greased cartridges, about flours polluted by the bone-dust of cows and pigs, about the intentions of the British to disarm the sepoys, about forcible conversions to Christianity, and about the inevitable end of British rule at the centenary of Plassey.[33] All these rumours circulating at the same time aggregated into one gigantic rumour. Untraceable in their origin and unverifiable in their import, the rumours moved in a powerful current, touching on issues that were profoundly close to indigenous sentiments. Like the great fear of 1789 in rural France which Lefebvre analysed, there spread in north India the alarm of a deliberate British plot to despoil the religion of Hindus and Muslims. One British officer stationed in Awadh wrote graphically about it:

> Government it was said had sent up cartloads and boatloads of, bone-dust, which was to be mixed with the flour and sweetmeats sold in the bazaar, whereby the whole population would lose their caste. The public mind became greatly excited. On one day, at Sultanpur, it was spread over the station that a boat had reached a certain ghaut on the river Gomtee laden with bone-dust, and the sepoys were hardly restrained from outbreak. A few days later, at the station of Salone, two camels, laden with ammunition, arrived at the house of Captain Thompson, the commandant. It was rumoured that the packages contained bone-dust and a panic spread through station. Not only the sepoys in their lines, but the domestic servants about their officers' bungalows, and the villagers and zemindars attending court, hastily flung away, untasted, the food which they had cooked and fasted for the day. At Lucknow, the rumours which were whispered about were perpetual, and the public mind was never allowed to rest. Now it was at one shop, the next day in another bazaar, that despatches of bone-dust had, it was asserted, been received. It was in vain that facts were opposed to this prevailing panic.[34]

The people were convinced that there was a move afoot to destroy their caste and religion. The programme of reform and Westernization so eagerly pursued and propagated by a generation of British administrators only fuelled such a belief. Rumours brought men together, stoked their suspicions, and engendered a common hatred and thereby led to common action.

There was one theme in all these rumours: a threat to religion. The sepoys saw their action as being in defence of their religion. In Meerut, 'small parties of cavalry troopers with cries of "Yah Ullah" and "Deen Deen" rushed into the city and called upon the people to join in a religious war against the infidels.'[35] A group of sepoys captured in 1858 were individually asked before the execution why they had taken to arms; each one of them individually replied, 'The slaughter of the English was required by our religion.'[36] In this context, the experiences of Ranjit Singh Bissein, a former havaldar of the 63rd Native Infantry is of some relevance. He was coming into Lucknow on 24 May when he passed a police outpost,

> the police [Ranjit Singh reported] ... were lounging on the charpoys. They called him to come and sit down and talk. They said they were new levies stationed there. He asked what duty was assigned to them. They said that they were to oppose any of the Sepoys ... and fight them. But they added, we shall not fight them. 'Kala kala admee sab eyk hyn. Deen kee bat hyn. Hum log kahi ko beydhuram ho.' All black men are one. It is a matter of religion. Why should we lose our religion?[37]

Religion served as the source of solidarity and fraternity. Religion for them was something that was imbricated with their entire life: It informed their world-view, it was their fountain of knowledge, it provided them with a practical code of ethics—it was, one could say following Marx, their *point d' honneur.*[38] British rule was seen as a challenge to an entire way of life. Thus the division of sepoys into Hindus and Muslims did not serve, contrary to British expectations, to disunite the rebels. In Lucknow, the sepoys could hail Birjis Qadr as their Krishna.[39] The British, and Christianity by extension, were identified as the common threat to a cherished and familiar way of life. In Sitapur, the name of the commissioner, Mr Christian became identified with the religion, increasing the wrath and fury of the rebels.[40]

I have been trying so far to draw out some of the general characteristics that informed the actions of the sepoys. These are, briefly, collectivity as revealed in the planning and coordination, a destruction that discriminated and extended itself by the logic of association, a violence whose chief modality was arson, and direct actions which were spurred on by rumours. In short, the mutinies were informed by a consciousness of a project of power, most obviously manifest in the singular way in which the sepoys wanted to destroy their dominators. All these features have parallels with the general features of peasant insurgency in the colonial period.[41] The sepoys were, in fact, behaving in exactly the same way as the peasants behaved when they took to arms time and again, against the dominant triad of *sarkar, sahukar,* and zamindar.

This similarity is not surprising. All the data that we have of the recruitment of the sepoys of the Bengal Army show that they were mostly drawn from the agricultural families of southern Awadh and eastern Uttar Pradesh.[42] This common background explains the easy communication across sepoy lines in north India and also the similar reaction of the sepoys to rumours. The sepoys were, to use a cliche, 'peasants in uniform' and so when they rebelled, they did so in exactly the same manner as their brothers in the villages did. This similarity also explains another thing. It puts into perspective the transformation of the mutinies into popular insurgency. Once the mutinies had struck and British administration had collapsed, in the words of one British officer, 'like a house made of cards',[43] the rebellion spread rapidly in the countryside and among the common people. The common people were waiting for the mutinies to initiate the uprising, in Meerut, to quote the official narrative again:

> Before a shot was fired, the inhabitants of the Sudder Bazar went out, armed with swords, spears, clubs, any weapon they could lay hands on, collected in crowds in every lane and alley, at every outlet of the bazars; and the residents of the wretched hamlets ... were to be seen similarly armed, pouring out to share in what they evidently knew was going to happen.[44]

They used these arms, as we have seen, against government property, against the White man, the zamindar, and the moneylender. In Kanpur, Nanak Chand described in his diary the plunder of all the houses of the mahajans and the rich.[45] What began as a mutiny transformed itself into a peasant rebellion. The sepoy-peasant continuum explains why the features of the mutiny were so similar to the features of peasant rebellions, and also why the sepoys' actions found such a direct and immediate echo in the countryside.

The sepoy, when he revolted, shed his uniform. In Meerut, most of the mutineers were in undress and 'they went to Delhi not, in military array, but in straggling disorder'.[46] In Kanpur, the sepoys broke out of their lines and tore off their regimental colours.[47] In short, the sepoys were rejecting the regimentation that had been imposed on them. The one thing they refused to surrender from their days in the Bengal Army was, of course, their arms. The peasant in uniform became the peasant with arms.

The rejection of the uniform and regimentation also has, perhaps, a greater significance. The act of mutiny was an act of negation, an act to eliminate individuals and a form of government that were seen as a threat to the social order. But this negation, even if it replicated the violence of the masters, was not a mere inversion, an empty act of imitation. In the rejection of the uniform, the regimentation, the colours—all those various signs by which an alien order had tried to separate the sepoy from his peasant brethren—there is the quest, however faint, or groping of an alternative identity which was perhaps entrenched in the shared common world of the peasantry. The alternative lay in that commonality, and it was that sense of collectivity that provided the uprising with its ultimate source of strength.

Notes

1. Eric Stokes, *The Peasant Armed: The Indian Revolt of 1857*, C. A. Bayly (ed.), Oxford: 1986, ch. 2.
2. Ibid., pp. 50, 54.
3. S. B. Chaudhuri, *Civil Rebellion in the Indian Mutinies, 1857–59*, Calcutta: 1957.
4. R. Mukherjee, *Awadh in Revolt, 1857–58: A Study of Popular resistance*, Delhi: 1984, p. 65.
5. Henry Lawrence to Canning, 3 May 1857, Foreign Dept, Secret Consultations, 18 December 1857, no. 565, National Archives of India, New Delhi (NAI).
6. J. W. Kaye, *History of the Sepoy War*, 1857–58, London: 1880; reprint, New Delhi: 1988, vol. 2, p. 244.
7. S. A. Rizvi and M. L. Bhargava (eds), *Freedom Struggle in Uttar Pradesh*, Lucknow: 1957, vol. 2, p. 14.
8. E. O. Bradford to Edmonstone, 2 July 1857, Foreign Dept Secret Consultations, 25 September 1857, no. 398, NAI.
9. Barrow's narrative in G. Hutchinson, *Narrative of the Mutinies in Oude*, London: 1859, pp. 127ff.
10. W. Edwards, *Personal Adventures during the Indian Rebellion in Rohilcund, Futtehghur and* Oude, 1858; reprint, Allahabad: 1974, p. 65.
11. R. H. W. Dunlop, *Service and Adventure with the Khakee Ressalah or Meerut Volunteer Force, during the Mutinies of 1857–58*, 1858; reprint, Allahabad: 1974, pp. 153–4.

12. *Narratives of Events Attending the Outbreak of Disturbances and the Restoration of Authority,* Calcutta: 1858, Meerut, p. 250, para. 152.
13. Mukherjee, *Awadh in Revolt,* pp. 36–7.
14. Ibid., p. 68 and note 19.
15. The massacre at Satichaura Ghat is analysed and reconstructed in R. Mukherjee, '"Satan let Loose upon Earth": The Massacres in Kanpur in the Revolt of 1857,' *Past and Present,* no. 128, August 1990.
16. Mukherjee, *Awadh in Revolt,* p. 70.
17. Hearsay's narrative in Hutchinson, *Narrative,* p. 97.
18. C. Ball, *The History of the Indian Mutiny,* London: n.d., pp. 299–300.
19. The evidence for this paragraph is taken from C. Hibbert, *The Great Mutiny: India 1857,* Harmondsworth: 1978, pp. 65, 69, 70, 72. In recronstructing the episode, Hibbert draws on G. W. Forrest, *Selections from letters, despatches and state papers in the Military Department of the Govt. of India 1857–58,* Calcutta: 1893–1912.
20. See Antonio Gramsci, *Selections from the Prison Notebooks,* edited and translated by Quintin Hoare and Geoffrey Nowell Smith, New York: 1971, pp. 196–200.
21. *Narrative of Events,* Meerut, p. 253, para 192.
22. Kaye, *Sepoy War,* vol. 2, p. 46.
23. W. H. Carey, *The Mohammedan Rebellion,* Roorkee: 1857, p. 9, quoted in R. Guha, *Elementary Aspects of Peasant Insurgency in Colonial India,* Delhi: 1983, p. 141.
24. *Narrative of* Events, Aligarh, p. 217, paras 36, 37.
25. R. Guha, *Elementary,* p. 141.
26. Quoted in Kaye, *Sepoy War,* vol. 2, p. 258.
27. S. N. Sen, *1857,* Delhi, p. 29.
28. Dunlop, *Service and Adventure during the Mutinies of 1857–58,* p. 36.
29. *Narrative of Events,* Meerut, p. 251, para 169; p. 252, para 171.
30. Ibid., p. 252, para 172.
31. G. Rude, *Paris and London in the 18th Century;* reprint, London: 1974, p. 26.
32. R. Cobb, *The Police and the People: French Popular Protest 1789–1820,* Oxford: 1972, pp. 88–9.
33. For rumours, see Mukherjee, *Awadh in Revolt,* pp. 72–6; for a general discussion on rumours in peasant insurgency see Guha, *Elementary Aspects,* pp. 251–77.
34. M. Gubbins, *An Account of the Mutinees in Oude and the Seige of the Luknow Residency,* London: 1858, p. 86.
35. *Narrative of Events,* Meerut, p. 251, para 170.
36. Ball, *History of the Indian Mutiny,* vol. 2, p. 242.
37. Foreign Department Secret Consultations, 26 June 1857, nos 52–4, Gubbins to Couper, 27 May 1857, Foreign Dept, NAI.
38. K. Marx, *A Contribution to the Critique of Hegel's Philosophy of Right,*

Introduction, in Karl Marx, *Early Writings*, L. Colletti (ed.), Harmondsworth: 1975, p. 244.

39. Mukherjee, *Awadh in Revolt*, p. 57.
40. Kaye, *Sepoy War*, vol. 3, p. 456.
41. Guha, *Elementary Aspects.*
42. Mukherjee, *Awadh in Revolt*, pp. 76–9.
43. Gubbins, *Mutinies*, p. 118.
44. *Narrative of Events*, Meerut, p. 251, para 165.
45. Nanak Chand's diary of events in Kanpur, printed as 'Translation of a Narrative of Events of Cawnpore', in *Narrative of Events in the NWP in 1857–58*, Calcutta: n.d..
46. *Narrative of Events*, Meerut, p. 253, para 184.
47. 'Synopsis of the Evidence of the Cawnpore Mutiny', in *Narrative of Events*, Kanpur; see also G. W. Forrest, *Selections from Letters*, vol. 2, pp. 156–8.

4 Seditious Letters and Steel Helmets*

Disaffection among Indian Troops in Singapore and Hong Kong, 1940–1, and the Formation of the Indian National Army

Chandar S. Sundaram

The Indian National Army (henceforth INA) was created during World War II to liberate India from British imperial rule. Its creation was a collaborative effort, which involved the nationalist elements of the nearly two million-strong Indian expatriate community in South-East Asia,[1] the imperial Japanese Army and Japanese government, and, most crucially, the approximately 45,000 Indian troops of the Indian Army captured by the Japanese during their lightning conquest of Malaya and Singapore in 1941–2.[2]

The Japanese saw the INA as an opportunity to appeal to the nationalistic feelings of Indians as a whole—not for any altruistic motive, but rather to destabilize, and possibly destroy, India's ideological and military allegiance to Tokyo's adversary, Britain. Although they had developed an appealing rhetoric based on the slogan 'Asia for Asians', as well as the concept of the 'Greater East Asia Co-Prosperity Sphere', the Japanese did not include India in the latter. Otherwise, they would have pushed on into India in mid-1942—when the British defence of India was in an extremely parlous state—instead of waiting until early 1944 to mount their offensives

* I thank DeWitt C. Ellinwood and Roger N. Buckley for their continuing friendship and encouragement. Kaushik Roy made some good suggestions on an earlier draft of this piece, which I have incorporated.

into north-east India. This makes credible the argument that their 1944 offensives, far from being the all-out 'March on Delhi' that the INA leadership believed them to be, had a rather more limited aim of securing the western perimeter of Japan's South-East Asian empire by neutralizing the Allied offensive build-up on the Indo-Burmese frontier.[3]

At it height, the INA numbered some 32,000 men, and 16,000 of them served in a losing cause in the Arakan, Imphal–Kohima, and Irrawaddy sectors of the Burma Front in 1944–5. Though it had 'allied army' status with the Imperial Japanese Army (hereafter IJA), the latter was contemptuous of the INA. This contempt manifested itself in the IJA's consistent minimization of the INA's combat deployment. Thus, the paltry INA units that were grudgingly permitted at the front did not have operational autonomy, and were largely deployed in outpost and line-of-communication roles, in piecemeal fashion.[4] Moreover, because of the INA's unimpressive combat record and the general distaste in academic circles for military history—even in its newer 'war and society' avatar[5]—most scholarly writing on the INA has highlighted its more successful political aspects.

Four monographs merit attention in this regard. Hugh Toye's *The Springing Tiger* depicts the INA as an extension of the life of Subhas Chandra Bose, its most famous and controversial leader. Kalyan Kumar Ghosh's *The Indian National Army* treats it as the 'second front' of the Indian struggle for independence from British rule, by focusing on the considerable political impact within India of the INA trials of 1945–6. Yet there never was that close connection or coordination between the 'mainstream' Indian independence struggle within India and the INA that the phrase 'second front' implies. Joyce Lebra looks at the INA more as a diplomatic 'jungle alliance' between the Japanese *Gaimusho* (foreign ministry) and expatriate Indians in South-East Asia.[6] Even the most recent monograph on the INA, Peter W. Fay's *The Forgotten Army*, which purports to depict it as 'India's Armed Struggle for Independence', devotes less than one-fifth of its 572 pages to the INA's combat experience. Then too, Fay dismisses the best archival source on the INA's military dimension, the Weekly Intelligence Summaries of the Allies' India Command, with a glib comment. Fay comments that relying on this source is rather like using the reports of the Pinkerton agency, which was employed by the American government to gather intelligence on the Confederacy during the American Civil War, to write a history of the Confederate Army of northern Virginia.[7] While this is indeed true,

Fay does not address the fact that sources on the INA's military dimensions from its own point of view are extremely patchy and scarce—due, no doubt, to the wholesale destruction of Axis records in the general confusion accompanying the end of the war in Asia in 1945. Researchers of the INA's military facets are therefore necessarily forced to use what James Belich has called 'one-sided evidence'—that is, evidence produced by the colonial state or the victors—to uncover the experience of the colonized, the losers.[8]

A similar bias holds sway in historical analyses of the INA's origins. While the roles of the Indian diaspora in South-East Asia and the Japanese in this have garnered much attention, what little we have on the role of the Indian *jawans* (soldiers) is mostly confined to memoir material.[9] Analyses of why Indian troops initially joined the INA in large numbers have generally looked at the state of the jawans in the aftermath of the Malayan campaign. These stress their basic desire for self-preservation[10] and their feelings of shock, abandonment, and disgust at the all-too-apparent failure of their British commanders to deliver the victory over the Japanese that they had earlier predicted with a racist arrogance. One of the most tragi-comic instances of the British underestimation of Japanese military capability comes to us from Air Chief Marshal Robert Brooke-Popham, the commander-in-chief of the British and Commonwealth forces in the Far East when the Japanese struck. Writing to a colleague in November 1941, he related that, while on a tour of Hong Kong a month earlier, he had had a '... good, close-up look ... [at] ... various sub-human specimens ... in dirty grey uniforms, which ... [he] ... was informed were Japanese soldiers'. Brooke-Popham noted smugly that: 'If these represent the average of the Japanese Army ... [he could] ... not believe that they would form an intelligent fighting force.'[11] And later, after the campaign, an Indian officer reported that he and his confrérès—both Indian and British—felt very frustrated at the British conduct of the defence of Malaya, which, to them, seemed to consist of one word: Retreat![12]

This study focuses on the state of the jawans in Singapore and Hong Kong in the months before the Japanese struck. Two main arguments will be advanced. First, that the Indian officers' and jawans' experience, attitudes, and individual and collective agency[13] during the period contributed to the emergence of the INA; and second, that the impetus for their actions arose in no small part from the poor leadership of their British superiors. Historians have consistently ignored this aspect of the INA's origins.[14]

The Seditious Letter and the 4/19th Hyderabad Regiment

The first case of disaffection we will examine concerns the 4/19th Hyderabad Regiment,[15] a line unit of the Indian Army that had been posted to Singapore in August 1939. It was part of the 12th Indian Brigade Group despatched from India at that time to defend imperial interests in the Far East. Though this particular deployment aroused the ire of the Indian nationalist, the use of Indian troops outside India was not new. Indeed, it began in 1762, when a force of Madras sepoys participated in the English capture of Manila during the Seven Years' War (1756–63). The practice really burgeoned from the 1860s onwards, when the Indian Army was used, in Lord Salisbury's famous phrase, as '... an English barrack upon Oriental seas from which ... any number of troops [could be drawn, paid for entirely by India, not by Britain].'[16] The Indian Army units, therefore, constituted an 'imperial fire brigade' used to further metropolitan 'defence' interests in places as far afield as China, Abyssinia, East Africa, Egypt, and even Malta. Yet the most significant use of Indian troops overseas came during World War I, when India recruited 1.4 million men—a larger contribution than was made by all the White dominions put together—and Indians saw action in France, Mesopotamia, Palestine, and East Africa. In the interwar period, Indian units fought in the Afghan War III, and, as war clouds gathered once again in 1938–9, were sent to various locations in the Middle East and South-East Asia. Moreover, from the 1920s onwards, there was a general feeling in London that India should contribute to imperial defence in a more systematic way than in the previous century, though very little was actually done about it until the outbreak of war in 1939.[17]

In April 1940, a letter written by an Indian Commissioned Officer (henceforth ICO) of the 4/19th Hyderabad Regiment came to the attention of British military censors in Singapore. The intercepted letter was addressed to an Englishwoman living in Patna. In it the ICO, Lieutenant Mohammed Zahir-ud-Din, expressed the hope that '... the [present] war might last for ten years, so that the British Empire ... [will] ... be so exhausted that [we] ... Indians ... [will] ... be able to turn the British out of [the] country.'[18] This was a clear example of sedition, which the *Manual of Military Law* defined as 'doing any act or publishing any words tending to bring into hatred or contempt, or to excite disaffection against, the Sovereign, or the government and constitution of the United Kingdom.'[19] This was not the first anti-British letter the lieutenant had penned. Indeed, British military intelligence had been keeping an eye on Zahir-ud-Din's correspondence with another woman living in Lahore, which contained numerous anti-British sentiments. Quite a ladies' man, Zahir-ud-Din also seems to have gotten himself involved with a German woman in Singapore. According to Captain K. S. Thimayya, a King's Commissioned Indian Officer (henceforth KCIO) of 4/19th Hyderabad who later rose to become chief of staff of the army of independent India, this woman had lived in India and had married an Indian. However, she subsequently left her husband, and India as well, resettling in Singapore. There she was employed by British intelligence, but they soon began to suspect that she was, in fact, a double agent working for the Axis powers. Since Zahir-ud-Din seemed to be well acquainted with her, British intelligence approached him and told him to report on the German woman's activities, contacts, and attitudes. The Indian lieutenant complied, but his reports on the woman painted her in such exemplary terms that they only served to convince British intelligence of Zahir-ud-Din's own potential for disloyalty.[20]

Even before the Zahir-ud-Din incident broke, things were not well in the unit. According to Thimayya, 4/19th Hyderabad—like all other Indian Army units—had been affected by the wholesale expansion of the Indian Army undertaken after the declaration of war. Projections called for the raising of five new divisions in 1941. New units needed officers, and in January 1940, a special form of commission, the Emergency Commissioned Officer (henceforth ECO), was introduced.[21] The officer training courses were shortened and an officer training school was opened at Belgaum, India, for the express purpose of training British ECOs. However, because pre-war planning had not envisaged such a large-scale expansion, no provision had been made for a certain proportion of officers and jawans to form the core around which the new units could be raised. Such a situation led to a process known as 'milking', where experienced KCOs and Viceroy's Commissioned Officers (henceforth VCOs) would be detached from active pre-war battalions to form new battalions, using drafts from training depots. The result was a high turnover of officers and a marked dilution of the *esprit de corps* of units.[22] As Thimayya observed, 'new officers for the battalion had come and gone quickly. With each turnover, the quality of the officers had decreased.' In particular, he singled out the new commanding officer and the second-in-command, who were 'old *Koi-hai*[23] types, still fighting the Mutiny of 1857' and distrustful of any liberal measures.[24]

One of these measures introduced by the British to tackle the situation was military Indianization, or 'the admission of Indians into the officer grades of the Indian Army in the same ranks as British officers'.[25] Since the inception of the Indian Army, Indians had been barred from the Indian Army's King's (or Queen's) Commissioned Officer—K(Q)COs—grades, which entitled members to command both British and Indian troops. The King's or Queen's Commission was therefore reserved solely for Britons. Indians, however, were officers, but in a subordinate officer grade, initially termed 'Native Officers', but officially designated the VCO class after 1858. Though VCOs provided the crucial liaison between the British officers and the Indian rank and file, the situation obtained where the seniormost VCO, even if he were a subedar major with forty years' service, would be junior to the newest British subaltern, fresh off the boat from England. Though ideas of elevating 'native' officers by giving them command responsibilities and even providing them with training in military colleges in India had been prevalent in Anglo-Indian military discourse as early as 1817,[26] these notions were rather vague. In any case, the 1857 Uprising, which in the minds of British military officialdom in India was put down through superior military leadership,[27] effectively put paid to any thought of military Indianization.

The issue of military Indianization only resurfaced in the 1880s, and was thereafter extensively debated and discussed by the highest aechelons of British political and military officialdom in India.[28] These discussions were spurred on, in part, by the importance attached to the issue by the newly emergent Indian National Congress which, from its third session in 1887, made military Indianization a major and consistent demand.[29] Yet it was only the stresses and strains placed on India by World War I that caused the bar preventing Indians from becoming KCOs to be finally broken in 1917.[30] Although announced by London in conjunction with a constitutional initiative designed to set India on the path towards self-government, a look at the sluggish and grudging record of military Indianization in the interwar period indicates that its adoption was merely a wartime expedient, fuelled by Anglo-India's need to secure the support of the moderate factions of the Indian nationalist movement.[31] With the closure of the Indore Cadet School in 1919[32] after only a year of operation, the only avenue open to an Indian who desired to become a KCO was attendance at the Royal Military College, Sandhurst, where only 10 places were reserved annually for Indian cadets yearly. Moreover, competition for these 10 places was by way of a long process of selection, and not by open examination.[33] By 1926, just 243 Indians had been deemed eligible to compete for the 83 Sandhurst vacancies available since 1919. Of the 83 Indians admitted in this period, 44 had successfully graduated, 18 were still enrolled at Sandhurst, 2 had died, and 19 had flunked. Moreover, 35 of the 83 admitted were 'martial races' from the Punjab.[34]

There was considerable pressure for increased military Indianization from moderate Indian nationalist politicians. In March 1921, one of them, P. S. Sivaswamy Aiyer of Madras, introduced a series of 15 resolutions relating to Indian defence matters in the recently created Indian Central Legislative Assembly.[35] Aiyer made four proposals regarding military Indianization that set the template for subsequent nationalist pressure on the subject: that all Indians—even those of the 'non-martial' races—be allowed to earn the King's Commission, subject of course to the prescribed standards of fitness; that as a start, 25 per cent of the King's Commissions granted annually go to Indians; that a school be established in India to prepare Indians for Sandhurst; and that a military college similar to Sandhurst be established in India.[36]

Such pressure led to the introduction of the Eight-Unit Indianization scheme in 1923. Under this scheme, King's Commissioned Indian Officers (henceforth KCIOs) were not posted throughout the Indian Army, but rather were funnelled into eight of its units, one of which was the 4/19th Hyderabad.[37] In practical terms, then, Indian KCIOs were segregated into a mere 6 per cent of the Indian Army's unit strength. Even within these eight units, the introduction of KCIOs was considerably retarded when compared to the posting of KCOs in non-Indianizing units. This was because the officer establishment of the eight units was constituted on the British rather than the Indian pattern, which meant that instead of having 8 KCOs and 12 VCOs, the Indianizing units would have 22 KCIOs and no VCOs. The KCIOs would thus receive their first posting as platoon commanders instead of company commanders, as their British counterparts in non-Indianized units would have done. It would therefore take them a considerably longer time than British officers of the Indian Army to rise through the ranks. This meant that it would take between 24 and 29 years for KCIOs to attain battalion command, with the rank of lieutenant-colonel, thus delaying the prospect of British officers and troops being commanded by Indians, or of British officers having to associate with many KCIOs in the regimental mess. Besides this racial motive, there was also a political one. It is clear that Anglo-Indian military authorities felt that using the British rather than the Indian pattern for the Indianizing units would surely raise the ire of those Indian communities who, under the 'martial race' theory formed the manpower pool of the colonial Indian Army. The 'martial race' theory was one of the key elements of the Raj's ideology. Essentially, it held that in India, unlike in Europe, only certain ethnic groups—'races' in colonial parlance—had the necessary moral qualities and physical characteristics to bear arms. Although 'martial' identities existed in pre-colonial India, the adoption of the 'martial race' ideology in colonial India rigidified these identities.[38] Official Anglo-India hoped that 'martial race' representatives—fearing that Indianizing on the British pattern, if adopted on an army-wide basis, would result in the extinction of the VCO class, thus closing off to them a significant avenue of social and professional advancement—would not be too supportive of Indianization.[39]

Moderate Indian nationalists in the Indian legislature were not impressed with the Eight Units scheme. Their consistent pressure, and official Anglo-India's concern at the alarming failure rate of Indian cadets at Sandhurst,[40] led to the formation of the 'Indian Sandhurst' (Skeen) Committee to examine military Indianization and suggest improvements. The Committee's report recommended that an 'Indian Sandhurst' be opened in 1933 with 100 vacancies, and that the number of seats open to Indians at Sandhurst be increased. It also recommended that the selection process be simplified so as to encourage more applicants from urban educated 'non-martial' backgrounds, and that Indianization be extended to the technical arms units—the artillery, engineers, and air force. Implementing these measures would result in half the Indian Army's officer corps becoming Indian by 1952. Most significantly, it recommended the abandonment of the Eight Units scheme, maintaining that KCIOs should be eligible to be posted to any Indian unit of the Army.[41]

Though applauded by the Indians,[42] the Skeen Report was rejected in London by a Cabinet sub-committee chaired by Lord Balfour, on the grounds that any quickening of military Indianization 'would have a disastrous effect on British recruitment, and possibly on efficiency...'.[43] Indeed, the only concessions the sub-committee offered were firstly to increase the number of Indian vacancies at Sandhurst to 25, and secondly to offer a very circumscribed number of vacancies to Indians at the Royal Engineer's Academy, Woolwich, and at the Royal Air Force Academy, Cranwell.[44]

By this time, it was becoming clear that increased military Indianization could not be denied indefinitely. In the late 1920s and early 1930s, there was a marked improvement in the performance of the Indian cadets at Sandhurst.[45] Moreover, in London, the new Labour government now cautiously accepted the idea of an 'Indian Sandhurst'. In 1931, the Eight Unit scheme was superseded by a 25 Unit scheme in effect, Indianizing a whole division. As this would demand a greater number of KCIOs than could be supplied from Sandhurst without radically altering the racial complexion of that institution,[46] the only solution was to set up an Indian Sandhurst. In 1932, therefore, the Indian Military Academy (hereafter IMA) opened at Dehra Dun. Thereafter, Sandhurst was not an option for Indians, who when they passed out of the Indian Military Academy would be designated Indian Commissioned Officers (henceforth ICOs). The IMA course lasted 2½ years, and comprised five terms. Forty cadets were admitted in each term 15 by open competition, 15 from the Army ranks, and 10 from princely states of India. Taking wastage into account, the IMA graduated, on average, 56 ICOs yearly. Yet the pace of Indianization was still slow. In October 1939, just over 8.9 per cent of the officer corps was Indian, and a mere 11 Indian officers had attained the rank of major.[47]

New KCIOs and ICOs expecting a welcoming atmosphere in the overwhelmingly British regimental messes of their home units were at times sorely disappointed. D. K. Palit, a KCIO whose nickname was 'Monty'—possibly in reference to Bernard Law Montgomery, who served for some time in India before becoming famous as the victor at El-Alamein—had this to say about 'race relations' during military Indianization's early days:

> When I joined my regiment, the [5/10th King George V's Own] Baluch [Regiment], the Commanding Officer, and the three seniors, company commanders, were British. I never went to their homes. Nobody ever asked me for a drink or tea or anything. We [Indian officers] lived amongst ourselves. We had our own social life .... We joined the club, of course, but we only went there for games. I never once saw an Indian officer ever share a table with a British officer or his wife.[48]

The commanding officer (hereafter CO) and second in command of the 4/19th Hyderabad did not like Indianization, as is evidenced by the fact that they were particularly hard on the battalion's Indian officers, subjecting their every action to the closest scrutiny. Thimayya himself came in for criticism. Once the battalion major shouted at him for not reporting to him promptly. Thimayya would not have minded this but for the fact that he received this tongue-lashing in front of the jawans. This Thimayya found galling, because the traditions of the Indian Army, and indeed of the British Army, held that it was considered the worst possible form of humiliation for an officer to be criticized by a senior officer in front of the troops. On another occasion, when Thimayya was called to the CO's office because of a minor infraction, the colonel's criticism developed into a full-scale diatribe against 'natives' such as Thimayya, who had the temerity to think they could be officers. In yet another incident, which happened on board the troop ship to Malaya, the battalion major shouted at Thimayya and two other Indian officers for sleeping on deck with the jawans, although the British officers were doing it too. As Thimayya later explained, the major's harangue was racist. Again, the fact that the major chose to humiliate them in front of the jawans was what really irked Thimayya.[49]

The interception of Zahir-ud-Din's seditious letter, therefore, seemed to confirm the distrust the battalion's colonel and major bore towards the Indian officers. When confronted, Zahir-ud-Din readily admitted authorship, thereby confirming that the sentiment expressed in the offending passage was a true reflection of his views. He was then promptly suspended from duty, pending court martial. This began the trouble. Initially, it was minor: off-duty jawans of the Ahir company of 4/19th Hyderabad[50] began to agitate peacefully for Zahir-ud-Din's reinstatement. When this agitation did not subside, Lieutenant General Lionel Bond, the General Officer Commanding (henceforth GOC), Malaya, requested that Zahir-ud-Din be sent back to India for court martial. Bond's reason for making such a plea, which was a departure from normal army procedure, was simple. He felt it imperative that the offending ICO had to be removed from Singapore before the loyalty of Indian troops there could be eroded any further.

Nevertheless, the damage had already been done. On 8 May 1940, the day Zahir-ud-Din departed for India, the Ahir company of 4/19th Hyderabad once again began to protest. The recurrence of agitation convinced the battalion's jittery CO that a full-blown mutiny was in the offing. Without bothering to consult either the KCIOs or ICOs under him, which would have been de rigeur in such situations, he ordered the Ahir company to be disarmed and replaced on guard duty by the Gordon Highlanders. Thereafter the weapons of the whole battalion were confiscated and the jawans were confined to their barracks. Such was the degree of concern that armed detachments from British Army units were detailed to guard 4/19th Hyderabad's barracks. These actions of the battalion commander greatly insulted the pride of the Ahir jawans, who reacted by mounting a sit-down hunger strike. Men of 4/19th Hyderabad's Jat and Kumaoni companies joined them in sympathy.[51]

The situation was clearly tense: jawans under suspicion, under guard, and on hunger-strike; the battalion's KCIOs and ICOs not on speaking terms with their commanding officer; and the battalion's morale, upon which depended its fighting effectiveness, ebbing by the day. Something had to be done—quickly and decisively—to restore harmony within the unit and to nip the crisis in the bud before word of it reached other Indian units in Malaya. This action came from the GOC, Singapore Fortress, who wisely ordered the commander of the 4/19th Hyderabad to immediately take the unit's Indian officers into his confidence and to work out a strategy to restore order. Accordingly, the battalion's senior Indian officers spoke to the jawans in soothing, conciliatory terms, reminding them of the basic wrongness of Zahir-ud-Din's actions, their loyalty to the Crown, and the dishonour their actions were bringing not only upon themselves, but on their families and communities as well. Though fairly basic, this strategy worked. On day three of the crisis, as a sign of renewed trust, the battalion's Kumaoni company was allowed to mount a quarterguard, with weapons. This day passed without incident, signalling an end to the difficulty.[52]

The Zahir-ud-Din incident did not go unnoticed by the highest echelons of the Raj. In London, Lord Zetland, the Secretary of State for India, feared that the crisis 'may well prove to be a serious matter', especially since the unit in which it occurred was an Indianizing one.[53] A Conservative Party politician who had been governor of the Indian province of Bengal during the critical years from 1917 to 1922,[54] Zetland's position seemed to echo that of Field Marshal Frederick Roberts, the Commander-in-Chief of India from 1885 to 1893, who expressed the opinion that Indian higher officers would be inclined to become disloyal to the Raj, either by leading a rebellion or, at the very least, by selling military secrets to Britain's enemies in Asia.[55] What focused Zetland's vague unease was the fact that, because of the Indian Army's wholesale expansion due to wartime exigencies, the Indian government was going to scrap the system of posting Indian officers into a small number of specified units, decreeing that 'Indian Commissioned Officers will be available for posting throughout the Indian Army, where their services can best be used'.[56] Undoubtedly, surmised Zetland, their willy-nilly distribution would increase chances of just such disaffection. Indianization was not wholeheartedly welcomed, as is evidenced by the fact that *Our Indian Empire*, a 170–page manual compiled by the General Staff, India, to familiarize British service personnel with India, made no mention of Indianization.[57]

Lieutenant-General Bond, the GOC, Malaya, also thought the situation serious. This was because he believed that the Zahir-ud-Din episode was a positive proof that disaffection in the Indian Army was now assuming an overtly political character, which could not, as in previous cases, be attributed to the abrogation of customs and traditions peculiar to Indian soldiery. Bond therefore asked the Commander-in-Chief, India, that the 4/19th Hyderabad be transferred back to India and replaced by a non-Indianizing unit. Furthermore, he asked, perhaps unrealistically, that only non-Indianizing units be assigned to his command.[58]

Bond had an additional reason for making these requests. He was alive to the fact that KCIOs and ICOs posted to Malaya Command were encountering racial discrimination at the hands of the English 'planterocracy' in colonial Malaya. Members of this class enjoyed a more exalted social position in colonial society than they would have had back home in Britain, or even in India. They were therefore naturally more zealous in protecting their privileges and exclusivity against 'natives' of all types.[59] In Malaya, therefore, a fairly rigorously enforced colour bar operated in social clubs, cinemas, and the railways. Any 'native' presuming an equality of class with the planterocracy, therefore, would be firmly rebuffed. An ICO of 1/14th Punjab Regiment, who later became an INA field commander, related the following story:

> At Alor Star [in northern Malaya] ... there was a club, and when our unit arrived there to be stationed, we heard that this club was open to officers. Now, usually, I would not be interested in such a club, but it had a small swimming pool. This excited me, for I very much liked to swim. But when I went there, I was told that Indians weren't allowed in the club, even if they were officers.[60]

Incidents such as these struck a fellow ICO of 1/14th Punjab as highly hypocritical. After all, he would write later in his memoirs, 'we were supposed to defend the very people who were discriminating against us'.[61] Another ICO felt:

> Greatly agitated by British war aims ... [I] could not convince [my] ... conscience that it was correct for Indians to shed their blood for an end that was not applicable to them. Even at the most critical period of her history, when she was utilizing India to fight for her own freedom, she [Britain] refused to consider the question of India's freedom. Instead, she ordered the arrest of Indian leaders, because they were guilty of asking Freedom for India.[62]

Discrimination against ICOs also extended to the professional sphere. The ICOs received less pay than their British counterparts, and received none of the additional overseas allowances that the latter received. For example, while an Indian lieutenant serving in Malaya received a monthly pay of Rs 400, inclusive of all allowances, his British counterpart was paid the basic salary of Rs 600 per month, to which was added Rs 180 in allowances. The resulting income was almost double what an Indian lieutenant received.[63] When some ICOs complained that they too should receive these additional overseas allowances because they were serving outside their homeland, no action was taken despite the fact that a pre-war Indian Army committee on the progress of military Indianization had identified wage discrimination between British KCOs and KCIOs and ICOs, as a major problem that needed amelioration.[64] Moreover, in Malaya, newly-arrived British ECOs were frequently promoted over the heads of the ICOs there, who possessed more extensive service records. This greatly irked at least three Indian officers, who later became INA field commanders.[65]

All of this created an atmosphere of ill will in at least two units—the 4/19th Hyderabad and 1/14th Punjab—if not in others. However, despite this simmering situation, the Army Headquarters, India rejected Bond's request regarding 4/19th Hyderabad. Indeed, one gets the impression from the commander-in-chief, India's reply that he thought Bond was overreacting. In his opinion, the situation at Singapore was definitely not as serious or as widespread as to warrant the recall to India of the 4/19th Hyderabad. Bond's plea for non-Indianizing units was also rejected.[66] Though the reasons for this were not made clear to Bond, certain plausible explanations suggest themselves. Bond's request might have been rejected on the grounds that, firstly, that other theatres, such as the Middle-East, had more priority regarding 'more efficient' non-Indianized units; secondly, Indianizing units, even when tainted by cases of disaffection, would be more than a match for the Japanese; thirdly, any move to replace

Indianizing units with non-Indianized ones would play very badly in India, upon whose continued and ever-increasing cooperation in the war effort Britain relied; and finally, more 'reliable' non-Indianized units would be needed to aid the civil power in the event of a general popular rebellion in India.[67]

The only recommendation the commander-in-chief was willing to make was the rather moderate one of instituting a board of enquiry to investigate the causes of the insubordination of the Ahir and Jat companies of the 4/19th Hyderabad. By early June, the board had completed its investigation of the matter. Responsibility for the incident was laid squarely at the feet of Lieutenant Zahir-ud-Din, who—the board averred—was 'politically educat[ing] ... the Ahirs'.[68] This was a clear violation of military law, which explicitly prohibited any person from endeavouring to seduce any person in His Majesty's regular, reserve, or auxiliary forces, or navy, from allegiance to His Majesty, or to persuade any person in His Majesty's forces to join in any mutiny or sedition.[69] Yet the board's finding seems a bit one-sided. Political education would have necessarily had to have been undertaken clandestinely. The required secrecy would have been very difficult to maintain in the regimental setting of the Indian Army, which thrived on rumour. In short, it is highly unlikely that the 4/19th Hyderabad's CO would not have known about Zahir-ud-Din's disloyal activities well before the interception of his seditious letter. Perhaps he did know, but being new to the unit was dismissive, given his already noted poor opinion of Indian officers.

The board's finding that the mutineers were encouraged by junior Indian officers seemed to point to a wider malaise. As a Sandhurst-trained Indian officer of the unit later commented:

> [t]he sympathy of the Indian officers was with the mutineers. Our anti-British feelings were intense. The war in Europe ... was going badly for the Allies, and most of us greeted the news of a British defeat with delight. The subaltern hotheads and the VCOs supported the mutiny of the Jats and the Ahirs, and were all for joining it. Fortunately, we older officers were able to keep them in line.[70]

However, the board did not pursue this line of investigation. Had it done so, the board's members might have uncovered the fact that relations between the 4/19th Hyderabad's CO and his Indian officers was at a low ebb. However, this would have required a deeper probing of the case, which the board seemed disinclined to undertake, perhaps because firstly it would have put British officers under scrutiny; and secondly it would have brought into question their focus on Zahir-ud-Din as the disaffection's sole instigator. Weight is lent to this analysis of the board's motives by its own admission that, because the battalion's ICOs and VCOs had closed ranks, expressing a reluctance to testify, no Indians apart from Zahir-ud-Din could be formally charged with sedition.[71]

From the point of view of this author, however, the significance of the Zahir-ud-Din incident lies in what occurred later. The board's only substantive recommendation—to immediately transfer the 4/19th Hyderabad out of Singapore—indicates that Bond was not the only senior British officer in Malaysia concerned about the reliability of the Indian units. However, the recommendation was not acted upon. When the Japanese attacked Malaysia on 8 December 1941, the unit was still there. Although in the ensuing campaign it generally fought creditably in a losing cause, it remains that the Zahir-ud-Din incident and the disastrous conduct of the campaign made the 4/19th Hyderabad more than a little susceptible to the blandishments of Mohan Singh and Fujiwara, the organizers of the INA, at Farrer Park. The battalion was among the ones that subsequently volunteered, almost to a man, to join the INA,[72] and one of its senior Indian officers—Major Niranjan Singh Gill—became the right-hand man of Mohan Singh when the latter became the Commander-in-Chief of the INA.[73]

Steel Helmets, and the Hong Kong and Singapore Royal Artillery

We now turn to the second case of disaffection, which involved Indian troops in Hong Kong and happened in December 1940–January 1941. It differed from the Singapore incident on three counts: firstly, it centred not on ICOs but on Indian 'other ranks' (IORs); secondly, it was more widespread than the Zahir-ud-Din affair; finally, it provided the crucial connection between the Japanese Army intelligence and a group of Sikh political extremists that eventually led to the formation of the INA. The disaffection at Hong Kong involved the 20th Heavy Battery of the 12th Heavy Regiment of the Hong Kong and Singapore Royal Artillery (hereafter HKSRA). The HKSRA was a regular unit raised to provide mobile, coastal, and anti-aircraft defences in Singapore and Hong Kong. Commanded by British officers and some VCOs, its rank and file consisted of jawans recruited in India under a special agreement with the Army Headquarters, India.[74]

The Hong Kong disaffection was initiated by Sikhs, the most famous of the 'martial races'. Perhaps because defeating them in the Anglo-Sikh wars of the late 1840s had been a near thing, British military authorities began recruiting Sikhs into the Indian Army beginning in the late 1840s itself.[75] From the start, the Sikhs' martial bearing and their loyalty to the 'Sarkar' impressed British officers. Moreover, the fact that Ranjit Singh's Khalsa army had trained Sikhs in current European tactical doctrine made them more attractive to British recruiters.[76] During the 1857 Uprising, Sikh warriors flocked to the British standard. Without their military support, it is safe to say that the British might well have been defeated by the rebellious sepoys, and the civil populations of Awadh and Rohilkhand. In the ensuing years, the British military authorities carefully tried to channel the Sikhs' martial identity and exclusivity. Recruiting was restricted to *keshdhari* (unshorn) Sikh men who had been baptized into the Khalsa. One British military official commented, not without some pride, that 'it is the British officer who has kept Sikhism up to its old standard'.[77]

However, in the early years of the twentieth century, Sikhs—whom the British regarded as the best educated of the martial races[78]—had begun to develop political consciousness. This initially centred on control of their gurdwaras, but soon expanded into involvement with the moderate Indian freedom movement championed by the Indian National Congress, as well as with more extremist Indian nationalist organizations that did not baulk at using violence. Indeed, British authorities in the Punjab noticed this propensity as early as 1907.[79] The Sikhs were also involved in creating the Ghadar, a revolutionary party created in 1913 by expatriate Indians on the Pacific coasts of Canada and the United States. The Sikh revolutionary activity continued even in the interwar period. It culminated in the bombing of the Central Legislative Assembly in New Delhi on 8 April 1929 by Bhagat Singh. A Sikh ICO who later joined the INA related to the author, 'Bhagat Singh's dramatic exploit ... and also his martyrdom by hanging inspired Sikh youths like me and my friends.'[80] The Sikh revolutionaries also directed their propaganda at their co-religionists in the Indian Army. A pamphlet which circulated among the Jat Sikhs at this time declared that the brave soldiers of the Khalsa had lost all sense of national honour, and advised that they must give up the British service and permit the '*feranghis*' [foreigners] no more to disgrace them, that they should be brave enough to expel the British.[81] It is little wonder, then, that an intelligence report commissioned by the Indian Army in early 1940 affirmed that some expatriate Sikhs were 'desperate revolutionaries ... involved in terrorist campaigns and covert sedition against British rule in India'.[82] It was therefore inevitable that some of this extremist propaganda would reach the ears of Sikh jawans posted in the Far East.[83]

The HKSRA disaffection arose over the question of headgear. In September 1939, with the declaration of war, the Mark 1 Steel Helmet was made standard equipment for the Indian Army. It was almost identical to the overturned shallow-soup-bowl-looking M.1916 model worn by the British and Commonwealth forces in World War I.[84] The Army Headquarters, India, and indeed all commands where Indian units were deployed, urged all Indian troops to 'realize the importance of this type of protection, and avail themselves of it in battle'.[85]

For Sikhs in the Indian Army, the implication of this order was obvious: in order to wear the steel helmets, they would have to cut their hair, thus violating their religious vows as baptized members of the Khalsa—vows that, as we have seen, British military authorities did much to foster. Indeed, some of the Sikhs of the HKSRA might have remembered a common slogan of their home region, which direly importuned them to 'guard their turban'.[86] It is hardly surprising, therefore, that they heartily jeered the Sikh Company of the 2/14th Punjab Regiment for carrying steel helmets as they disembarked at Hong Kong in October 1940. Around that time too, Sikh soldiers in Hong Kong began to exhibit a reluctance to move crates of army stores, for fear that they contained steel helmets.[87] Repeated incidences of such reluctance forced the GOC, Hong Kong—General Grasett—to issue an order to the effect that 'steel helmets ... be carried by all ranks to whom they are issued, whether British, Indian, or Chinese'.[88]

Standard procedure for general orders was that they be read out to all assembled ranks in a particular command, and this was duly carried out in Grasett's command on 19 December. Assembled troops were then required to sign a register to signify that they had been present and had heard the order read. Any hopes that the order would be well received were dashed when a Sikh havildar-major of the 20th Heavy Battery of the 12th Heavy Regiment of the HKSRA refused to sign the register. After making repeated entreaties, the unit's commanding officer had no option but to dismiss the troops. Later that same day, he called a meeting of all his VCOs and Indian NCOs. At this meeting, he explained to them that signing the register did not signify agreement with a certain order, but was merely to show that a soldier had been present when an order was communicated. The next morning, 20 December, the 20th Heavy Battery was once more called out on parade and the Sikh jawans were again called upon to sign the register. This time, the havildar-major who had initially refused to sign relented, affixing his name to the register. However, now the unit's senior havildar refused. After refusing to heed repeated orders to sign the register, the senior havildar was relieved of his duties, placed under arrest, and escorted to the guardroom, where he was to be detained under guard. Upon witnessing this, the remaining 85 Sikhs of the 20th Heavy Battery mounted a collective insubordination by marching in good order to the guardroom where their senior havildar was detained. Here they stayed, in show of support for the senior havildar.[89]

The commander of the 20th Heavy Battery, clearly concerned by the worsening situation, asked the commanding officer of the 2/14th Punjab to address the recalcitrant Sikhs. On the morning of 22 December, this was done. In his lecture, he alerted the Sikhs to the full implications of their insubordination. He focused especially on the damage their action was doing to their *izzat*. Soldiering was always a coveted profession in India, one that carried with it izzat—an Urdu word denoting honour, reputation, glory, and prestige. Izzat manifested itself in an informal code of conduct, which stressed steadfastness, bravery, and loyalty. Any abrogation of this creed—as this insubordination undoubtedly was—would only bring shame, not only upon the violator, but on his community as well.[90] When the address was over, the 85 Sikhs were given one more opportunity to sign the register. Only two came forward. The remaining 83 were then escorted to the guardroom, where they were placed under close arrest. Then they launched a hunger strike.[91]

The arrest and confinement of the 83 Sikhs was supposed to put an end to the crisis. However, its effect was just the opposite. On 22 December, Sikh jawans of the Hong Kong Rifles refused to handle crates containing steel helmets. That evening, the Sikhs of two batteries of the 5th Anti-aircraft Regiment, HKSRA, refused food. On 24 December, these same jawans refused to parade; although upon second thought they did in fact go to the parade ground. Over the next 24 hours, numerous acts of Sikh insubordination occurred in all HKSRA units stationed in Hong Kong. Although these protests were peaceful, by 28 December Grasett expressed fears that as many as 800 Sikhs in his command might actually mount a violent mutiny.[92]

These fears proved unfounded, and the crisis eventually lost momentum. It is unclear exactly what happened. However, two possibilities present themselves. First is the possibility that the Sikhs began to become convinced by the repeated entreaties and dire warnings of their British officers, to which they would have surely been subjected. Secondly, a compromise might have been reached, whereby the Sikhs could keep their *kesh* (hair), thus preserving their dual identity as martial jawans and devout Singhs. Such an outcome seems the most likely, especially when one considers that a similar incident involving Sikh troops in France during World War I had been defused in a similar way.[93] Perhaps, too, the military authorities realized that the costs of alienating the martial Sikhs were too great for the Indian Army to bear, especially in the midst of a war.

Subsequent investigation into the HKSRA disaffection pinpointed factors external to the army as causing it. Responsibility was pinned on certain Sikh priests who, it had been discovered, had been filling the heads of Sikh soldiery with seditious propaganda along the lines of Ajit Singh's pamphlet. Also, sources of this propaganda—which played on the themes of Indian nationalism and Sikh identity—were found to be more widespread than initially thought. The inquiry found that seeds of incitement were present in the Hong Kong police force, in which a number of Sikh constables served, and among the colony's expatriate Indian community. Moreover, it was maintained that known Indian nationalist extremists were actively disseminating anti-British propaganda among Indian troops, and that they were aided and abetted in their activities by German and Japanese spies who were known to be operating in the area. Further inquiries revealed that certain VCOs were quite uneasy about the adoption of the steel helmets, and that they had deliberately concealed the complaints of the Sikh troops from their British superior officers.[94]

Yet what is really noteworthy about this investigation is what it did not emphasize. First, it did not admit the basic insensitivity to Sikh sensibilities displayed by the introduction of steel helmets. British military authorities had seemingly forgotten that Indian troops had always been 'edged tools'[95] to be handled with care. It had also seemingly slipped their minds that one of the main causes of the 'Sepoy Mutiny' a century before had been the rumour that cartridges for the new Enfield rifles were coated with animal fat offensive to both Hindu and Muslim sepoys (see Chapter 2).[96] Second, by placing most of the blame for the crisis on shadowy cloak-and-dagger spies and revolutionaries, the investigation seemed to deny the fact that the jawan was a mature, thinking individual, capable of acting as an idependent agent. This denial of agency is consistent with the prevalent ideology—some would say 'mythology'—of the colonial Indian Army, in which the home of the slow-witted, but fiercely steadfast and brave sepoy was the regiment, whose British officers were both his 'mother' and his 'father' (mai-bap). Thus, the regimental 'family' tradition would preclude any disaffection or revolt on the part of the sepoys. This is why news of the INA hit some British officers—especially those with long familial associations with the Raj and its army—especially hard.[97]

The court martial of the 83 Sikh artillerymen began on 17 January 1941, and lasted a month. Sentences varied, from seven years' penal servitude for havildars to one year's hard labour for the gunners. All sentences included reduction to the rank of private soldier, where applicable. However, only 11 of the 83 sentences were carried out; the rest were suspended.[98] The question remains, why was the treatment lenient. Four explanations are plausible. First, at no point did the disaffection turn violent, and involve loss of life. Indeed, the acts of defiance the Sikh soldiers undertook resembled those of Gandhian *satyagrahis*.[99] A rash and severe response on the part of the Army to peaceful protests would have only further alienated the Sikhs, who might then very well have escalated their disaffection into all-out violent mutiny. Jallianwallah Bagh had made its mark. Second, the leniency might have been a tacit and somewhat shame-faced admission that the imposition of steel helmets on otherwise loyal Sikh troops was essentially wrong-headed. The third possibility was that it was a corollary of the mai-bap ideology. The 'child-like' sepoys could be easily led astray by the devious and conspiratorial machinations of Indian 'ring-leaders'. Once these malcontents had been identified and dealt with, and the sepoys given a good dressing down, it was argued that they would see the error of their ways and return to the regimental fold.[100] Finally, the leniency might have been the result of sheer manpower needs. At that time in the war, when British manpower resources were stretched to the limit, and with the Hong Kong garrison's needs woefully low on the British list of priorities, Grasett might have decided that his garrison could ill afford the loss of 83 experienced artillerymen.

Yet the major impact of the HKSRA incident lies in the chain of events that it set in motion. In December 1940, while the steel helmet trouble was gaining momentum, three Sikhs escaped from British custody in Hong Kong and made their way to Canton, then under

Japanese occupation. These Sikhs were not soldiers but civilians, and they had been arrested by the Hong Kong police for disseminating seditious propaganda among Sikh jawans. Upon reaching Canton, the three lost no time in presenting themselves at the Japanese 21st Army's headquarters there. They asked the Japanese authorities to assist them in travelling to Bangkok, the capital of Siam. When asked why Bangkok, they responded that they intended to join forces there with a Sikh revolutionary cell that called itself the Independent League of India, whose stated purpose was to overthrow the Raj by any and all possible means, including violence. This piqued Japanese interest. By this time Tokyo was planning to incorporate all of South-East Asia, with its considerable mineral and agricultural resources, into the Japanese empire. The Japanese military and political planners thought that this would necessarily involve war against the Western powers—Britain, America, and Holland—who controlled the regions that they wanted.[101] To make their takeover easier, Tokyo thought that establishing contact with dissident anti-colonial movements in South-East Asia would be advantageous. The Independent League of India fits the bill perfectly. The man who arranged passage for the three Sikhs to Bangkok was Major Fujiwara Iwaichi, an officer with the Japanese Army intelligence. In September 1941, Fujiwara himself proceeded to Bangkok, where he and his team, F. Kikan, established closer ties with the Independent League. Thus, as a result of the HKSRA incident, a link was forged between the Japanese Army and Sikh dissidents in Bangkok. It was a link that would ultimately lead to the creation of the INA.[102]

Conclusion

The two instances of disaffection described in this article provide evidence that all was not well with the Indian officers and troops stationed in the Far East before the outbreak of the Pacific war. Legally speaking, both the Zahir-ud-Din and HKSRA cases were mutinies, which are defined as implying 'collective insubordination, or a combination of two or more persons to resist or to induce others to resist lawful military authority'.[103] Yet they present differing facets of insubordination.

In writing his seditious letter, Zahir-ud-Din was perhaps exhibiting progressive tendencies in Indian society. I use the word 'perhaps' here because of the impossibility of knowing exactly why Zahir-ud-Din penned those seditious words. As a commissioned officer in His

Majesty's Indian Forces, he would have surely been instructed in military law at the Royal Indian Military Academy. Because a good part of military law and The Army Act are concerned with infractions arising out of mutiny or sedition, it is inconceivable that Zahir-ud-Din would not have known the full implications of his action. The argument that since the anti-British sentiments were contained in a private letter, they were admissible under 'freedom of speech' does not hold water: for one thing, it was wartime, and the Defence of India Rules, suspending civil rights and freedom for the duration of the conflict, had already been enacted. In any case, the modern notion of freedom of expression did not apply in colonial India even in peacetime, especially in the early part of the twentieth century, when the Indian nationalist movement was in full swing.

The plausible explanations for Zahir-ud-Din's sedition are these: that he was stupid, arrogantly believing that British military censors would not intercept his seditious remarks; that, being young and impetuous, he was greatly agitated by the discrimination against Indians in Malaysia and, perhaps more importantly, by the poisoned atmosphere within his own unit; that he was, in some measure, an Indian nationalist, attempting to introduce 'modern' ideas to the jawans, in much the same manner as the Army Educational Corps did for the Tommy. No doubt this last reason was why his men held him in such high regard as to agitate for his release.

Yet responsibility also lay with the British, both structurally and situationally. Structurally, there was the slow and grudging pace of Indianization even after it had been adopted as official policy by the Indian government in 1917. A British general who would eventually become the last commander-in-chief of the pre-independence Indian Army remarked in 1940, '[t]he Indian has always thought ... that we never intended ... [Indianization] ... to succeed, and expected it to fail.' According to him, this view had something to it, because of 'the way in which each new step [or advance in Indianization policy] ... had to be wrested from us, instead of being freely given'.[104]

The officer in command of the 4/19th Hyderabad and his second-in-command, who were both British, made no secret of their dislike of Indianization to the ICOs serving under them. They were out of touch with the realities of the day and had lost the ability of man management, which is crucial to the success of a professional officer. Tongue-lashing of the ICOs in front of jawans was detrimental to unit morale and exhibited a lack of professionalism. The decision to disarm and confine the Ahirs to their barracks without first consulting the ICOs was also a clear error, and would have been seen by any officer—Indian or otherwise—as an unmistakeable snub. The Army Headquarters, India, must also accept some responsibility for not complying with General Bond's request that the tainted unit be transferred back to India. However, Bond was himself a little naïve in asking for only non-Indianizing units, given the fact that Britain's military manpower resources were, at that particular juncture, stretched to the limit.

Responsibility for the HKSRA disaffection lies more squarely with the British. While it is true that the Sikhs were the ones that rose up, one must remember that the order they were protesting against was one that would have required them to lose a part of their traditional religious identity. Moreover, this identity fit neatly with their image as a 'martial race', which, to a certain extent, was a tradition invented by the British military establishment in India.[105] Indeed, though it is not known exactly where the steel helmet order originated, this author would not be surprised if it sprang from some War Office staff officer with no prior knowledge of the Indian Army, or its history. That the most severe crisis in British rule—the 'Mutiny' of 1857—had been sparked by rumours of a similar assault on the sensibilities of Indian soldiers is too obvious a point to need making.

The general officers in command of garrisons have certain discretionary powers. It is unknown whether General Grasett had had any prior experience commanding Indian soldiery; if indeed he had, he would have surely realized the threat posed by steel helmets to Sikhs, and used his discretionary powers to ameliorate the situation instead of overreacting with fears of a violent mutiny. Officially, Grasset was routinely replaced when his tour ended in December 1941, but perhaps his failure to gauge the HKSRA situation correctly was not unrelated to his departure from the Far East.[106]

Yet there was also ferment amongst the Sikhs themselves. Sikh organizations such as the Shiromani Gurdwara Prabandhak Committee (SGPC) and the Akali Dal were politicizing the Sikh world view. Moreover, among the Sikh diaspora in North America and South-East Asia, ideologies more revolutionary and extremist than either the SGPC or the Akali Dal had emerged. The British military intelligence was aware of the existence of Sikh revolutionary cells. The British civil authorities in Hong Kong had in fact apprehended some Sikhs and charged them with spreading seditious propaganda amongst Sikh troops, but no effective countermeasures seem to have been taken. Was there a disconnect between the civil and military authorities in Hong Kong, just as there was at Singapore? Alternatively, did an overweening smugness—the notion that 'what could a bunch of crazed revolutionaries do against the might of the British Empire'—rule out any effective action?

The two incidents discussed in this article did not, by themselves, lead to the formation of the INA. That occurred only with the conjunction of the political situation in India and the unmitigated disaster of British Far Eastern strategy. Yet, both these cases of disaffection indicate a change in the Indian Army's military culture. The jawan was beginning to assert his agency in more sophisticated and political ways than he had done before. Perhaps the most significant indication of this was that both the Zahir-ud-Din and HKSRA incidents were non-violent. This was quite unlike the violent mutiny of the 5th [Indian] Light Infantry, which occurred in Singapore in February 1915. This incident was precipitated by the fears of the mostly Muslim jawans of the unit that they were going to be transferred to either Egypt or Mesopotamia to fight against their Ottoman co-religionists. Thus, while it was similar in some ways to the incidents described in this article, by being violent from the outset, it displayed none of the political sophistication of either of them.[107] However, as early as the nineteenth century, a high Anglo-Indian military official had foreseen the need to treat the jawan as 'an intelligent agent',[108] yet the bulk of the Indian Army's British military leadership willfully or unknowingly failed to comprehend this until it was too late, and the INA was already a fact. This was not at all an atypical attitude among British officers in India in the early twentieth century. In fact, Philip Chetwode—the Commander-in-Chief of India, under whose aegis the Royal Indian Military Academy, Dehra Dun, was opened—expressed dismay at the number of senior and junior British officers under his command who seemed to be afflicted with what he called 'brain sickness.' He explained that this was characterized by 'narrow interests ... bounded by the morning parade, the game they happen[ed] to play, and purely local ... matters.' Brain-sick officers were 'quite unaware of the larger aspects of what ... [was] ... going on in India around them, and still less of the stupendous events ... that ... [were then] ... in the process of forming an entirely new world'.[109] The INA was part of that process—part of what Paul Scott, the 'prose-poet of the Raj in decline', termed 'the movement of India from the nineteenth to the twentieth century'.[110]

NOTES

1. The vast majority of the Indian expatriate community in Asia made Burma and Malaya their home. Smaller communities existed in Thailand, Hong Kong, the Dutch East Indies, and Japan. See US Government Office of Strategic Services: Research and Analysis Branch, *Report 1595: Indian Minorities in Southeast and East Asia*, Washington: 1944, pp. 1–2.
2. A recent treatment of the Malayan campaign is Malcolm Murfett, *et. al.*, *Between Two Oceans: A Military History of Singapore from First Settlement to Final British Withdrawal*, Singapore: 1999, Chapters 7–8. Also useful are Tsuji Masanobu, *Singapore: The Japanese Version*, Sydney: 1960; and H. P. Willmott, *Empires in the Balance: Japanese and Allied Pacific Strategies to April 1942*, Annapolis: 1982.
3. For an interesting and sympathetic first-hand Japanese insight into the INA's formation, see Lieutenant General Fujiwara Iwaichi, *F. Kikan: Japanese Intelligence Operations in Southeast Asia during World War II*, trans. Akashi Yoji, Hong Kong: 1983. On Japanese attitudes towards 'Greater East Asia', see Joyce Lebra (ed.), *Japan's Greater East Asia Co-Prosperity Sphere in World War II: Selected Readings and Documents*, Singapore: 1975. For an interesting perspective on India's place in Japanese designs, see Robert Craigie, 'India and the Co-Prosperity Sphere', 14 October 1942 [F1073/845/23], Public Record Office, Foreign Office (henceforth PRO FO) 371/38133. The best account of the Japanese offensives into north-east India in 1944 is Louis Allen's *Burma: The Longest War, 1941–1945*, London: 1984.
4. Chandar S. Sundaram, 'A Paper Tiger: The Indian National Army in Battle, 1944–1945', *War and Society*, 13(1), 1995, pp. 35–59.
5. The 'War and Society' school—or the 'New' military history—transcends the parameters of the older military history, which focused on the course of military operations, tactics, strategies, weapons, and generalship in a didactic, lessons-oriented way, by problematizing war as the military activity of societies. The last decade has witnessed the burgeoning of the 'New' military history of colonial South Asia. See Douglas Peers, *Between Mars and Mammon: Colonial Armies and the Garrison State in Early Nineteenth Century India, 1819–1835*, London: 1995; Seema Alavi, *The Sepoys and the Company: Tradition and Transition in Northern India*, Delhi: 1995; Peter Stanley, *The White Mutiny: British Military Culture in India*, New York: 1998; Chandar S. Sundaram, 'Reviving a "Dead Letter": Military Indianization and the Ideology of Anglo-India, 1885–1891'; Kaushik Roy, 'Logistics and the Construction of Loyalty: The Welfare Mechanism in the Indian Army, 1859–1913', and Vivien A. Kaul, 'Sepoys' Links with Society: A Study of the Bengal Army, 1858–95', in P. S. Gupta and A. Deshpande (eds), *The British Raj and its Indian Armed Forces, 1857–1939*, Delhi: 2002.

Relatively new general surveys of the Indian Army are David Omissi, *The Sepoy and the Raj: The Indian Army, 1860–1940*, Basingstoke: 1994, and T. A. Heathcote, *The Military in British India: The Development of British Land Forces in South Asia, 1600–1947*, Manchester: 1995.

6. See Hugh Toye, *The Springing Tiger*, Oxford: 1959; Kalyan Kumar Ghosh, *The Indian National Army: Second Front of the Indian Independence Movement*, Meerut: 1969; Joyce Lebra, *Jungle Alliance: Japan and the Indian National Army*, Singapore: 1971; Gerrard H. Corr, *War of the Springing Tigers*, London: 1975.
7. Peter Ward Fay, *The Forgotten Army: India's Armed Struggle for Independence, 1942–1945*, Ann Arbor: 1994, p. 563. The India Command Weekly Intelligence Summaries Fay mentions are available in London—L/WS/1/1433 and 1576, British Library, Oriental and India Office Collections [BL(OIOC)]. For a useful corrective to Fay, which makes extensive use of the summaries, see Sundaram, 'A Paper Tiger'.
8. James Belich, *The New Zealand Wars and the Victorian Interpretation of Racial Conflict*, Auckland: 1986, pp. 330–5.
9. For memoir material on INA veterans, see A. C. Chatterji, *India's Struggle for Freedom*, Kolkata: 1946; Shah Nawaz Khan, *My Memories of the INA and its Netaji*, Delhi: 1946; M. G. Mulker, *INA Soldier's Diary*, Calcutta: 1947; Mohan Singh, *Soldiers' Contribution to Indian Independence*, Delhi: 1974; M. Z. Kiani, *India's Freedom Struggle and the Great INA*, Delhi: 1996; G. S. Dhillon's two unpublished pieces, 'The Changi Garrison' and 'Nehru Holds the Irrawaddy'; and Fay, *Forgotten Army*; I include Fay's book here because in it the story is told almost wholly from the points of view of the INA veterans Prem and Lakshmi Saghal.
10. See Hugh Toye, 'The Indian National Army, 1941–45', *Indo-British Review*, 16(1), 1989, pp. 73–87, for a thorough treatment of this aspect. This was also the view of the colonial government in the aftermath of World War II. See Governor General (War Department) to Secretary of State for India, 11 August 1945 [telegram 10234], part 3, para 6, in N. Mansergh, E. W. R. Lumby, and P. Moon (eds), *The Transfer of Power, 1942–1947*, vol. 6, London: 1974.
11. See John W. Dower, *War Without Mercy: Race and Power in the Pacific War*, Toronto: 1986, p. 99. For a fictionalized account of Singapore on the eve of the Japanese attack, which nonetheless captures the essential 'feel' of the English community there, see J. G. Farrell, *The Singapore Grip*, London: 1978.
12. Note by an Indian Emergency Commissioned Officer, n.d., 208/819A, PRO FO.
13. The focus on the agency of peasant and subordinate groups in colonial India has been pioneered by Ranajit Guha and his colleagues in *Subaltern Studies: Writings on South Asian History and Society*,

vols 1–7, New Delhi: 1982–94. As David Omissi has ably pointed out, Guha and his group have focused almost wholly on peasant resistance to the Raj, but not on Indians that sided with it, such as those who served in the Indian Army. See David Omissi, *Sepoy and the Raj*, pp. xix, 113–52. The present essay contributes to remedy this deficiency.

14. This neglect extends to this day. For example, see Alan Warren, 'The Indian Army and the Fall of Singapore', in B. Farrell and S. Hunter (eds), *Sixty Years On: the Fall of Singapore Revisited*, Singapore: 2002, pp. 284–6. I thank Karen Ann Leong, Singapore History Consultants, for sending me a copy of this article.
15. The 19th Hyderabad Regiment originated in the Hyderabad Contingent, a force raised by the Hyderabad Nizami (state) at the insistence of the East India Company (hereafter EIC), and trained and equipped on the British pattern. The Contingent was eight battalions strong when, in 1853, it was folded into the East India Company's Madras Army. Over the next 50 years, recruitment into the Contingent reflected the general reorientation northward, and the Hindu–Muslim ratio of its rank and file was fixed at 3:2. The Kitchener reorganization of 1903 abolished the Hyderabad Contingent, but not its constituent battalions. Nineteen years later, in 1922, these battalions were once more grouped together, forming the 19th Hyderabad Regiment. For more information, see John Gaylor, *Sons of John Company: the Indian and Pakistani Armies, 1903–91*, New Delhi: 1993, pp. 194–8.
16. Great Britain, *Parliament, Debates (Commons), 1867*, Third Series, vol. 190, col. 406.
17. Though wide-ranging, the use of the Indian Army as an imperial fire brigade from 1762 has not yet been systematically studied. This brief précis has been compiled from the following: John O. Rawson, 'The Role of India in Imperial Defence beyond Indian Frontiers and Home Waters, 1919–1939', unpublished DPhil thesis, Oxford University, 1976; G. Pythian-Adams, *The Madras Regiment: 1758–1958*, Wellington: 1958, p. 24; Philip Mason, *A Matter of Honour: An Account of the Indian Army, its Officers, and Men*, London: 1974, pp. 65, 242; S. D. Pradhan, 'The Indian Army and the First World War', in Pradhan and DeWitt Ellinwood (eds), *India and World War I*, New Delhi: 1978; Keith Jeffery, *The British Army and the Crisis of Empire, 1918–1922*, Manchester: 1984, p. 1.
18. Viceroy of India to Secretary of State for India, 27 May 1940, L/WS/1/391, OIOC.
19. Great Britain, War Office, *Manual of Military Law*, 6th edition, London: 1914, p. 16.
20. Viceroy of India to Secretary of State for India, 27 May 1940, L/WS/1/303, OIOC; Humphrey Evans, *Thimayya of India: A Soldier's Life*, New York: 1960, pp. 167–8.

21. Gautam Sharma, *Nationalization of the Indian Army: 1885–1947*, New Delhi: 1996, p. 175.
22. On 'milking', see S. N. Prasad, *Expansion of the Armed Forces and Defence Organization: 1939–1945*, New Delhi: 1956, pp. 64, 82–3.
23. Literally, 'Who's There?' in Hindustani. Though defined in H. Yule and A. C. Burnel, *Hobson Jobson: A Glossary of Colloquial Anglo-Indian Words and Phrases*, 1886; reprint, Calcutta: 1990, p. 750, as 'the popular distinctive nickname of the Bengal Anglo-Indian', it was, by the 1940s a term of derision levelled at those Anglo-Indians who seemed haughty, self-centred, and imperious to fellow Britons, and especially to Indians. As the Thimayya quote demonstrates, the typical Koi-hai was also thought to live in the past.
24. Evans, *Thimayya*, p. 158.
25. This was how Indianization was defined by General Frederick Roberts, Commander in Chief of the Indian Army from 1885 to 1893. See Sundaram, 'Memorandum on a Proposal of the Government of India to Appoint Native Gentlemen to the Commissioned Ranks of the Army in the Same Grades as European Officers, 29 July, 1886', in *Correspondence of General Frederick Roberts*, Simla/Calcutta: 1890–1893, part VI(i), L/MIL/17/5/1615, OIOC.
26. John Malcolm to Thomas Munro, 30 August 1817, in Malcolm Collection, MSS, EUR F/151/120; India Office Tract 552, OIOC; Letter to the Rt. Hon. Sir John Cam Hobhouse, BART ... from Lieutenant-Colonel John Briggs, Madras Army, 1836, OIOC; Henry M. Lawrence, 'The Military Defence of Our Empire in the East', *Calcutta Review*, 2(3), 1844, pp. 154–5. These officers' ideas are analysed in detail in C. S. Sundaram, 'A Grudging Concession: the Origins of the Indianization of the Indian Army's Officer Corps, 1817–1917', unpublished PhD thesis, McGill University, 1996, pp. 64–71.
27. See for example, 'Note by Ashley Eden', 8 February 1886, para 3, in Enclosures to Secretary of State for India's Military Despatch, no. 88 of 1886, 15 April 1886, in L/MIL/3/950, OIOC.
28. See C. S. Sundaram, 'Preventing Idleness: The Maharaja of Cooch Behar's Proposal for Officer Commissions in the British Army for the Sons of Indian Princes and Gentlemen, 1897–1898', *South Asia*, New Series, 18(1), 1995; Sundaram, 'Martial Indian Aristocrats and the Military System of the Raj: The Imperial Cadet Corps, 1900–14', *Journal of Imperial and Commonwealth History*, 25(3), 1997; Sundaram, 'Reviving a Dead Letter: Military Indianization and the Ideology of Anglo-India, 1885–1891', in P. S. Gupta and A. Deshpande (eds), *The British Raj and its Indian Armed Forces: 1857–1947*, Delhi: 2002. See also Mark H. Jacobsen, 'The Modernization of the Indian Army, 1925–1939', unpublished PhD thesis, University of California, 1979, pp. 223–43; David Omissi, *Sepoy and the Raj*, chapter 5.

29. See Sundaram, 'A Grudging Concession', pp. 81–5, 126–8; Satyendra Sinha and Mazar-ul-Haque, 'Commissions for Indians in the Army', *Indian Review*, vol. 17, 1916, pp. 113–16.
30. Great Britain, *Parliament, Debates (Commons)*, 5th Series, 1917, col. 1696.
31. The evolution of the official mind's thinking on Indianization in 1914–1917 is analysed in 'A Grudging Concession', pp. 266–334.
32. The Indore Cadet School opened in 1918, and by the time it closed in 1919, 39 Indians trained there had received King's Commissions, but only in their temporary probationary form. For reports on these cadets, see L/MIL/7/19018, OIOC.
33. For the details of the selection process, refer to Government of India, *Report of the Indian Sandhurst Committee, 1926*, London: 1927, pp. 8–10.
34. *Report of the Indian Sandhurst Committee*, p. 10.
35. These resolutions were issued in response to the report of the Esher Committee. For a summary of the Esher Committee's conclusions, see Stephen P. Cohen, *The Indian Army: Its Contribution to the Development of a Nation*; reprint, Delhi: 1990, pp. 77–8. The Indian Central Legislative Assembly (CLA) was the lower house of the bicameral Indian legislature created by the 1919 reforms. The CLA was not entirely democratic. Of its 145 members, 104 were elected, the rest being Government of India appointees. Representation among the elected members was based on community and class, not population. Thus, 30 seats were reserved for Muslims, 9 for 'Europeans', 7 for landowners, and 4 for commercial communities. No seats were specially reserved for India's Hindu majority. See S. R. Mehrotra, *Towards India's Freedom and Partition*, New Delhi: 1979, pp. 159–69.
36. Government of India, *Central Legislative Assembly, Debates*, 1921, vol. 1, pp. 1449–50; P. S. Gupta, 'The Debate on Indianization, 1918–1939', in Gupta and Deshpande (eds), *British Raj and its Indian Armed Forces*, p. 229. Of these proposals, the only one rapidly acted upon was the third. The Prince of Wales Royal Indian Military College was opened in March 1922, with the aim of 'giving prospective [Indian] candidates for the [Indian] Army an education, commencing from an early age and on English public school lines, such as would fit them not only for the [Sandhurst] entrance examination but also for the subsequent ordeal of the Sandhurst course of training, and for their future association in the Army with British comrades'. See *Report of the Indian Sandhurst Committee*, pp. 7–8.
37. The other units selected for Indianization in 1923 were: 7th Light Infantry, 16th Light Cavalry, 2/1st Madras Pioneers, 5th Royal Battalion, 5th Maratha Light Infantry, 1/7th Rajput Regiment, 1/14th Punjab Regiment, 2/1st Punjab Regiment. See *The Army of India and its Evolution*, Calcutta: 1924, p. 165.

38. Despite its centrality in the world view of Anglo India, the 'martial race', has not received commensurate attention in T. R. Metcalf's *Ideologies of the Raj,* Cambridge: 1994. The classic imperialist formulation of the theory is G. F. MacMunn, *The Martial Races of India,* London: 1935. For a modern and balanced analysis, see Omissi, *Sepoy and the Raj,* pp. 1–75.
39. See Government of India, *Central Legislative Assembly, Debates,* 1923, 3(iii), pp. 2419, 2549; Omissi, *Sepoy and the Raj,* p. 178; Sundaram 'A Grudging Concession', pp. 343–45. The racist assumptions underlying the Eight Units scheme are plainly exposed by the comments of General Rawlinson, the commander-in-chief under whose imprimatur it was introduced. In his private diary, he referred to Indians as 'nothing but a lot of sheep, and a few thousand British soldiers could conquer central, southern, and eastern India today, just as they did 150 years ago under Clive'. See Rawlinson Diary, 8 February 1924, Rawlinson Collection, National Army Museum, 5201–33–24.
40. The failure rate for Indian cadets at Sandhurst in the period 1919–25 stood at 30 per cent. See *Indian Sandhurst Committee Report,* p. 10.
41. *Indian Sandhurst Committee Report,* pp. 22, 28, 34. For an excellent analysis of the *Indian Sandhurst Committee Report,* see P. S. Gupta, 'The Debate on Indianization, 1918–1939', in Gupta and Deshpande (eds), *British Raj and its Indian Armed Forces,* pp. 238–59.
42. See Sir P. S. Sivaswamy Aiyer, 'Indian Sandhurst Committee Report', in K. A. Nilakanta Sastri (ed.), *A Great Liberal: Speeches and Writings of Sir P. S. Sivaswamy Aiyer,* Bombay: 1965, pp. 391–8. This article originally appeared in the *Indian Review,* vol. 28, 1927.
43. Jacobsen, 'The Modernization of the Indian Army', p. 238. Significantly, the Cabinet sub-committee's membership included Lord Birkenhead and Winston Churchill, both of whom were vehemently opposed to any devolution of political, and particularly military, power to Indians. For Birkenhead and Churchill on India, see Carl Bridge, *Holding India to the Empire: The British Conservative Party and the 1935 Constitution,* New Delhi: 1986.
44. Omissi, *Sepoy and the Raj,* p. 181.
45. See, for example, 'Results of the Examination of Indian Cadets at the Military Academies in Britain, June 1931', L/MIL/7/19100, OIOC. The evidence in this document runs counter to Omissi's blanket contention that '... the results of sending to Sandhurst had not been encouraging'. The 14.6 per cent failure/resignation rate among Indian cadets at Sandhurst between 1919 and 1931 that Omissi cites here is half that of the figure cited in note 40, and indicates a vast improvement, thus undermining his point. See Omissi, *Sepoy and the Raj,* p. 184.
46. While British military authorities were comfortable having a few Indians at Sandhurst, this statement indicates that they would have

been considerably perturbed had the trickle developed into a flood. See Omissi, *Sepoy and the Raj*, p. 184.

47. In actual numbers, out of a total Indian Army Officer Corps of 4424, only 396 were Indian. See B. Prasad (ed.), *Official History of the Indian Armed Forces in the Second World War, 1939–1945: India and the War*, Delhi: 1966, pp. 259–60.
48. Quoted in Z. Masani, *Indian Tales of the Raj*, Berkeley: 1987, p. 25. See also Major General D. K. Palit, 'Indianization: A Personal Experience', *Indo-British Review*, 16(1), 1989, pp. 59–64.
49. Evans, *Thimayya*, pp. 167–8.
50. The Ahirs were a 'martial race'. The 4/19th Hyderabad was a mixed-class battalion, into which different 'martial races or classes' of Indians were recruited. Thus in 1940, the unit comprised an Ahir company, a Jat company, and a Kumaoni company. The somewhat imprecise nature of the 'martial races' is shown by the fact that while the Ahirs and the Jats were castes, the term 'Kumaoni' was regional, denoting the population of Kumaon, a region to the south-east of Kashmir.
51. C. S. Sundaram, 'Soldier Disaffection and the Creation of the Indian National Army', *Indo-British Review*, 18(1), 1990), pp. 155–6.
52. Evans, *Thimayya*, p. 168; Sundaram, 'Soldier Disaffection', p. 156.
53. Letter, Secretary of State for India to Viceroy, 9 May 1940, L/WS/1/391, OIOC.
54. R. J. Moore, 'British Policy and the Indian Problem: 1936–1940', in Moore, *Endgames of Empire: Studies of Britain's Indian Problem*, Delhi: 1988, p. 68.
55. Sundaram, 'A Grudging Concession', pp. 130–8; General Frederick Roberts, Memorandum on Military Education for the Natives of India, 18 May 1888, paras 18–20, L/MIL/17/5/1615, part 6(1), OIOC.
56. Government of India, press communiqué, 17 June 1940, in L/MIL/7/19112, OIOC.
57. General Staff, India, *Our Indian Empire: A Short Review and Some Hints for the Use of Soldiers Proceeding to India*, 4th edn, 1940, Lahore: 1942. See also the comments of J. S. Arora, an ICO who later led India to victory in the 1971 war, in Masani, *Indian Tales*, pp. 24–5.
58. Secret cipher telegram, General Officer Commanding, Malaya, to Commander-in-Chief, India, 9 May 1940, L/WS/1/391, OIOC.
59. See K. Ballhatchet, *Race, Sex, and Class under the Raj*, London: 1980; Robin Moore, *Paul Scott's Raj*, London: 1990. As late as 1943, a handbook designed for British soldiers going to India had a section on the 'Danger of Assaulting Indians'. See *Our Indian Empire*, pp. 76–8.
60. Interview with Gurbax Singh Dhillon, 27 July 1984.
61. Kiani, *India's Freedom Struggle*, pp. 25–8.
62. S. Section CSDIC(I): Report No. 1007 on H/1050 Mohan Singh, 1/14 Punjab, Appendix B, WO 208/833, Public Record Office (henceforth PRO).

63. Shah Nawaz Khan, *My Memories of the INA*, pp. 4–5; interview with P. K. Sahgal, 29 July 1984.
64. One of the witnesses called before this committee who urged the equalization of pay between British and Indian officers was Major K. M. Carriappa, a KCIO who had, at that time, rendered 19 years' service, and who, eleven years later, became independent India's first Chief of Army Staff. The Committee's recommendations were not carried through because of the advent of war in 1939. However, perhaps as a result of the need to raise morale in the wake of the INA, and the Indian Army's drubbing in Malaya and Burma, the pay of KCIOs and ICOs was revised upwards, and they were now entitled to additional pay at the same rates as British officers. See Sharma, *Nationalization of the Indian Army*, pp. 165, 177.
65. Interview with Gurbax Singh Dhillon, 23 July 1984; Dhillon, *Why I Joined the INA: Different States of Mind*, Lahore: 1946, pp. 3–5; Khan, *My Memories of the INA*, pp. 4–6; Kiani, *India's Freedom Struggle*, p. 11.
66. Secret cipher telegram, Commander-in-Chief, India, to General Officer Commanding, Malaya, 10 May 1940, L/WS/1/391, OIOC.
67. According to Burton Stein, the very swiftness with which the Raj moved to quell Gandhi's Quit India agitation in 1942 revealed that the authorities had been planning for just such an eventuality since at least the beginning of the war in 1939. Burton Stein, *A History of India*, Oxford: 1998, p. 354; Telegram, Lieutenant Colonel Cawthorn to Major Mackenzie, 15 April 1942 [3062/Cipher 14/2], in N. Mansergh and E. W. R. Lumby (eds), *India: The Transfer of Power, 1942–1947*, vol. 1, London: 1970, pp. 176–7. A total of 57½ infantry battalions—the equivalent of around 46,000 men—were deployed as internal security troops to put down the Quit India agitations. See Arun Bhuyan, *The Quit India Movement: The Second World War and Indian Nationalism*, New Delhi: 1975, p. 95.
68. Secret cipher telegram, General Officer Commanding, Malaya, to Commander-in-Chief, India, 6 June 1940, L/WS/1/391, OIOC.
69. Great Britain, Parliament, *The Army Act* (44 and 45 Vict., ch. 58), part I, section 7.
70. Evans, *Thimayya*, p. 169.
71. Secret cipher telegram, General Officer Commanding, Malaya, to Commander-in-Chief, India, 6 June 1940, L/WS/1/391, OIOC.
72. Besides 4/19th Hyderabad, the following Indian units volunteered, almost to a man, to join the INA in the recruitment drive that followed the meeting at the Farrer Park race course in Singapore on 17 February 1942, at which Fujiwara and Mohan Singh made the INA's existence public to a gathering of 45,000 Indian prisoners of war: 2/17 and 3/17 Dogra; 3/18 Garhwal Rifles; Kapurthala Infantry; Hong Kong and Singapore Royal Artillery; 1/14, 5/14 and 6/14 Punjab; 2/9 and 4/9 Jat;

2/16 and 3/16 Punjab; and various Royal Indian Army Supply Corps and Indian Army Ordnance Corps detachments. See Sundaram, 'The Indian National Army: A Preliminary Study of its Formation and Campaigns', unpublished MA thesis, McGill University, 1985, pp. 73–4.

73. Murfett, *et al., Between Two Oceans*, p. 345; Combined Services Detailed Interrogation Centre, India [hereafter: CSDIC(I)], Red Fort, Delhi; *A Brief Chronological and Factual Account of the Indian National Army*, p. 13, L/WS/2/45, OIOC.

74. S. W. Kirby, *The War Against Japan*, vol. 1, London: 1957, p. 113. This source, which seems to be the only secondary reference to the HKSRA's origins, functions, and composition, states that it comprised only mountain and medium batteries, and not heavy batteries. Likewise, the Kirby source, perhaps because it was an 'official' history, does not mention the HKSRA incident; nor, for that matter, does it mention the Zahir-ud-Din affair. However, a few lines on the HKSRA disaffection are included in L. James, *Raj: The Making and Unmaking of British India*, London: 1997, pp. 543–4.

75. Omissi, *Sepoy and the Raj*, p. 95. On Sikhs, their religion, and early history, see J. S. Grewal, *Sikhs of the Punjab*, Cambridge: 1990; I. Banga (ed.), *Five Punjabi Centuries, Polity. Economy, Society and Culture, c. 1500–1990: Essays for J. S. Grewal*, New Delhi: 1997; and J. F. Richards, *The Mughal Empire*, Cambridge: 1993. On the Anglo-Sikh wars of the 1840s, see H. C. B. Cook, *The Sikh Wars: The British Army in the Punjab*, London: 1975; E. R. Crawford, 'The Sikh Wars, 1845–1849', in B. J. Bond (ed.), *Victorian Military Campaigns*, New York: 1967; and B. S. Nijjar, *The Anglo-Sikh Wars, 1845–1849*, New Delhi: 1976.

76. V. G. Kiernan, *European Empires from Conquest to Collapse, 1815–1860*, Leicester: 1982, pp. 51–2, 70.

77. G. F. MacMunn, *The Armies of India*, London: 1911, p. 135.

78. A. E. Barstow, *Recruiting Handbooks for the Indian Army: The Sikhs*, Calcutta: 1928; Sundaram, 'Soldier Disaffection', p. 158.

79. Denzil Ibbetson, 'Report on the Political Situation in the Punjab, 30 April 1907', quoted in Grewal, *Sikhs*, p. 153. Ibbetson was governor of the Punjab in 1907–8. On Sikh politics in this era, see Harjot Singh, 'From Gurdwara Rakabganj to the Viceregal Palace: A Study of Religious Protest', *Punjab Past and Present*, 14(1), 1980; Mohinder Singh, *The Akali Movement*, Delhi: 1978.

80. Interview with Gurbax Singh Dhillon, 24 July 1984. The best source on the Ghadar party is Harish K. Puri, *The Ghadar Movement: Ideology, Organization and Strategy*, Amritsar: 1983. On Bhagat Singh, see Kamlesh Mohan, *Militant Nationalism in the Punjab, 1919–1935*, New Delhi: 1985; and Bipan Chandra, *et al., India's Struggle for Independence*, New Delhi: 1988, chapter 20.

81. This pamphlet was written by Ajit Singh, a revolutionary Jat Sikh leader based in Lahore. See Omissi, *Sepoy and the Raj*, pp. 126–7.
82. 'A Note on the Sikhs', para 2, in L/WS/2/44, OIOC.
83. 'Note on the Sikhs', para 2; 'Survey of the Sikh Situation Affecting the Army', L/WS/1/303, OIOC.
84. Andrew Mollo and Malcolm MacGregor, *Army Uniforms of World War 2*, Poole: 1973, plate 214, pp. 30, 179.
85. Extract from General Orders by General Archibald P. Wavell, Commander-in-Chief, Middle-East, 11 October 1940, L/WS/1/303, OIOC.
86. The actual slogan was 'O Jat, guard your turban'. See: *Sepoy and the Raj*, p. 127
87. S. W. Kirby, *Singapore: The Chain of Disaster*, London: 1971, p. 290.
88. Secret cipher telegram, General Officer Commanding Hong Kong, to Commander-in-Chief, India, 22 December 1940, part I, paras 2, 4, L/WS/1/303, OIOC.
89. Secret cipher telegram, General Officer Commanding, Hong Kong, to Commander-in-Chief, India, 22 December 1940, part I, para 5, L/WS/1/303. For an indication of the procedures involved, see Great Britain, War Office, *Manual of Military Law*, 6th edn, London: 1914, p. 27.
90. Omissi, *Sepoy and the Raj*, pp. 77–84; Mason, *A Matter of Honour*, p. 127.
91. Secret cipher telegram, General Officer Commanding, Hong Kong, to Commander-in-Chief, India, part II, 22 December 1940, para 2, L/WS/1/303.
92. Secret cipher telegram, General Officer Commanding, Hong Kong, to War Office, London, 28 December 1940; secret cipher telegram, General Officer Commanding, Hong Kong, to Commander-in-Chief, India, 28 December 1940, L/WS/1/303.
93. S. L. Menezes, *Fidelity and Honour: The Indian Army from the Seventeenth to the Twenty-First Century*, New Delhi: 1993, p. 349.
94. Secret cipher telegram, General Officer Commanding, Hong Kong, to Commander-in-Chief, India, 23 December 1940; secret cipher telegram, General Officer Commanding, Hong Kong, to War Office, London, 17 February 1941, paras 1–4, L/WS/1/303.
95. Henry Lawrence, 'The Military Defence of our Indian Empire', in Lawrence, *Essays Political and Military, Written in India*, London: 1859, pp. 154–5.
96. The literature on the 'Sepoy Mutiny' is vast. Among the best works are Surendranath Sen, *Eighteen-Fifty-Seven*, Calcutta: 1958; C. A. Bayly (ed.), Eric Stokes, *The Peasant Armed: The Revolt of 1857*, Oxford: 1986.
97. The mai-bap relationship, and what happened to it in World War II, is most brilliantly evoked in a novel. See Paul Scott, *The Day of the*

Scorpion, 1973; reprint, London: 1983, pp. 385–406. See also R. J. Moore, *Paul Scott's Raj*, London: 1990, pp. 83–5.

98. Secret cipher telegram, General Officer Commanding, Hong Kong, to War Office, London, 17 February 1941, para 4, L/WS/1/391, OIOC.
99. Literally, those who undertake *Satyagraha* (truth-force), the technique of non-violent non-cooperation evolved by Gandhi to fight the British, whom it frustrated and perplexed. The literature on Satyagraha is voluminous. Good introductions are J. M. Brown, *Gandhi: Prisoner of Hope*, New Haven: 1989; Dennis Dalton, *Mahatma Gandhi: Nonviolent Power in Action*, New York: 1993; David Arnold, *Gandhi*, Harlow: 2001.
100. This is probably why CSDIC classified the vast majority of INA personnel captured at the end of the war as 'Whites'—misguided soldiers, who were induced to join by the wilier and less numerous 'Greys' and 'Blacks'. See Governor General of India to Secretary of State for India [Telegram 10234], 11 August 1945, part i, para 1, in N. Mansergh, E. W. R. Lumby, and P. Moon (eds), *India: The Transfer of Power, 1942–1947*, vol. 6, London: 1976.
101. For an interesting perspective concerning this see C. Thorne, *The Issue of War: States, Societies, and the Far Eastern Conflict of 1941–1945*, London: 1985, pp. 15–17.
102. Fujiwara Iwaichi, *F. Kikan*, pp. 1–50.
103. Great Britain, *Manual of Military Law*, London: 1914, p. 15.
104. Lieutenant General Claude Auchinleck to Leo Amery, 12 October 1940, L/MIL/7/19156, OIOC.
105. On 'invented traditions' generally, see Eric Hobsbawm and Terence Ranger (eds), *The Invention of Tradition*, Cambridge: 1983, especially pp. 1–14.
106. B. Greenhous, *C Force to Hong Kong*, Toronto: 1997, p. 15.
107. See Omissi, *Sepoy and the Raj*, pp. 148–9. Fuller accounts of the mutiny of the 5th Indian Light Infantry can be found in Corr, *Springing Tigers*, chapter 1; L. James, *Mutiny: In the British and Commonwealth Forces, 1797–1856*, London: 1987, chapter 7. These latter two are popular, not scholarly, treatments.
108. Lieutenant General George Chesney, Memorandum [on Sir A. Eden's Memoranda of 6 July 1885 and 8 February 1886], 20 May 1886, para 3, L/MIL/7/19019, OIOC.
109. C. Thorne, 'The British Cause and Indian Nationalism in 1940: An Officer's Rejection of Empire', *Journal of Imperial and Commonwealth History*, 10(3), 1982, p. 355. A comparison of Chetwode's 'brain-sick' officers with Thimayya's Koi-Hai types described earlier reveals that they were essentially one and the same.
110. Paul Scott to J. A. E. Heard, 8 October 1975, in R. J. Moore, *Paul Scott's Raj*, London: 1990, p. 106. The 'prose-poet' title is Robin Moore's. See also p.116.

Section II

Military Culture and Society

5

The Military Enters Indian Thought*

Stephen P. Cohen

Three variables seem to account for Indian attitudes toward the British-Indian military structure. The first is the culture in which an individual or group seeks to define its status. Is the referent culture traditional or Western? Or is it an amalgam of the two: a neotraditionalism looking forward for means but backwards for ends? The second variable is the degree to which a group or individual values the military. Is the military a prime value (an end) or an instrumental value (a means) to the group?[1] The third variable is the degree of xenophobia or nationalism: in the Indian context, to what extent was the group anti-British?

The movement of these three parameters was profoundly affected both by British policy and by events outside India. B. B. Misra describes the progressive Westernization of India under British-inspired economic, social, and educational reforms.[2] These reforms created an Indian 'middle class', tied intellectually, professionally, and economically to the West. At the same time Western attitudes towards the role of the military developed in India, especially after the Indians gained an understanding of their own army and the armies of Britain, Japan, and—after 1917—Russia. The need for understanding their army increased after the possibility of home rule, dominion status, or some other form of relative autonomy was raised. The Indian leadership soon realized that control over the military was closely related to control over other important levers of the state.

* First published in Stephen P. Cohen's *The Indian Army: Its Contribution to the Development of a Nation*, New Delhi: Oxford University Press, 1990; reprint 1991, pp. 57–87.

Finally, the modern, and to some extent the traditional, sectors of Indian society became progressively more radical towards the British.

Two major sets of attitudes developed towards the military: traditional militarism and gradualism. Both attitudes shared one assumption: that the British were in India to stay, and that their presence was not inherently evil. This assumption was challenged during and after World War I by more radical perspectives.

Traditional Militarism

There are two fundamentally different sets of Indian attitudes towards the British-Indian military structure, both of which may legitimately be labelled Indian militarism: 'modern militarism' and 'traditional militarisim'. 'Modern militarism' emerged in Bengal and western India, and spread to other regions, especially to the intellectuals, bourgeosie, middle classes, and professional families.[3] Modern militarism stressed the value of the military as a national universal solvent, as an expression of the national will, and demanded equalitarian recruitment.

'Traditional militarism' resulted from regional traditions and the recruiting practices of the British. It was confined to those castes and military classes which exercised the use of arms as a matter of birth and right, and was unevenly distributed throughout India—the Punjab being at one extreme, Madras and Bengal at the other. Traditional militarism is usually confined to specific castes, while other castes have no desire to abandon their traditional occupations for military life. In the Punjab, for example, the Chuhras, or untouchable sweepers, traditionally have not joined either indigenous military organizations or the Indian Army except as sweepers, yet former Chuhras who have been converted to Sikhism (Mazbhi Sikhs) have a long—if tenuous—history of military activity as sepoys.[4]

At the turn of the nineteenth century, traditional militarists fell into two categories. First, members of classes which were no longer recruited, or recruited only in very small numbers; and second, those classes which constituted the army, but which sought even greater status as commissioned officers.

After the British radically changed the base of recruitment late in the nineteenth century, many classes were no longer taken into the military. Over a period of years, these classes remained a large, and at times pathetic, group. After the 1890s they were again recruited, only to be once again dropped from the army list.

A typical such group was the Mahars, an untouchable caste from present-day Maharashtra. They comprised a sizeable portion of the armies of the Maratha chieftain Shivaji, served as hereditary local policemen, and were thus a 'natural' martial class. Heavily recruited in the pre-Mutiny years, the Mahars constituted a fifth to a quarter of the entire Bombay Army.[5] A number of distinguished leaders of the Mahar community in the nineteenth century had at one time served in the Army, many as non-commissioned officers. One of these was the father of modern India's leading untouchable politician, B. R. Ambedkar, who had in fact grown up in a military cantonment.[6] In the reorganization of the recruiting base of the Indian Army in the late nineteenth century, Mahar recruitment was rapidly terminated, until there were only a few serving by 1900, practically none by 1914.[7]

The Mahars—like many other classes in the same position— were anxious and resentful when they were dropped from the army list. They were resentful because they felt they were being insulted, and they were anxious lest they suffer setbacks in other areas of government recruitment. Their reaction to their plight was typical—protests were essentially supplicatory: petitions, negotiations, speeches, editorials in sympathetic newspapers, and delegations to the authorities. These tactics were to be expected from groups which sought to retain or recover a privileged place in the British Raj (or Rule, as the British Indian Government was called).

Ambedkar's biographer describes the protests of his father in 1892; Ambedkar himself later took up the cause of Mahar recruitment when he entered Indian politics after World War I. In 1910, the Conference of the Deccan Mahars petitioned the Secretary of State for India—the document deserves to be quoted at length for its style as well as its content:

> We, the Mahar inhabitants of India, residing in the Bombay Presidency, have experienced the vitalizing influence of the general awakening of our Indian people, and long to participate in the new privileges which have been granted by our illustrious Emperor and King to the people of our country, in accordance with the declarations of our late Empress, Queen Victoria the Good, in the celebrated Proclamation of 1858. We do not aspire to high political privileges and positions, since we are not educationally qualified for them, but humbly seek employment in the lowest grades of the Public Service, in the ranks of Police Sepoys and of Soldiers in the Indian Army.
>
> We are making no new demands; we do not claim employment in services in which we have not been engaged before. Indeed, some few of our people do still hold positions in the Police Force .... So also have our people

> been employed in the Indian Army from the very commencement of the British Raj in our country, and they have risen to the highest positions by their valour and good conduct.
>
> But the present changes in the Indian Army have been most prejudicial to the interests of our people. We have been excluded from the Military Service entirely, for reasons unknown to us.[8]

The Mahars continued their plea by offering to serve in segregated regiments or in Muslim regiments if high-caste Hindus objected to their presence; they anxiously stated that they were not 'essentially inferior' to their fellow Indians, and that in fact many Mahars were now Christians. Rather optimistically, they continued that 'the kindly touch of the Christian religion elevates the Mahar at once and forever socially as well as politically, and shall not the magic power of British Law and British Justice produce the same effect upon us, even as followers of our own ancestral faith?' The petitioners offered to serve in any capacity in the military, even as menial servants or as mule drivers, if they could not again serve as sepoys.

The Mahars were also concerned with the effect that dropping them from the recruitment rolls would have on their status in western India. An important theme of their petition was that the British not accede to caste prejudice and discriminate against the lower castes, such as the Mahar community.

The petition of the Mahars was parallelled by petitions from other classes and castes, many with a distinguished military past. Maharashtrian Brahmins, Tamils, Telugus, Coorgs, and numerous other groups were cut from the army list. At a session of the Indian National Congress in 1891, the great western Indian leader Bal Gangadhar Tilak advocated 'organizing throughout the more warlike races of the Empire a system of militia service'.[9] At a later Congress session, at Bankipore in 1912, two Telugus spoke feelingly about the exclusion of their community from the Madras Presidency army list—they were particularly shamed because Muslims and 'Pariah-Christians' were recruited ahead of their own people.[10] They cited Hindu scripture in support of their contention that the Brahmins were a warlike race and invoked the ancient Hindu lawgiver Manu to refute Lord Roberts' alleged slights against the Telugu people.

The castes and classes which the British did recognize as traditionally warlike had different concerns. The prime objective of Punjabis, Muslims, Sikhs, Dogras, Jats, and Rajputs—to mention only the most prominent groups in the reorganized Indian Army—was to place their sons in a position where they might rise to the rank of commissioned officer. Similarly, many hundreds of aristocratic families had had martial traditions (especially in the Punjab), and contributed troops to the Indian Army (or maintained their own army under the control of the British). They also sought a position alongside the British officer, commensurate with their status in Indian society.[11]

The British had long been aware that the structure of the Indian Army was liable to produce tensions unless great care was taken to appease the leadership of the recruited castes by providing avenues of advancement for able Indians within the military. Before the establishment of the sepoy system, petty Indian noblemen were allowed to raise and lead their own men in battle—a practice which the all-British King's Commissioned Officer (KCO) corps eliminated. Under the sepoy system, Indians could become the Viceroy's Commissioned Officers (VCOs), but they could never be promoted to senior appointments (all held by the British KCOs). The VCOs generally could not speak English and were untutored in modern theories of warfare. Their entire military careers had been spent within one regiment, and their experience was limited. In addition, they were usually too old to begin new military careers as KCOs, even if they had been permitted to do so.

The problem of accommodating Indian opinion remained, however, and several alternatives were proposed over the years. In 1836, Lieutenant Colonel John Briggs of the Madras Army argued for increased association of Indians with the military at the higher levels, and the Indianization—in part—of the officer corps. Briggs suggested that military colleges be established for the sons of native officers, and that professional and loyal Indians gradually replace the British officers, freeing the latter for more sensitive political jobs.[12] A few years later, Henry Lawrence took up the argument:

> There is always danger in handling edged tools, but justice and liberality forge a stronger chain than suspicious and niggardly policy. We hold that no place or office should be absolutely barred to the Native soldier .... Legitimate outlets for military energy and ability in all ranks, and among all classes *must* be given .... The question is only whether justice is to be gracefully conceded or violently seized. Ten or twenty years *must* settle the point.[13]

Lawrence saw many able Indians leaving British service and hiring themselves out to Indian rulers. It was these men who had to be retained and controlled.

The Mutiny of 1857 put an end to such speculation for several years. The British were worried about the quality of their own officers, and few who had served during the Mutiny were eager to place Indians in positions of command.

Yet the problem persisted, and pressure for change came from both the Indians and the British.[14] The first step towards the Indianization of the King's officer corps came in 1901 with the establishment of the Imperial Cadet Corps. In 1905, a special form of King's Commission 'in His Majesty's Native Indian Land Forces' was instituted for Indians who had qualified through the corps.[15] It was different from the VCO primarily in method of entry. The VCO had to serve for several years in the ranks as a sepoy before receiving his commission. The new commission was somewhat more suitable for an Indian 'gentleman', as he had only to attend an elite military academy. The commission only carried the power of command over Indian troops, and those who held it could not rise above the level of squadron or company officer. The main instigator of the cadet corps was Lord Curzon, who saw in it a means of providing a military career for those

> whose pride of birth or surrounding prevents them from embracing a civil profession, whose interests lie naturally on the side of the British Government, but whose sympathies are in danger of being alienated, and their energies dulled by the absence of any field for their natural ambitions.[16]

These individuals would come from the princely and noble families of India; they would not be from 'the newer aristocracy, who, if the criterion were one of wealth or education, or precocity in European manners, would flood us with a stream of applications supported by every sort of examination test, but resulting in the very last type of young officer that we should desire to procure'.[17]

The basic difficulty of Indianizing the officer corps was to set up criteria for determining the qualifications of prospective officers. This problem was not solved until World War II. The martial classes argued on political grounds: they had been loyal in the past, and must be kept loyal in the future. Yet what if loyalty was not accompanied by professional competence—which was to come first? Indianization posed a challenge to the standards of the British officer corps, and to their feeling of superiority over the Indians.

Despite the urging of civilian officials, the British military was reluctant to acknowledge the value of the small cadet corps and regarded it as a major encroachment upon their exclusive world. But just as important, it was not entirely satisfactory to the Indian officers. If they could only command Indian troops, their status was dearly inferior to that of the British officers who, as KCOs, could command British as well as Indian troops. Even if they were to be trained in India, at an 'Indian Sandhurst', many thought they could never be fully equal to their British colleagues. But to the Indians from traditional martial classes, the challenge was learning to adapt their martial background to the technical and professional requirements of a modern military organization. As the Indian Army modernized, the tension between the two sets of skills and values increased.

GRADUALISM

'Instrumental gradualism' was the second important strand of Indian thought on military matters to emerge before World War I. The gradualists were the forerunners of the Indian defence experts who came to prominence after 1920. They were 'established' members of Edwardian India, with close personal and intellectual ties with Britain and British thought, and constituted the loyal opposition to official British policy in India. They regarded military and defence matters as important but secondary to budget cutting, government jobs for Indians, and the removal of moral and social slights. The best expression of their views can be found in the records of the early sessions of the Indian National Congress—an organization founded in 1885 by a Britisher to enable loyal, educated Indians to ventilate their grievances even as they expressed their support for the Raj.

The first Congress, held in Bombay in 1885, set the tone for many years to follow:

> That in the opinion of the Congress the proposed increase in the military expenditure of the empire is unnecessary, and regard being had to the revenue of the empire and the existing circumstances of the country, excessive.[18]

The mover of the resolution, P. Runiah Naidu of Madras, stressed the loyalty of the natives of India to the Queen and their thanks for the 'blessings conferred on us by British rule'.[19] He and other delegates claimed that the Russian threat would be met by mass volunteering because of this deep loyalty of the Indians to the British. Naidu argued that the poverty-stricken condition of the country required the government to rely upon such volunteers in a crisis, to cut the size of the Indian Army, and to significantly reduce the British element of the army in India.[20]

The high cost of the Indian Army was a recurrent theme (although dwindling in intensity) until the 1920s but another problem concerned many delegates. At the second session of the Congress, it was suggested that the government initiate a system of volunteering. However, the speech by the mover of the resolution, Raja Rampal Singh, went beyond the content of the resolution itself. After timidly apologizing for being at variance with his government, and after stressing the Indians' gratefulness for British rule, he came to his main point:

> but we cannot be grateful to it for degrading our natures, for systematically crushing out of us all martial spirit, for converting a race of soldiers and heroes into a timid flock of quill-driving sheep (*prolonged shouts*). Thank God things have not yet gone quite so far as this. There are some of us yet, everywhere, who would be willing to draw sword, and if needful lay down our lives ... for the support and maintenance of that Government to which we owe so much.[21]

The possibility of saving money by a voluntary system or recruitment was clearly a secondary motive for Rampal Singh and many others. His main concern was that arms be given to the upper classes so that their self-reliance would not deteriorate further than it had since the Mutiny. It was not a matter of tradition or of money alone, but of honour.

The same concern was behind the resolution urging repeal of the Arms Act in 1888. The majority of delegates, led by Sir Pherozeshah Mehta, succeeded in passing the resolution over the opposition of most British and a few Indian delegates. The real issue was the loss of self-respect.[22]

Another objective for many Indian moderates was increasing the number of government positions open to Indians. Their main interest was in the Indian Civil Service. Indians had theoretically been eligible for the Indian Civil Service since the Charter Act of 1853; but none were recruited until 1871, when four were taken into the elite corps. In 1879, as a result of agitation in both England and India, a statutory civil service was created and the number of Indians rapidly increased—by 1915, there were 63 Indian Indian Civil Service members, 5 per cent of the total.[23] Although all lower ranks of the Indian Army were made up of Indians, they did not reach the 5 per cent level in the officer corps until the 1930s, and even then were crammed into the lower levels of the hierarchy. Not until the twentieth century was there much pressure from urban India for increased places in the officer corps; but by that time, Indianization was seen as something more important than prestige or jobs—Indianization had become linked to home rule and independence.

A leading spokesman for the moderate position was G. K. Gokhale. He dealt annually with military problems in his budget speeches before the Imperial Legislative Council.[24] His major concern was the reduction of the heavy defence expenditure—or at least a larger contribution by Britain, since the Indian Army was often used for imperial purposes. His most important contribution to the debate on defence, however, foreshadowed arguments which are still encountered in India today. Gokhale had some familiarity with foreign military systems. He argued that the mercenary Indian Army must be replaced by a cheaper, more effective citizens' army. Japan was an especially attractive model after that nation's triumph over Russia in 1905. If the British would establish a short-service citizens' army, they would save a great deal of money; but more important, they would heal India's wounded self-respect.[25]

The British refused to reconsider the organizational premises of the Indian Army. Although some concessions were made to the martial classes in the form of token commissions in the officer corps, there was no attempt to resume recruitment of those classes which had been dropped, or to broaden the base of the army, let alone make it a 'citizens' army'. The army was especially reluctant to experiment with untried castes or with the new Indian middle classes, either as soldiers or as officers. They might well have, for World War I, placed intolerable strains upon the capacity of the martial classes to produce recruits in adequate numbers, and this crisis led the British to make promises which they were reluctant to carry out after the war.

World War I

Percival Spear remarked that 'the First World War forms the portal through which India entered the stage of the modern world'.[26] It was a bloody entry for the Indian Army, which served in Europe, the Middle East, and Africa. More than 36,000 soldiers were killed and 70,000 wounded. Indian Army personnel won 16 Victoria Crosses—the highest award bestowed by the British Empire—and 99 Military Crosses for numerous deeds of heroism and gallantry.[27] The army suffered inordinate losses due to its obsolete equipment and inadequate training against major military powers; but as an army and on an individual level, the Indian expeditionary force performed magnificently.

Although the impact of World War I on Indian society was important and diverse, two developments particularly affected both the traditional military groups and the more Westernized gradualists. The first was the scope and intensity of recruitment. Classes which had been dropped from the recruitment lists were again recruited, as well as new classes which had never been recruited. Second, the British made promises to induce recruitment.

THE MARTIAL RACES IN WORLD WAR I

One of the early casualties of World War I was the 'system of recruiting the martial races' theory. Although the war verified the warlike characteristics of the classes designated as 'martial', it also demonstrated that other classes, given adequate training and leadership, performed equally. It also revealed that the base of recruitment was far too narrow, and that threats, extortion, and a variety of promises were necessary to raise adequate numbers from the martial classes.

Between August 1914 and November 1918, the Indian Army more than tripled in size—from 1,55,000 to more than 5,73,000 men. Nearly 7,40,000 sepoys served at one time or another during the war. The bulk of the army was drawn from those classes that had traditionally been recruited, the largest being the Punjabi Muslims, who contributed more than 1,36,000 men. Sikhs (88,000), Rajputs (62,000), Gurkhas (55,000), and Jats (54,000) also provided significant numbers. Lesser contributions were made by Dogras (23,000), Pathans (28,000), Hindustani Muslims (36,000), and Ahirs (19,000).[28] Seventy-five 'new' classes were 'tried' during the course of the war, including many groups which in fact had had long and distinguished military histories.[29]

There had been several warnings from within the military establishment in India (as well as from Indian civilians) that the base of recruitment was too narrow. In 1892, one officer of the adjutant-general's branch advised that 'recruiting for the Native Army was practically breaking down toward the end of the Afghan War, and although at present a sufficient supply of men is forthcoming, I am of [the] opinion that it; will again break down when stress is put on it'.[30] Between 1892 and 1914, conditions of service had improved greatly; but even so, the last pre-war inquiry into army affairs (the Nicholson Army Commission, 1912) found that in the event of a 'serious war', recruitment might fall off unless steps were taken to improve the attractiveness of the army to the sepoys. They suggested that Sikh recruitment be reduced, and that sparsely represented classes such as Deccani Brahmins and Nagas be recruited, as long as the efficiency of the army was not diminished.[31] These suggestions, however, remained unimplemented.

The greatest problem was the recruitment of the Jat Sikhs. Although there were fewer Sikhs recruited from the Punjab than Muslims, the Sikhs had been contributing a higher percentage of their available manpower to the army. They were experiencing important social changes by way of the militant Akali reform movement in the early part of the twentieth century, and were regarded as one of the more recalcitrant and pugnacious classes.[32] In addition, the Jat Sikhs had been the target of early nationalist propagandizing, and many were impressed by the news before World War I that several retired Sikh sepoys had destroyed their medals and discharge certificates in a wave of anti-British sentiment in America and Canada. Restrictions on Indian immigration to Canada and the *Kotaga Maru* incident fed conspiratorial sentiment, and copies of revolutionary newspapers filtered back to the villages of the Punjab.[33] These papers were followed by the revolutionaries themselves. Acts of violence were committed during the first years of the war, but they were effectively dealt with by the British with the assistance of Punjabi—especially Sikh—gentry. Returning sepoys, who had had an opportunity to compare British and French treatment of their colonials, created additional unrest.

The final two years of the war brought enormous pressure upon civilian and military officials to speed the flow of recruitment from the Punjab. Sir Michael O'Dwyer, Lieutenant Governor of Punjab, toured the countryside from division to division, district to district, exhorting the youth of the martial classes—especially the Sikhs—to come forward. In numerous speeches, he argued that India's cause was that of Britain: therefore India should contribute a proportionate number of soldiers, which he calculated to be three million.[34] He threatened that conscription would be necessary if Indians would not volunteer. A quota system was informally introduced and the threat of conscription was used as an incentive. O'Dwyer praised the districts which had contributed large numbers of troops and shamed those that did poorly, especially with the taunt that Bengal had provided a 'keen and capable' unit. He attempted to stir Jat Sikhs by pointing to the rise in Mazbhi (untouchable) Sikh recruitment: 'if regard be had to available numbers the Mazbhi Sikhs have far surpassed the Jats ... do the Jats view the Cavalry of Mazbhis with equanimity?'[35] If the Punjabis—especially the Sikhs—really wanted true izzat, they must obtain it through service to a noble and just cause (*khidmat*). The promise of further commissions as officers, however, may have been more effective in recruiting Sikhs than all the threats of the British.

As regards the further grant of King's Commissions, the Government of India have already laid their proposals before the Home Government and we may be sure that they will receive early and sympathetic consideration. Meantime, eleven representatives of leading martial tribes have received commissions in the King's Indian forces within the last few months, but the number to be granted will naturally depend in a great measure on the response to the call for recruits. We have often been told by those who claim to understand the Indian mind [a reference to Indian politicians?] that the one thing wanted to open the flood-gates of recruiting is the grant of King's Commissions. The next few months should show whether that view is correct.[36]

There were, of course, other material incentives for joining the army or for assisting the British in the recruitment effort. Former soldiers received relatively liberal pensions, and those who served the British with distinction or who were officers were given grants of land, jagirs, and were further rewarded by having their relatives favourably considered for recruitment.[37]

Although the Punjab had performed magnificently, the manpower needs of the war were staggering, and the British turned to many 'nor-martial' classes. Of the 75 new classes which the army recruited, many were either closely related to classes already on the army list (Dogra Jats, Mahtam Sikhs, Punjabi Brahmins, Punjabi Hindus, Punjabi Christians, south Punjabi Muslims, west Punjabi Muslims, and Oudh Rajputs) and many were formerly recruited classes (Mahars, Telugus, Bhils, Bengalis, Moplahs). Although some results were not satisfactory (the Bengal regiment mentioned by O'Dwyer was so unsuitable and unreliable that it was not put into action in Europe), by and large they performed as well as the older classes:

The war has proved that all men are brave, that the humblest follower is capable of sacrifice and devotion; that the Afridi, who is outwardly the nearest thing to an impersonation of Mars, yields nothing in courage to the Madrasi Christian .... These revelations have meant a general levelling and the uplift of classes hitherto undeservedly obscure.[38]

For any who cared to examine the performance record—still available in the unit histories of 'non-martial classes' which participated in the war—it was clear that with adequate leadership and training, virtually any group could be successfully employed somewhere in the military. Nevertheless, the system of recruiting the 'martial races' persisted up until World War II. It was invoked in the developing debate over *swaraj* (home rule for India), and the retention of defence matters in the hands of the British long after other political functions were turned over to Indians or shared with them.

RAISING OF HOPE

The most significant by-product of India's great material and manpower contribution to the Allies in World War I was the pledges and promises offered by the British to the Indians. In retrospect, it is clear that there were mixed motives behind these promises: they were a reward for past effort, but were also inducement for further endeavour. As the need for Indian assistance declined with the termination of hostilities, elements in both the British and Indian governments procrastinated in fulfilling these pledges. Nowhere was this postponement more obvious and blatant than in the Indianization of the officer corps. At the height of the war, Indians who held the Viceroy's commission were made eligible for the King's commission. This eligibility for advancement was a direct inducement to the recruited classes to increase their efforts in the war, although it meant little in practical terms. By the time an Indian was made a VCO, he was already advanced in age: he could never hope to rise far as KCO, and would have been ill trained for a major promotion. Another significant step was taken in 1917, when 10 vacancies at the Royal Military College, Sandhurst, were ordered reserved each year for suitable Indians. The British did not attempt to chart out the effect of these programmes on the Indianization of the Army as a whole. The King's commissions were reserved for 'selected representatives of families of fighting classes which have rendered valuable services to the State during the War', that is, the 'martial races'. Indianization was seen as a reward for services rendered, not as a process in the evolution of India towards self-government.[39]

These limited rewards for faithful service were announced the same year as another important policy was set down. The Secretary of State for India, Edwin Montagu, announced in the House of Commons:

> The policy of His Majesty's government, with which the Government of India are in complete accord, is that of the increasing association of Indians in every branch of the administration, and the gradual development of self-governing institutions, with a view to the progressive realization of responsible government in India as an integral part of the British Empire.[40]

Shortly after the announcement, Montagu visited India and, with the Viceroy, Lord Chelmsford, attempted to give effect to the statement:

It is not enough merely to assert a principle. We must act on it. The services of the Indian army in the war and the great increase in its numbers make it necessary that a considerable number of commissions should be given .... Race should no more debar him from promotion in the army than it does in the civil services .... We feel sure that no measures would do so much to stimulate Indian enthusiasm for the war.[41]

While in India, Montagu found Commander-in-Chief Sir C. C. Munro interested in the cause of Indianization, but not enthusiastic over it. Munro had attempted to get Indian officers into service clubs (most of which resented their presence), but had his own ideas about recruitment. Montagu wanted to open up an 'Indian Sandhurst' and enable any qualified Indian to obtain a commission. However, Munro stipulated that first priority should go to the sons of servicemen. According to Montagu, Munro and the military regarded the demand for commissions as 'political'.[42]

A start had been made. In addition to the quota of 10 vacancies per year at Sandhurst, some King's commissions were given to specially selected noncoms, officers, and graduates of the Cadet College, Indore. Major General Iskander Mirza, who became president of Pakistan, was among those in the first category. The first Indian Commander-in-Chief of the Indian Army, General K. M. Cariappa, was in the latter group.[43]

Both methods of obtaining the King's commission were temporarily disastrous for the cause of Indianization: selection was not careful enough, and many of the first Sandhurst cadets were unprepared for life abroad. A series of accidents had the result that few cadets graduated successfully.[44] Above all, there was no set policy for the pace and objective of Indianization. Only in 1928 was Indianization linked to the progress of India towards self-government and dominion status.[45]

Postwar Retrenchment

After the termination of hostilities, the Indian Army reverted to its peacetime manpower level and there were second thoughts about some of the promises made concerning Indianization.

A decision had to be made as to which classes and castes would remain on the recruitment list, and which would be dropped. Apparently no serious thought was given to an army with a relatively wide base of recruitment. The number of sepoys in the Indian Army dropped from 5,00,000 in 1918 to 1,20,000 in 1923.[46] The cut was made almost entirely in the classes recruited for the first time during the war, or among those who had formerly been recruited and dropped, and then newly recruited for the war. The Mahars had been recruited in 1914–18, and after a brief period under two Madras battalions, were given their own unit, the 111th Mahars. To the consternation of the Mahar community, this unit was disbanded. Another untouchable class, the Mazbhi Sikhs, was similarly again recruited during the war and then gradually 'retrenched', although the last Mazbhi unit was not disbanded until 1932. Bengalis, Madrassis, and non-Punjabis were most vulnerable to these cuts. Undoubtedly the increasing political awareness in Bengal and Madras influenced the termination of recruitment from these regions, although the Punjab was also no longer politically quiet. The increase in recruitment from the lower castes and 'non-martial regions', which was repeated during World War II, seems to bear out the hypothesis of several scholars that participation in military affairs is closely related to the intensity of warfare and the rate of social change.[47] High intensity demanded greater numbers and lower castes eventually get an opportunity to serve in the military, an opportunity denied to them during peacetime.

The major political issue which faced the British, however, stemmed not from the administrative decisions which rather automatically dropped 'non-martial races'—but from the political promises of intensified Indianization. After the termination of hostilities, the British hedged on the promises made under the pressure of war. This retreat was the subject of a political dialogue between the British and those Indians still regarded as loyal to the British Raj.

The report of the Esher Committee (1920) indicated the wide disagreement between these groups.[48] The committee which had been appointed to examine the future of the military in India was composed of high-level British civilian and military officials, and had two Indian members. It rejected increased democratic control over the military, proposed strengthening the Commander-in-Chief's position, rejected a broadly-based recruitment pattern, and only cautiously encouraged an educational build up which would qualify Indians for Sandhurst. While paying lip service to the 1917 declarations on the future status of India, the committee proposed little which would have actually led to an Indian officer corps. The question of Indianization was, in fact, evaded, except in the minutes by the two Indian members.

The minutes indicated the split in approaches to military matters between Indian moderates and the spokesmen for the 'martial classes'.

Sir Krishna Gupta criticized the committee for ignoring Indianization. He urged the opening up of all branches of the army to all Indians on the basis of ability alone. A short-service, self-reliant military organization, backed, by an extensive territorial force, with a broad system of pre-service military education was required to help 'achieve this goal of national unity and full responsible government'.[49]

On the other hand, Sir Umar Hayat Khan, a Punjabi landowner and a leader of Muslim conservatives, went even further than the British and urged extreme caution in any innovations in the military. His minute contained both direct and implied criticisms of Sir Krishna's argument: a long-service army, recruited exclusively from the 'martial races' was best officered by Indian officers drawn from the same 'reliable' martial races. Sir Umar Hayat, hardly an advocate of Indian self-reliance or independence, argued that maintaining and intensifying the present system was necessary for the political safety of the British, and for military efficiency.[50]

The Sivaswamy Aiyer Resolutions

Fortunately for the growing number of progressive moderates interested in military affairs, the first Legislative Assembly under the new constitution sat after the Esher Committee's report had been released. Sir P. S. Sivaswamy Aiyer[51] took advantage of the opportunity and introduced 15 resolutions on the Esher Committee's report at the end of the first Assembly. The resolutions present a clear picture of what sophisticated Indian moderates and liberals wanted in defence matters. The resulting debates on the resolutions give some indication of different attitudes.[52] Most members were absent from Calcutta at the end of the session, and the government lost its majority. After attempting to modify the resolutions by amendment, it gave up and accepted them almost *in toto*. The British later felt it was a 'tactical' mistake.

One of Aiyer's resolutions called for restrictions on the uses of the Indian Army—that it be used for Indian defence, internal or external, but not as a British imperial police force. Another called for the substitution of a civilian member in the Viceroy's Executive Council for the commander-in-chief, paralleling British practice. Other resolutions called for a cut in defence expenditures and covered minor matters which had been or were going to be adopted by the government in any case.

Two crucial resolutions led to extensive debate, and were to have serious political repercussions. The first, resolution no. 7, called for the admission of Indians into all branches of the Indian military and suggested that 'every encouragement should be given to Indians—including the educated middle classes—subject to the prescribed standards of fitness, to enter the commissioned ranks of the Army'.[53] It also suggested that a quota of 25 per cent of new King's commissions be reserved for Indians.[54] The second proposed the establishment of preliminary military training to prepare Indians for Sandhurst, and the establishment of an 'Indian Sandhurst'.[55]

The latter resolution was accepted by the government. In an unusual intervention, the Commander-in-Chief, General Henry S. Rawlinson, gave his support to the part of the resolution calling for Indian facilities for pre-Sandhurst training. Rawlinson also stated that he was eager to see facilities for higher military training established, especially for the sons of Indian officers. He inadvertently referred to the proposed institution as a 'college', and his statement that at no distant date 'we shall be able to establish a College on these lines as suggested in the Resolution' made it appear as though he expressly hoped that an 'Indian Sandhurst' would be established.[56] This was not in fact his view, for he later explained that he had in mind an expanded version of the old Imperial Cadet College, which was not able to produce KCOs.

The resolution calling for increased commissions for Indians was amended by the government, with the strong support of the many Punjabi representatives, Sikhs and Muslims alike:

> and in granting King's Commissions, after giving full regard to the claims to promotion of officers of the Indian Army who already hold the commission of His Excellency the Viceroy, the rest of the commissions granted should be given to cadets trained at Sandhurst. The general rule in selecting candidates for this training should be that the large majority of the selections should be from the communities which furnish recruits to the army and, as far as possible, in proportion to the numbers in which they furnish such recruits.[57]

The amendment carried by one vote. The alignment of debaters was not unexpected: on one side were a former British Indian Army officer who had served with Punjabi units, three Sikhs, and a Punjabi Muslim. Opposing the amendment were a former British-Indian Army officer who had served in the technical services and sappers (Madras), a Bengali Muslim, and a Punjabi Hindu of a non-martial caste.

The advocates of the amendment presented several reasons for drawing officers exclusively from the 'martial races'. First, men of the 'martial races' could only be handled by officers of the same race—they cited disastrous incidents in which VCOs of one race tried to command troops of another. Second, the martial races were entitled to the lion's share of the officer commissions because they had made the greatest sacrifices in the war. Third, for financial reasons, it would be easier to recruit from the races presently serving than to attempt to search all of India for the right type of officer. Fourth, for disciplinary purposes, it was necessary to assure recruits from the 'martial classes' the possibility of promotion to officer status; sepoys were already grumbling that not enough King's commissions were going to Punjabis. Finally, they argued that the amendment did not rule out the possibility of a military career for sons of non-military families, but only established a priority which was just and necessary.

The amendment aroused the representatives of the 'martial classes'. Khan Sahib Mirza Mohammad Ikramulla Khan, for example, related how his father, his uncle, his brother, and his son had served the British loyally for years in the Indian Army. He explained that the army needed men from families such as his, for they possessed 'the great military qualities of courage, perseverance and endurance which are the product of social heredity, of moral traditions: they are not to be learned in any school or from books'.[58] How could the army be officered by 'the sons of lawyers and shopkeepers and others who, whatever may be their virtues, those virtues are not the iron virtues of our old martial classes'?[59]

The Sikhs were equally adamant. They felt strongly that when the time came for distributing commissions, those classes who had shed their blood were going to be shortchanged. Where were the 'non-martial classes' when the blood was flowing? One Sardar (Bhai Man Singh) ridiculed the 'airy idealism' which held that India consisted of one nationality. He argued that India was made up of many classes and races, and not even among the 'martial races' could men of one race officer troops of another.[60]

The opponents of the amendment and of selective recruiting pointed out many of the obvious flaws in these arguments. It was ludicrous to claim that 'martial classes' could only be officered by members of the same class, for the British had been commanding all of the various classes for years and no one seriously thought they could be dispensed with overnight. The Bengalis and 'non-martial Hindus' argued that their communities should get an opportunity for military service, as long as the selection was based on fair criteria. Equal competition should be allowed, regardless of community. They and others argued that men of merit should be made officers, whether they were British or Indian, 'martial' or 'non-martial'. Selection on this basis would be the best guarantee of maintaining discipline, even among 'martial' troops. Proponents of equal opportunity in recruitment did not raise the question of rewarding the 'martial races' for the extra loss of life and blood in World War I. This moral obligation on the part of the government was the weakest point in the progressives' argument. In their demand for commissions, the representatives of the 'non-martial races' stressed the unity of the Indian nation, and denied the strictness of the division between classes. They argued that the 'non-martial classes', had as much suitable officer material as the 'martial classes', untapped and waiting to be used, and that officer commissions required skills for which birth was irrelevant. Both the traditionalists and gradualists could base their arguments on army efficiency.

When the Government of India and the Commander-in-Chief accepted the Sivaswamy Aiyer resolutions, they committed themselves to their implementation. Severe obstacles to this implementation developed on both political and administrative levels: neither the British government nor the British officers in the Indian Army were happy with it. We shall not examine the administrative problems raised by Indianization here, but we will discuss the political objections.

Commander-in-Chief Rawlinson formed a military committee to implement the Indianization resolutions passed by the Legislative Assembly.[61] The committee proposed an immediate statement of intention to Indianize, and a policy of progressive Indian self-reliance in defence matters, including the eventual replacement of British by Indian officers. In addition, it recommended that recruitment be broadened to include youths from the 'new' India: professional and middle-class families were to be eligible, and were to be inducted into all branches of the army.

These proposals—which merely detailed a resolution already accepted by the Government of India—were not satisfactory to the Home government. An alternative to the Rawlinson proposals was suggested by the Secretary in the Military Department of the India Office, Lieutenant General Alexander Cobbe, and later supported by the Secretary of State for India, Viscount Peel.[62]

Cobbe revived all the stock arguments for restricting commissions: a large influx of Indians into the officer corps would have a 'detrimental' effect on the 'efficiency of the military machine'. As proof, he cited incidents during World War I when Indian troops, deprived of their British leadership, showed a tendency to deteriorate seriously and quickly ... few, if any, Indians apparently having the natural aptitude for leadership possessed by the average Englishman'. He neglected to point out that various Western armies had fared equally poorly after losing their officers, and that much of the French Army had, in fact, at one point mutinied. Cobbe believed that the social structure of India would never permit a suitable combination of indigenous troops and officers:

> It is an unfortunate fact that the fighting races of India, from which the Indian Army is recruited, are the very classes who are most backward as regards education, and on the other hand those classes whose educational qualifications are the highest are generally regarded as lacking in martial qualities.[63]

Cobbe argued that Indianization must proceed with great caution, and that Indians should not be given the King's commission. Instead, Indian officers might be limited to a few units or, better still, confined to a dominion force, composed of retired troops, with a British commander. British officers would be allowed to volunteer for this force, which would gradually replace the regular Indian Army. This plan would permit Indians to serve as officers and would avoid the embarrassment of Indians serving alongside British officers or, even worse, Indians commanding the few British ranks found in some units of the Indian Army.

The Cobbe scheme was received with dismay by the Government of India. The Viceroy, Lord Reading, replied by telegraph that the Rawlinson plan had in effect been accepted publicly by the Government of India. Indian opinion would not tolerate any backsliding on the Indianization issue, which the Viceroy called 'the crucial test of our sincerity in the policy of fitting India to advance towards the goal of self-government'.[64]

This exchange—marked by the difference in perspective and priorities which so often characterized Home and Indian correspondence—was resolved in favour of the Viceroy. The idea of a dominion force was abandoned, and eight units were earmarked for the Indianization 'experiment'. The government had earlier partly fulfilled one resolution and established the Prince of Wales Royal Indian Military College in 1922. This was not in fact a college, but a pre-Sandhurst institution run along the lines of an English public school.[65]

The Indians were temporarily satisfied with these schemes. Preference was clearly to be given to youths from the 'martial classes', but 'non-martial groups' were eligible for commissions as well. However, Indians who were attentive to defence policy matters soon realized that there were serious flaws in Rawlinson's 'eight-unit scheme'.

To the members of the 'martial classes' military service was more than a prestigious occupation—it bordered on a moral obligation, and might also have been a path for religious fulfilment. Furthermore, the attitudes that we have characterized as traditional militarism permeated several levels of the 'martial regions': lower castes tended to emulate the 'martial' posture of higher castes. As these castes became socially mobile, they sought places within the military on the basis of real or contrived martial traditions.

Under the Raj, the spokesmen for the 'martial classes' had a powerful instrument of leverage: their loyalty and cooperation was vital if recruitment were to proceed smoothly and if the sepoys were to remain loyal. The spokesmen did not need to threaten non-cooperation to obtain concessions from the government. The government willingly reserved places in the officer corps for their sons. The implied threat of non-cooperation still exists to a lesser degree today —the bulk of India's and Pakistan's armies are still recruited from the 'martial classes'. Electoral politics have enabled representatives of regional martial classes—whatever political party they belong to—to press their demands and resist broadened recruitment at the highest levels of government.

The other set of attitudes discussed in this essay—the instrumental gradualism—also persisted to the last decades of the British Raj, and in a modified form still exists today. Three men whose careers overlapped formed the core of this attitude: P. S. Sivaswamy Aiyer, Motilal Nehru, and H. N. Kunzru. Kunzru is still active, productive, and interested in military matters, despite his advanced age. Others were almost as active: Mohammed Ali Jinnah (in the earlier years of his career), Nirad C. Chaudhuri, Umar Hayat Khan, M. S. Moonje, Amarnatha Jha of Allahabad University, and a handful more. Some of these men were occasionally taken into the confidence of the government, allowed to examine classified documents, and generally treated with great respect, for they were in most cases highly regarded by the British for their knowledge. Some of them, particularly Motilal Nehru, were politically influential. Over the years, a small pool of expertise was built up outside of the official circles of government and yet not closely linked with the vigorous elements of the nationalist movement. These men were on occasion able to mount knowledgeable attacks upon government policy, and because these attacks were well informed, they were particularly embarrassing for the government. This group further provided an important link between the British-dominated Government of India and the nationalist movement. The relatively loyal opposition of these gradualists to the British may have been scorned by the more militant nationalists, but their presence continually reminded the British that there were indeed 'reasonable' Indians, and that compromise was necessary to maintain the fading power of the gradualists. Compromises in the area of military affairs—especially Indianization—may have appeared insignificant, but they did result in the creation of a small but well-trained contingent of Indian officers. Although few in number, they were able to replace the British with little loss of administrative efficiency.

Two institutions established by the British enabled the two sets of attitudes to the military to survive. The Legislative Assembly provided a haven for the loyal moderates. There they were treated with deference and respect, and their suggestions on military matters were politely received—if not always acted upon. As the nationalist movement grew, however, the power of the moderates rapidly dwindled, and they spoke with growing bitterness as the years passed. Kunzru was clearly frustrated and even angered in his role in the ill-fated Indianization Commission of 1939.

The Indian Army itself was the second institution and the stronghold of the traditional militarists. With its links to the Indian countryside and its own fertile recruiting grounds, it was a vehicle for the expression of grievances and the instrument for the fulfilment of growing aspirations among the recruited classes. The army protected the interests of these classes, who reciprocated with an almost unbroken record of loyal, competent service. When this link was partly broken in World War II, the effect was shattering to both parties.

A strong tie had been forged. The army in India was permanently linked to the state. The state protected and provided for the military sectors of Indian society, and the army was left free to perform its prime functions of defence and internal security. Allegiance to the army meant permanent allegiance to the state and the idea of a state. Ironically, the British grossly underestimated the desire on the part of Indians from 'non-martial' as well as 'martial' classes to commit themselves to this relationship.

NOTES

1. See Alfred Vagts, *A History of Militarism,* rev. edn, New York: 1959, and especially, Hans Speier, *Social Order and the Risks of War,* New York: 1952, pp. 230ff.
2. B. B. Misra, *The Indian Middle Classes,* New York: 1961.
3. See Speier, p. 231.
4. See Stephen P. Cohen, 'The Untouchable Soldier: Caste, Politics and the Indian Army', *Journal of Asian Studies,* 28(3), May 1969, for further data on this caste.
5. See Sir Patrick Cadell, *History of the Bombay Army,* London: 1938, and Lieutenant Colonel Tugwell, *History of the Bombay Pioneers,* London: 1938, Appendix 2.
6. Dhananjay Keer, *Dr. Ambedkar: Life and Mission,* 2nd rev. edn, Bombay: 1962, pp. 11–12.
7. Tugwell, *Bombay Pioneers.*
8. Reproduced in H. N. Navalkar, *The Life of Shivaram Janba Kamble,* Poona: 1930, pp. 142–57. I am grateful to Eleanor Zelliot for this reference.
9. *Proceedings of the Seventh Indian National* Congress, Nagpur: December 1891.
10. See the speeches of the mover, C. V. S. Narasimha Raju of Vizagapatnam, and of Prakasa Rao.
11. This demand was pressed through the Indian Army itself (which had strong links to the Indian countryside because of its recruiting apparatus) and later through caste associations and 'front' organizations such as the Anjuman-i-Islah-i-Rajputan-i-Hind (All-India Rajput Conference). The Anjuman enjoyed the official patronage of the commander-in-chief, Punjab officialdom, and other high British officials. See *Papers Relating to Constitutional Reforms in India,* Calcutta: 1908, vol. III, 1465.
12. Lieutenant Colonel John Briggs , Madras Army, *Letter to the Rt. Hon. Sir John Hobhouse, Bart., President of the India Board,* privately printed: 1836, p. 38. Copy in India Office Library.
13. *Essays, Military and Political,* London: 1859, pp. 24, 276.
14. Sir George Chesney, *Indian Polity,* 2nd edn, London: 1870, p. 353.
15. The cadet corps was a military parallel to the Statutory Civil Service. It was also designed for the younger sons of princes and nobles. But 'no one can make people give equal esteem to a service for where there are not sufficient candidates and to another of men picked by keen examination'. Philip Woodruff, *The Men Who Ruled India,* vol. II: *The Guardians*; reprint of 1954 edn; London: 1963, p. 167.
16. *Lord Curzon's Memorandum on Commissions for Indians,* 4 June 1900, Bengal Military Letters and Enclosures, vol. 639, enclosure to Letter

no. 103 of July 1900, *India Office Library*; reprinted in C. H. Philips (ed.), *The Evolution of India and Pakistan, 1858-1947*, London: 1962, p. 518.

17. Ibid., p. 521.
18. *Proceedings of the First Indian National Congress*, Bombay: October 1885, pp. 52ff.
19. Ibid.
20. The concern over the defence budget was shared by the Government of India. See Mishra, *Indian Middle Classes*, p. 363
21. *Proceedings of the Second Indian National* Congress, Calcutta: December 1886, p. 93.
22. *Proceedings of the Fourth Indian National Congress*, Allahabad: December 1888.
23. Sir Edward Blunt, *The I.C.S.: The Indian Civil Service*, London: 1937, pp. 53ff.
24. Printed in G.K. Gokhale, *Speeches*, Madras: 1909?.
25. Speech on the Budget, 1906, Gokhale, *Speeches*, p. 174.
26. *The Oxford History of India*, Oxford: 1958, p. 779.
27. Brig. Rajendra Singh, *History of the Indian Army*, New Delhi: 1963, pp. 121ff.
28 These figures are from the official but unpublished history of recruitment during World War I: *Recruiting in India Before and During the War of 1914*–1918, Army H.Q., India, October 1919, Appendix 9. The volume used is in the Archives of the Ministry of Defence, Government of India.
29. Ibid., Appendix 13.
30. Ibid., p. 16..
31. Ibid.
32. For the government view of Sikh unrest, see Major A. E. Barstow, *Sikhs*, Calcutta: 1928. This volume is one in a series of Handbooks on the Indian Army prepared for all classes.
33. The *Kotaga Maru* was a Japanese steamer chartered by 376 immigrants for a voyage to Canada. All but 30 were Sikhs. Upon arrival, they were refused permission to land although they fulfilled the extraordinarily rigorous requirements set by the Canadian government. After considerable hardship and two months in Canadian waters, they returned to India. Upon arrival (in late September, 1914), they were forced to proceed back to the Punjab. Some Sikhs refused, and in a police firing, 21 were killed. The rest were handcuffed and shipped to the Punjab by rail. This incident presaged a considerable flow of returning immigrants. Khushwant Singh, *The Sikhs*, London: 1953, pp. 124ff.
34. Sir Michael O'Dwyer, *War Speeches*, Lahore: 1919, speech of 4 May 1918.
35. Ibid., speech of 17 April 1918.

36. Ibid., speech of 4 May 1918.
37. At the end of World War I, 4,20,000 acres of land were distributed among 5902 VCOs and other ranking Indian officers. Over 14,000 persons received *jangi inams*—special pensions—for two 'lives', i.e., the amount (10 rupees per month for a VCO) was passed on to the next generation. Specially selected VCOs received 200 jagirs. These jagirs included: (a) grants of land with full proprietary rights, yielding a net annual income of 400 rupees, and assignment of land revenue for three lives; (b) pensions amounting to 150 rupees upto the third generation, and (c) 200 VCOs were granted honorary KCOs. The KCO received double the ordinary VCO pension upon retirement. One wonders about the economic and social impact of these awards in the Punjab, where most of them were granted. Data from monograph, Bisheswar Prasad (ed.), 'Honours and Awards', Adjutant General's Branch, India and Pakistan: Combined Inter-Services Historical Section, 1947?, on file in the Ministry of Defence, Historical Section Archives, New Delhi.
38. Edmund Candler, *The Sepoy*, London: 1919, pp. 1–2.
39. The quote and evaluation are from the Preliminary Draft Report of the Indianization Committee of 1938–9. The report, in manuscript form, is in File 601/12810/H of the Archives of the Ministry of Defence, Historical Section, Government of India. The Indianization Committee was appointed subsequent to a resolution adopted by the Legislative Assembly on 2 September 1938, calling for a re-examination of the process of Indianization. Although the committee sat, heard testimony, and did preliminary work on its report, its efforts were interrupted and then terminated by the outbreak of war.
40. Reprinted in Philips, *India and Pakistan*, pp. 264-5. For a study of the background and implications of the declaration, see S. R. Mehrotra, 'The Politics Behind the Montagu Declaration of 1917', in C. H. Philips (ed.), *Politics and Society in India*, London: 1963, pp. 71–96.
41. Great Britain, *Report on Indian Constitutional Reforms*, Cd. 9109 (1918), pp. 209–10.
42. Edwin S. Montagu, *An Indian Diary*, Venetia Montagu (ed.), London: 1930, pp. 201, 352ff.
43. Cariappa graduated from Daly College, Indore. He was one of 39 cadets given the King's Commission in December 1919. Cariappa was from a 'martial class', (a Kodava from Coorg) which had supplied a few troops to the army. He was the first Indian graduate of Staff College (Quetta), the first to hold a Grade II appointment, and the first Indian battalion commander. A later commander-in-chief, General K. S. Thimayya was a cousin of, Cariappa. Another Coorgi, Cheppudira Ponnappa, retired as a brigadier in 1951. For details about Cariappa's life, see I. M. Muthanna, *General* Cariappa, Mysore: 1964.

44. During 1918-26 only 243 Indians competed for the 83 positions at Sandhurst. The Skeen Committee calculated that the dropout rate of Indians was 30 per cent compared with only 3 per cent for Britishers. Indian Sandhurst Committee, *Report*, 14 November 1926, Calcutta: 1927.
45. Speech of Lord Birdwood. India Legislative Assembly, *Debates*, vol. II (1928), 8 March 1928.
46. For specific figures by year and class, see *Recruiting in India*, and *The Army in India and its Evolution*, Calcutta: 1924, various appendices.
47. For a discussion of this question, see Stanislaw Andrzejewski, *Military Organization and Society*, London: 1954. Also, Marion J. Levy, Jr., *Modernization and the Structure of Societies*, Princeton: 1966, vol. II, 600–1.
48. *Report of the Committee to inquire into the Administration and Organization of the Army in India.* Cmd. 943, 1920 [The Esher Committee].
49. Ibid., p. 103.
50. Ibid., p. 101.
51. A leading moderate from Madras who maintained a consistent interest in military affairs for many years.
52. India, Legislative Assembly, *Debates*, vol. I, part 2 (1921), 28 March 1921.
53. Ibid., p. 1739.
54. Ibid.
55. Ibid., p. 1753.
56. Ibid., p. 1754.
57. Ibid.
58. Ibid., p. 1742.
59. Ibid., p. 1743.
60. Ibid., p. 1746.
61. The activities of Rawlinson's Military Requirements Committee are recorded in: Government of India, Army Dept., Proceedings, December 1923, nos 85–111, subject: Indianization of the Indian Army, Ministry of Defence, Historical Section, Archives, file 601/10798/H.
62. Ibid., Cobbe Memorandum, 14 September 1921, and telegram, 29 November 1921, Secretary of State to Viceroy.
63. Ibid., Cobbe Memorandum.
64. Ibid., Viceroy to Secretary of State, India, 18 February 1922.
65. The British believed that a public school education in India was an absolute requirement for becoming an army officer if an education in Britain was impossible. This belief was paralleled by similar beliefs in regard to the ICS and the colonial service. The British believed a public-school education particularly necessary for Indian boys whose upbringing had made them unsuitable for the rigours and self-discipline of army life. This belief was shared by Indians, and has been put into practice both in India and Pakistan—the RIMC (Royal Indian Military

College) has been renamed Rashtriya (National) Indian Military College, and is the military-oriented public-school equivalent of the nearby Doon School. For a study of the public school in the colonial service see Robert Heussler, *Yesterday's Rulers*, Syracuse: 1963.

6

Contested Identities and Military Indianization in Colonial India (1900–39)*

Anirudh Deshpande

Introduction

Military Indianization was the commissioning of Indians in the British-Indian Armed Forces as King's Commissioned Officers (KCO).[1] This article does not claim to present and analyse all the views on Indianization, some of which, in certain forms, date from the early nineteenth century. For practical purposes, genuine Indianization after the Great War (1914–18) would have implied the recruitment of Indian officers as KCOs in the Indian armed forces and the *accelerated replacement* of costly British officers with Indian officers. This paper is influenced by the fact that the Great War was a watershed in the Indianization debate and created the historical potential for real Indianization. However, this potential remained unexploited for reasons outlined below. It was in the 1920s that the colonial military discourse in India found its most systematic and resolute opponent in the vehement nationalist demand for Indianization. British schemes of Indianization before the Great War, such as the Imperial Cadet Corps (ICC) created by Lord Curzon, had been designed for ceremonial and symbolic purposes. In the omnipresent colonial quest for loyalty, and in accordance with what the British considered

* First published in *Contemporary India*, 1(1), January–March 2002, pp. 99–131.

A draft of this paper received the Partha Sarathi Gupta Award in the Modern India and Countries Other than India Section at the Indian History Congress, Kolkata, 2–5 January 2001.

'martial' in India, these schemes served a limited number of Anglicized Indian aristocrats who were fond of, and obviously impressed by, a lifestyle involving uniforms, parades, polo, and shikar.[2]

After the Great War, the British seriously considered the possibility of developing Commissioned Officers (COs) from the ranks of the Viceroy's Commissioned Officers (VCOs), most of whom belonged to the agrarian 'martial races'. This contrasted with the earlier attempts to recruit a limited number of aristocratic Indians as officers. British thinking remained preoccupied with the 'martial races' throughout the Indianization debate in response to the issues raised by the politicized Indian middle class. After the Mutiny of 1857, the British had gradually evolved the theory of the 'martial races' hand in hand with the Punjabization of the Indian Army to pursue their military and political interests in India. At the turn of the century, the theory of the 'martial race' had become an almost unshakeable orthodoxy in the higher ranks of the colonial military establishment. Since this theory was considered essential for the successful functioning of the professional and largely non-political Indian Army, any attempt to undermine it was perceived by the British an attack on the guarantee of their Indian Empire. Hence, Indianization of the Indian Army appeared to signal the beginning of the end of British rule in India for the vast majority of British officials and public.

On the other hand, Indianizing the Indian Army—sustained by Indian revenues as it was—was an essential element of the discourse of self-government preferred by a significant number of prominent Indians after the Great War. On both sides of the debate, the question of national and social identities was considered important. The British resistance to Indianization was predicated upon the rigid colonial classification of Indians into 'martial' and 'non-martial' groups. This semi-historical classification had been slowly and carefully cultivated after the Mutiny of 1857.[3] In contrast, and in opposition to the pseudo-scientific colonial discourse on the subject, much of the Indian opinion on Indianization represented a 'subaltern' attempt to fashion, and even historically reclaim, identities denied to the colonial subjects by their foreign masters.

INDIANIZATION, 1905–25

Significant aspects of Indian military history between the two World Wars were most certainly influenced by Indian opinion. Politically-articulate Indians began to pressurize the Government of India

(GOI) on matters of military reform soon after 1918, primarily because they had supported Britain during the Great War. This demand for reform was predicated upon popular Indian hopes aroused by the colonial war effort. Furthermore, as part of a broader agenda, the Indians highlighted the role of military reform in a scheme of self-government promised to India during the War. But the Indianization issue was older. Commissioning selected Indians was discussed in Calcutta at a conference held immediately after the Imperial Durbar in 1911. In it, Sir Horace Smith Dorrien, representing the War Office, had categorically stated that Indians had to be trained at Sandhurst to be granted the KC. By implication, it was emphasized that training in India would produce inferior officers and thereby strengthen racial prejudice in the army. A course at Sandhurst, in comparison, was held capable of ushering in some equality between Indian and British subalterns to begin with. It was the fond hope of paternalists such as Smith that, after training at Sandhurst, Indian subalterns—like their counterparts in the Anglicized Indian Civil Services (ICS)—would start 'their regimental careers with the manners and ideals of English gentlemen'.[4]

This was easier said than done. To the War Office, the House of Commons, and the British Officers of the Indian Army, Indianization was anathema for obvious reasons. The matter was considered so 'delicate and risky' that the War Office's opinion on granting commissions even to the sons of Indian princes was described by Morley as 'hopelessly narrow'. Morley confessed to Hardinge that the War Office did not 'comprehend the nature and content of the demand for a career of useful activity in the Native Army' and therefore its suggestion on the matter were 'sure to be hopelessly wide of the mark'.[5] It was true that in 1905 a symbolic commission for Indian aristocrats and 'gentlemen' had been conceded in His Majesty's Native Indian Land Forces. This inferior commission, authorizing command only over Indian troops, was not fodder enough for an ambitious Indian middle class.[6] By 1911 the War Office, with great reluctance and the approval of the King and Viceroy, had agreed to grant a KC in special cases to a Sandhurst-returned Indian of 'high rank' in the ceremonial Household Cavalry. However, as Hardinge pointed out to Morley, this was not what the Indians wanted.[7] The Viceroy knew that giving commissions in the Household Cavalry was 'no solution at all' to a serious problem which was becoming politicized: 'It is a question that will certainly become acute before very long unless something is done to satisfy the aspirations of these younger men, and I think that the nettle should be grasped at once and the movement held in check before it becomes too powerful.'[8]

Regarding the opposition to Indianization amongst British officers, Montagu expressed reformist views even before the Great War ended. British soldiers and officers disliked the idea of serving under Indians. This militated against the times. If Britons could be subordinated to Indians in the Civil Service, according to Montagu, 'it was ridiculous to think that soldiers could maintain out of date privileges'. Montagu was aware of the obstacles in the path to Indianization. But, in his considered view, reform had to prevail over racial prejudice in keeping with the changing times. The Indianization experiment had to be 'inevitably tried' even in 'a certain atmosphere of prejudice' because soldiers were not the most liberal-minded of men. Moreover, there were other problems waiting to surface, because added to the ideological burden of the previous century was the fear of ragging at Sandhurst. After all, if Indians were selected for commissions, it was important to make them comfortable; otherwise the British would be saddled with the charge of scuttling the scheme in the beginning. Hence the Viceroy was asked to explore avenues of granting commissions to Indians in India.[9] This implied the eventual establishment of a military college in India fashioned after Sandhurst.

The wartime promise of Indianization justified the Indians who launched a strident campaign for it in the Legislative Assembly soon after 1918. Earlier, on 20 August 1917, while Indian regiments raised with the help of Gandhi and Tilak were fighting for Britain, the Secretary of State announced in the Commons that the 'gradual development of self-governing institutions with a view to the progressive realization of responsible Government in India' would be encouraged by all means after the War.[10] This reformism was also reflected in the Montagu-Chelmsford Report, which discerned in India 'an ever growing discontent with [administrative] measures which were resented as evidence of racial discrimination'. Prominent among these was the exclusion of Indians from the commissioned ranks in the army:

> Indian officers form a separate establishment from the British officers, and the highest and the most experienced of the former rank lower than the most junior of the latter .... The services of the Indian army in the war, and the great increase in its numbers make it necessary that a considerable number of commissions should now be given.[11]

In 1918, the Royal Military College in Sandhurst was totally dominated by the British. Sandhurst training was necessary for acquiring the King's Commission in the Indian Army. But the realization that setting up 'a military training school in India' might 'be desirable' in future to satisfy the Indians was growing. Due to the influence of the widely publicized Montagu-Chelmsford declarations, 10 vacancies per annum were reserved for Indians at Sandhurst. However, the sources admit, this was 'more a gesture than the inauguration of a policy'.[12] And this gesture predictably failed to satisfy the Indians, who soon started demanding substantial concessions. In March 1921, under growing Indian pressure, the Legislative Assembly adopted a crucial resolution on the matter, moved actually by the government.[13] According to this resolution, all arms of the Indian services were to be opened to Indian commissioned officers *in the near future*. Further, unofficial Indians were to assist the authority which would nominate Indians to an entrance exam for admission to a training school producing Indian commissioned officers *in India*. In the beginning, 25 per cent of all the commissions granted per year were to be given to Indians and the pay of *all commissioned ranks* was to be set on an Indian basis to counter the serious charge of racial discrimination. In addition, adequate facilities were to be created soon for the preliminary training of Indians selected for Sandhurst, and steps would be taken to finally establish a military college in India on the lines of Sandhurst. The Indians were later supported by the 'far-reaching recommendations' of the Report of the Military Requirements Committee (1921), which advocated gradual Indianization based on the development of military education in India.[14] It held that since dominions such as Australia and Canada had their own military colleges, it was only fair that India, with a large standing army, should ultimately establish a college to produce officers economically. Furthermore, since middle-class Indians would, in all probability, be admitted to the Indian services, Indianization appeared to their leaders the 'natural corollary' of self-government in India.[15]

It would have been extremely embarrassing for the GOI to ignore the Assembly Resolution of 1921. Hence it was left with no choice but to frame provisional plans for Indianization. Evidence clearly proves that men such as Montagu were rare and on their own, the British would *never* have taken Indianization seriously. The credit for putting Indianization on the post-Great War reform agenda goes to those Indians who fought for it in the 1920s. After the resolution of 1921 was accepted by the GOI, two Indianization plans were drafted by the army, whereas the third was produced by the Shea Committee appointed by the GOI for the purpose.[16] Let us first look at Gail Wigram's paper on Indianization, placed before the GOI in 1921.

Wigram pointed out that Indianization was the most vital part of British policy in India after the Great War, and the friendship between the GOI and influential Indians depended on it. Expressing the worries of the Indian armed forces, he also assumed that military reform would enable the Indian taxpayers to 'shoulder the burden of high military expenditure more cheerfully and willingly'.[17] Nonetheless, it was difficult to grant the KC to Indians in an army wedded to traditions and favoured classes. Indianization also raised the problem of finding suitable Indians for higher military training. The issue was serious because, firstly, the Indian politicians were demanding the establishment of an 'Indian Sandhurst' in the *near future*; and, secondly, they expected the rate of granting commissions to Indians to *accelerate*. Commissions were being demanded in all the services, including the artillery—which, following the policy dictated by the rebellion of 1857, was controlled by the British. The issue was delicate, because the transformation of the Indian Army and substantial Indianization in the context of mass nationalism could have meant the end of British rule in India. Nonetheless, it had to be undertaken with minimum damage to British interests in India in the given political context.[18]

The best way of doing so was to first rationalize theory on the basis of age-old stereotypes. Keeping this in mind, Wigram repeated the assertion that during the Great War the subedars and jamadars had demonstrated their dependence on British officers for initiative and leadership. The British officer possessed important public-school attributes. He knew how to 'play for the side' with a 'sense of duty'. Indians, in contrast, were found 'noticeably deficient' in this public spirit.[19] Thus it was implied that large-scale Indianization carried the risk of military inefficiency. The solution to this was to be found in the Unit Scheme. Under this scheme, the army would be Indianized unit by unit, with the Indianized units ultimately comprising a Dominion Army. Indians would receive a Dominion Commission, instead of the KC, and gradually this Dominion Army would expand into a sort of national army of India. Since Indianization 'would do more to drive India out of the Empire than anything else', slowing down the reform process was essential to British interests.[20] The merits and demerits of this unrealistic proposal notwithstanding, the Indians, who wanted to eliminate British officers from the Indian Army as quickly and economically as possible, would have opposed this scheme.

In 1921, another scheme based on the assumption that Indians were racially and socially inferior to the British was proposed by Lt. Gen. Cobbe (Secretary, Military Department, India Office, Whitehall). Cobbe knew very well that British officers and men hated even the idea of taking orders from Indians and this, according to him, *could be interpreted* by Indians as racial discrimination. The British, however, were apparently justified in thinking so because in the army, as elsewhere, they generally considered Indians inferior. Expanding upon the dangers of Indianization, Cobbe stated that it would diminish the supply of British officers to the Indian Army and thereby make it inefficient. Furthermore, the likelihood of friction arising between the Indian and British officers made their permanent coexistence in units a bad idea. These adventurous experiments would weaken the army and undermine the security of British rule in India in the ultimate analysis. Instead, a defence of British politeness lay in devising a policy designed to satisfy Indian opinion without unduly disturbing British officers. And this could only be done by dividing the Indian Army into a Dominion Army and an Indian Army. In the beginning, a brigade would be Indianized and the number of British officers in it would gradually decrease. Finally, somewhere in the not-so-near future, more Indianized brigades would form the Dominion Army to replace the Indian Army in a self-governing India.[21] Cobbe's plan, it is easy to see, was similar to the Unit Scheme suggested by Wigram.

While the Dominion Army plan was being examined by a sub-committee of the Imperial Defence Committee, the Shea Committee appointed by the GOI went about the business of examining Indianization.[22] Opposing the Dominion Army concept on economic and moral grounds, it concluded in favour of a careful transition *within* the Indian Army. In its opinion, Indianization had to start slowly, but ultimately Indian officers would have to be appointed to units irrespective of their class composition. Firstly, Indianization would begin in certain carefully-selected infantry and cavalry regiments of the army with the intention of subjecting the Indian subalterns to the toughest conditions prevalent in the army. This, it was assumed, would satisfy the advocates of Indianization.[23] Later the ancillary services, such as supplies etc., would be Indianized. In the interest of military and political stability—and the unmentioned British vested interests in the Indian Army—the number of Indians would increase very slowly in proportion to British officers. The carefully worded conclusion of the Shea scheme militated against the *acceleration* of Indianization desired by the Indians. It was also not free of the racist bias evident in the submissions of Wigram and Cobbe examined above. Indianization was conceived by the Shea Committee as the means for 'ensuring the steady organic growth *of units* in which capacity for *command by and of subordination to members of their own race* shall become inherent in Indian officers and soldiers'[24] (emphasis added).

Arguing along the lines taken by the Esher Committee, the Shea Committee recommended using the class of the largely rural VCOs as a potential source of Indian KCOs.[25] Since there was little to prove that middle-class and educated Indians made good officers, Indianization had to secure 'the good-will and interests' of the 'fine body of Indian officers of the existing type'. Hence, following the conservative approach favoured by British military policy in India, the Shea recommendations were 'framed with a view to securing to the Army a continuance of the services of Indian officers already serving and of, ensuring an adequate future supply of officers from the same sources'.[26] The Shea scheme of complete Indianization envisaged a process spread over 42 years, in three stages of 14 years each. The scheme also envisaged the establishment of an Indian military college to produce Indian commissioned officers. After 42 years, according to the Shea Committee, 21 cavalry regiments, 4 pioneer and 94 infantry battalions, 20 artillery batteries, and 33 engineering units would stand completely Indianized. This effort would require 5464 officers at a wastage rate of 3.5 per cent per annum throughout the period. The scheme, beginning in 1925, was supposed to end in 1967. The annually desired output from the Indian military college would be 111 officers from 1925 to 1938. In the third stage, the number of cadets enrolled at the Indian College, which would open and replace Sandhurst from 1925 onwards, would reach its peak. On reconsideration, probably because the year 1967 appeared distant even in the official visions of decolonization, a revised 30 year schedule was suggested by the Committee.[27] Despite all its faults, some credit must be given to the Shea Committee for suggesting a time frame and rate of Indianization for the first time. However, as we shall see, by clearly mentioning the setting up of an 'Indian Sandhurst', it played into the hands of the Indians perhaps a trifle unwittingly.

While the Shea Committee thrashed out the details of Indianization, the Viceroy sent a resume of its lines of inquiry to the Secretary of State, stating that since the matter was of 'great importance and perplexity', he wanted the Sub-Committee of the Imperial Defence Committee, to consider the direction which Shea was taking. Cobbe's plan, which would most probably have necessitated extra expenditure on a Dominion Army, was rejected by the GOI because of the problems the military budget was raising in India.[28] A revealing and highly discursive correspondence between the GOI and London followed.

Whitehall was unhappy with the GOI's objections to Cobbe and desired more knowledge of its position on the matter. Even the economic arguments failed to convince the British government. By November 1921, and obviously to accommodate the Home government, General Rawlinson had, in fact, formulated a Unit Scheme on the basis of the Shea findings. Now the Secretary of State wanted to know why the Unit Scheme was considered economical by the GOI. The Viceroy, reiterating the bias inherent in Cobbe's plan, explained the Indian position further. Cobbe had sponsored an untrustworthy brigade which was 'useless' from a 'military point of view'. Moreover, Indian opinion and the budget inveighed against the measure. Compared with this, Rawlinson's scheme appeared practical and would give Indians a chance to work under British officers without unduly harming their interests. Furthermore, the Viceroy assumed, the Unit Scheme would satisfy the Indians in a way by suggesting a time frame of Indianization desired by them.[29] However, he forgot to add that Indian opinion was not necessarily reconciled to the Unit Scheme, and ultimately, his assumptions were challenged by the Indians. Events soon proved that merely suggesting a time frame was not enough to deter Indian opposition to the official schemes of Indianization.

The Viceroy failed to convince the Secretary of State, who asserted—somewhat ironically—that the Dominion Army would engender esprit de corps among Indians due to the sense of *nationalism* and *patriotism* inherent in it. Furthermore, the rising efficiency in the Dominion Army would eliminate the risk of letting Indian officers command Britons. But the Viceroy remained categorical in pointing out that Indian pressures and the legislature did not favour increases in military spending. Simultaneously, the demand for Indianization was growing and the press was criticizing the GOI's excessive military spending. In such trying times, a besieged satrap could only refer to the 'grave embarrassment' a deficit of 40 crore rupees was causing to his government.[30] The post-Great War financial condition of the GOI was actually quite serious. Although British India had decided to maintain peace with Afghanistan, and some troops were being retrenched on the advice of the Military Requirements Committee, widespread civil disobedience in India put the brakes on large-scale retrenchment in 1921. The government, facing the largest civilian unrest in its history, nonetheless expressed the hope of 'seriously weakening' the 'pernicious agitation' to win some respite in future. But, it was understood, in the near future the Raj would be forced to deliver a 'severe blow' to a movement which was threatening the roots of British rule in India.[31] Indianization, as part of this counter-nationalist strategy, had to be politically, socially, and economically safe.

London responded with a terse and imperious definition of reform. The outpost was asked to remain vigilant because the announcement of reforms could not be interpreted to mean that the British were even remotely thinking of retreating from India: 'Such an idea, if it exists, is a complete fallacy and its continuous existence can only lead to intensified challenges to our authority and to a decline in morale among the services.' British authority had to prevail at all costs because only a peaceful, loyal, and successful working of reforms would lead to self-government. Indianization could be promised, conceived of, and put into practice keeping this in mind. Extreme caution in military matters and unwavering fidelity to tradition were the touchstones of British military policy in India. The historical continuities governing the Indian services since the previous century could not be overlooked in a fit of enthusiasm for the cause of political India produced by the War. In sum, therefore, and at best, the Imperial government was only willing to tolerate a compromise between the schemes of Indianization present before the GOI. In keeping with these imperatives of British rule in India, only four battalions could be selected initially for an Indianization experimental.[32] Wartime promises made to the Indians were to be shelved for the time being.

The Viceroy did not accept this sermon happily. The British Government, he quickly rejoined, had misconstrued the intentions of his government which were based, in fact, on Imperial policy declarations. The Raj, as the experience of British rule in India showed, also had to be benevolent to survive:

> We find ourselves therefore entirely unable either to comprehend or subscribe to the position that the acceptance of a practicable programme, which has been prepared by our own military advisers, can be interpreted as implying a concession to a suggested policy of retreat from India.[33]

Indian opinion on army reform had to be placated or else the GOI faced the danger of losing more allies in India. In March 1921, the Central Legislative Assembly had passed a resolution saying that in future 25 per cent of all officer recruits per year would be Indians. A year later the Indians were demanding substantial concessions and a miserly four-unit scheme would compromise British credibility at a moment when danger was pressing from below. Since the GOI needed collaborators in its effort to overcome the Gandhi-led Non-Cooperation Movement, permission was sought to urgently proclaim a broader scheme as soon as possible. But these entreaties fell on deaf ears. In response, Whitehall remained quiescent. 'If pressed, your argument would be that policy be dictated by dissent,' answered the Secretary of State. The Imperial government, the Secretary made it quite clear, was 'not prepared to commit' itself 'to a particular programme of Indianization' until the loyalty and efficiency of Indian officers was proven. Initiatives could be sanctioned but substantial Indianization would depend only on their results. New experiments were welcome and even the number of Indianizing units could be increased, but Indians were not to be commissioned just because they were Indians:

> It is, we are convinced, just as wrong in the interests of Indian development to give inefficient Indians opportunities the results of use of which will discredit their country as it is to deny efficient Indians the opportunity of serving their country with credit.[34]

For much of 1922, discussions continued between Delhi and London on features of the scheme to be finally announced. In the summer of 1922, the Viceroy dispatched the summary of the Eight Unit Scheme to the India Office stating that four units would be 'nugatory' and even eight units was a 'narrow basis' to begin with. Permission was needed to announce the Eight Unit Scheme in the Assembly as the beginning of total Indianization of the army.[35] The salient features of the Eight Unit Scheme were provided by Rawlinson, the Commander-in-Chief in India, and an avowed opponent of Indianization. From 1923, Indian KCOs would be appointed to the selected Eight Units as Squadron or Company Officers at par with British Officers of the same age and rank. From 1926, only Indian officers would be appointed to these units. It was thought that in the beginning of 1927, all squadron or company officers of these Eight Units would be Indians. After this, promotions would be based on tests, after which the Indians would begin replacing the senior British officers of these units. In the final stages, the Indian KCOs would also start replacing the VCOs. The GOI planned to wait till the eight units were completely Indianized before assessing the scheme. But the scheme was obviously designed to safeguard British interests, and Rawlinson made this much clear to the Shea Committee on 25 January 1922 in the following words: 'However the experiment must be made and all we can do is to give it every possible assistance whilst at the same time preserving the *vested interests* of the British officers in the Indian Army'.[36] (emphasis added).

An extremely modest programme of Indianization would have discouraged Indians from preparing for an army career, and 10 vacancies at Sandhurst were not enough to satisfy them. The possibility that the VCOs in the Indianizing units would be threatened when Indian officers started replacing them could not be ruled out. This would also cause discontent both in the more or less loyal VCOs as well as the Indian KCOs being demoted in comparison with their British counterparts.[37] The Unit Scheme proved unpopular with the Indians although the units chosen represented a cross-section of the Indian Army. But that made no difference to the charge of 'segregation' levelled against the scheme by the Indians. The pace of Indianization calculated for these units was so slow that it would have taken them roughly 22 years to become totally Indianized, and that too after the replacement of the VCOs by young Indian KCOs starting their careers lower down compared with British officers posted in other units. The scheme was not destined to last that long, thanks to World War II. By 1926–7, as the supply and frustration of Indian officers grew, growing Indian allegations of 'segregation' and service discrimination necessitated a review of Indianization.[38] In the meantime, the Unit Scheme inadvertently enhanced the reputation of Indian officers despite British intentions to the contrary.[39]

Indians had always maintained that Indianization would ultimately be decided by the development of military education in India. Hence, while the Eight Units were being tried, they began to focus on the creation of an 'Indian Sandhurst', which had also been mentioned by the Shea Committee. In December 1924, the Assembly accepted a resolution proposing the establishment of an 'Indian Sandhurst' moved by Venkatapatiraju.[40] Having conceded Eight Units, the government on its part tried its best to slow down the reform process. Hence it reasserted the shibboleth that since an Indian college would most certainly dampen army efficiency, it was better to train Indians at Sandhurst. Furthermore, an Indian commission would be unacceptable to British personnel who, the GOI stated, would continue to swear by the superiority of the KC. The government also opined that it would be 'monstrously uneconomical' to start a military college in India for only 10 cadets. Here the Commander-in-Chief completely agreed with it. Rawlinson's opposition to an Indian college smacked of racism: 'If I wanted to ensure the failure of the scheme for Indianization I would create an Indian Sandhurst tomorrow.'[41] In fact, this military bluntness left some of the members of the Viceroy's council 'rather disturbed'. Rawlinson also denounced Indianization in the Assembly in the following words:

> One of the first difficulties with which we are confronted is that it is no simple matter to create a national army in India, because India is not a nation.[42]

Coming from the Commander-in-Chief, such abrasiveness went a long way in fortifying Indian opposition to the official schemes of Indianization. In the event, the view that the British were obviously prejudiced against military reform in India gained ground. But Rawlinson's views exemplified the ideology of the establishment to which he and his predecessors, such as Field Marshal Roberts, belonged. These ideas comprised the core of a military discourse fashioned in India by the British since the nineteenth century.

The Skeen Committee: A Borrowing of Perceptions

However, nation or no nation, it did not take very long for the British to realize that the matter was 'quasi-political, quasi-military' and, as usual, some of them wanted a committee to be set up to examine the possibility of opening a Sandhurst-type military college in India. Several officials also believed that it was the government's duty to remove the 'ignorance' and 'prejudice' about the subject. Since the GOI had never rejected the Assembly resolution of March 1921, retreating from it in 1925 would have lowered its credibility further. In the meantime, the Auxiliary and Territorial Force Committee, formed on the advice of Indian members, demonstrated Indian initiative in military matters. But, as events proved, the government still had fight left in it. Afraid of substantial Indianization, it opposed the Indian stand on the subject in the Assembly in February 1925. Although all, Indian non-official members were pressing for an 'Indian Sandhurst', some of them desired more information on the matter before deciding the issue. This division amongst Indians reprieved the government, which noted with pleasure that some of these men were forced 'to acknowledge, in their minds at any rate, that further enquiry and careful constructive work by an expert committee would be required' before an Indian military college was established.[43] For the moment, and to the GOI's relief, more Indianization appeared indefinitely postponed. However, the situation could hardly be misinterpreted to assume that the Indians were diluting, their long-held demand for accelerated Indianization. Leaders such as Jinnah, for instance, believed that serious constitutional advance in India was impossible without complete Indianization of the Indian armed forces.

A crisis was precipitated on 3 March 1925, when Jinnah threatened a vote of censure because the GOI's Indianization policy in the past had been 'disingenuous, dilatory and inadequate'. This was enough to convince the authorities that agitation was 'boiling up' on the issue. Though an 'Indian Sandhurst' was a Cabinet affair, the majority of the Viceroy's Council supported the idea of at least forming a committee to examine the possibility of establishing an 'Indian Sandhurst' in the near or distant future. But pockets of resistance remained. Rawlinson, as usual, preferred a committee of 'limited scope' to collect 'evidence regarding the supply of young officers to the army and the best means of giving them their military education'. This worsened matters, and finally Jinnah's 'guillotine' fell on the government. On 14 March, he forced the home member to commit that the GOI would soon appoint a committee of inquiry to speed up the process of Indianization. Pushed into a corner, as Army Secretary E. Burdon noticed, it became necessary for the GOI 'to put the matter in train'. Consequently the formation of the Skeen Committee was announced in July 1925. The way Jinnah, as a secular nationalist, attacked the Commander-in-Chief in the Assembly in February 1925 is worth remembering:

> You come here with one excuse or another, and you tell us that there is this difficulty and that, that there is this to be done and that to be done .... Has there ever been a proposal which we have suggested which was not rash ... when have you Englishmen ever agreed with us and said that any proposal we make is not rash? You say, 'It is rash, be cautious'. We have been 150 years under this government. You have deprived the people of India of arms. What have you done.[44]

The Skeen Committee (also known as the Indian Sandhurst Committee) was formed to probe the three main and related issues of Indianization. It had to recommend ways of improving the supply of Indians to the commissioned ranks of the Indian Army; it had to decide whether establishing an Indian Sandhurst was a practicable idea. Finally it had to say whether an Indian military college, if opened in the future, would replace Sandhurst as the source of Indian KCOs.

To begin with, and in keeping with nature of its membership, the Skeen Committee criticized the Eight Unit Scheme and the general condition of education in India. But the result of its submissions was not spectacular and the period of Indianization it suggested was not very different from the one mentioned by the Shea Committee's plan. The Skeen Committee opined that the Eight Unit Scheme had neither produced significant results nor generated enthusiasm for Indianization in India. Coming closer to the British position on the matter, it asserted that Indians educated in public schools could make excellent officers. Hence, in its scheme, an 'Indian Sandhurst' would succeed in an education system formed by the spread of public schools, presumably dominated by the Indian middle class. The Committee also wanted the GOI to shoulder the responsibility of developing military education in India as part of general education. This was held up as the primary responsibility of British rule. After all, asserted the Skeen Committee, the culpability of British policy in discouraging the growth of military traditions in many regions of India could hardly be ignored. Since a general 'disarmament of the people' under British rule had diminished the military impulse among the educated Indians, it was the government's duty to develop a 'more comprehensive and widely diffused' military tradition in India. In fact, under Indian influence, the committee ended up calling British policy the 'general root cause' of the ills which plagued military recruitment in India.[45]

The Skeen Committee found educational standards in India quite low compared with the system of elite-dominated public schools prevalent in Britain. These privately owned and run public boarding schools, which catered for various needs of the British bourgeoisie, were widely believed to develop initiative and independence in young boys. Members of the committee visited England to observe this system at close quarters. Some of these members had personal experience of such schools. Not surprisingly, they were extremely impressed with what they saw. Furthermore, publicized European praise of these English schools was harnessed to the argument to make the case of developing public schools in India stronger.

The low publicity of military affairs and opportunities in India and the prohibitive cost of training abroad added to the problems created by insignificant investment in Indian education. The selection of candidates for Sandhurst was so 'rigidly official' that it was found 'seriously objectionable' by many witnesses before the Skeen Committee. In England, special arrangements had been made to promote NCOs to the commissioned ranks, but in India nothing of the sort had been done. The Committee ignored the fact that this may have been done because the British Army had, due to reasons stated by Barnett, become unpopular in the British middle classes in the 1920s. Since Indianization had to depend upon the 'co-operation and good will' of the VCOs of the Indian Army, it was necessary to keep their interests in mind.[46] However, paying lip-service to the VCO interests in keeping with stated British policy objectives was one thing, and actually converting VCOs into KCOs quite another. The matter might have raised crucial questions of class and caste. How, we are tempted to ask, would the Westernized public school-educated urban middle-class Indian co-exist with largely rural 'less' educated and more native VCO-turned-KCOs in the same officer cadre? This problem and its potential consequences were not discussed by the official and non-official advocates of VCO interests. If the problem between Indian and British officers was racial, the problem between Indian officers and aspirant VCOs was bound to be that of class and its attendant upbringing.[47]

The Skeen Committee felt that the Eight Unit Scheme made Indianization unpopular by encouraging an 'invidious form of segregation'. It noted that a lecture given at Sandhurst in 1925, which actually claimed that the Eight Unit Scheme was a slow process favourable to British interests in the Indian Army, had been widely misinterpreted in some popular works on India. Many British officers openly expressed the fear of losing control over Indian troops in the event of effective Indianization. The Skeen Committee dismissed these apprehensions and recommended more Indianization. It recommended that the number of seats for Indians at Sandhurst be doubled in 1928 and *increased* thereafter. The artillery, air, engineer, signal, and armoured sections of the Indian armed forces had to be Indianized. As a step in this direction, seats were demanded at Woolwich for training in artillery and Cranwell for training in the air force. The committee recommended the opening of an Indian military college in 1933. However, to maintain the Sandhurst connection, 20 seats for Indians would remain there. Following all this, according to the Skeen Committee's estimates, 50 per cent of all officers in the Indian services would be Indian by the year 1952.[48]

The submission of the Skeen Committee Report in 1927 was followed by a policy declaration as usual. The Commander-in-Chief, Field Marshal, Sir William Birdwood, announced the official policy of Indianization, incorporating some of the Skeen recommendations in March 1928. Twenty vacancies were reserved at Sandhurst for educated Indians. And. to satisfy the Skeen Committee *and* long-held opinion of the military establishment, five seats were specially opened for selected VCOs at Sandhurst. Six seats were reserved at the artillery college in Woolwich and six at the RAF college in Cranwell for selected Indians. These were the only concessions the British were willing to make in response to recommendations made by an official committee. Further progress, the government repeated, would depend upon the results of these new concessions. Despite the opinion of the Skeen Committee, the GOI stated its unwillingness to abandon the Eight Unit Scheme which was, in fact, to be given a 'full and fair trial'.[49] In fact it was maintained that upon supply outstripping demand in these Indianizing units, Indian officers would replace the VCOs as platoon commanders to form homogeneous units on the British model. In sum, the government planned to intensify Indianization of selected units in opposition to the Indian demand for extensive Indianization. In practice, this meant the formation of a Dominion Army because the eight units would in any case have formed a 'segregated' army alongside the British-led Indian regiments. Why British subalterns could not join Indian regiments as VCOs to model them on the British Army pattern was a question the GOI did not answer while sermonizing to the Indian officers on the issue.

Deceptive Policy and the Nationalist Critiques of Indianization

A decade after the Montford Report of 1918, the main issues of Indianization remained unaddressed by British policy. In the meantime the eight units upon which the policy of Indianization hinged raised more questions. Nobody knew what would happen when Indian KCOs reached higher positions of command in the Indianizing units. How would they be ranked alongside senior officers of other units? Would the Indianizing units be trusted during war? Would Indian officers relish the idea of replacing the VCOs in the event of British subalterns not doing so in other units of the Indian Army? Policy had no answer to these questions in 1928. The atmosphere was also vitiated by the senseless pronouncements made by the government which, for instance, suggested that there was no need to recruit VCOs in the Indianizing units. This insensitivity to Indian needs was based on the racist presumption that desperate Indian subalterns would not mind replacing their subordinates and hence start their careers at a level much lower than that of British subalterns. This would have directly influenced seniority in the officer cadre and thereby the issue of higher command.

But by far the biggest blow to Indian aspirations was the rejection of an 'Indian Sandhurst'. This thwarted the acceleration of Indianization. However, the sorely disappointed Indians were left with no choice but protest. Jinnah's adjournment motion in the Assembly, carried by 70 (to 41) votes, soon after Birdwood's announcement, highlighted the longevity of Indian support for rapid Indianization.[50] Due to the decision to intensify the Eight Unit Scheme, only one out of eight Indian officers could hope to command units in future (whereas before 1928, approximately one out of three Indian officers could have expected command). The possibility that increased competition due to deliberate policy would generate bitterness in the officers corps and undermine military efficiency could not be ruled out. Among jawans too, with promotion to the VCO rank closed in the Indianizing units, disaffection would grow.[51] This could only end up lending credibility to British opinion according to which Indians did not comprise officer material and Indianization was a threat to military efficiency.

Parts of the classified discussion and official thinking on Indianization in 1927 support the charge of dishonesty levelled against the British by Indians such as Jinnah. For example, Lord Irvin, wrongly blaming Indianization for the reluctance of young Britons at Sandhurst to join the Indian Army, confided to Lord Birkenhead that the British policy on Indianization was guided more by helplessness than anything else:

> We are all moreover so limited by the pledges of our predecessors, definitely to concede a certain measure of Indianization, that it is not likely to be possible to give any absolute guarantees, which would bring reassurance in this way to the hesitating young men at Sandhurst.[52]

The Viceroy also emphasized the need for more propaganda to influence the British recruits who were hesitating because of the unattractive service conditions in India. Furthermore, the effect of falling prices on the British Army was discouraging recruitment to the Indian Army amongst the limited number of recruits in Britain.

Earlier a boy could join a good British regiment only if he could spare £300 a year. In the 1920s, falling prices in England 'inevitably' militated against a Briton voluntarily exiling himself to India. The impressionable British subalterns had to be given inducements and told that the British element in the Indian Army was bound to be great, or perhaps greater than in the Civil Services, and that Indian defence would be the *real* Imperial problem of the future.[53]

The decisions of 1928 can be placed in better perspective if we see how the Viceroy's Council reacted to the Skeen Committee Report in 1927. At the outset, it had become clear that the GOI had to increase the number of commissions offered to Indians because of the specific conditions prevalent in India and the official commitments made during the Great War. While discussing the Skeen Report, the Viceroy's Council could use three methods of posting Indian officers to the Indian Army. The first, as the Skeen Committee suggested, was to post them anywhere they liked. For obvious reasons guiding long-term British policy, this was impossible. The second was to post a maximum of 23 Indian KCOs to more units. Thirdly, it was thought desirable to give Indians a Dominion commission within the Eight Unit Scheme, making them replace the VCOs and British officers in the gradual course of time. Great caution was required in doing so because Indians disliked even the idea of being given an inferior commission. But to a government which had all along been biased against Indianization, other matters too were crucial. Irwin expressed the fear of inefficiency once again in the following words:

> The real point of principle and substance, as it seems to me, is that you should do nothing to impair the efficiency of other units than those in which you are already conducting your experiment.[54]

Considering this, the Viceroy's Council, despite the Commander-in-Chief's opposition, agreed (in Irwin's words) 'upon a formula which, while not specifically mentioning the eight units 'meant' substantiallv the same thing'. The compromise lay in the Indian KCOs replacing the British KCOs upwards and Indian VCOs downwards in the eight units. The demand for seats at Woolwich and Cranwell had been conceded, but was dismissed contemptuously by Irwin:

> We also decided to ask for admissions to Woolwich and Cranwell. As regards the first, I don't think, if you accede to our request, it is the least likely that for years to come any Indians—or at least not more than an odd one—will succeed in qualifying.[55]

This meant that the GOI, instead of addressing the criticism of the Indian education system made by the Skeen Committee, saw educational backwardness as a buffer against Indianization.

Left to British policy, Indianization would have stagnated at the level of 1928. However, under considerable Indian pressure, some decisions were taken by the Sub-Committee of Defence (no. VII) at the Round Table Conference in 1931. This committee involved Indian delegates to the Round Table such as T. B. Sapru, M. R. Jayakar, B. S. Moonje, and M. A. Jinnah. Its 'definite resolutions' demanded steps 'to increase substantially the rate of Indianizing the Indian Army'. But Jinnah found this resolution too general and wanted a clear picture of the *pace* of Indianization. This committee also called for the urgent establishment of an Indian military college. The GOI was asked to form a Committee of British and Indian experts to 'work out the details of the establishment of such a college'. The Committee was also 'unanimous' in its view 'that the declaration must not be taken as a mere pious expression of opinion', but immediately after the conference 'steps should be taken to deal effectively with the recommendations made'.[56]

Consequently, a committee of experts under the Commander-in-Chief, General Sir Philip Chetwode, was appointed in May 1931. But the Dominion Army concept remained influential. Indianization would now cover a *complete division* of all arms and a cavalry brigade with proportionate provisions for ancillary services, staff, etc. with an intake of 60 officers per year. Since the Eight Units 'were not' popular with either the Indian public or the young Indian officer', ostensibly for the first time 'a real start with an Indian Army as a fighting proposition, and not merely an experiment' was being made. An 'Indian Sandhurst' was evaded and policy was mentioned in familiar phrases:

> In dealing with the expansion of Indianisation, our object is to create a recognised combatant force on a purely Indian basis, which would in time replace a force of a similar size in the Imperial Army. For it is by the gradual replacement of Imperial fighting formations alone that India will be able eventually to assume responsibility for her own defence .... Our first task is to create a steady flow of fine young officers.[57]

The disappointed Indians protested. Six Indian unofficial members of the Chetwode Committee submitted 'dissertations' of dissent summarizing the Indian position on Indianization.

According to Chotu Ram, S. N. Mukarji, and Abdur Rahim, the Chetwode Scheme contradicted the Round Table Resolutions which mentioned steps to 'increase substantially the *rate of Indianisation*'. In contrast, the plan to replace the VCOs with Indian KCOs made the 'apparent increase' in Indianization 'entirely illusory'. There was no point in slowing down Indianization, because in the Indian Army 17,000 non-Indians were serving as officers at the cost of the Indian taxpayers. Furthermore, the future military college proposed by the committee contained no provision for naval and air training. The minutes were critical of the 'experiment' referred to by the Chetwode Committee because it negated the spirit of the Round Table Resolutions—replacing the VCOs by Indian KCOs in the Indianizing units would reduce efficiency by denying promotion to the jawans and thereby adding to their service grievances. In such circumstances, enterprising young men would not join these units.[58]

B. S. Moonje asserted that after the Round Table Conference, the GOI had forgotten that Indians 'wanted to be the architects of their own destiny'. The Conference had claimed, *inter alia,* that soon Indians would become responsible for their defence and governance. Quoting extensively from the Defence Sub-Committee resolutions, Moonje highlighted the difference between the theory and practice of reform. Fixing the annual intake to the future college at 60 was a 'sad though highly instructive disillusionment' because no one knew who actually had the authority to fix the intake. The GOI was being presumptuous in fixing the intake because the Sub-Committee had clearly spelt out the functions of the Expert Committee. In any case, compared with the number suggested by the Shea Committee, 60 appeared at best parsimonious. With 60 per cent of the candidates being nominated, this concession violated the Skeen Committee recommendations which wanted nominations restricted to 20 per cent:

> This system of nomination perpetuates the myth of the artificial distinction of martial and non-martial classes. It serves as a handle for the people to charge the Government with the policy of 'Divide and Rule'. It propagates the poison of communalism in the body politic of India. It emasculates large sections of the people and as a reaction serves to create what may be called swelled head in those who are generally enlisted in the Army. It strikes at the very root of the conception of a national Army, and perpetuates the system of a mercenary Army which is the inevitable concomitant of a foreign government.[59]

A comprehensive critique was provided by Sir P. S. Sivaswamy Aiyer and Major General Raja Ganpat Rao Raghunath Rao Rajwade. Both criticized the limits imposed upon the Chetwode Committee's scope of inquiry by the GOI. The fact that the Commander-in-Chief emphasized the details of an 'Indian Sandhurst' before and not *the pace of Indianization* smacked of authoritarianism. Hence it appeared that in deciding the terms of reference of the Committee the central issue of Indianization was ignored by the government. The GOI also failed to realize that Indians would reject cosmetic changes and refute the illogical arguments favouring them:

> The validity of these arguments will be examined later on. They are considered by Indians to be more specious than sound, but they appeal to the average British layman. The British mind is essentially empirical and wishes to build upon the results of experience and is content to solve the problems of the day without looking forward beyond tomorrow. 'Sufficient unto the day is the evil thereof' is a maxim which more or less accurately expresses the mentality of the average Englishman .... If the Empire had to face the danger of another world war on the same scale as the Great War, there can be little doubt that England would be obliged to train India for her own defence within a much shorter period.[60]

Furthermore, the myth of 'martial' and 'non-martial' races could not withstand historical scrutiny. Undermining this myth suggested that British policy on the subject was responsible for diminishing military initiative in the Indians. Since the nineteenth century, the British had considered it 'necessary to impress upon the mind of the Indian soldier a conviction of his permanent racial inferiority to the British soldier. But a different reading of history suggested that military qualities were predicated upon suitable opportunities and training. Since the theory of the 'martial races' had evolved to suit the 'policy of combining absolute political safety with the maximum of military efficiency', the government relied on reports such as the one presented by the Simon Commission on military matters. This was unfortunate, because the Simon Commission showed 'no intelligent analysis or appreciation of the various causes affecting recruitment' in India. Even the climatic theory explaining martial behaviour—according to which cold and 'bracing' climates produced martial people, explaining martial behaviour—was baseless:

> If this were a valid argument the British and the Gurkha soldier should not be enlisted for service in India or in expeditions to other tropical countries. During the wars in foreign lands in which Indian troops were employed, nothing was heard of unadaptability of the Indian soldiers to the climatic conditions of other countries.[61]

British military thought, conditioned by the geographical location of Britain, did not appreciate the importance of a national army, whereas historical experience showed that a national army was morally stronger than a 'merely professional army drawn from particular classes'. Since the Indian military situation, with India's long land and sea frontiers, was similar to that of the Continental powers, only Indianization could develop a national army in India. The argument for segregation, which blighted the prospects of a national army, was based on untenable colonial myths, racial discrimination, and British arrogance. Even the fear that British subalterns would ignore the Indian Army if commissions were given to Indians was substantiated only in the case of the aristocratic and exceptionally haughty Britons. Considering this, the Indian position on military recruitment was categorical: even if all Britons disliked Indians getting the KC, India would have to be 'prepared to face the situation and learn to do without British recruitment'. No matter what the British said, the real cause of segregation, expressed in the Eight Unit Scheme, was the deep-rooted British apprehension that 'the Englishman's prestige with the native troops themselves would be gone, if they were ever placed under other than British command'. The policy of segregation treated Indian officers *as a class*, but nothing proved the superiority of British officers *as a class.* In fact evidence and the observations of none other than Lord Roberts after the Boer War revealed serious deficiencies in British officers and training methods.[62]

The reference to the Boer War, which revealed several drawbacks of the British military model, was most apposite. Our study of the Boer War suggests that the 'martial races' theory could only have been sustained by the relative isolation of the North-West Frontier Province (NWFP)—the main battle-cum-training ground of the Indian Army. Criticizing the British system of training officers, Major General R. S. S. Baden Powell had said the following to the Royal Commission on the war in South Africa:

> Junior officers should be given responsibility from their first entry into the service. They should be made to really command their unit, however small, and be answerable for its efficiency and success .... The so-called chain of responsibility is too often one of irresponsibility.[63]

Other distinguished officers such as Roberts (who was instrumental in keeping the focus of the Indian Army on the NWFP and the 'Punjab Classes'), Kitchener, and Hamilton were equally, or even more, critical of British field officers. Kitchener said the following about staff and regimental officers:

There appears to be too often a want of serious study of their profession by officers who are, I think, rather inclined to deal too lightly with military questions of moment .... I should like to point out, further, that in the higher ranks also there seems to be a want of that professionalism which is essential to thorough efficiency.[64]

A tendency to shirk responsibility was noticed in the entire officer corps. Routine over-subordination of juniors to the seniors, in the words of the report 'blighted the development of their self-reliance and power of decision'. Major General Sir Henry Colvile called the 'want of initiative' the greatest fault of the British officers. How much the British officers had actually learnt from skirmishing with tribesmen on the highly romanticized NWFP was mentioned by Sir Ian Hamilton (Military Secretary in South Africa). He also attacked the peacetime training methods of the British Army:

The previous practical peace training of Aldershot proved itself quite unsuited to the requirements of South African warfare. This training was *calculated* to stunt rather than to develop the initiative of company officers, section leaders, and men[65] [emphasis added].

The African Wars proved that success in modern warfare depended upon the discipline and individuality of troops. Hence the Australians, Canadians, and New Zealanders did extremely well in the Boer War because, compared with the average British recruit, they had 'more individuality'.[66] But despite this criticism and the experience of a World War, the mentality of British officers did not change. After the Great War, senior officers of the Indian Army such as Lieutenant General Corbett blamed this mentality for the rising discontent in the Indian Army. In his opinion, the racist attitude of most young British officers, who were 'apt to consider themselves infallible with little reason for doing so', alienated the Indians, with serious consequences. For example, young British officers in the Indian Army regularly reprimanded the VCOs and NCOs in front of jawans. This was deeply resented because British subalterns, also new to the army and therefore prone to making mistakes, were 'not treated in this way'.[67]

The government, as mentioned earlier, also wanted to abolish the VCO rank in the Indianizing units. This was disliked by the Indians. However, because such arguments emerged *after* Indianization started, made the Indians suspect them even more. Indeed the official concern for the VCOs appeared hypocritical: 'The military authorities are so full of tenderness for the Viceroy's commissioned officer that they wish to improve his class out of existence'.[68] But this criticism did not make an impression on the British even after the IMA opened. At the third session of the Indian Round Table Conference in 1932, a specific time frame for Indianization was yet again excluded from policy: 'The view was stated on behalf of His Majesty's Government that the pace of Indianization must continue to be regulated by stages, while it was pointed out that a programme of Indianization already exists which extends much further than the previous stage and looks forward to still greater developments in future.' Besides Indianization, the Indians also desired some legislative control over the deployment of the Indian Army but the British were categorical on this point. It was 'implicit in the reservation of Defence' that the Viceroy remained supreme in the decisions involving the deployment of Indian troops anywhere in the world.[69]

Conclusion

Among many Anglophile Indians, a certain fondness and nostalgia for the so-called British sense of fair play endures to this day. This paper has exposed British justice in an important Indian matter for all its worth. This has been done by underscoring the colonial context of military Indianization in British India. The ideological contours of the Indianization problem made sure that Indians, as colonial subjects, were denied their due share in the colonial Indian Armed Forces. Indian and British critics might argue that Indianization was, after all, a policy matter which only affected the English-educated Indian middle classes.[70] However, in our opinion, that would amount to overlooking the racism of the British position on Indianization. The point would also undermine the importance of treating the vast majority of Indians as *social subalterns* in relation to the British during the colonial period.

Our story of Indianization asserts that the British disliked the idea of giving the power of command to Indians in the Indian Army for obvious reasons. The fear of losing control over a predominantly Indian army, and the consequent descent into anarchy, had always been there since 1857. This fear virtually governed British military policy in India since the Mutiny. Conceding the power of command to Indians in the army threatened the carefully cultivated 'natural' superiority of the British officers. These fears became heightened in the political context of the disturbed 1920s and sharpened some of the British positions on Indianization. But the British discourse on Indianization was predicated upon ideological mechanisms of colonial control which had evolved in the nineteenth century. The division and classification of Indians into social groups identifiable on the basis of certain characteristics—from the British viewpoint—was an important element of colonial rule in India. Hence certain Indians were said to have criminal tendencies while others were upheld as non-criminal. Some Indians were martial, most were considered non-martial. Many were decadent, some were mercifully not. The classification of what was martial in India informed colonial military thought till the very end of the British Empire and became the basis of an identitarian conflict between the excluded Indians and the British. A large number of Britons continued to believe that Indians could be classified into martial and non-martial groups even as empirical evidence accumulated against these beliefs. Hence the Indianization schemes were suffused with a racism best summed up by General Auchinleck in 1939. 'In my opinion', he wrote to Amery,

> we have been playing a losing hand from the start in this matter of 'Indianisation'. The Indian has always thought, rightly or wrongly, that we never intended the scheme to succeed and expected it to fail. Colour was lent to this view by the way in which each new step forward had to be wrested from us, instead of being freely given. Now that we have given a lot we get no credit because there was little grace in our giving.[71]

Non-symbolic Indianization began with the Great War. It was explicit in the promises made to Indians by the British in their hour of crisis. However, this magnanimity was short-lived. Indianization was barely touched upon by the powerful Esher Committee. London wanted to revert to token Indianization. Left to itself, reform would have ended there. However, the Indians who launched a vigorous campaign for *accelerated Indianization* represented an influential political class. The consequence was the Eight Unit Scheme, which segregated Indian officers in selected units which were officially considered inferior to the rest of the army. The criticism of this scheme led to the appointment of the Skeen Committee whose recommendations, it is well known, were influenced by Indian opinion. Nonetheless, every step of Indianization was extracted from the Raj. In 1932, after the Round Table deliberations, the Indian Military Academy (IMA) opened but the Indians remained unhappy. This reservation was expressed in well-researched, revealing, and critical commentaries produced by Indians associated with the Chetwode Committee. These commentaries comprise a pursuasive counter-colonial discourse. The opening of the IMA has recently been called 'a very carefully worked out deception plan which did not deceive anyone'.[72] This is so because the Indian commissioned officers coming from the IMA began to replace the VCOs in the units selected by the Divisional Scheme. *This did not amount to the acceleration of Indianization and the replacement of British KCOs with Indian officers across the board.* The Divisional Scheme was an avatar of the Unit Scheme. This Scheme remained operational till 1939 and can be held responsible for the shortage of trained officers faced by the Indian forces in 1939–40. To overcome this shortage, created primarily by British policy between the wars, the government created the cadre of emergency commissioned officers to tide over World War II.

Notes

1. This article is a much revised chapter of my unpublished PhD thesis 'British Military Policy in India, 1919–1945', Centre for Historical Studies, Jawaharlal Nehru University, New Delhi: 1996. Drafts were presented in Jawaharlal Nehru University (1997) and Nehru Memorial Museum and Library (1998), where the late Professor Partha Sarathi Gupta was present. It is dedicated to his exemplary scholarship and professional commitment.
2. Some of the racial problems associated with later Indianization were anticipated in these token schemes. One of these was the difficulty of making British soldiers and subalterns salute and obey these Indian officers.
3. I call the theory of the 'martial races' a semi-historical classification simply because military traditions, like other traditions, change. They transform temporally when troops of a particular community or region are deployed *or not deployed* in combat zones. State policy, over time, can make 'martial' or 'non-martial' troops. Hence, in the 1880s and '90s, the advocates of the 'martial races' conveniently pointed towards the 'unmartial' Madras Army. The system of regional recruitment and deployment followed after 1857 consigned the Bombay and Madras armies to non-combat zones. In contrast the Punjabized regiments of the Bengal Army were regularly deployed against the Afghans and Frontier Pathan tribesmen. This gave them a more or less recent martial 'history', i.e., the historical content of the 'martial race' classification. The fictional content was, of course, provided by the favoured notions of colonial anthropology which coloured the Indian Army's *Caste Handbooks.*
4. *Confidential Simla Records—3 no. 601/10482/H.A.D. Case no. 29147. 1927, nos 333–341 and Appendix Subject: Proposed formation of a well equipped Military College in a suitable locality in India to train*

Indians for the Commissioned ranks of the Indian Army and Appointment of Indian Sandhurst Committee, HS. Recent work covering Indianization comprises the following: Partha Sarathi Gupta (posthmous) and Anirudh Deshpande (eds), *The British Raj and its Indian Armed Forces, 1857–1939,* New Delhi: 2002. Lt Col Gautam Sharma, *Nationalisation of the Indian Army, 1886–1947,* New Delhi: 1996; and B. P. N. Sinha and Sunil Chandra, *Valour and Wisdom: Genesis and Growth of the Indian Military Academy,* New Delhi: 1992. Indianization is discussed by almost all the standard histories of the Indian Army, but a specific bibliography cannot miss Lt Gen. S. L. Menezes, *Fidelity and Honour: The Indian Army from the Seventeenth to the Twenty First Century,* New Delhi: 1993; T. A. Heathcote, *The Military in British India: The Development of British Land Forces in South Asia, 1600–1947,* Manchester: 1995; and David Omissi, *The Sepoy and the Raj: The Indian Army, 1860–1940,* London: 1994.

5. Morley to Hardinge, 19/5/1911, Morley Collection (microfilm), Acc. no. 1614, National Archives of India (NAI), New Delhi.
6. Committee on the Indianization of the Officer Ranks of the Indian Army (Secret), 18/8/1939, Draft Report, File no. 601/1281/H, p. 2, HS. Also known as the Indianzation Committee Report 1938–9.
7. Hardinge to Morley, 23/3/1911, Morley Collection. The Viceroy understood the problem better than many of his contemporaries: '... what Indians want is that the sons of important people should be allowed to have commissions in the Native Army. They do not in the least want to be in the British Army, and I hope that this will be borne in mind and that you will be able to come to a solution of this much vexed question on that basis.'
8. Ibid. The cause of concern was also a Resolution of the All-India Muslim League passed in its 1911 annual session, urging the government to increase commissions for the 'sons of Ruling Chiefs and scions of other noble houses' to which Hardinge referred.
9. Montagu to Viceroy, 3/8/1917, Montagu Papers (microfilm) Acc. no. 1930, NAI. Opposition to the Indians gaining commissions in the Indian Army continued despite the services rendered to the British cause by the Indians during the Great War. In his letters to Chelmsford dated 16 May and 3 July 1918 (Acc. no. 1930), Montagu touched upon the subject again, saying that while the War Office was opposed to the grant of commissions to Indians, the military members of the Army Council also expressed their 'grave displeasure' on the issue. Taking the fear of racial discrimination into account, Montagu also advised posting Indian commissioned officers to units where they could find some of their own people. Later they could be transferred to other units. The matter had to be handled very carefully because early failures would retard the scheme for many years and British officers of at least one unit did not like the appointments.

10. 601/1079/H, 1923, GOI Army Dep. Org. *Proceedings*, December 1923, nos 86–111, Sub: Indianization of the Indian Army. Gail Wilgram's Confidential Note (GS File 11795)—Indianization of the Indian Army separately inducted in these proceedings, HS.
11. Montagu Chelmsford Report, cited by Wigram, op. cit.
12. Notes from Appendix, 601/10482/H. Army Dep. *Progs* A. March 1927, Secretary of State to GOI, Telegram no. 28, 5 April 1918, [HS]: Indianisation Committee Report 1938–39, p. 4.
13. 601/10482/H, Army Dep. *Progs*, Appendix; Indianisation Committee Report 1938–39, pp. 5–6. The Prince of Wales Royal Military College was opened in Dehra Dun in March 1922 to provide 70 cadets with public school education. A cogent nationalist position on military reform soon after the Great War was presented in the famous Sivaswamy Aiyer Resolutions, accepted by the GOI in March 1921—see Legislative Assembly Debates, 1, 11, Official Report, 1921, NMML, pp. 1683–1762—Debate (28.3.1921) on 15 seminal resolutions on the Esher Committee Report. Aiyer had formulated these resolutions in 'critical but constructive' vein.
14. For a summary of these 'confidential' recommendations see Sharma, *Nationalisation of the Indian Army*, pp. 64–6.
15. 601/10482/H, 12810/H, Army Dep. *Progs*.
16. The Committee appointed by the commander-in-chief was headed by Lt Gen. Shea, acting Chief of General Staff, and is referred to as the Shea Committee hereafter. Ref: SECRET Indianization of the Indian Army, Report of a Committee appointed by His Excellency the Commander-in-Chief in India, Delhi, 1922 in the Army Dep. *Progs*, 1923, nos 85–112, Sub: Indianisation of the Army.
17. Our account of Wigram's paper is based on a printed copy of it in the Army Dep. *Progs*, 1923 (see General Rawlinson cited by Wigram).
18. Wigram's paper, op.cit., p. 4.
19. Ibid., p. 10.
20. Ibid.
21. SECRET PAPER—Indianization of the Indian Army by A. S. Cobbe, sent to the Chamberlain Committee from Whitehall, 14 September 1921, Army Dep. *Progs*, 1923.
22. Telegram from the Secretary of State to Viceroy, no. 5960, 21/22 November 1921, Army Dep. *Progs*, 1923.
23. The move could easily have been conceived with the intention of making it backfire. Had the Indian subalterns faltered in these hardened fighting formations, their failure would have been held up by the colonial authorities to the advocates of Indianization as an example of Indian military ineptitude.
24. Shea Committee Report, p. 4. On p. 11, the familiar moral argument of British superiority followed: 'In the absence of a conscious, mature and homogeneous national spirit in India the moral factor most

essential to the creation of a "Dominion Army" does not exist, and only in units of the regular army are to be found those moral influences arising from a history of service and achievement in war which are a most valuable reinforcement to the national spirit.'

25. I have examined the Esher Committee Recommendations in detail in Gupta and Deshpande (eds), *The British Raj and its Indian Armed Forces, 1857–1939.*
26. Shea Committee Report, p. 9.
27. Ibid.
28. Viceroy to Secretary of State 24 November 1921, Telegram no. 2005, Army Dep. *Progs,* 1923.
29. Secretary of State to Viceroy, 29/30 November 1921, Telegram no. 6088 and Viceroy in reply 8 December 1922. Telegram no. 48c, Army Dep. *Progs,* 1923.
30. Secretary of State to Viceroy, 8/10 December l921, Telegram no. 6219; Viceroy in reply Telegram no. 43, 11 January 1921 and Viceroy to Secretary of State, 5 February 1922, Telegram no. 19, Army Dep. *Progs,* 1923.
31. Viceroy to Secretary of State, 5 December 1992, op. cit.
32. Secretary of State to Viceroy, 14/15 February 1922, Telegram no. 674, Army Dep. *Progs,* 1923.
33. Viceroy to Secretary of State, 18 February 1922, Telegram no. 262, Army Dep. *Progs,* 1923.
34. Secretary of State to Viceroy, 22/23 February 1922, Telegram no. 807, and Viceroy in reply 25 February 1922, Telegram no. 300, Army Dep. *Progs,* 1923. On foreign policy and Indianization, the reservations and advice of the Home Government were accepted by Delhi 'with great regret'. Even in Waziristan, the Imperial government was very regretfully allowing the GOI to abandon the unfavourable forward policy.
35. Viceroy to Secretary of State, 16 March 1922, Tel. no. 836–F, and Secretary of State in reply, 20/21 March 1922, Tel. no. 1213, Army Dep. *Progs,* 1923.
36. SECRET 1922 Simla Army Dep. Separate no. 45, 3/8/1922: Dispatch to His Majesty's Secretary of State for India, Sub: Indianisation of the Indian Army. The Viceroy sent the summary of the Eight Unit Scheme to the Secretary of State on 28/7/1922, Tel. no. 999 (Simla) Army Dep. *Progs,* 1923.
37. Army Dep. Separate 45, op. cit, p. 5, warned against communal combination of Indian officers and men even though the nationalists had never raised the issue: 'It is conceivable that a demand might be made under any scheme of Indianization for officers to be distributed to units on a communal basis. We should, in anticipation, for reasons which it is hardly necessary to specify, definitely exclude this possibility.'

38. This aspect of Indianization was noticed by the Indianization Committee of 1938–9. The units chosen were: 7th Light Cavalry; 16th Light Cavalry; 2/1st Madras Pioneers; 4/19th Hyderabad Regiment; 5th Marathas (MLI); l/7th Rajput Regiment, l/14th Punjab Regiment, and 2/lst Punjab Regiment. Byron Farwell, *Armies of the Raj,* London, 1989, p. 298, mentions that the scheme 'was not a success'; Stephen P. Cohen, *The Indian Army,* New Delhi: 1990, p. 84, draws attention to the fact that the scheme only temporarily satisfied the Indians; Y. Longer, *Red Coats to Olive Green,* Longmans: 1974, p. 199, points out the extremely limited benefits of the scheme.
39. As a breach in the commissioned ranks, the Eight Units Scheme opened visions of success besides providing India her first batch of post-World War II generals. By concentrating Indian officers in a few units, and not dispersing them into obscurity, the scheme gave the jawans a chance to judge them. It is probably true, also because the chosen eight units were mixed, that working within the scheme exposed Indian officers to a cross-section of the Indian Army. Personal details of this experience are recorded in the following H. Evans, *Thimayya of India: A Soldier's Life,* New York: 1960, pp. 102–3; Gen. J. N. Chaudhuri, *An Autobiography as narrated to B. K. Narayan,* Delhi: 1978, p. 54; and Lt Gen. S. P. P. Thorat, *From Reveille to Retreat,* New Delhi: 1988, pp. 1–47.
40. *Confidential Simla Records—3 no. 60l/l0482/H. A.D. Case no. 29147, 1927*—GOI, Army Dep. Organisation. *Proceedings* A, March 1927, nos 333–341 and Appendix—Subject: Proposed formation of a well equipped Military College in a suitable locality in India to train Indians for the Commissioned Ranks of the Indian Army. Appointment of the Indian Sandhurst Committee, 1925–26, HS (hereafter ADP 1927).
41. ADP 1927, section on *loci classici of* Indianization. These views were expressed in 1925, the year Rawlinson died.
42. Viceroy Reading to Lord Birkenhead, Secretary of State for India, 12 March 1925, in the Birkenhead Collection (microfilm), Acc. no. 1948, NAI.
43. ADP 1927; M. M. Malviya and M. L. Nehru were among such men.
44. ADP 1927, Skeen Committee Report (Report of the Indian Sandhurst Committee, Simla: 1927), chapter on the background of Indianization; *Legislative Assembly Debates,* vol. V, part II, Official Report, Delhi, 6 March, 125 (NMML)—Debate on Indian Sandhurst, Resolution *RE* Establishment of a Military College, 19 Feb. 1925, pp. 1220–73. The participants in this debate were B. Venkatapatiraju, Sir Sivaswamy Aiyer, M. A. Jinnah, M. M. Malviya, E. Burdon (Army Secretary), Colonel J. D. Crawford (European member from Bengal), Captain Ajab Khan (Non-official member from Punjab) and M. L. Nehru.
45. Skeen Committee Report, pp. 12–13.

46. Ibid., pp. 14–16.
47. This contradiction was resolved in favour of the Indian middle class in the Indian republic. Commissioned officers receive their commissions after being trained at the Indian Military Academy (IMA), Dehradun (the equivalent of Sandhurst). The cadet entrants to Dehradun come from the National Defence Academy (NDA), Khadakvasala (near Pune), where boys straight out of school train for the three services before finally being commissioned in a particular one. The admission to NDA is based on an open entrance exam, which is much easier for public school-educated boys to clear in comparison with boys educated at the ill-equipped and neglected government schools.
48. Extracts of the Sandhurst Lecture are present as Appendix III of the *Skeen Report.* Apprehensions of British officers were articulated by Valentine Chirol, whose *The Modern World Series,* India: 1926, was quoted by the Committee. SECRET 1922 Simla Army Dep. *Progs* Separate no.45, op. cit. See the KCO time-scale/age as follows: Beginning as lieutenant at 20, captain at 29, major at 38, and lieutenant colonel at 46. Even the complement of officers carried by an infantry battalion of the army was not very high: it had 12 officers comprising one commandant (lieutenant colonel/colonel), one second in command (lieutenant colonel/major), four company officers (lieutenant/captains), one adjutant officer (lieutenant/captain) one quartermaster officer (lieutenant/captain) Skeen Committee Report, pp. 23–33, called for public schools, scholarships, and special arrangements for the sons of the VCOs in India.
49. Indianization Committee Report, 1938–39, p. 22; *Legislative Assembly Debates,* vol. 1, Official Report, Delhi, 1–27 March 1928, announcement of government policy and general military review by Commander-in-Chief, 8 March 1928, pp. 1175–87. Certain concessions in accordance with the Skeen recommendations would be granted to India; but with time, 'the scheme would have to be reconsidered and, if necessary, revised from the stand-point of efficiency'. This left M. L. Nehru 'cold', and 'completely shattered' Jinnah's faith in the bona fides of the British Government'.
50. *India in 1927–28: A Statement prepared for presentation to Parliament in accordance with the requirements of the 26th Section of the Government of India Act (5 and 6 Geo V. (chap. 61),* Calcutta: 1928, p. 311; government policy on Indianization remained doubtful in this period—*India 1930–31: A Statement prepared for presentation to Parliament ...,* Calcutta: 1932, p. 43, referred clearly to 'extraordinary difficulty, indeed the impossibility, of establishing a coherent, efficient, and reliable army officered by Indians within the time desired by the critics of the Government'. The Storeman Scheme, as the same source, p. 28, pointed out was a good example of minor Indianization attempted by the GOI. The Storeman Scheme was designed to replace British

Other Ranks (BORs) by Indians as assistant storekeepers in the Indian Army Ordnance Corps and was 'financed' by reducing the number of Indian sepoys in the same department! According to the report this made 'it appear as though little or no increase in the Indian establishment' was actually being made.

51. 1/5 Correspondence and notes about Sikh troubles in the Indian Army, The Papers of Lt Gen. Thomas William Corbett, Churchill Archives Centre, Cambridge. Elements of British recruitment policy geared to achieve a favourable balance in the units also led to growth in intrigue and discontent. For instance during the late 1920s, the policy of balancing Manjha and Malwa recruits in the Sikh cavalry was linked to discontent among Sikh troops. During court martials, promotions, and recruitment, British officers could also easily be accused of favouritism. In fact the situation was serious enough for a certain officer Reynolds to write to Corbett that the Sikh troops were well behaved in face, but extremely hesitant to use force against religious leaders. Reynolds was asked to exercise caution in promoting men because in at least one cavalry squadron, promotions were being considered at the last moment and names 'calculated to reduce the efficiency of the Sqn.' were being mentioned, presumably by the Indian VCOs.
52. Viceroy Irwin to Lord Birkenhead, 28 March 1927, Birkenhead Collection, op. cit., Acc. no. 1949.
53. Ibid.
54. Irwin to Birkenhead, 14 July 1927, Acc. no. 1949.
55. Ibid.
56. Indian Round Table Conference, 12 November 1930–19 January 1931, *Proceedings*, London, 1931 [Cmd. 3778], Sub-Committee no. VII, whole conference held on 16 January 1931, p. 395.
57. *Chetwode Committee Report*, p. 21; Indianisation Committee Report 1938–39, p. 31; *Progress Report on the armed forces for 1929–30*, 601/10848/H, Secret, Delhi: 1930 [H] tells us that the long-awaited Kitchner College was opened in July 1929 to prepare NCOs for VCO rank and as platoon commanders; *India in 1931–32, A Statement prepared for presentation to Parliament ...*, Calcutta: 1933, section on Indianization mentions that the Indian Military Academy opened in Dehra Dun in October 1932 with the aim of taking in 40 cadets every two years—of these 12 were to be selected by open competition, 3 were to be nominated by the Commander-in-Chief from among the other qualifiers of the exam, 15 were to be serving soldiers of the Indian Army (including the auxiliary and the territorial Forces), and 10 were to come from the Indian states forces.
58. Minutes by Chotu Ram, S. N. Mukarji, and Abdur Rahim appended to the *Chetwode Committee Report.*

59. Minutes by B. S. Moonje, appended to the *Chetwode Committee Report.* Earlier Indians had vehemently opposed the Simon Commission Report on similar grounds. Even Nirad C. Chaudhuri (*Thy Hand Great Anarch: India 1921–1952.* London: 1987, p. 321), called the report 'a dishonest document'. Even before the Indian Military College Committee (Chetwode Committee) had concluded its report in July 1931, Chaudhuri wrote a series of well-informed articles criticizing the 'martial races' theory in *The Modern Review* between 1930 and 1931. Later, in an article in the same *Review* for October 1931, he examined the Chetwode Report, finding it 'an ungenerous and unintelligent sneer'. Earlier, in a letter to Sir Sivaswamy, he had warned against the British attempts to 'convert' Indian 'cadets into imitation polo-playing English subalterns, weaned away from their habits and tradition, which will make them as ineffective or offensive as the majority of the Indian members of the services'. In fact Chaudhuri emerged as a publicist because of his acclaimed articles on the 'martial races'. A precise summary of his involvement in the Indianization issue is given in *Thy Hand Great Anarch,* pp. 319–28.
60. Minutes by Sivaswamy Aiyer and Major General Rajwade appended to the Chetwode Commitee Report.
61. Ibid. The example of the Duke of Wellington doing with the 'scum of the earth' in the Peninsular War was given by Aiyer and Rajwade.
62. Minutes by Sivaswamy Aiyer and Major General Rajwade appended to the Chetwode Committee Report.
63. *Report of the Royal Commission on the War in South Africa,* vol. III, 1904 [Cmd.1791, CUL], Minutes of Evidence, pp. 424–5: Powell's view was very critical. Angered by the fact that very few of the British officers or men knew 'how to sharpen a sword or how to keep it sharp on service', he emphasized the educational reform of the officer corps, and the promotion of battlefield resource and cunning as opposed to the existing overemphasis on barrack square drill, form and deadening routine.
64. *Report of His Majesty's Commissioners appointed to inquire into the Military preparations and other matters connected with the War in South Africa, 1903* [Cmd.1789, CUL], pp. 53–4.
65. Ibid., pp. 55–6.
66. Ibid., p. 79; this was the view of none other than Field Marshal Lord Roberts.
67. 1/5 Correspondence and notes about Sikh troubles in the Indian Army (1928), Corbett Papers. Corbett's advice to young officers was simple: 'We cannot all be interpreters in the language. A far more important factor is knowledge of human nature and justice tempered by cool judgement and the milk of human kindness. If British officers consider themselves exempt from the standards of smartness in dress, punctiliousness and

general military thoroughness demanded of them, slackness and inefficiency are bound to occur in the Regiment.'

68. Minutes by Aiyer and Rajwade, op. cit.
69. *Report on the Indian Round Table Conference (Third Session), 17 November, 1932–24 December, 1932*, London: 1933 [Cmd.4238, CUL], pp. 45–7.
70. In some sense this 'creamy layer' argument is used against affirmative action (policy of reservation) these days. There is some merit in it, although it is significant to note that affirmative action must begin somewhere for a 'creamy layer' to develop in the first place. In the colonial context, therefore, a policy of Indianization involving relatively small sections of the Indian middle class would have constituted a progressive development.
71. Auchinleck to Amery, quoted in Menezes, *Fidelity and Honour*, pp. 338–9.
72. Sharma, *Nationalisation of the Indian Army 1886–1947*, Preface.

7

Martial Gurkhas*

The Persistence of a British Military Discourse on 'Race'

Lionel Caplan

INTRODUCTION

There can be few ideas which convey British imperial attitudes to questions of 'race' as succinctly as the view that martial qualities inhere only in particular populations. While the notion of martial groups may have pre-dated European arrival in South Asia, it was during the latter part of the colonial period that the 'theory' was elaborated and became the principal basis for military recruitment into the (British) Indian army. Moreover, it persisted well into the twentieth century, and in certain instances—I am thinking particularly of the British Brigade of Gurkhas—it endures to this day. In this article I explore how the martial race idea informed enlistment strategies in respect of the Gurkhas, and more generally British military discourse about these legendary warriors from Nepal. The texts I examine are those written—and still being written—by British officers who have commanded Gurkhas in war and peace: regimental histories, personal war memoirs, autobiographies, and (principally) popular accounts of these soldiers and their exploits which feed the public appetite for military adventure and exotica.

* First published in Peter Robb (ed.), *The Concept of Race in South Asia*, New Delhi: Oxford University Press, 1995, pp. 260–81.

Acknowledgements: Fieldwork in Nepal in 1988 was funded by the Nuffield Foundation, while expenses incurred in Britain in connection with this research were met from a grant provided by the School of Oriental and African Studies (SOAS). I am grateful to both bodies for their assistance. I am also indebted to Pat Caplan and David Arnold for comments on an earlier version of this paper.

The theory of martiality is too well known to need elaboration here, and so we might only remind ourselves that it was predicated on the idea that while the 'military instinct' is inherent in Europeans (especially the British), the same could not be said for all the diverse peoples of the Indian subcontinent. The theory had two main strands based on the idea of natural qualities, emphasizing that martiality was an inherited trait and therefore an aspect of 'race'.[1] In this conception, a martial race, to quote Cynthia Enloe, flags an ethnic community as inherently inclined towards military occupation—it possesses some special characteristic embedded in its physical make-up, in its 'blood' (1980, p. 39). In the nineteenth century, blood was widely regarded as the substance responsible for the transmission of hereditary features, so that all members of a particular race would be endowed with the same qualities (Robb ed., *The Concept of Race in South Asia*, Delhi: 1995; Street, 1975, pp. 7 and 77). Martiality (along with other characteristics) was thus deemed to be inherited in the blood. In this sense, martial theory did not emerge *sui generis* to meet specific military needs in the nineteenth-century Indian context. Rather, it has to be understood as but one manifestation of the wider European doctrine of biological determinism or scientific racism, which gained at least some of its currency from contemporary anthropological ideas about race, culture, and evolution (see Fox, 1985, pp.150–3; Bolt, 1984, pp. 129–30; Street, 1975, p. 5).

A second strand in martial thinking introduced a climatic-environmental element. The most favoured argument was that we find warlike peoples in hilly, cooler places while in hot, flat regions races are timid, servile, and unwarlike (see Creagh, p. 233).[2] Both these strands of martial thought could be and were employed in the designation of Gurkhas as a martial people. So after 1857, the British felt the need to reconsider the suitability of certain previously-favoured groups (such as the men from Awadh) for military enlistment; there was a dramatic fall in the number of battalions recruited from traditional areas in the east and south, and a corresponding rise in the numbers recruited from the north (Omissi, 1991, p. 12). The intellectual justification for the revision of enlistment policy was provided by senior military figures such as Field Marshal Lord Roberts and Lieutenant General G. F. MacMunn, whose ideas on martiality were shared, according to Mason, by 'nine out of ten' British officers and 'perhaps more' (Mason, 1974, p. 348; Roberts, 1897/2; MacMunn and Lovett, 1911; MacMunn, 1932). Alongside the new bias towards north India, attention was increasingly focused on Nepal.[3]

MARTIAL NEPALIS

In Nepal, the notion that some groups are more suited to military occupations than others pre-dates the flowering of the 'martial race' theory in nineteenth-century British India. Prithvi Narayan Shah, the ruler of Gorkha at the time of the invasion of the Kathmandu Valley in the third quarter of the eighteenth century, and regarded as the 'father' of modern Nepal, is reported to have favoured the idea that only four *jat* ('castes' or 'tribes') should be enlisted in his army—namely, the (caste) Thakuris and Khas (Chetris), and the (tribal) Gurungs and Magars—and that the priestly (Brahman) and lowest ('untouchable') groups should be excluded (Stiller, 1989 [1968], p. 44).[4] The ethnic or jat composition of the Nepalese Army at the time of his conquest of the valley of Kathmandu is a matter of some uncertainty and much speculation. While there is widespread agreement that Chetris and Thakuris provided the bulk of the officer class, opinions as to the identities of the other ranks are mixed. Bennett, for example, in her study of a rural area in central Nepal points out that the high castes ('Chetri-Bahuns') regard themselves as having formed the bulk of the conquering army of Prithvi Narayan Shah (1983, p. 10). This reinforces Kirkpatrick's observation that in the latter part of the eighteenth century, Brahmans and Chetris 'compose[d] the army of the state' (1811, p. 183). Others, such as Shaha, insist that the Gorkha Army included Magars and Gurungs as well as Chetris and Thakuris (1986, p. 5), which view accords with that attributed to the Gorkha king himself in *Dibya Upadesh* (see above).

A series of Nepalese government orders issued during the 1814–16 war with the East India Company also suggests that not all groups were expected or allowed to fight. While 'weapons-bearing castes' were instructed to report with their swords, shields, bows, arrows, and muskets, members of the ('untouchable') blacksmith caste (Kami) were required to make themselves available for metal work at munitions factories and forts; Damais (musicians)—also 'untouchables'—were instructed to bring their musical instruments to accompany the troops; and Brahmans were ordered to recite scriptures and pray for victory.[5] Subsequently, most Western (and especially military) authors have come to insist on, though they do not provide much evidence for, a preponderance of Magars and Gurungs in the Nepalese forces at the outbreak of the Anglo-Nepal War (see Vansittart, 1894, p. 213; Pemble, 1971, p. 26). This may simply be a case of reasoning *ipso post facto,* since following the war, as we shall see, Magars and

Gurungs were singled out as pre-eminently suited for military occupations, and became the principal groups enlisted as recruits. One British Gurkha officer, writing about the war, argues:

> we may surmise that the Nepalese troops opposed to [the East India Company's Generals] Gillespie and Ochterlony were the pick of their service and composed to a great extent of the classes (for example Magars) we value so much nowadays [Shakespear, 1913, p. 379].

Probably the first European to refer to Nepal's 'martial tribes' was Hamilton (1819, p. 19), and from the Anglo-Nepal war, during which the British 'discovered' the fighting qualities of their Nepalese opponents, certain ethnic groups were regularly labelled in this way. Like those in north India, they were believed to have something in their make-up, in their blood, which made them inherently inclined towards military occupations. So Nepalese deserters and prisoners were recruited into special Gurkha battalions even during the Anglo-Nepal war, and several decades later, following the Mutiny, the numbers of Gurkha units and recruits increased. Hodgson, who was at the British Residency in Kathmandu during the third and fourth decades of the nineteenth century, labelled particular groups as 'martial classes' (1833, p. 220) and urged their recruitment. Hodgson's classification had a very pragmatic political motive (that is, fear of a resurgence of Nepalese militarism), but in time the underlying reason for his plea disappeared in the general rhetoric surrounding the development of 'martial race' ideas in the Indian Army. Significantly, the Nepalese warriors on whom British admiration was lavished were the ordinary soldiers and not their officers. The view was becoming widespread that, as Lord Roberts was later to pronounce, 'eastern races ... do not possess the qualities that go to make leaders of men' (1897, p. 444). So the Nepalis could only realize their enormous martial potential under the tutelage, supervision, and leadership of British officers (see Northey, 1937, p. 196). Shortly after the Anglo-Nepal war, the Nepalese government actually offered to place units of its army—with their own officers—at the disposal of the Company; but the British refused, and insisted on recruiting only ordinary riflemen, who would be commanded by British officers.

The notion of Gurkhas as a martial race developed fully towards the end of the nineteenth century. British officers enthusiastically proclaimed the virtues of their soldiers. 'Their fighting qualities,' wrote the author of the first handbook on Gurkhas, 'are *nulli secundus* amongst the troops we enrol in our ranks from the varied classes of our Indian Empire' (Vansittart, 1894, p. 249). They are, he later added in his revised handbook on the Gurkhas, 'natural fighters', and, moreover, the cool and bracing climate of the Nepalese hills produced a robust character, physically as well as morally superior to that of any Hindu of the plains or valleys (1915, p. 10).

By the end of the nineteenth century, regiments were permitted to enlist men only from the martial tribes or classes described by headquarters. As India had been, Nepal was divided into ethnic units and a particular set of characteristics was attributed to each on the basis of personal observations. This was especially extemporaneous in the case of Nepalese groups, since British recruiting officers were unable to visit the country (which was closed to all foreigners until after 1951), and so had no first-hand knowledge of it. Nonetheless, a few officers became avid ethnographers, producing handbooks in which ethnic differences were stressed and highlighted (see, for example, Vansittart, 1915; Morris, 1933; Gibbs, 1947). Military authors disregarded the ethnic and linguistic heterogeneity of the various groups inhabiting the middle hills of Nepal (on which all recruitment was concentrated). Differences were rendered insignificant by the premise of a common 'biology' and environment, which transmitted the collective martial inheritance. Indian army handbooks, as Omissi points out, were part of 'the urge to measure, codify and classify the Indian population' so that 'India could be comprehended (and therefore controlled)...' (1991, p. 19). The tendency was to attribute to whole groups particular characteristics (such as martiality) which, as we have already noted, were thought to be passed on from generation to generation. Stereotyped ethnic identities were thus carefully cultivated over many years, and continually reiterated and reinforced both in the literature produced by military writers, and orally within the informal contexts of British officers' interaction (such as the mess).

These strategies of division and classification have been seen as part of 'the instinctive defence mechanism of imperialism, an understandable tendency to seek out those groups who might be relied upon by the colonial power and exclude those who could not' (Omissi, 1991, p. 8; see also Enloe, 1980, p. 25). But whatever the practical politico-military implications of these policies, it is important not to overlook or dismiss the content of the martial ideology itself, which came in time to be regarded as a 'truth emergent from the nature of society itself' (Des Chene, 1991, p. 75).

The Martial Groups of Nepal

For some years, Hodgson's identification of martial groups in Nepal formed a recruiting blueprint, and mainly ('tribal') Magars and Gurungs were taken. Indeed, at one point, the Nepalese prime minister is reported to have begged the Indian army not to insist so exclusively on enlisting only members of these two communities, since the areas of western Nepal in which they lived were becoming denuded of their young men (Husain, 1970, p. 246). Hodgson's other specified martial class, the (higher caste) Khas (or Chetris)—which implied the (royal caste of) Thakuris as well—whom he deemed to be somewhat less desirable because of their 'brahmanical prejudices' and devotion to the House of Gorkha (Hodgson, 1833, p. 220), were lightly recruited before the Mutiny, but hardly at all for several decades after it (Cardew, 1891, p. 136). Although a special regiment was formed for high-caste groups in 1893, the Gurkhas still drew their numbers predominantly from among the Magars and Gurungs who, Vansittart asserted, were 'by common consent recognised as the *beau ideal* of what a Gurkha soldier should be' (1894, p. 223).

Even some 'tribal' groups who shared a common middle-hill environment as well as many aspects of history, language, and culture with the Magars and Gurungs were not initially labelled 'martial'. Peoples of the eastern hills, such as the Rais and Limbus, while acknowledged as good fighters and taken into para-military units such as the Burma Military Police and the Assam Rifles, were deemed too headstrong and quarrelsome, and so too undisciplined, to be labelled real martial classes. These latter groups, however, were gradually re-classified as martial. Another Tibeto-Burman community, the Tamangs, who were even closer to the Gurungs and Magars in terms of both geographical propinquity and culture–history, did not acquire a martial label until the middle of this century (see Gibbs, 1947), although the latest Gurkha handbook declares that the Tamang 'makes an excellent soldier' (Leonard, 1965, p. 113). While early handbooks tended to blame Tamang dietary habits (they were reputed to eat beef) for the virtual ban on their enlistment, more recent handbooks admitted that the principal region of Tamang settlement in central Nepal was closed to recruitment on the insistence of the Nepalese government (Gibbs, 1947, p. 21). Pahari suggests that these areas were closed because they immediately surrounded the capital, and the country's political rulers exercised a virtual monopoly on Tamang labour, which was in 'bondage to the state and Kathmandu elites'. Thus while they were relatively numerous in the Nepalese police and army, their number in foreign armies was 'disproportionately low' (Pahari, 1991, p. 9). The implication is that British recruiting policy and the theory of martiality on which it was based took account of such circumstances. In similar fashion, they acquiesced in the tea-planters' request not to interfere with their labour pool for the tea gardens, and for a time recruitment was prohibited in Darjeeling, where members of a number of Nepalese martial communities had migrated (Vansittart, 1915, p. 157). By the commencement of World War I, Magars, Gurungs, Rais, and Limbus were acknowledged as the principal 'Gurkha tribes', Thakurs and Khas were still being listed as such, and another Tibeto-Burman group, the Sunwars, had been added to the list (ibid., p. 47).

Thus, despite the notion that martiality was 'bred in the bone' and/or environmentally determined by the climate, of the middle hills, the identity of Nepalese fighting groups—such as those in India (Dewey, 1992; Omissi, 1991, p. 10)—did not remain static over time, and was subject to various 'external' influences. Nonetheless, martiality was perceived to be the key ingredient in enlistment. Ragsdale estimates that approximately 60 per cent of men entering Gurkha service between 1894 and 1913 were recruited as Magars and Gurungs, 27.5 per cent as Rais and Limbus, while all other ethnic communities (including Khas and Thakuris) contributed about 12.5 per cent of recruits (1990, p. 13).

The Place of Martiality

British officers with the Gurkhas also stressed the importance of 'place' in certifying groups and individuals as 'martial'. Thus, a group which was normally deemed martial could only be so in its own native territory. There was a belief that when, for example, Gurungs or Magars migrated to the east of the country from their original homes in western Nepal, as many of them did, they somehow ceased to retain the qualities which characterized them as martial in the first place. Military writers make statements such as 'Gurungs of Eastern Nepal are practically not Gurungs at all', or 'the Magars of Eastern Nepal are ... very much inferior to those of Central Nepal ... in all respects' (Vansittart, 1915, pp. 78, 86); or again, Magars and Gurungs outside their native habitat are 'usually of inferior quality and are not normally enlisted' (Northey, 1937, p. 94). Such assertions were usually not accompanied by any explanation, but where a reason was given it was that intermarriage had occurred—so the blood which carried the military qualities had been contaminated. Officers with the Gurkhas shared the general British abhorrence of 'miscegenation' and insisted on recruiting 'unsullied' members of the martial classes. Vansittart refers to the Magars' 'proper habitat' west of the Kathmandu Valley, where 'undoubtedly the best and purest Magars are found' (1915, p. 82). But one section (the Gharti) was pronounced 'more mixed' than other (pure) Magar sections, and so those responsible for enlistment were warned to be cautious when confronted with members of the former group (Vansittart, 1894, p. 230). Similarly, recruiters were informed that, whereas Thakurs were 'good material', the Hamal Thakur or progeny of a Thakur and Brahman 'should not be enlisted by any regiment' (Vansittart, 1915, p. 62).

British officers in the Gurkhas believed in the idea that character could be fundamentally influenced by place. For years they debated the respective merits and traits of 'western' and 'eastern' Gurkhas (see Smith, 1973, p. 40). Men belonging to regiments recruited in western Nepal were (thought to be more phlegmatic but of better humour, while those enlisted from the eastern side of the country were comparatively dour and quicker to anger. While explanations for these attributes were seldom given, when pressed at interview, officers might account for the differences in terms of settlement patterns or the productivity of land.

The significance of 'place' also featured centrally in the longstanding debate about the martial quality of 'line boys', the sons and grandsons of soldiers who had been born in the family 'lines' of the Gurkha battalions, had been to school, and had experienced the 'fleshpots' of India before independence, and later those of Malaya, Brunei, or Hong Kong, where the regiments subsequently were quartered. The view was widespread among British officers that contact with towns corrupted a Gurkha's purity and simplicity, and so his fighting ability; and elaborate precautions were taken by recruiters to enlist only young men from the more remote parts of the Nepalese hills. The literature is replete with speculations about the extent of martial deterioration as a result of growing up in the lines. MacMunn reasoned that if such a boy had a Gurkha mother he would have 'sucked in' the regimental tradition with her milk, and kept most of the warlike traits of his father for at least one generation (1932, p. 199). Similarly, early Gurkha handbooks reported that, while their physique did not deteriorate much in a single generation, their morality did, so that 'they are often men of loose habits, and are not dependable, the chief characteristics of the Gurkha being almost entirely absent from their characters .... There is no doubt that the real Gurkha despises them ...' (Morris, 1933, p. 126; see also Vansittart, 1915, p. 92). Another military author concluded that by the second generation, the line boys could hardly achieve the standard of the 'hill-bred article' as far as things such as morals and dependability were concerned (Northey, 1937, p. 195).

This prejudice against line boys developed fully in the latter part of the nineteenth century alongside the general British preference for what were assumed to be simple villagers, and the distrust of literate or semi-literate urban dwellers. In the middle of the nineteenth century, the Gurkha regiments had actually seemed anxious to recruit line boys. In a letter to the Deputy Adjutant-General of the Indian Army, the then Commander of the Sirmoor (Gurkha) Battalion reported that he was 'encouraging men to bring their families with them, so as to have boys on the lines. These lads .... I find just as good in the Field as the fresh Goorkah from Nepaul ... and far more intelligent ...'.[6] But within a few decades—and especially following the Mutiny—any idea of favouring men raised in the lines or in towns had disappeared. It was the 'extra wild Goorkhalees' who were now regarded as the 'most trustworthy'.[7] Uneducated youths from the hills were definitely preferred to educated young men from the plains—that is, towns (Forbes, 1964, p. 158). 'If we were to judge by the Gurkha soldier', wrote one senior British officer, 'then we would conclude that mankind is happiest and most honest where ... civilising influences are least' (Tuker, 1957, p. 3). The most severe deterioration in martial qualities was assumed to occur among what one author called the 'flotsam and jetsam who have drifted into the big cities' (Gibbs, 1947, p. 5). In Calcutta, we are informed, 'evil communications corrupt good manners', and the Gurkha declines rapidly (Nortbey, 1937, pp. 195–6; see also Morris, 1933, p. 126).[8]

Masculinity

The rhetoric of martiality embraced an idealized notion of masculinity. Indeed, the two terms were occasionally used interchangeably. MacMunn, for example, might refer to martial classes as 'manly' classes (1932, p. 358). Martial races possessed obvious masculine qualities which the non-martial races lacked. The British, we are told, found the 'fighting races' more attractive than the 'passive, supine Hindus ...' (Parry 1972, p. 50). Said (1985, p. 23) has pointed out that the Orient was routinely described as feminine, and Inden has recently reiterated that imperial India was widely imagined as a female presence, lacking Western (masculine) rationality. Hinduism was seen to exemplify a mentality favouring the passions over reason and will, 'the two inevitable components of world-ordering rationality' (1990, pp. 85–9). In the novels of empire, too, the people of India were seen as 'volatile and passionate', quintessentially female qualities (Mannsaker, 1983). Even male dress was described as graceful but essentially feminine (Tarlo, in press). The widely held perception was therefore of European (masculine) reason dominant over an Indian (feminine) nature.

The military authors who created the discourse on Gurkhas discovered in non-martial India the very antithesis of manhood. The merchants and town-dwellers lacked 'guts' (MacMunn, 1932, p. 345), while the intelligentsia were dismissed as effeminate (ibid., p. 354). Masters tells us that south Indians, who inhabited what the British termed the 'sloth belt', were all thought timid (1956, p. 145). But the Bengalis, as Robb notes in his introduction to this volume, had the worst of it. They were castigated as 'soft' (Roberts, 1897/2, p. 383), 'languid and enervated' (Oldfield, 1974 [1880], p. 262), and 'hopeless poltroons' (MacMunn and Lovett, 1911, p. 130).[9] MacMunn made it plain that the British had little regard for them, reserving their 'respect and affection for martial classes' (1932, p. 345).

Nepal came out rather well in the masculinity stakes. It benefitted especially by contrast, since it bordered on the homeland of what one military writer called the 'least masculine' of India's people—in Bihar and Bengal (Tuker, 1950, p. 626). Nepalis also compared well against the 'effeminate races of the South' (Roberts, 1897, p. 442). The contrast between plains and hills, moreover, served almost as a metaphor for masculine–feminine distinctions. The hills bred robust and sturdy men, who looked down on men of the plains as soft and supine (Forbes, 1964, pp. 54–5; see also Bayly, 'Caste and "Race" in the Colonial Ethnography of India', in Peter Robb (ed.), *The Concept of Race in South Asia*, Delhi: 1995; on Elliott). One British officer wrote to his mother, after his transfer to the plains from the regimental station in the hills of what is now Pakistan, that 'all the locals seem half-dead after the Pathans ... [T]he Pathan has his faults but is a man anyway.'[10]

Nepal itself has, since the Anglo-Nepal war, been consistently portrayed by the British very much in masculine terms. Vansittart conveys the image by noting, for one thing, that the purity of Nepal's soil (as compared to that of India) had not been sullied by the 'foot of the Mohamedan conqueror'—it is interesting that he does not consider India's soil as having been 'sullied' by the British conqueror—and, for another, that the Nepalis had fought the Company 'in fair conflict like men'. Even Nepal's lingua franca (Khas-kura or Gurkhali, as the British writers called it) had a hard, masculine quality: 'terse, simple ... very characteristic of the unlettered but energetic race of soldiers and statesmen who made it what it is' (Vansittart, 1915, pp. 10, 32, and 67).[11]

Military writers also conveyed the manliness of the country in two main kinds of trope. In one, Nepal was seen as a 'military state' in which a military 'outlook' pervaded every section of society, so that the whole ethos of the Nepalese state was perceived to consist in militarism. Hodgson wrote not only of the 'martial propensities' and 'martial habits' of the highland tribes, but more generally of the 'warlike enthusiasm of the people' (1833, p. 205). He referred to the 'exclusive military and aggressive genius of the Gorkha institutions, habits and sentiments' (see Hasrat, 1970, p. 234). Campbell, the Assistant Surgeon at the British Residency in Kathmandu during much of Hodgson's tenure, also detected a natural propensity for the masculine activity of warfare, and the 'abhorrence of all the military tribes in Nepal to engaging in other pursuits than that of arms ...' ibid., p. 226). And the theme was taken up by British military writers. One wrote of the Government of Nepal as a 'purely militarist government of a purely military people' (Bruce, 1928, p. xxiii).

In a second kind of trope, these authors stressed the contrast between what they perceived as the pervasive obsequiousness of Indians—especially those who inhabited the plains—and the spirit of independence found among the martial people of Nepal. It is not only the Gurkha as an individual or member of a martial group who possess the qualities associated with autonomy and self-reliance, but the whole political ambience in which he has lived for generations. These military writers therefore contrast the colonial subjugation of India, on the one side, with what they term Nepal's spirit of independence, on the other, a spirit which was thought symptomatic and generative of the Kingdom's military strength, dignity, and (by implication) masculinity. Nepal, wrote Woodyatt, 'enjoys complete independence' (1922, p. 158), while according to Morris it is a 'completely independent country and in no way subject to the orders of the Government of India ...' (1935, p. 425). Northey, for his part, insists that in light of Nepal's independent status, the British Resident in Kathmandu occupies an 'entirely different position from that of a Resident in a native state in India' (1937, p. 59). But of course the Treaty of Sagauli, which concluded the Nepal-East India Company war of 1814–16, had imposed the Resident—the only representative of an outside power permanently stationed in the country—who kept an eye on Nepal's internal affairs, and for over a century severely restricted its right to conduct its own foreign policy. Nepal's independence was clearly limited to the extent allowed by the British (Mojumdar, 1973; see also Rose, 1971, pp. 171–2; Des Chene, 1991, pp. 153–8).

The Persistence of Martial Thinking

Although the 'martial race' theory was effectively suspended during both World Wars—in order to achieve the massive recruitment targets set by the Indian Army—the end of hostilities on both occasions saw its return as the main basis of enlistment. Omissi shows that, after World War I, the Indian Army 'returned to its pre-war ethnic mix', and that 'martial race' thinking was not abandoned. If the theory was no longer the colonial strategy it had once been, it had nonetheless become a 'habit of mind' (1991, pp. 21–2). If anything, it received a fillip with the publication in 1932 of MacMunn's volume on *The Martial Races of India.*

Even World War II, in which over 2,00,000 Nepalis of every description took part, appears not to have seriously shaken the confidence of British military thinkers and authors in the soundness of the theory of martiality, since it persists in providing the basis of recruitment to the Brigade of Gurkhas in the post-colonial British Army. The section of the Nepalese population from which recruits are sought continues to comprise only a tiny proportion (some 6 per cent) of the total population of the country, and the area in which this population is found (the middle hills) constitutes about one-third of the total area of Nepal (Edwards, 1978, p. 228). Gibbs' manual on the Gurkhas, prepared in 1943 and published just after World War II, defines the 'true Gurkha' as 'a man of the martial clans of Nepal' (1947, p. 6), and lists those ethnic groups which provide true Gurkhas. Similarly, Leonard's handbook of 1965—prepared for a post-war, post-Indian independence generation, and recommended to British officers joining the Gurkhas even today—has a table listing the districts in which ethnic groups who supply

Gurkhas are to be found, with comments about their martial qualities. Thus, Gurungs, in one administrative area, are said to be available only in small numbers and 'are not of the best type', while Magars in another area are numerous and 'of good type'. Even particular clans are labelled: in Palpa there are 'excellent' Thapa Magars, but 'careful selection is necessary and the foothills must be avoided' (Leonard, 1965, pp. 138–9). These reproduce the kinds of assessments offered by Vansittart in his 1915 handbook: this Thapa clan 'needs careful enlisting' or that Thapa clan 'should not be enlisted' (see above). Thus, on the basis of evaluating a few individuals at one point in time, entire groups inhabiting large tracts of territory continue to be stereotyped as fit or unfit for martial tasks. The latest handbook also indicates the persistence long after the end of World War II of ideas about the significance of place, with statements insisting that, for example, Thakurs in eastern Nepal must be cautiously selected because it is not their 'natural habitat' (Leonard, 1965, p. 139). Finally, the underlying theory of martiality is reiterated and reinforced when the same author traces the origin of the martial spirit in Nepal to the 'infusion of north Indian blood into the brave, but unenterprising hill tribes' (ibid., p. 27).

Recent military contributors to the literature on Gurkhas still refer to 'martial tribes' (see Bredin, 1961; Davis, 1970; Niven, 1987) and express a traditional view on line boys. Thus, although the prejudice against the latter is said to have eased somewhat following World War I (see Woodyatt, 1922, p. 194), Cross continues to insist that because of being raised away from their villages, line boys simply do not possess the 'inherent chemistry engendered by an upbringing in the hills' which enables them to 'make good if they are enlisted', although he shares the widespread opinion that the education they receive in British Army schools 'is useful when technicians and specialists are being recruited' (Cross, 1986, pp. 133–4). Writers also continue to refer to the 'demanding environment' of the middle hills which form the 'hard, stoical, self-disciplined but cheerful characteristics of the Gurkhas who join the British Army' (Edwards, 1979, p. 222). The image of autonomous and independent men produced by harsh surroundings also endures. According to one military writer, these qualities are found quintessentially among the Gurungs, described as nomadic pastoralists who, like the Pathans, were:

> a tribe of warriors, preferring the spoils of war to the tedium of weaving blankets, tilling the fields and minding their flocks. Moving about amid the

remotest Himalayan steeps and valleys .... Perched on the heights, with their flocks ... [even today] the more solitary herdsman seldom comes into conversation with other folk [Tuker, 1957, p. 33].

Like many an anthropologist, these military writers see in this imagined pastoralism what Rosaldo refers to as the 'idealized characteristics of a certain masculine imagination—fierce pride', a warrior spirit, rugged individualism ...'(1986, p. 96).

An alternative to the Gurkha as pastoralist 'free spirit' is the image of the soldier as 'yeoman'. The Gurkhas, writes one post-colonial military author, 'were freehold yeoman farmers' who had 'bred in them a spirit of independence' (Forbes, 1964, p. 55). As Green has pointed out, the English also believed themselves to be a nation of yeoman soldiers (1980, p. 34), and the label was frequently attached to the martial classes in the Indian and especially the pre-Mutiny Bengal Army (see Peers, 1991, p. 551). However misleading this application of a category delineating nineteenth-century British society to contemporary South Asian contexts, it is meant to imply, among other things, that these martial people have come from the middle order of the agricultural classes, and thus share the pride and self-esteem thought to characterize the small landowner. As one senior British officer who had served with the Gurkhas commented in an interview: 'We only recruited people with land, and not landless labourers, so we creamed off the best—the independent yeomen'.

Men seeking enlistment in the Gurkhas are by now well aware of these British predilections for rural recruits possessing the idealized characteristics of a martial people. So, although many young Gurungs, for example, nowadays want to join the Gurkhas precisely to escape the village and to have money to live well in what *they* regard as modern and civilized conditions (that is, the towns), they feel obliged to present themselves to recruiters as rustics, and to stress their martial qualities—that is, to play up to the British image of the ideal Gurkha (see Des Chene, 1991). In other ways too, the Gurkhas reproduce the rhetoric of martiality created by the British. While in Nepal in 1988, I was told by one former soldier that the governments of other countries regularly request Nepal to send quantities of Gurkha semen/seed *(biu)* so as to acquire their martial attributes. Like others labelled martial, then, Nepalis who were, are, or seek to become Gurkhas are, as Fox observes, compelled 'to adapt to British beliefs about them' (1985, p. 4).

Discussion and Conclusion

Dawson has drawn attention to the durability of the image, within Western cultural traditions, of the soldier as paragon of masculinity. In the Indian colonial context this ideal 'became intimately bound up with ... the imagining of imperial identity, in which the Englishman enjoyed a natural, racial superiority over the ... peoples who had been subordinated to British imperial power' (1991, p. 119). The representation of Gurkhas by their British chroniclers in strongly martial–masculine terms may be seen therefore as a recognition in the Gurkhas of those very qualities which enabled the British to fashion an empire.

The discourse on martiality, grounded in nineteenth-century biological determinism, has survived with some slight modifications into the period post Indian independence and quite different scientific presuppositions.[12] Some scholars have from time to time declared the end of martial theory, but it endures in British writings about Gurkhas, although 'races' have become 'tribes' or 'classes', and the language of disdain for non-martial people has turned softer. Certainly, ethnological knowledge has grown as British officers have come into contact with a wider cross-section of Nepalese hill society, and personally gained access to many parts of the country previously closed to them, and this has been reflected in recent publications. Yet the portrait of Gurkha 'character'—in terms of inherent qualities of martiality—has remained remarkably consistent (see also Des Chene, 1991, p. 81). Despite the many changes in the home environments from which the soldiers originate, and in the politico-military contexts within which the Brigade itself is situated, the Gurkhas appear caught in a time warp woven by their military chroniclers. While some officers informally contradict, even disclaim, many of the stereotypes offered in the literature, latter-day texts continue to essentialize the Gurkhas in much the same way as they did in the past.

Why should this be so? Why should ideologies generated within and fostered by an imperial context continue to pervade post-imperial military writings? One answer may simply be that images and perceptions of others tend to persist through time, despite the changing political and ideological environments in which they arose in the first place. This is especially so where those who represent others exercise dominion over virtually all aspects of their subjects' lives.

The officers, from whose ranks emerge those who perpetuate the discourse on Gurkhas, control the enlistment, training, assessment, promotion, disciplining—and so ultimately the livelihoods—of their soldiers. Such omnipotence would encourage most authors to rest secure in the authenticity of their depictions.

Furthermore, tenacity of discourse is implied in the nature of the relationship between the writer and audience of such militaria. The Gurkha literary 'genre' presupposes certain expectations on the part of the reader, to which the author responds (Green, 1980). There is, in other words, something of a conspiracy between writer and audience to preserve these Gurkha 'fictions', in the sense of their consistency over time.

But the perseverance of this discourse on martiality might also be understood against the background of political and military upheavals following World War II: fundamental changes in the size and role of the British army consequent on post-war economic and power realignments, and the rapid collapse of the empire. These developments had direct consequences for the Gurkhas, which were manifested in the traumatic division of regiments between the armies of Britain and independent India in 1947–8. Some 20 years later, the end of 'confrontation' in South-East Asia (in which the Gurkhas had played a vital role) had further repercussions for the Brigade. Sometimes described as the British Army's last great colonial battle, this was followed not only by dramatic alterations in the size and dispositions of the Gurkha regiments, but by a felt transformation in the officers' attitudes towards their calling, encouraged in part by changes in the composition of the officer corps itself. This period is perceived as heralding the rise of the career officer, for whom service with Gurkhas was only one of several possible stages in the course of professional advancement, and the corresponding demise of the regimental officer, devoted above all to his unit, his colleagues, and his Gurkha soldiers. During interviews with former officers who served during the period up to and including 'confrontation' in South-East Asia, they would invariably refer to the hostility shown by even the most senior officers to 'careerism', perceived as an insidious threat to the regimental focus of the British Gurkha officer. In the words of one: 'In the 1960s we were extremely reactionary. The company commanders in those days were wartime officers who were totally devoted to Gurkhas, and you were distrusted if you went to staff college.' Another recalled: 'In the days of Confrontation we never thought of leaving. Nobody went outside his regiment, thought of going away even for career reasons. It was only when Confrontation ended that people began getting career-minded.'

The great majority of officers who moulded the discourse and authored the literature on Gurkhas—including the most recent texts—spent their formative years in this kind of colonial or neo-colonial setting, and regarded themselves as zealously attached to 'their' Gurkhas. Against the background of what appears to these officer-authors as retrogressive change, the continuity of Gurkha portraits might therefore be understood as their attempt to preserve an image of something which no longer obtains, but which they feel should be cherished. In this respect, these Gurkha depictions are like the pre-World War I travel books which sought to retain the illusion of bygone places which had long since passed out of existence (Fussell, 1980, p. 226). Through textualization, a disappearing world might be preserved (Clifford, 1986, p. 112).

Finally, it has to be noted that in numerous ways Gurkhas have been depicted as honorary Europeans, possessing the most endearing qualities of their public school-educated British officers—courage, humour, honour, and so on. Their virtues, moreover, were consistently emphasized in contrast to the negatively-evaluated qualities of non-martial Indians (and Nepalis) who represented 'Otherness' for these authors (Caplan, 1991). The image of Gurkhas as inherently martial thus reflects the way in which British officers have for a very long time perceived themselves, and the endurance of such an image may be read as an attempt on the part of the latter to situate their own sense of identity in what would seem to be a timeless and unchanging 'racial' essence.

Notes

1. In the view of Bingley and Nicholls, authors of a military handbook on Brahmans, 'fighting capacity is entirely dependent on race ...'. *Caste Handbooks for the Indian Army: Brahmans*, Calcutta: 1918, p. 47.
2. Heathcote points out that this hypothesis, that 'hard countries breed hard men', goes back at least as far as Herodotus and was popular in the post-Mutiny Indian context because of its simplicity. T. A. Heathcote, *The Indian Army: The Garrison of British Imperial India, 1822–1922*, Vancouver: 1974, p. 93.
3. Since the focus of this essay is on the specific discourses generated by British Gurkha officers, I cannot consider the varieties of martial race theorizing in India, or their development over time.
4. According to *Dibya Upadesh,* Prithvi Narayan at first planned to

include the brahmans among his army to attack the valley, but it reports that his uncle advised him that if he did so, there would be 'sin everywhere' (Stiller, 1989 [1968], p. 40). Thereafter, the brahmans were not included in his fighting jat.

5. Regmi Research Series, 16, 1984, pp. 11–12. Chakravarti argues that brahmans served as soldiers and commanders of armies in ancient India and were frequently represented as such in the epic literature (1941, 78–9). And of course the Bengal Army in the eighteenth and nineteenth centuries included many brahmans, a fact of which the Nepalis would certainly have been aware. It is therefore possible that while brahmans were not compelled to bear arms in Nepal, many in fact did so.
6. Major C. Reid to Major Norman, 25 January 1858, Letter Books, 2nd KEO Goorkhas.
7. Lieutenant Colonel D. Macintyre, CO 2GR, to Adjutant General, 1 February 1878, Letter Books, 2nd KEO Goorkhas.
8. The same prejudice applied to Muslims in north India, who would not be recruited if they lived in towns. Omissi points to the irony of declaring such men to make poor soldiers when they could not be enlisted in the first place (1991, p. 10).
9. The frontispiece of Woodyatt's (1922) book on the Gurkhas contains a photograph of a British Gurkha general dressed (presumably for a costume party) as a 'Native Clerk', with dhoti and kurta, waistcoat, turban, and umbrella. The resident British community of the period would immediately have recognized the stereotype of the 'baboo', and no doubt found it immensely amusing.
10. Unpublished letters, Oriental and India Office Collections of the British Library.
11. In his study of masculinity, Seidler points out that masculine language is seen as 'deeply instrumental' (1989, p. 63).
12. Cohen suggests that 'no one believes in this enlightened age in the theory of martial castes' calls for a Gilbert and Sullivanesque response: well, hardly anyone—except the military. Cohen suggests that the theory of martiality is still 'widespread' in independent India (1971, p. 47). Though officially discredited, it appears to survive in the ways its soldiers are organized and portrayed. Not only are they still grouped in ethnic regiments, but military authors continue to list the special qualities of each, using terms made familiar by the British (see, for example, Das, 1984).

References

Names preceded by an asterisk (*) are British officers who served with Gurkhas.

Bennett, L., *Dangerous Wives and Sacred Sisters*, New York: 1983.

Bingley, A. H. and A. Nicholls, *Caste Handbooks for the Indian Army: Brahmans,* Calcutta: 1918.

Bolt, C., 'Race and the Victorians', in C. Eldridge (ed.), *British Imperialism in the Nineteenth Century,* London: 1984.

*Bredin , A. E. C., *The Happy Warriors: The Gurkha Soldier in the British Army,* Gillingham, Dorset: 1961.

*Bruce, C. G., Foreword to W. B. Northey and C. J. Morris, *The Gurkhas: Their Manners, Customs and Country,* London: 1928.

Caplan, L., '"Bravest of the Brave": Representations of "the Gurkha" in British Military Writings', *Modern Asian Studies,* vol. 25, 1991, pp. 571–97.

Cardew, F. G., 'Our Recruiting Grounds of the Future for the Indian Army', *Journal of the United Service Institution of India,* 20(86), 1891, pp. 131–46.

Chakravarti, P. C., *The Art of War in Ancient India,* Dacca: 1941.

Clifford, J., 'On Ethnographic Allegory', in J. Clifford and G. E. Marcus (eds), *Writing Culture: The Poetics and Politics of Ethnography,* Berkeley: 1986.

Cohen, S. P., *The Indian Army: Its Contribution to the Development of a Nation,* Berkeley: 1971.

Creagh, Sir O'Moore, *Indian Studies,* London: n.d..

Cross, J. P., *In Gurkha Company: The British Army Gurkhas, 1948 to the Present,* London: 1986.

Das, Chand, N., *Traditions and Customs of the Indian Armed Forces,* New Delhi: 1984.

*Davis, P., *A Child at Arms,* London: 1970.

Dawson, G., 'The Blond Bedouin: Lawrence of Arabia, Imperial Adventure and the Imagining of English-British Masculinity', in M. Roper and J. Tosh (eds), *Manful Assertions: Masculinities in Britain since 1800,* London: 1991.

Des Chene, M. 'Relics of Empire: A Cultural History of the Gurkhas, 1815–1987', PhD thesis, Stanford University: 1991.

Dewey, Clive, 'Racism and Realism: The Theory or the Martial Caste', unpublished paper given to the SOAS workshop on 'the Concept of Race in South Asia', 2 December, 1992.

*Edwards, J. H., 'Nepal and the Brigade of Gurkhas', *Royal Engineers Journal,* vol. 93, 1979, pp. 220–30.

Enloe, C. H., *Ethnic Soldiers: State Security in Divided Societies,* Harmondsworth: 1980.

*Forbes, D., *Johnny* Gurkha, London: 1964.

Fox, R. G., *Lions of the Punjab: Culture in the Making,* Berkeley: 1985.

Fussell, P., *Abroad: British Literary Travelling between the Wars,* New York: 1980.

*Gibbs, H. R. K., *The Gurkha* Soldier, Calcutta: 1947.

Green, Martin, *Dreams of Adventure, Deeds of Empire,* London: 1980.

Hamilton, F. H., *An Account of the Kingdom of Nepal*, Edinburgh: 1819.

Hasrat, B. J., *History of Nepal: As Told by its Own and Contemporary Chroniclers*, Hoshiarpur, Punjab: 1970.

Heathcote, T. A., *The Indian Army: The Garrison of British Imperial India, 1822–1922*, Vancouver: 1974.

Hodgson, B. H., 'Origin and Classification of the Military Tribes of Nepal', *Journal of the Asiatic Society*, vol. 11, 1833, pp. 17–24.

Husain, A., *British India's Relations with the Kingdom of Nepal 1857–1947*, London: 1970.

Inden, R., *Imagining India*, Oxford: 1990.

Kirkpatrick, W., *An Account of the Kingdom of Nepaul*, London: 1811.

*Leonard, R. G., (for the Ministry of Defence), *Nepal and the Gurkhas*, London: 1965.

MacMunn, Sir G., *The Martial Races of India*, London: 1911.

MacMunn, Sir G. and A. C. Lovett, *The Armies of India*, London: 1911.

Mannsaker, F., 'Early Attitudes to Empire', in B. Moore-Gilbert (ed.), *Literature and Imperialism*, Roehampton: 1983.

Mason, P., *A Matter of Honour: An Account of the Indian Army, its Officers and* Men, London: 1974.

*Masters, J. *Bugles and a Tiger: A Personal Adventure*, London: 1956.

Mojumdar, K., *Anglo-Nepalese Relations in the Nineteenth Century*, Calcutta: 1973.

*Morris, C. J. (compiler), *Gurkhas: Handbooks for the Indian Army*, New Delhi: 1933.

*Morris, C. J. 'Some Aspects of Social Life in Nepal', *Journal of the Royal Central Asiatic Society*, vol. 22, 1935, pp. 425–46.

Niven, Col B. M., *The Mountain Kingdom: Portraits of Nepal and the Gurkhas*, Singapore: 1987.

*Nothey, W. B., *The Land of the Gurkhas or the Himalayan Kingdom of Nepal*, Cambridge: 1937.

Oldfield, H. A., *Sketches from Nepal: Historical and Descriptive with an Essay on Nepalese Buddhism and Illustrations of Religious Monuments and Architecture*, Delhi: 1974 [1880].

Omissi, D., '"Martial Races": Ethnicity and Security in Colonial India 1858–1939', *War and Society*, vol. 9, 1991, pp. 1–27.

Pahari, A., 'Ties that Bind: Gurkhas in History', *Himal*, 4(3), 1991, pp. 6–12.

Parry, B., *Delusions and Discoveries: Studies on India in the British Imagination 1880–1930*, London: 1972.

Peers, D. M., '"The Habitual Nobility of Being": British Officers and the Social Construction of the Bengal Army in the Early Nineteenth Century', *Modern Asian Studies*, vol. 25, 1991, pp. 545–69.

Pemble, J., *The Invasion of Nepal: John Company at War*, Oxford: 1971.

Ragsdale, T. A., 'Gurungs, Goorkhalis, Gurkhas: Speculations on a Nepalese Ethno-history', *Contributions to Nepalese Studies*, vol. 17, 1990, pp. 1–24,

Roberts, Field Marshal Lord, of Kandahar, *Forty-one Years in India: From Subaltern to Commander-in-Chief*, London: 1897.

Rosaldo. R., 'From the Door of his Tent: The Fieldworker and the Inquisitor', in J. Clifford and G. Marcus (eds), *Writing Culture: The Poetics and Politics of Ethnography*, Berkeley: 1986.

Rose, E. L., *Nepal: Strategy for Survival*, Berkeley: 1971.

Said, E., 'Orientalism Reconsidered', in F. Barker *et al.*, *Europe and its Others*, vol. 1, Colchester: 1985.

Seidler, V., *Rediscovering Masculinity: Reason, Language and Sexuality*, London: 1989.

Shaha, R., 'The Rise and Fall of Bhimsen Thapa: The War of 1814–16 with British India and its Aftermath', *Rolamba*, vol. 6, 1986, pp. 2–7.

*Shakespear, L. W., 'The War with Nepal: Operations in Sirmoor, 1814–1815', *Journal of the United Services Institute of India*, vol. XLII, 1913, pp. 369–79.

*Smith, E. D., *Britain's Brigade of Gurkhas*, London: 1973.

Street, B., *The Savage in Literature: Representations of 'Primitive' Society in English Fiction 1858–1920*, London: 1975.

Stiller, L. F., *Prithinarayan Shah in the Light of Dibya Upadesh*, Kathmandu: 1989 [1968].

Tarlo, E., *Dress and Undress in India: The Problem of 'What to Wear' in the Late Colonial and Modern Era*, London: in press.

*Tuker, Sir F., *While Memory Serves*, London: 1950.

——, *Gorkha: The Story of the Gurkhas of Nepal*, London: 1957.

*Vansittart, E., 'The Tribes, Clans and Castes of Nepal', *Journal of the Asiatic Society of Bengal*, 63(2), 1894, pp. 213–49.

——, *Gurkhas: Handbooks for the Indian Army*, Calcutta: 1915.

*Woodyatt, N., *Under Ten Viceroys: The Reminiscences of a Gurkha*, London: 1922.

8

Two Masculine Worlds Compared

The Army Cantonment and Jaipur Rajput Male Society in Late Colonial India

DeWitt C. Ellinwood

Mrinalini Sinha's work on 'Colonial Masculinity' in late nineteenth-century Bengal reveals that questions of British masculinity and Indian male effeminacy were very much an issue.[1] Sinha's work makes clear the 'moral imperialism' that denigrated Indian men, especially Bengalis, and both depressed and elevated Indian women's situations.[2] The tension concerning these concepts produced vigorous, contentious argument. When we turn from that Bengal scene to the two masculine worlds of Amar Singh of Jaipur and the cantonment society of the British officers, there is no such contention. Amar Singh was a Rajasthani Rajput serving in the army in early twentieth-century India.[3] Neither Rajputs nor British officers worried seriously about effeminacy in their midst.[4] A vigorous masculinity was implicit and explicit in their views and lives.

Questions of gender, masculinity, femininity, and related matters recently have become the subject of lively historical, psychological, and social analysis.[5] Despite the strength of custom in both societies, changes were taking place in practice and ideas in the nineteenth and twentieth centuries. Masculinity, as recent studies emphasize, has a history, involving change and creation.[6] Extensive studies have been made of British masculinity of the period. However, such study has focused more on Britain itself and on imperialist qualities than on the British officers and men in the Indian Army, a specific social group. However, many men from the latter service have written autobiographies or been the subjects of biographies, vividly recording military masculinity.

Scholars are producing an increasing body of work about Indian masculinity during the same time period. The major focus of the scholars working on India has been on the region of Bengal, the centre of British government and of extensive Indo-British interactions. Perhaps this emphasis also comes from the sharpness of the contrast between the images of effeminate Bengali *babus* and manly Englishmen. Views of Indian masculinity on a wider scale also have tended to stress the imperial view that contrasted manly Englishmen with unmanly, immature natives. Philippa Levine also stresses the number of distinctions made in colonial masculinities in India and elsewhere.[7] Scholars have paid less attention to other Indian regions. Rosalind O'Hanlon provides an eighteenth century, pre-colonial, north Indian perspective, thus suggesting comparisons with the changing colonial concepts.[8]

The colonial military offers a special subculture of masculinity. Ideas and practices of masculinity were evolving in both countries, and one issue is how British ideas affected Indian concepts. For the colonial military, many have analysed the British 'martial races' notion.[9] The 'martial races' included, most prominently, the Pathans, Rajputs, Punjabis (Sikhs, Muslims, and Hindus), and Gurkhas; but they also included less well-known classes such as Dogras, Gahrwalis, and Hindustani Muslims. The British military, in its gradual nineteenth century development of the 'martial races' concept, adapted Hindu and Indian caste and religious concepts to fit their needs. Extensive literature exists concerning Sikhs, Pathans, Gurkhas, and Rajputs. Although these works about the 'martial races' are not focused on questions of masculinity, they often include information relevant to the subject. The concept of 'masculinity' is a new social science concept, so it did not directly appear in contemporary writings. The term 'manliness' was more common at the time. The Indian Army produced a series of 'Caste Handbooks' about groups recruited by the army.[10] Material about Rajputs and Rajputana (now Rajasthan) is particularly relevant to this study. Important historical studies exist of various Rajput and other Indian notions and practices of martiality, a central element in Indian notions of masculinity.[11]

This essay analyses and provides information on Rajput concepts and expressions of manliness, and British military ideas and practices relating to masculinity. Our point of entry into these societies and their connections is Amar Singh, born in 1878. His sense of manhood and manliness took shape under Rajput guidance, but he was exposed significantly to Anglo-Indian ideas and practices from 1900 onward. As a reference point for our study, we can use a definition of masculinity developed from a study of northern India:

> That aspect of a man's social being which is gendered: which defines him as a man and links him to other men and conditions other aspects of his identity, such as of class, occupation, race, and ethnicity. Masculinity is therefore at once a public social status, a role within family and household, a subjective identity, and a rhetorical trope in public discourse.[12]

Many studies of gender also emphasize the power relationships—meaning, in most cases, the dominance of men over women. Another element needing consideration in discussions of masculinity is the 'material' aspect. One careful analyst of the concept points out that with 'definitions, or theoretical perspectives of masculinity, the question arises: how does this quality relate to what men do, to men's material practices? ... Most versions tend to divert attention away from material practices, whether in work, sexuality, violence, or elsewhere, and away from a materialist or materially based analysis of gendered power relations.'[13] Our study will touch on both concepts and material expressions of masculinity.

Because masculinity was not an issue for the British military or the Rajput aristocracy, men in these societies did not separate their definitions of masculinity from their views of themselves as gentlemen and officers. If there were British officers who did not fit the mould, they were little heard of. Now, however, we know of examples of serious homosexuality among British officers.[14] By way of contrast, an active heterosexuality was 'the demonstrable proof of the masculinity so crucial to the maintenance of the colonial enterprise'.[15] Aristocratic Rajput male society assumed 'manliness', as their tradition called for it, though Amar Singh's diary reveals less than manly qualities in some individuals. Speaking as a manly Rajput, he once said with annoyance that 'the people of Jaipur have not much go in them. They are very effeminate and one comes across rare examples of manliness'.[16] When British officials looked at Rajputs and other members of the 'martial races', they acknowledged their masculinity. Yet they qualified this admiration with the view that such Indians did not possess the manly and leadership qualities necessary for serving as army officers. The Rajputs considered British military personnel to be manly, but this did not detract from their own sense of manliness. This mutual acceptance of and admiration for masculinity was another part of the picture of colonial masculinities in early twentieth-century India. As we will see, 'masculinity' and 'martiality' in both these societies emphasized honour or izzat, courage, vigour, loyalty, and expressiveness.

Amar Singh, a commissioned army officer, though in an ambiguous body—'Native Indian Land Forces', 1905–17—lived in both these worlds: the Rajput aristocratic male world, and the British Indian military world. They mutually reinforced his masculinity.[17] In some ways, Amar Singh was not a typical Rajput. He was typical in his love of hunting, riding, and polo, and in his concern for family and honour. He was unusual because he read voraciously both Western and Indian literature,[18] and because he kept a diary. Also, he was critical of certain common Rajput traits—heavy drinking, indulgence with 'dancing girls' and mistresses, inattention to estates, and leisured lives spent without purpose. He had received a somewhat unusual upbringing. At the age of 10, his father sent him from his home in Jaipur to his father's friend in Jodhpur, Sir Pratap Singh. Pratap, a member of the Jodhpur royal family, was an extraordinary man who mixed Indian and British cultures in his own way.[19] The British admired Sir Pratap, and he played up to them without losing his Indian individuality and Rajput identity. Sir Pratap instilled in his group of young proteges the value of discipline, along with a broad sense of Rajput identity, and also skill in horsemanship, polo, and the martial arts. Even more influential on the thinking of the young Amar Singh was his education under an exceptional tutor, Ram Nath Ratnu. Ratnu was a member of the Charan or bardic caste. He had received some English-type education and had a high sense of morality, personal honour, and the value of literary and historical study.[20]

Amar Singh did not return to live with his family in Jaipur until he was married at the age of 23. Thereafter, his grandfather and father played larger roles in his life. Both men exhibited a strong sense of duty and service to the princely government, along with political, diplomatic, and social skills. This combination of influences gave Amar Singh a sense of manliness that combined literary interests, morality, martiality, and equestrian skills. He also exhibited a vigorous sense of personal and family honour. Although he was not bellicose by nature and preferred peaceful relationships, he hoped for a military career. His sense of self was that of a martial Rajput. Under Sir Pratap, he became a resaldar, a junior commissioned officer, in the Jodhpur Lancers. As a member of this Jodhpur State Imperial

Service Cavalry,[21] he participated with the British and Indian forces in putting down the Boxer uprising in China. This service gave him modest experience in battle and in facing an enemy.

Amar Singh's involvement with British culture and the British military reinforced and modified his masculine and martial attitudes. His first significant exposure to the British came in China between 1900–1. Closer and more extensive contact with Britishers and British lifestyles took place after he entered the Imperial Cadet Corps in 1902. In this institution, the British officers were commanders and teachers. The Indian cadets were given modest military training along with training in military social skills. The small size of the institution generated intimate connections. Amar Singh became close to one instructor, Captain Cameron, with whom he shared an interest in horses and Shakespeare. The Indian Army appreciated and encouraged his equestrian skills and knowledge. Life with British officers generally nourished his gentlemanly qualities and sometimes stimulated his literary interests. He did not enjoy the British officers' 'manly' taste for drink and for occasional carousing in the officers' mess. Similarly, he disliked Indian 'singing girls' and the heavy drinking enjoyed by many of his Indian friends. The British assumed his martiality as a Rajput aristocrat, but they did not develop leadership skills in him or his Indian peers meaningfully until 1917. He was a squadron commander in the 16th Cavalry Regiment; from early 1919 to April 1921. In the end, in April 1921, he received an unfavourable report from his commandant and left the army in anger.[22] While his 16 years in the army gave him status, honour, and some martial experience, it left him with a distaste for life in the British-Indian Army. Nonetheless, he was delighted to become, in 1923, the commander of a modernized Jaipur State Cavalry and then to command all the Jaipur state forces in the early 1930s.[23]

The masculine aspects of Amar Singh's two 'worlds' and the ways in which they were reinforcing and in which they differed are notable. The 'worlds' we deal with were both elite realms.[24] They influenced senses of masculinity among subordinate groups, but the masculinities of other groups, such as sepoys and British 'Tommies' (enlisted men), deserve separate study.[25] There were some obvious differences between the two 'worlds'. The military cantonment, in which most military life was lived, was an artificial colonial creation.[26] A central characteristic of the cantonment was that personnel at any cantonment or post were transient. While patterns and values were similar in all such centres, the personnel changed regularly. By way of contrast, Rajasthani Rajput male society was dispersed but continuous. It changed slowly through the maturing of young males and the arrival of death. Its peripheries were less well defined than those of the cantonment, but for practical purposes the boundaries were knowable. As the British had been present in India and Rajputana for many years by 1900, the two societies had intermingled in many ways. Although the colonial power and culture were dominant, Rajput traditional identity retained much of its autonomy, particularly because most Rajputs lived in the semi-independent princely states.

Let us now look at the meaning of masculinity, at the socially inculcated self-concepts of these two societies. Manliness was highly prized among the British in India, particularly among military officers. A recent study of nineteenth- and twentieth-century Britain observes that English 'manliness' embraced 'qualities of physical courage, chivalric virtuous fortitude with additional connotations of patriotic virtue'.[27] The chivalric element, in the sense of willingness to offer one's life as a sacrifice, is explored extensively in British history in a book called *Bloody Good: Chivalry, Sacrifice and the Great War.*[28]

British society expected officers also to be self-confident and to be able to lead men both by example and by direction. Dependability in service and morality were important. Furthermore, British masculinity involved perseverance and the ability to carry through in professional responsibilities and in friendship. Such a view implied courage and strength in the face of battle and other dangers. 'The stiff upper lip' and 'playing the game' were not just cliches for this society. Put differently, Christopher Bayly describes 'moral independence' as the touchstone for imperial rule and, implicitly, for colonial masculinity.[29] In many situations—in battle, in hunting, and in the relaxations of the regimental mess—an element of liveliness and going beyond the rules was permissible, even encouraged. At one farewell party reported by Amar Singh with distaste,

> the officers began getting rowdy in the beginning. And toward the end most of them had as much as they wanted & some even more. Whitehall got drunk and began fighting & hit Hamilton rather a bad knock .... It was the cheeriest & noisiest night I have ever had anywhere yet. I am afraid there are many more like this in front of me.[30]

Various studies of late nineteenth- and early twentieth-century masculinity in Britain point out the nature and significance of this constellation of ideas. Honour was a manly characteristic for the British, although not as strongly and explicitly stressed as in Rajput society. Combined with a sense of duty, it dominated much of the thinking about the officers' working life. Also, British honour demanded a kind of gendered chivalry, a protective attitude towards British women and the view that officers should not talk about women in less than honourable terms, especially in the mess and in public. Autobiographies and other writings of British army officers and officials, and their biographies, reveal this cluster of ideas.[31]

Christianity had been a notable element in middle and late nineteenth-century British masculinity. However, it was not as evident in the early twentieth-century cantonment as it had been in the earlier British community in India. Most British officers thought of themselves as members of the Christian faith, usually the Anglican community. Churches were attached to cantonments, and military regiments sometimes attended service as units. In the Mhow Cantonment church, for example, the pews include slots for rifles. Observing life in the Mhow Cantonment, Amar Singh, a Hindu with a distaste for Christianity, wrote little about British religiosity except occasional references to Sunday services. On the contrary, he cited the antipathy of his first general, O'Moore Creagh, for all clerics, east or west.[32] This view struck a favourable chord with Amar Singh, who also was critical of many clergy, including Hindu priests.

In his book *Soldier Heroes*, Graham Dawson tells how imperial heroes and their stories helped to mould British boys and men of this period. He discusses nineteenth- and twentieth-century figures, such as Henry Havelock and T. E. Lawrence. The British of those times also looked back to such historical heroes as the Duke of Marlborough, Lord Clive, and King Henry V.[33] The Rajputs thrived on stories of Rajput historical heroism, most commonly told in poetry by their Charans. One famous Rajput hero admired by Amar Singh was Rana Pratap Singh, sixteenth-century ruler of Mewar (Udaipur).[34] Pratap Singh consistently resisted the Mughal armies of Emperor Akbar, even after defeats. Legend credited another sixteenth-century Rajput leader, Bappa Rawal, with founding the Guhilot clan of Rajputs and with being the first Guhilot ruler to occupy the later famous fortress of Chitor, in the Mewar region.[35]

While this Charan and heroic tradition retained some vitality in the early twentieth century, contemporary Rajputs' conceptualization was based largely on Colonel James Tod's early nineteenth-century *Annals and Antiquities of Rajasthan*.[36] Tod's stress on heroism in battle, feudal relations and loyalties, and insistence on honour at any price set the modern sense of manhood and *Rajputai* (Rajput code of conduct). A particular type of heroism noted by Tod and revered by Amar Singh and other Rajputs was *jauhar*. Jauhar was self-immolation of women in the face of defeat or dishonour. Surprisingly, two of the most famous cases of jauhar were committed by the women of the famous Udaipur fort of Chitor.

The Rajput ideal of manliness was similar on many points to the British image, but it was subtly different. Part of this difference was due to the fact that British power had robbed most Rajputs of their freedom to be warriors and to fight. Their hallowed traditions included fighting to defend their clan, to establish power over peoples and territories, and to assert the claims of Rajput nobles against their Rajput rulers. Nineteenth-century British treaties with Rajput rulers established the British Raj as sovereign and placed the princes or chiefs in a subordinate, though semi-independent position. Some of them got the titles of maharaja and maharana. The British wished to prevent military conflict both between and within the states. Beyond delimiting opportunities for Rajputs to exercise military prowess, British power weakened the ties (sometimes called feudal) between the chiefs and their kin and clansmen, their nobles.[37]

Some Rajputs served in the army, but until the time of Amar Singh and his peers, they had no hope of serving in the regular officer corps. They were enrolled in the army as the Viceroy's Commissioned Officers (VCOs), Non-Commissioned Officers (NCOs), and sepoys (ordinary soldiers).[38] All holders of the lower officers' ranks were subordinate to the King's Commissioned Officers (KCOs, all British until 1905). The nobler Rajputs would not accept the subordinate position of the VCOs and NCOs. Consequently, it was not until the creation of the Imperial Cadet Corps in 1902 and the subsequent commissioning of its graduates that they entered military service under the British. Amar Singh connected the limitations placed by the British on the Rajputs' governance and military activities to a weakening of Rajput quality. Implicitly, this meant a decline in what he saw as manly qualities. Visits to his wife's family *thikana*, Satheen in Jodhpur state, and to Idar, a princely friend's Rajputana state, confirmed Amar Singh's view that aristocratic Rajput society was in decline.[39] Once, meeting a young Rajput who was drinking heavily in the morning, he lamented that 'he is absolutely ignorant about his traditions or of any sort of knowledge .... It makes one grieve when one sees to what a low level the Rajputs have sunk.'[40]

Amar Singh, in turn, sought to uphold Rajput ideals, and he spoke of peers who were worthy Rajputs. While the battle tradition had largely disappeared, the prestige of service to a ruler, Rajput or British, continued as a desirable occupation for a manly Rajput. Amar Singh's family was a service and landholding family in Jaipur,[41] and his ambition was to receive an appointment in the state, preferably as head of its modest military forces. Along with court and service positions, landholding remained a major defining element for elite Rajputs, whether they were called *sardars*, *thakurs*, *thikanedars*, or *jagirdars*. However the tradition continued that Rajputs of the landed class did not themselves farm or concern themselves seriously with agricultural development. Amar Singh and his family were among the exceptions. The young Indian officer thought regularly about how to make the family estates productive, profitable, and attractive. The diary contains extensive essays on projects to improve the estate and make it more attractive, efficient, and economically viable.[42]

During the early twentieth century, the Rajput princes continuously put pressure on their sardars and sought to take some of their landholdings from them. This happened to Amar Singh's family, causing a continuing tension with the ruler and his government. Estate maintenance, as well as changes in landholding, and favour or disfavour from princes affected family status, honour, and income. Sometimes the British intervened in such disputes, usually to the benefit of the chiefs. Amar Singh's family felt that using all their contacts, particularly those with Britons, was appropriate in order to recover villages lost earlier to their ruler.[43]

Despite some poor exemplars of their breed, Rajputs admired a strong individual, one with self-confidence and vigour. The main characteristic of a Rajput was a concern with honour. Jayasinhji Jhala's dissertation on a Rajput clan and state in Gujarat exhaustively explores the Rajput code. Drawing on the Mahabharata, the great Indian epic that features five heroic brothers and fighters,[44] Jhala lists 'bravery, chivalry, charisma, fortitude, expertize, steadfast(ness) in battle, generosity, unflinching devotion to God...' as the key Rajput attributes.[45] Over time, the Rajputs were assimilated into the Hindu *varna* (caste) system as kshatriyas—warriors and rulers. The kshatriyas were ranked second in the varna ranking system, below the brahmins. By the early twentieth century, however, bravery and steadfastness in battle had receded, while honour, prestige, and concern with status predominated.

Steadfastness in life was not a major emphasis for Rajputs, and Amar Singh often noted the whimsical nature of Rajput princes and aristocrats. A sense of self-confidence continued, and elite Rajputs thought themselves superior to other Indian classes—businessmen, servants, and even brahmins. Amar Singh's diary comments were frequently critical of brahmins. He did not speak of brahmins as unmanly, but he was distasteful of their greed and lack of cleanliness. Self-indulgence in drink, drugs, and sex were regarded as appropriate to Rajput males, part of their manly prerogatives. Amar Singh showed no interest in sexual indulgence or alcoholic excesses, though he sometimes accompanied friends on rounds of nightly entertainment by 'singing girls' and prostitutes in Bombay. At home in Rajputana, he drank mainly on festive, religious, or family celebratory occasions. In the army setting, where drinking was a common part of officers' lives, the Indian captain drank more frequently, though not heavily.

On religious matters, the Indian officer held a mixed view. Amar Singh shared General Creagh's antipathy for clerics, including most brahmins and *sadhus* (holy men, ascetics). This may have had something to do with his sense of the value of an active life. It also reflected his distaste for dirtiness in temples and temple priests, and for the cupidity of many priests he met. However, he also was a practising Hindu in some ways. His nephew Mohan Singh says that Amar Singh's religious life was expressed primarily in his reading, and the diary supports this analysis, especially through the reports on his wide reading of religious works. However, he participated in religious ceremonies and festivals, although his interest in them seemed more an interest in Indian traditions than in spirituality. Still, in his diary, he sometimes recorded the saying of prayers. We cannot tell how regular this practice was. In any case, he considered religious life to be a proper part of a Rajput's manly existence. Some Rajput rulers, notably the princes of Udaipur, Kashmir, and Alwar were noted for their support of Hinduism.[46]

This listing of manly characteristics in the two societies provides only part of the story of their concepts and practice of masculinity. Actions exhibited and reinforced ideas of masculinity. In the field of profession or 'work', the two cultures were somewhat distinctive from each other. British masculinity in India was considered most appropriately expressed in the military and, to some lesser degree, in civil government. The British officials approved of European businessmen and missionaries, but they did not consider them to be their equals; they were not considered so manly. Many scholars and writers have noted the strong appeal of the military to nineteenth- and twentieth-century Britons. By 1900, social shifts within Britain meant that landholding, while still desirable, no longer was as central to military service or masculine dignity. For Rajputs, the military remained a desirable, though limited, outlet. Consequently, Amar Singh felt the full dignity of his appointment to the army and wished only that it might lead to a military career in Jaipur State. His membership in the respected British-Indian Army's officer corps enhanced his male Rajput dignity and honour.

Interest in horses was a significant activity that exhibited Rajput manliness. Riding, hunting, and, somewhat less frequently, polo were daily fare for some Rajputs, notably for Amar Singh. Their equestrian interest extended to the trading, selling, giving, and lending of horses. Amar Singh often trained horses for friends and other officers. Giving a horse (as well as other gifts, including motor cars) to other princes or to nobles was particularly appropriate for a Rajput prince. The Rajputs valued and admired gift-giving. Amar Singh judged his Rajput peers partly according to their interest and skill in horsemanship. When he met friends—such as the maharajas of Idar and Kashmir—who showed no interest in riding, he was seriously disappointed.

Here again, British and Rajput activities and senses of masculinity joined. Men shared an interest in sports that defined men. The interest in equestrian activities was especially characteristic of the British cavalry officers and of Amar Singh.[47] Cavalry regiments and some princes had polo teams, which competed in tournaments in Indore, Meerut, and elsewhere. Many autobiographies, including that of Winston Churchill,[48] testify to the great love, even obsession with, polo on the part of British officers. Hunting was an expected diversion for British officers. The young officer Archibald P. Wavell (later Field Marshall and Governor General of India), was a subaltern in India from 1903 to 1908. He testified to the centrality of hunting to the British officer's life, observing that 'every one gets as a matter of course 10 days leave every month for shooting and I fancy as much more as he likes to apply for ...'[49] Another officer expressed a similar view: 'Unless a subaltern [junior officer] went out shooting it was considered that he lacked some military virtue ...'[50] With the leisure that he had while drastically underemployed in the Indian

Army, Amar Singh seldom spent a day without at least one of these activities and often two of them. Most of his hunting and riding were informal in nature; this was true as well for the British officers. Summarizing the views of Lord Baden-Powell and Theodore Roosevelt, John MacKenzie says that 'hunting required all the most virile attributes of the imperial male—courage, endurance, individualism ... sportsmanship ... resourcefulness, a mastery of environmental signs and a knowledge of natural history'.[51]

Pig-sticking, a special form of hunting, called forth the skills and courage of horsemen. Pig-sticking was not a simple sport.[52] The wild boar, especially the male, was one of the craftiest, toughest, speediest, and most dangerous of India's wild creatures. It hid in bush and woods and could turn rapidly. If cornered, it likely would charge, and its sharp tusks were a vivid danger. Riding on horseback after the boar on rough ground was a challenging task, and the first hunter to spear the boar was honoured. Baden-Powell, the well-known army officer, hunter, writer, and founder of the scouting movement, devoted an entire book to the sport.[53] Amar Singh had a passionate love for this sport, and he distinguished himself in 1902 by participating very well in the national Kadir Cup competition.[54] Formally organized *shikar* (hunting) for large game such as tigers[55] was infrequent, often taking place in association with visits by Indian princes or British dignitaries. The 16th Cavalry in the New Delhi Cantonment, in which Amar Singh served, had hunting hounds. They were used both for organized hunts and for small group hunting. The relevance of these equestrian avocations to traditional military officer patterns, especially those of the cavalry, is clear. The Indian officer corps had adequate leisure to enjoy them, as Wavell's statement shows. The association of riding and hunting with the land made them appropriate for landowners, such as the Rajputs and British, with extensive leisure.

The games of the British public schools, such as cricket and rugby, were less common in this South Asian setting. However, officers sometimes joined ordinary soldiers on regimental football teams. In the cantonment and in the upper-class Anglo-Indian community of Jaipur, other popular sports were tennis and badminton.[56] These were not so closely associated with manliness, for both British men and women and such partly Anglicized Indians as Amar Singh joined in these diversions.

Another area of life that helped define masculinity for Britons and Rajput comprised family, the position of women, and sex. Manhood for both groups called for the protection of women and the family, as well as for actions that supported the family's honour and position. For British officers, this involved a fairly strict moral code, despite aberrations displayed by individuals or at social centres such as Simla. While also insisting on the primacy of family, the Rajput tradition accepted polygamy, concubinage, and additional male sexual liberty. The Rajputs did not favour homosexuality, but they generally accepted it.[57] Masculinity for both elites meant belief in the predominant position of the male. Women were subordinate in both societies, whatever their individual ability to exert power within the family. Many studies of gender stress the central issue of power; the power that men had over women.[58] In these two societies, power clearly lay in the hands of men. In Rajput society, the eldest male family member exercised this power. This elder held power over women, of course, but he also had dominant authority over other men in the family. Amar Singh knew how to get around some of his grandfather's commands or wishes, but he respected him and never directly challenged his grandfather's authority. Such a pattern was not so clear in the British officer corps. Although many British military families served over generations in India, they were dispersed. Of course, the army was thoroughly hierarchical, and the senior officers wielded power according to their ascending rank.

British women had a degree of social equality and freedom in the cantonments and imperial cities. They mixed with men at home and on social, ceremonial, religious, and sporting occasions. No doubt women were important to the effective psycho-social operation of the cantonment. However, their familial and social roles in Indian military settings were limited by the extended absences of children, and sometimes of themselves. Wives and children spent time both in England and in schools at Indian hill stations. The frequent and often extended absences of children from cantonments made the British experience of masculinity less intergenerational than that of Rajputs or British home society. Some British-Indian military families were resident over many generations, so that family relationships might be maintained. Others, without such ties, were largely without relationships with an older British generation.

By way of contrast, Rajput family life was continuously intergenerational, while the system of purdah restricted upper-class Rajput women to the *zenana*. Here they passed their days in a strong familial society of other women, women servants, and children, with limited visits by men. Only occasional family social events or religious festivals provided them with opportunities for wider mixing and activities outside the zenana. Within the zenana, the eldest woman, the mother or grandmother, held sway. However, she was dependent on the financial dispensations and wishes of the patriarch. Rajput males believed this system supported the family and, implicitly, it strengthened a vigorously masculine society. Amar Singh accepted the system of purdah and expressed only modest interest in change along lines seen in British society. He did envy the freer association and conversation of the sexes and of friends in British society. In fact, he dreamt of a future life at the family home in Kanota. There, he envisioned that he and his wife would live a freer, though still custom-centred, life along with his brothers and their wives.[59] Some evidence exists of a more active life for some Rajput elite women, and activities outside the zenana. Laxmi Kumari Chundawat, the wife of a Rajput noble in Bikaner state, speaks of hunting when she was a girl and a young woman. She reports that such a practice was widespread in Rajput aristocratic families.[60]

Amar Singh's diary reveals important intergenerational relationships, although his long absences on army service restricted such social interactions. Amar Singh had great respect for his grandfather and father, who provided notable male models for his life. He also respected his mother, but he did not find in her as many admirable qualities as those exhibited by his male elders. His long absences kept him from enjoying the company of his children (all but one of whom died in infancy) and his nephews and nieces. Clearly he was affectionate towards them and also towards his one sister. Furthermore, as the oldest son, he felt a concern for the education and upbringing of the boys, especially of his oldest nephew, giving attention to their education and training. His efforts in this regard necessarily were limited, however, because of his time away from home. Clearly, affection and concern for the children were part of his masculine make-up. The deaths of his children found him restrained in emotion, probably reflecting both his limited contact with them, and his masculine and personal stoicism. He mourns other deaths, but does so in quiet fashion.[61]

Seen from a different angle, all these elements of masculinity add up to societies in which most interactions by men were with other men. Life was an overwhelmingly masculine experience for them. In the cantonment or on the frontier, army officers shared their working and sporting lives with other men. Some British women were equestrians, but their numbers were apparently small. Social life for bachelor officers centred on the mess, the site of eating, drinking, and socializing. Only rarely were women invited to the mess as guests. Married officers, of course, had a broader gender experience. However, the army discouraged officers from early marriage, so the number of officers' wives and daughters in cantonments was relatively small.

The Rajput elite males lived lives with regular, though restricted, interaction with women. These women included their mothers, sisters, wives, and concubines. They also included female servants, though the latter served mainly in the female zenana.[62] Aristocratic Rajput men spent their days with their peers and, for some purposes, with male servants.[63] Female companionship was regular, but much less extensive than that with other men and was hedged in by custom. Amar Singh was deeply in love with his wife, but he could only visit her late at night or on special occasions. When he and his wife were in the presence of their elders, custom forbade them from showing affection for each other. Amar Singh's brothers and his best friend, a cousin, provided his main companionship when he was at home.

In the cantonment as well, the Indian officer's working and sporting lives were overwhelmingly masculine. He met other British officers' wives at social events, over tea, at tennis, and at celebratory events at gymkhanas. Apparently Amar Singh's only friendships with British ladies were with the wives of some of his commanding generals at the Mhow Cantonment. They might call him to tea, talk with him at length, ask him to help with various tasks, or exchange gifts with him. Most unmarried British officers may have had more limited contact with the wives of fellow officers. The diary recorded very little interest on the diarist's part in the British women of the Mhow post, other than the generals' wives and an occasional visitor. Nor did he report gossip about sexual mores or peccadilloes in the cantonment. Also, he did not indicate how he, as a married officer, dealt with his extended separation from his wife.

Male companionship, then, was central to masculinity and to these masculine 'worlds'. For the British officers, it meant companionship or at least a modicum of cooperation in their professional lives. Their leisure time was spent with fellow officers talking, drinking, and participating in sports. For Rajput men, male companionship occupied most of their waking hours. Thus, they carried out their functions as government servants or as owners of estates, spent time at home or in their gardens talking over affairs of the day and gossiping, hunting and riding, and drinking. A notable feature of Rajput male society was that other male relatives played a central role in their lives, even when individuals did not care for each other. Amar Singh was continuously at odds with one uncle (his father's cousin), Thakur Roop Singh, head of the related Naila family. Because that uncle was a senior member of the family and a leading government official, the nephew necessarily spent time with him. Family members and peers were a continuing part of an individual's life, though individuals could make choices of companionship. For British officers, relationships were transitory in any one setting, though over a professional career, long-lasting friendships and associations developed. Membership in a particular regiment and its officers' mess helped establish deep associations.

These patterns of masculinity were significant elements of the Indian society of the late colonial period. They perpetuated two patriarchal and hierarchical societies. However, their interaction produced changes in each. For the most part, this was change wrought on Rajput notions and practices by the British. Such change came through the ending of traditional Rajput military life and the inculcation of British attitudes in Rajput soldiers and rulers. Young Indians of various 'martial classes' (including Rajputs) and a few from 'non-martial' classes who became commissioned officers experienced socialization, especially professional socialization, on the British masculine–officer model. Both traditions moulded Amar Singh's life.

World War I brought unexpected changes to the Indian Army.[64] One innovation which occurred in 1917 was the opening of full commissioned officer status to nine young Indians, including Captain Amar Singh. This promotion raised their professional socialization to a new level. Henceforth, they could learn and practice the power of command, a key characteristic of British officers' masculinity.[65] These young Indians were accepted with some hesitation into the new status. They seem to have fitted in socially without serious difficulty, but there were more questions about their leadership abilities. For example, a summarized confidential report about one of Amar Singh's peers made these observations: 'Capt. Aga Cassim [Shah]. 8th Skinner's Horse. Good manners, & has been well received by all ranks. Is weak & diffident, & lacks confidence in his own judgment, but [Divisional Commandant] considers that with more experience these defects may be remedied.'[66]

Today's South Asian militaries continue to exhibit habits and characteristics of British military masculine professionalism.

Horsemanship has declined, as it has elsewhere, but patterns of socializing and drinking remain, along with dress patterns and regimental organization.[67] Apurba Kundu has portrayed aspects of the contemporary situation in his work, *Militarism in India: The Army and Civil Society in Consensus.* Stephen P. Cohen in *The Pakistan Army* provides historical perspective on the Pakistan Army after 1947.[68]

Rajput traditions have changed, as well. Careers in the military are now open to both lower- and upper-class Rajputs. A number of Amar Singh's relatives have had military careers, and Rajput officers have held high posts in independent India's military branches. With the passage of land reform bills, aristocratic Rajput landholding has declined in amount and significance. Notably, a number of Rajput families have converted their homes and palaces into hotels. By this means, they secure a source of income in contemporary India and are able to maintain their noble and princely residences.[69] Some princes, princesses, and aristocrats have turned to politics, continuing the Rajput tradition of political power in the new democratic forms.[70] Rajput class consciousness and the tradition of command continue to operate. However, they do so in a context in which many other castes and classes have achieved improved social, economic, and political positions. A sense of Rajput identity and leadership remain. Moreover, despite modifications, the pattern of isolation for noble Rajput women continues, as does male dominance. In sum, South Asian traditions and new ideas and situations have produced new South Asian 'masculinities', combining traditional customs and views with new ideas and practices.

Notes

1. Mrinalini Sinha, *Colonial Masculinity: The 'Manly Englishman' and the 'Effeminate Bengali' in the Late Nineteenth Century*, Manchester: 1995. Another work on Bengal is Indira Chowdhury, *The Frail Hero and Virile History: Gender and the Politics of Culture in Colonial Bengal*, New Delhi: 1998. A relevant work that looks primarily at British writing about India is Revathi Krishnaswamy, *Effeminism: The Economy of Colonial Desire*, Ann Arbor: 1998. Ashis Nandy has explored the subject in, for example, *The Intimate Enemy: Loss and Recovery of Self under Colonialism*, New Delhi: 1983. Both feminist and gay studies have helped to stimulate the study of masculinity.
2. In addition to Sinha's book, these essays by her are relevant: Mrinalini Sinha, 'Gender and Imperialism: Colonial Policy and the Ideology of

Moral Imperialism in Late Nineteenth Century Bengal', in Michael S. Kimmel (ed.), *Changing Men: New Directions in Research on Men and Masculinity*, Newbury Park: 1987, pp. 217–31; Sinha, 'Gender in the Critiques of Colonialism and Nationalism: Locating the "Indian Women"', in Ann-Louise Shapiro (ed.), *Feminists Revision History*, New Bruinswick: 1994, pp. 246–75. A series of essays on women in Indian history is Kumkum Sangari and Sudesh Vaid (eds), *Recasting Women: Essays in Indian Colonial History*, New Brunswick: 1989.

3. Amar Singh was a Rathore Rajput. His family moved in the nineteenth century from the Jodhpur state to the Jaipur state in Rajputana (now Rajasthan). The King's Commission given to him in 1905 was in the Native Indian Land Forces. This commission allowed him a very restricted power of command. He received a full commission in 1917 and retired in 1921. See DeWitt C. Ellinwood, 'A Rajput Aristocrat in Imperial Service: Ambiguous Relationships', *Indo-British Review*, 15(2), 1988, pp. 91–101.
4. In his diary, Amar Singh expresses distaste for homosexuality, but he accepts it as part of his society. The British officials at the Imperial Cadet Corps were concerned about it and dismissed some students because of it. See Susanne Hoeber Rudolph and Lloyd I. Rudolph, with Mohan Singh Kanota, *Reversing the Gaze: Amar Singh's Diary as Narrative of Imperial India*, Delhi: 2000, pp. 279–80, 288–91.
5. For India, see Mrinalini Sinha, 'Giving Masculinity a History: Some Contributions from the Historiography of Colonial India', in Leonore Davidoff, Keith McClelland, and Eleni Varikas (eds), *Gender and History: Retrospect and Prospect*, Oxford: 2000, pp. 27–42. A good example of the study of masculinity, gender, and related issues in India is Partha Chatterjee and Pradeep Jeganathan (eds), *Community, Gender and Violence: Subaltern Studies*, vol. 11, New York: 2000.
6. Michael Roper and John Tosh (eds), *Manful Assertions: Masculinities in Britain since 1800*, London: 1991.
7. Philippa Levine, *Prostitution, Race and Politics: Policing Venereal Disease in the British Empire*, New York: 2003.
8. Rosalind O'Hanlon, 'Issues of Masculinity in North Indian History: The Bangash Nawabs of Farrukhabad', *Indian Journal of Gender Studies*, vol. 4, 1997, pp. 1–19.
9. The 'martial races' or 'martial classes' notion was pervasive in British thought in the late nineteenth century and early twentieth century. It derived partly from strong exposition by Lord Roberts, Commander-in-Chief, 1885–93 (Frederick Sleigh, Earl Roberts, *Forty-one Years in India: From Subaltern to Commander-in-Chief*, London: 1897, 2 vols). A classic statement is available in Lieutenant General George MacMunn, *The Martial Races of India*, London: 1933. Nirad C. Chaudhuri, newspaperman and writer, made one of the earliest Indian analyses of the idea in the following articles: 'The Martial Races of India', Part I,

Modern Review, July 1930, pp. 41–51; Part II, September 1930, pp. 295–307; Part III, January 1931, pp. 67–76; Part IV, February 1931, pp. 215–28. A recent study of the 'martial races' concept as seen in the Army Caste Handbook on the Gurkhas is Mary Katherine DesChene, 'Language and Practice in the Colonial Indian Army', paper presented at the Institute for Global Studies in Culture, Power and History, John Hopkins University, 7 December 1993. Also see M. K. DesChene, 'Relics of Empire: A Cultural History of the Gurkhas, 1815–1987', PhD Thesis, Stanford University, 1991. Chandar S. Sundaram examines the notion carefully in his dissertation, 'A Grudging Concession: The Origins of the Indianization of the Indian Army's Officer Corps, 1817–1917', PhD Thesis, McGill University, 1996. Also see his paper, 'Orientalism and Invented Tradition: Intellectual Underpinnings of the Martial Races Ideal', Conference on South Asia, University of Wisconsin, Madison: 19 October 1995. Another sound evaluation is David Omissi, '"Martial Races": Ethnicity and Security in Colonial India, 1858–1939', *War and Society*, vol. 9, 1991, pp. 1–27. Lloyd Rudolph sees Tod's *Annals and Antiquities of Rajasthan*, with its glorification of Rajput military valour, as an intellectual source for the 'martial races' theory. See Rudolph's 'Producing and Reproducing Rajasthan: Why Colonel Tod Represented Rajasthan the way he Did and its Consequences for Imperial, Nationalist and Rajput Historiography', in Varsha Joshi (ed.), *Culture, Communities, and Change*, Jaipur: 2002, pp. 28–9.

10. A. H. Bingley, *Handbook on Rajputs*, 1899; reprint, Delhi: 1986. The 1899 edition was reprinted in 1918 at Calcutta. A later version is B. L. Cole, *Rajputana Classes*, Simla: 1922.
11. Dirk Kolff, *Naukar, Rajput and Sepoy: The Ethnohistory of the Military Labour Market in Hindustan, 1450–1850*, Cambridge: 1990; Malavika Kasturi, *Embattled Identities: Rajput Lineages and the Colonial State in Nineteenth-Century North India*, New Delhi: 2000. Stewart Gordon, *Marathas, Marauders, and State Formation in Eighteenth Century India*, Delhi: 1994, discusses martiality among different groups, particularly Marathas, in central and southern India.
12. O'Hanlon, 'Issues of Masculinity in North Indian History', p. 3.
13. Jeff Hearn, 'Is Masculinity Dead? A Critique of the Concept of Masculinity/Masculinities', in Mairtain Mac an Ghaill (ed.), *Understanding Masculinities: Social Relations and Cultural Arenas*, Buckingham: 1996, pp. 202–17.
14. Ronald Hyam, *Empire and Sexuality: Studies in Imperialism*, Manchester: 1980, pp. 128–34.
15. Levine, *Prostitution, Race and Politics*, p. 153.
16. 'Notes about My Last Leave of 103 Days. XXVI, Pertap Singhjee of Kama', 28 July 1907, Amar Singh's Diary (hereafter ASD). Pertap Singh was a friend of Amar Singh from their stay at the Imperial Cadet Corps. Emotionally, Amar Singh identified more with Jodhpur.

17. I have worked extensively with the diary of Amar Singh for the years of his military career, 1905–21. On this basis, I have written *Between Two Worlds: A Rajput Officer in the Indian Army, 1905–21, Based on the Diary of Amar Singh of Jaipur*, Lanham, Boulder: 2005. Professors Susanne and Lloyd Rudolph have worked intensively with the diary and have drawn on it for many writings. Some of these are collected in their work, *Essays on Rajputana: Reflections on History, Culture and Administration*, New Delhi: 1984. They also have written, with Thakur Mohan Singh Kanota, nephew and heir of Amar Singh, *Reversing the Gaze*. Mohan Singh owns the diary, located in his Kanota village fort home near Jaipur. Microfilm copies of the diary are in the Nehru Memorial Museum and Library in New Delhi and in the Joseph Regenstein Library, University of Chicago.
18. Amar Singh's reading ranged over a number of genres. The major ones were novels, history, poetry (primarily Rajasthani *dohas*—couplets), and Shakespeare's plays.
19. For his life, see: R. B. Van Wart, *The Life of Lieutenant-General H. H. Pratap Singh*, London: 1926; Dhananjaya Singh (great-great grandson of Sir Pratap), 'Of Boy-Kings and a Grand Old Man', in his book, *The House of Marwar*, New Delhi: 1994; anon., *A Brief Account of the Life of His Highness the Maharaja Col. Pratap Singh of Idar, K. C. B., G. C. S. I., Ll. B., Maharajdhiraj of Jodhpur and Aide-de-Camp to His Majesty the King-Emperor Edward VII*, Bombay: 1902.
20. These points are well set forth in Rudolph and Rudolph, *Reversing the Gaze*.
21. Such princely state forces were modest in size. Nonetheless, they could be called on for active duty with the Indian Army, as they were in the Boxer Rebellion, World War I, and World War II.
22. Amar Singh's original appointment in 1917 was to the 2nd Cavalry. However, this regiment was overseas. Therefore, he was 'seconded' to the 16th Cavalry and served with them until he left the army in 1921. The negative report given to Amar Singh by his colonel is not available, and the diary does not describe it. Although Amar Singh left active service in 1921, the army allowed him to remain on leaves until 1923, when he became eligible for an army pension. *The Quarterly Indian Army List, April 1923*, Calcutta, p. 881.
23. On Amar Singh's retirement in 1936, the maharaja of Jaipur designated him major general of the Jaipur State Forces. *Report on the Administration of Jaipur State for the Year 1936–7*, Allahabad: 1937, p. 6.
24. In *Colonial Masculinity*, Sinha emphasizes the intermingling of gender ideas and practices with those of nation, gender, race, class, etc.
25. An example of the study of ordinary British soldiers is Ilana R. Bet-El, 'M and Soldiers: British Conscripts, Concepts of Masculinity and the Great War', in Billie Melman (ed.), *Borderlines: Genders and Identities*

in War and Peace, 1870–1930, New York: 1998, pp. 73–94. For sepoys during the British period, the best book is David Omissi, *The Sepoy and Raj: The Indian Army 1860–1940*, Basingstoke: 1994.

26. Cantonments and the work and life that went on therein have been studied modestly. Officers' autobiographies tell something about them, but leave much unsaid. A lucid, wry account of life in Lansdowne, a small hill cantonment, is in John Morris, *Hired to Kill: Some Chapters of Autobiography*, London: 1960. Many details of daily cantonment life appear in Dermot M. Killingley and Siew-Yue Killingley (eds), *Farewell the Plumed Troop: A Memoir of the Indian Cavalry, 1919–1945*, Newcastle-upon-Tyne: 1990. A pioneering study by an historical sociologist is Anthony King, *Colonial Urban Development: Culture, Social Power, and Environment*, London: 1970. In her book, *The Making of Colonial Lucknow, 1856–1877*, Princeton: 1984, pp. 48–55, Veena Talwar Oldenburg provides a clear account of the post-Mutiny Lucknow cantonment. Mulk Raj Anand, the novelist, tells of growing up in a Punjab cantonment in his autobiographical novel, *Seven Summers: The Story of an Indian Childhood*, Bombay: 1950. A recent study on legal and administrative aspects is T. Jacob, *Cantonments in India: Evolution and Growth*, New Delhi: 1994. Kenneth Ballhatchet's well-known *Race, Sex and Class under the Raj: Imperial Attitudes and Policies and Their Critics, 1793–1905*, London: 1980, provides extensive analysis of late nineteenth-century cantonment acts, which were concerned with British troops, prostitution, and venereal disease. Interest in women's history has evoked further study on this topic, for example, Alan Johnson, 'Cantonments, Women and the Discourse on Health in Colonial India', unpublished paper, Conference on South Asia, University of Wisconsin, Madison: November 1994. The other major setting for military life in India was that of the frontier. Similar in many ways to peacetime locations, frontier military life was even more exclusively masculine.

27. J. A. Mangan and James Walvin (eds), *Manliness and Morality: Middle Class Masculinity in Britain and America, 1800–1940*, Manchester: 1987, p. 1. Their authors thus summarize the analysis of Norman Vance, *Sinews of the Spirit: The Ideal of Christian Manliness in Victorian Literature and Religious Thought*, Cambridge: 1985. Mangan has written extensively on the connections between games, public school socialization, manliness, and imperialism. An excellent example is his work, *The Games Ethic and Imperialism: Aspects of the Diffusion of an Ideal*, New York: 1986. Another study of English manliness is John Tosh, *A Man's Place: Masculinity and the Middle-Class Home in Victorian England*, New Haven, Connecticut: 1999.

28. Allen J. Frantzen, *Bloody Good: Chivalry, Sacrifice, and the Great War*, Chicago: 2004. In this work, Frantzen explores Christian concepts of sacrifice, art, and war memorials as well as other aspects of the topic.

29. C. A. Bayly, *The Imperial Meridian: The British Empire and the World, 1780–1830*, London: 1989, p. 151.
30. 8 December 1918, ASD.
31. Two quite different examples of autobiographies are these: a serious work by O' Moore Creagh, *The Autobiography of General Sir O'Moore Creagh*, London: 1924; a light-hearted work by Francis Yeats-Brown, *The Lives of a Bengal Lancer*, New York: 1930. Creagh was commander-in-chief, 1909–14. He was also Amar Singh' first and favourite commander.
32. 'Notes about My Last Stay at Mhow. XI. Talks with the General', 9 September 1905, ASD.
33. Graham Dawson, *Soldier Heroes: British Adventure, Empire and the Imagining of Masculinities*, London/New York: 1994. This sense of heroism is nicely stated in Mangan, *Games Ethic*, pp. 50–1. Here, the heroism of ancient Greece and Rome are invoked as well.
34. In 1914, Amar Singh read a biography of Rana Pratap Singh, probably R. C. Dutt, *Rajaputa Jibana Sandhya*. This work was translated into English as *Pratap Singh, The Last of the Rajputs: A Tale of Rajput Courage and Chivalry*, Allahabad: 1943.
35. Michael W. Meister, 'Art Regions and Modern Rajasthan', in Karine Schomer, Joan L. Erdman, Derrick Lodrick, and Lloyd I. Rudolph (eds), *The Idea of Rajasthan: Explorations in Regional Identity*, vol. I, *Constructions*, Columbia, Mo.: 1994, pp. 144–5.
36. Lieutenant General James Tod, *Annals and Antiquities of Rajasthan, or the Central and Western Rajput States of India*, London: 1920, 3 vols. It was published originally in 1829 and 1832. Amar Singh thought this was the best book for Rajputs to read.
37. British support for the princes troubled Amar Singh. The diarist vividly expressed his concern in 'A Few Notes that I Wrote out for General Sir O'Moore Creagh ... at Mhow', 17 September 1905, ASD.
38. In the infantry, the Viceroy's commissioned officers (VCOs) were subedar, subedar major, and jemadar. The cavalry officers were resaldar and resaldar major. The Indian non-commissioned officer ranks were dafadar, dafadar major, havildar, havildar major, and naik.
39. 'Notes about My Last Leave of Three Weeks. VI. Visit to Satheen', 4 March 1917; 'Notes about My Last Visit to Himmatnagar', 27 April 1917, ASD.
40. 'Notes about My Last Leave of Ten Days. XVII, Khendela Raja's Son', 13 March 1918, ASD.
41. Amar Singh's grandfather and two granduncles migrated to Jaipur in the mid-nineteenth century. They migrated from an arid estate in Jodhpur. They gained major appointments in Jaipur and received jagirs or estates in the state. Robert Stern in *The Cat and the Lion* surveys nineteenth- and twentieth-century Jaipur history.

42. While at home, Amar Singh spent a great deal of time working on these projects, along with his brother Sardar Singh, the estate manager. After these visits, he often wrote extensive 'Notes' or essays on the subject, frequently devoting a section to each of the villages and their lands.
43. Both the diary and detailed histories of Rajput states are replete with evidence of these concerns, e.g., 'Notes about My Last Christmas Leave, XIV, Col. Showers', 31 December 1909, ASD.
44. The Mahabharata features a dramatic conflict between two sets of royal cousins, climaxing in a grand battle. It is the longest Indian epic. The other great Indian epic is the Ramayana, which tells the story of the god-king Rama and his culminating battle with the demon-king Ravana.
45. Jayasinhji Jhala, 'Marriage, Hierarchy and Identity in Ideology and Practice: An Anthropological Study of Rajput Society in Western India against a Historical Background, 1090–1990 AD', 2 vols, (PhD dissertation, Harvard University, 1991, chapter 2, part I, p. 21. Also relevant are these works: Schomer, *et al.*, *Idea of Rajasthan*, 2 vols; Richard D. Saran and Norman P. Ziegler, translators and annotators, *The Mertiyo Rathors of Merto, Rajasthan: Select Translations Bearing on the History of the Rajput Family, 1462–1660*, Michigan Papers on South and Southeast Asian Studies, no. 51, 2 vols, Ann Arbor: 2002.
46. Alwar was known for his support of Hinduism, despite his personal peccadilloes and immorality. Ultimately, in 1933, these failings and problems in his state led the British to force him off the throne. Barbara Ramusack, *The Princes of India in the Twilight of Empire: Dissolution of a Patron-Client System, 1914–29*, Columbus: 1978, pp. 179–80, 289, note 91. Amar Singh discussed the maharaja of Alwar in 'Notes about My Last Visit to Alwar. X, The Maharaja', 28 August 1910, ASD.
47. An interesting chapter on 'The Imperial Hunt in India' appears in John MacKenzie, *The Empire of Nature: Hunting, Conservation and British Imperialism*, Manchester: 1988; also see Mackenzie, 'The Imperial Pioneer and Hunter and the British Masculine Stereotype in Late Victorian and Edwardian Times', in Mangan and Walvin (eds), *Manliness and Morality*, pp. 176–98. A popular book on British sport in India is Major General J. G. Elliott, *Field Sports in India: 1800–1947*, London: 1973. This work includes descriptions of animals and birds that were popular for hunting. The topic of hunting and sport has been less studied for Rajputs and other Indians.
48. Winston Churchill, *My Early Life: A Roving Commission*, New York: 1958.
49. Archibald Wavell, Letter to his sister, 11 October 1907, quoted in Harold E. Raugh, Jr., 'Training Ground for a Future Field Marshall: Wavell in the Boer War and Edwardian India, 1900–1908', *Journal of the Society for Army Historical Research*, 72(289), 1994, p. 16.

50. Brigadier R. C. B. Bristow, *Memories of the British Raj: A Soldier in India*, London: 1974, p. 73.
51. MacKenzie, *Empire of Nature*, pp. 50–5.
52. Amar Singh regarded pig sticking as the most exciting form of hunting—for example, [Shikar Notes], Kanota, 14 August 1913, ASD. Yeats-Brown gives vivid descriptions of polo in *Lives of a Bengal Lancer*, pp. 71–85 and pig-sticking (pp. 86–103). Another contemporary source on pig-sticking is Major A. E. Wardrop (Royal Horse Artillery) (with chapters by others), *Modern Pig Sticking*, London: 1914. Pig-sticking is discussed in MacKenzie, *Empire of Nature*, pp. 186–89.
53. Baron Baden-Powell of Gilwell, Robert Stephenson Smyth Baden-Powell, *Pig sticking; or Hog Hunting: A Complete Account for Sportsmen and Others*, Pall Mall: 1889. Baden-Powell is famous as the founder of the Boy Scout Movement. He had a distinguished career in the British Army, including service in South Africa and India. See his autobiographical work, Robert Stephenson Smyth Baden-Powell, *Memories of India; Recollections of Soldiering and Sport*, Philadelphia: 1915. Baden-Powell's views on manliness and manly activities have received wide scholarly attention—for example, Mangan, *Manliness and Morality*, *passim*.
54. See Rudolph and Rudolph, *Reversing the Gaze*, pp. 255–60. Also, see Chandar S. Sundaram, '"Martial" Indian Aristocrats and the Military System of the Raj: The Imperial Cadet Corps, 1900–1914', *Journal of Imperial and Commonwealth History*, 25(3), 1997, p. 423.
55. Amar Singh's younger brother, Colonel Kesri Singh, was famous for tiger hunting and wrote on the subject, *The Tiger of Rajasthan*, Bombay: 1959; *One Man and a Thousand Tigers*, New York: 1959.
56. Another 'manly' game that Amar Singh enjoyed was billiards. He purchased a billiard table for his home in Kanota and played with his brothers. Golf, croquet, and bridge, however, had no appeal to him. On the other hand, he learned new Patience games from generals' wives, while his family played chess and *helma* (Chinese chequers) at home. 30 Jan. 1912, ASD.
57. For discussion of homosexuality in the Imperial Cadet Corps, see Rudolph and Rudolph, *Reversing the Gaze*, pp. 278–91.
58. For example, Ghaill, *Understanding Masculinities*.
59. 'Notes about My Last leave of Ten Days. VIII. My Wife', 1 April 1906, ASD.
60. Frances Taft (ed.), Laxmi Kumari Chundawat, *From Purdah to the People: Memoirs of Padma Shri Rani Laxmi Kumari Chundawat*, Jaipur: 2000. Laxmi Kumari Chundawat reports that these royal women hunted: the maharani of the late Maharaja Bhopal Singh of Udaipur, the present rajmata of Kota, and Rajmata Gayatri Devi of Jaipur (email letter to DeWitt Ellinwood from Rani Laxmi Kumari Chundawat, 5 October 2002).

61. An example of Amar Singh's comments on the death of a relative is 'Notes about My Last Leave of Thirty-Six Days. VI. [Uncle] Bheem Singhjee's Death', 31 December 1917, ASD.
62. The diary contains references to men, especially in their old age, who become closely attached to, or even dominated by, female servants. 'Notes about My Last Leave of Twelve Days, I. The Idea, III. Mukand Singhjee Sahib's Death', 30 December 1918, ASD.
63. Work with male estate servants was a continuous part of life for Amar Singh when at home, and for his brother, Sardar Singh, who managed the family estate. On the other hand, one of Amar Singh's younger brothers fraternized with servants, thereby dismaying his elder brother.
64. See DeWitt C. Ellinwood, 'The Indian Soldier, the Indian Army, and Change, 1914–18', in DeWitt C. Ellinwood and S. D. Pradhan (eds), *India and World War I*, New Delhi: 1978, pp. 141–76.
65. There are many autobiographies and biographies of Indians who became Indian Army officers before Partition in 1947. Examples include C. B. Khanduri, *Field Marshal K. M. Cariappa: His Life and Times*, New Delhi: 1995; Major General D. K. Palit, *Major-General A. A. Rudra: His Service in Three Armies and Two World Wars*, New Delhi: 1997; General Mohammed Musa, *Jawan to General: Recollections of a Pakistani Soldier*, New Delhi: 1985.
66. Handwritten summaries, in File M 45349, 1918, 'Confidential Reports on Indian Officers Granted King's Commission', L/MIL/7/19017, Oriental and India Office Collection, The British Library, London.
67. A useful way to discover continuity between the British-Indian Army and the post-independence armies of the subcontinent is to look at Stephen P. Cohen's two histories: *The Pakistan Army*, Berkeley: 1984, and *The Indian Army: Its Contribution to the Development of a Nation*, Berkeley: 1971. For a psychoanalytic perspective see Nandy, *The Intimate Enemy*.
68. Apurba Kundu, *Militarism in India: The Army and Civil Society in Consensus*, London: 1998. Historical perspective on the Pakistan Army since independence is provided by Cohen, *The Pakistan Army*.
69. Thakur Mohan Singh, nephew and heir of Amar Singh, has converted Amar Singh's garden home outside Jaipur's city walls, into the Narain Niwas Palace Hotel. In addition, he has turned part of the family fort-home in Kanota into a hotel. For this development, see Barbara Ramusack, 'Tourism and Icons: The "Packaging of the Princely States of Rajasthan"', in Catherine Ella Blanshard Asher and Thomas R. Metcalf (eds), *Perceptions of South Asia's Visual Past*, New Delhi: 1994, pp. 235–55.
70. Gayatri Devi, the last maharani of Jaipur, illustrates this transformation. She joined the Swatantra political party and was elected to the Lok Sabha (House of the People, popularly elected), the lower but most powerful chamber of India's Parliament. Her husband, Maharaja Man

Singh, kept aloof from political parties, but he was elected by the Rajasthan Legislative Assembly to the Rajya Sabha (Council of the States; nominated and elected by state legislatures), upper chamber of the Parliament. Later, Maharaja Man Singh served as Indian Ambassador to Spain. [Maharani of Jaipur, Gayatri Devi, *A Princess Remembers: Memoirs of the Maharani of Jaipur*, Philadelphia: 1976]

Section III

From Small War to World War

9

'Passing it On'
The Army in India and Frontier Warfare, 1914–39

Tim Moreman

Between 1849 and 1947, the inhabitants of the mountainous no man's land between the administered areas of the North West Frontier Province (henceforth NWFP) and Afghanistan posed a continuous threat to the security of British India. In many respects, this local and immediate problem of tribal control overshadowed the more distant threat of war with Afghanistan or Czarist Russia (later USSR) on the Indus frontier, which happened to be the most sensitive strategic frontier of the British Empire. The frontier tribes tied down large numbers of British and Indian troops in a long series of inconclusive skirmishes and major campaigns. What was known to generations of imperial soldiers as variously hill warfare, tribal warfare, mountain warfare and, perhaps most commonly, frontier warfare had distinctive characteristics. It was the most prevalent form of actual combat carried out by British and Indian troops in India. In this essay, the changing characteristics of such operations during this period—caused by improving tribal military effectiveness and changes in the organization, equipment, and training of imperial troops—will be charted. In particular, the article will demonstrate how the lessons learnt by the British armed forces during these operations were passed on to successive generations of officers and men in the form of official specialized training manuals and systems of instruction.

The Tribal Threat and the Army in India

The basic characteristics of frontier fighting had long been known to the imperial troops. They first came into direct contact with the devoutly Muslim and heavily armed trans-border Pathan tribes after the British annexation of the Punjab in 1849. These Pathans repeatedly raided areas under direct British administration and attacked trading caravans. To specifically protect the trans-Indus areas, a localized armed force, named the Punjab Irregular Force (hereafter PIF), was raised. This force was renamed the Punjab Frontier Force (henceforth PFF) in 1865. It quickly learnt, during a long series of 'butcher and bolt' punitive military expeditions, that fighting in mountainous terrain against tribal *lashkars* (war parties/bands) posed a range of problems very different from those encountered in conventional warfare. When operating in tribal territory, the Indian troops were tied down by the need to protect long, vulnerable, and cumbersome columns of pack transport carrying food, water, and ammunition on which they depended in the barren hills. Freedom of movement was thus restricted to the valley floors, while the lightly-equipped tribesmen operated with comparative freedom on the hill sides. Lack of reliable intelligence and maps made it difficult for the British to select suitable objectives, while the difficult climate and endemic diseases in tribal territory often inflicted heavier casualties than the opposing tribesmen. On the other hand, the tribesmen were well acquainted with fighting in their mountains. This familiarity reinforced their relative strengths—mobility, flexibility, and superior marksmanship—in the elusive guerrilla warfare against the slow-moving Indian columns.

By trial and error, the PIF evolved a series of specialized principles and minor tactics tailored to local conditions in tribal territory. To meet tribesmen on equal terms, its infantry regiments developed light infantry skills—skirmishing, skill at arms, marksmanship, self-reliance, and fieldcraft—modelled on those of their opponents. Mountain artillery batteries were equipped with light ordnance capable of being dismantled and transported in the hills on muleback. When operating in tribal territory, the heart of the tactical problem for the British and Indian troops lay in bringing the tribesmen to battle and preventing their harassment of the cumbrous, self-contained main body of the imperial columns. Offensive tactics were emphasized at all stages of a campaign so as to bring the enemy to battle and to demoralize the tribal opposition. Yet this often proved impossible, forcing recourse to the destruction of villages and crops. It was quickly discovered that the key to success lay in controlling the flanking high ground and dominating the surrounding terrain by fire. Outlying pickets would shield vulnerable British columns as they moved by 'crowning the heights' on either side of the route of march, withdrawing to rejoin the main body only when it had passed by. Initially, the short range (300 yards) of Pathan firearms meant that pickets were seldom overlooked by other positions within the tribesmen's effective range, and were secure except from direct assault. The evacuation of a picket, when tribesmen would seize the vacant position and attack the retreating garrison, was, however, the point of greatest danger. To prevent successful tribal attacks, the posting and withdrawal of pickets involved considerable skill and led to the development of elaborate codes and drills by the PIF. At night, encampments located on the valley floors would be surrounded in a similar manner by pickets intended to keep the tribesmen at arm's length. Elaborate field defences consisting of a perimeter wall constructed from rocks, stores, or bales of fodder encompassed each camp to stop rushes by swordsmen, to provide cover from sniping, to shelter sleeping troops, and to prevent infiltration by rifle thieves. The withdrawal of the British and Indian columns represented the biggest tactical difficulty for any expedition. Tribal attacks on rearguards normally intensified, making their extraction under fire the greatest problem for the commanders. All these necessitated the development of further tactical drills. The brutal treatment frequently meted out to the British or Indian dead and wounded by tribesmen exerted a powerful influence on hill warfare, necessitating rapid counterattacks to recover the dead bodies and prisoners, as they could not be allowed to fall into enemy hands.[1]

These principles and minor tactics were a comparatively simple and pragmatic response to hill warfare. A combination of repeated practical experience and specialized training directed solely towards hill warfare made the imperial units highly effective as guardians of the administrative border of the Punjab (later the North West Frontier Province). Yet, because the PIF was a local force under the control of the Punjab government rather than the military authorities until 1886, these methods were not passed on to the regular army in a coherent manner. Until the 1880s and 1890s, when regular troops were deployed in the Punjab for the first time in large numbers, mountain warfare remained the prerogative of the frontier regiments. Following the 1897–8 Tirah campaign, when British and Indian regulars suffered comparatively heavy casualties at tribal hands, a range of specialized official manuals for frontier warfare were produced and appropriate training introduced during the early 1900s.[2] This was of particular importance when the PFF was finally de-localized in 1903 (greatly simplifying the organizational problems caused by maintaining a specialized force) and made available for service throughout India.

In 1908, this new approach to training for colonial warfare on the frontiers of India was thoroughly vindicated during the Zakka Khel and Mohmand expeditions, when small, lightly equipped, and highly trained columns of regular troops inflicted heavy casualties on the opposing tribesmen. Nevertheless, in 1909, the specialized manuals promulgated following the 1897–8 campaigns were abandoned by the newly formed General Staff in India. In accordance with a decision made at the Imperial Defence Conference, it was decided that *Field Service Regulations* (hereafter *FSR*) will be adopted as the basis of training for all the imperial armies.[3] Thenceforth, British and Indian troops relied for guidance in frontier fighting on the general principles of war and six condensed paragraphs that only provided a bare outline of the specialized tactics required in tribal territory.[4] This important change, however, had no significant impact on the efficiency of the Army in India which, by 1914, contained large numbers of officers and men who had considerable experience and a long tradition of frontier fighting.

World War I quickly exposed the shortcomings of this approach to training for frontier fighting, when most highly experienced pre-War regular regiments were sent overseas. Their under-officered and poorly equipped replacements were far below their standard of training in mountain warfare, causing serious concern to the military authorities as unrest spread in the hills during 1915. When British Territorial Army (henceforth TA) regiments, whose officers lacked any real military knowledge or training, were deployed in the NWFP, the inherent limitations of relying solely on the principles of war and limited information contained in the *FSR* to govern frontier warfare training were exposed. As a stop-gap measure, the Mountain Warfare School was opened in May 1916, using innovative teaching methods specifically to train cadres of TA officers and non-commissioned officers (hereafter NCOs) in frontier fighting. These officers were required in turn to instruct their own units.[5] Despite this development, a serious lack of uniformity was evident in applying the principles and minor tactics of mountain warfare during operations conducted by the 1st (Peshawar) and 2nd (Rawalpindi) divisions in November 1916. This was highlighted at a conference in Delhi, 22–24 February 1917, when Major General William Bunbury called for definite rules to be laid down as he believed lack of uniformity was a source of serious danger in the field. Other senior officers, however, openly opposed publication of a special manual or any additions to the *FSR*. Lieutenant General Arthur Barrett, General Officer Commanding (hereafter GOC) Northern Command, closed this discussion by observing:

> I think there is no doubt that mountain warfare is a science. I have always regarded it as a thing very much like a game of chess which wants a great deal of skill to avoid mistakes, but at the same time it is not a science that can be said at any one time to have reached its finality. We are always going on evolving new things and a great many of these points that have been raised have been evolved gradually from experience. We must not assume that the stage we have reached now is the last stage of the process .... We must remember that the increased armament of these tribes that we fight against will go on modifying our rules and systems.[6]

A series of disastrous skirmishes in Waziristan during the spring further underlined the need for specialized training. On 2 May 1917, the GOC Northern Command warned: 'If we employ troops inexperienced in hill warfare, it appears to me that incidents in the Gomal are likely to be repeated .... To frontier warfare the second reserve is quite untrained.'[7] Despite further efforts to improve training by the Mountain Warfare School during 1917 and 1918, by the end of World War I the efficiency of the border garrisons had plummeted far below pre-War standards.

The Lessons of the 1919–20 Waziristan Campaign

The Army in India quickly repulsed the short-lived Afghan invasion in May 1919, but the ensuing tribal rising in Waziristan (where various militias raised to police tribal territory mutinied) was a far more difficult proposition.[8] Before 1914, the army had relied on quality rather than quantity when units were deployed to punish local inhabitants. Now the opposite was true due to the diminution of training. Heavy casualties were inflicted on the raw, ill-trained Indian troops comprising the Derajat Column when punitive operations were finally carried out in the winter of 1919–20. In the heaviest fighting ever witnessed in tribal territory, imperial troops were nearly defeated at Palosina, 19–21 December 1919, by well-armed and trained Mahsud and Wazir lashkars, whose ranks included a significant number of ex-servicemen from the Indian Army. A skillful combination of fire and movement was employed with deadly effect against the demoralized Indian troops by the tribesmen, who also engaged in desperate hand-to-hand combat whenever an opportunity offered.[9] Writing on 13 January 1920, Major General Skipton Climo, GOC Waziristan Field Force, observed:

> Those who do not know India and the frontier, and even some who have fought on the frontier in pre-war days, but lack the knowledge and imagination to realize that conditions have altered with the great improvement of the armament of the tribesmen, cannot understand or believe the standard of training that is required for the Infantry in the conditions that now prevail on the Frontier to-day. To such, the belief is natural that the mere frontier tribes cannot be formidable opponents to modern troops nor can they believe that the standard of training or method of tactics that succeeded in the great war can, in former cases, be insufficient for and, in the latter cases, be inapplicable to a Frontier campaign.[10]

The possession of large numbers of modern .303 service rifles transformed the fighting effectiveness of Pathan lashkars. It altered the characteristics of frontier warfare by slowing down every phase of operations and dramatically increasing imperial casualties. In response, a slow, deliberate, and heavily contested advance of only 2–4 miles a day was adopted as the Derajat Column advanced deeper into Waziristan. This heavy fighting taught British officers that existing methods had to be adapted and new tactics ought to be developed to ensure victory. The latter included the widespread use of permanent pickets on all commanding positions within effective rifles range (1000–1500 yards) of a column, a fixed line of communications to service spiralling logistical requirements, and the widespread use of night operations to nullify the effect of tribal riflemen. Despite deploying large numbers of men and support from modern aircraft, 3.7″ pack Howitzers, and Lewis light machine guns, by the end of the hostilities, the Waziristan Force had 366 dead, 1683 wounded, and a further 237 men missing.[11] This unprecedented 'butcher's bill' indicated that a new era had begun in frontier warfare. Henceforth, all operations in tribal territory clearly had to be deliberate, governed by a fixed line of communication, and carried out by large numbers of troops except where very light opposition was encountered.

The near disaster in Waziristan and the fact that large numbers of regular troops were deployed on the frontier following the Third Afghan War, as part of the newly-organized Covering Troops, convinced the Indian General Staff that it had to act quickly to restore the Army's efficiency in mountain warfare. On 1 February 1920, the Mountain Warfare School was reopened at Abbottabad to provide sufficient trained instructors for imperial units. Under the command of Colonel William Villiers-Stuart, it ran a series of courses during the spring, summer, and autumn of 1920, beginning with an explanation of the basic principles of war—a deliberate attempt to avoid over-specialization—before introducing the modifications required in their application to 'trans-border' warfare. Members of the Directing Staff emphasized the importance of individual skills—skill at arms, self-reliance, vigilance, and personal judgement—to overcome 'trans-border' loneliness. Particular attention was directed towards various modifications of tactics and the lessons derived about the employment of modern equipment in mountain warfare during the recent fighting in Waziristan, as confusion existed in the minds of many officers.[12] Although the Mountain Warfare School proved a highly successful expedient, it was not retained by the Army in India as a permanent training establishment. In accordance with normal British practice, at the end of the year, the commanding officers were once again made responsible for training, under the direction of the staff of the formations to which they belonged.

The military authorities realized that it would take some time before the efficiency of regular British and Indian units was restored to pre-War standards. Indeed, the intrinsic difficulties were such that re-establishment of the PFF was briefly considered by the high command on several occasions during the early 1920s, as it was widely accepted that specialized troops would be more effective in tribal territory.[13] Following the closure of the Mountain Warfare School, the provision of an authoritative source of guidance to units periodically serving tours of duty in the tribal areas was of considerable importance. It was clear that something more was needed than the *FSR*, as the 1920 provisional edition still referred to 'savage warfare' solely in terms of fighting against opponents reliant on shock tactics, and its small section on mountain warfare lacked the detail required by inexperienced junior officers and NCOs. As a temporary measure, a small pamphlet was hurriedly prepared in 1920 for units garrisoned in the NWFP and Baluchistan. A revised edition was published in January 1921, and 15,000 copies were issued. The pamphlet laid down general rules governing the conduct of 'uncivilized' warfare, as well as the general principles governing military operations against the trans-border Pathan tribes for all three arms of service. It covered picketing; protection on the march; protection of the lines of communication, camps, and bivouacs; and night operations. Moreover, it provided tentative guidance regarding the use of new equipment such as Lewis guns.[14] For units in action in Waziristan, the HQ of

Wazirforce also produced and distributed its own tactical notes tailored to conditions in that area.[15] Several unofficial textbooks discussing frontier fighting also appeared during the early 1920s, written by experienced Indian Army officers to assist their junior colleagues.[16]

The low-intensity fighting that dragged on inconclusively in Waziristan between 1920–4 ensured that many British and Indian units gained practical experience of mountain warfare. When combined with specialized instruction, this meant that by 1924 most of the units had reached a semblance of their pre-War standard of training.[17] It also supplied valuable practical experience about the capabilities and limitations of new equipment hitherto utilized only in small quantities on the North-West frontier (aircraft, machine guns, motor transport, and modern mountain artillery). Many officers were eager to employ other military technology originally developed on the Western Front. For example, gas warfare was investigated in 1919–20, and tanks were given trials in tribal territory with mixed success during the early 1920s. Due to the terrain, most heavy weapons and equipment, however, could not be employed except on or near the growing network of roads built in accordance with new government policy in Waziristan and the NWFP. Other factors militated against the use of more destructive types of military equipment. As Colonel Frederick Keen reminded readers of the *Journal of the United Service Institution of India* (hereafter *JUSII*), the inhouse journal of the army in India, in 1923:

> We should realize, as we have perhaps not done in the past, that in fighting the Pathans we are engaging in civil war and that it is to our advantage that enemies of to-day should be turned into our friends of to-morrow .... In a word, our coercive measures should always be directed with a view to eventual pacification and control.[18]

A combination of drastic cutbacks in the military budget and lack of skilled Indian personnel, however, decided the issue by preventing the acquisition of large quantities of new arms and equipment. The infantryman and pack mule still reigned supreme in frontier warfare. As Captain Mervyn Gompertz concluded in the *Army Quarterly* in 1925:

> One cardinal fact remains. The use of the Lewis gun enables a reduction in the strength of piquets and to increase fire effect; the motor vehicle and the tractor may speed up operations; wireless telegraphy may add the personal touch; the glider may become the infantry of the air to assist the infantry of the ground: yet the age long principle remains that it is the soldier who will win or lose the frontier.[19]

The need for authoritative up-to-date guidance in frontier fighting for the large numbers of imperial troops deployed in close contact with the trans-border Pathan tribes had been clearly demonstrated between 1919–24. Although the revised 1924 edition of the *FSR* incorporated a chapter dealing with warfare in 'undeveloped' and 'semi-civilized countries', it was clearly accepted by the military authorities in India that the general principles of war and the small section on mountain warfare that it contained was an insufficient basis for training. In response, the lessons learnt in Waziristan since 1919 were compiled at Army Head Quarter (hereafter AHQ) that year and incorporated in a new manual intended to complement the *FSR* and the training manuals for the various arms of service.[20]

The *Manual of Operations on the North West Frontier of India*, published in 1925, reflected the important changes that had occurred in frontier warfare since World War I. No fewer than 35,000 copies were printed and by October 1925 had been issued to units serving throughout India. Its pages reflected the Indian Army's extensive experience of frontier operations, and brought up to date the existing doctrine and system of training caused by improved tribal tactics, leadership, and equipment, as well as changes in the organization, training, and equipment of imperial troops. It represented a significant improvement over solely relying on the *FSR* as the basis of all training, although it still discussed the conduct of mountain warfare with close reference to the principles of war. This manual included chapters describing the trans-border Pathans and tribal territory; fighting troops and their characteristics; protection on march and when halted; the organization and protection of lines of communication; the conduct of attack and withdrawal for all three arms; foraging and demolitions; as well as administrative routine in camp and on the line of march. It emphasized the importance of appropriate training for all three arms of service, especially with regard to the development of individual skills of self-reliance, vigilance, and initiative to overcome the peculiar difficulties encountered when fighting in tribal territory. The use of the Royal Air Force (hereafter RAF) in cooperation with troops was discussed, and it even went on to cover the employment of tanks in hill warfare, although they were still unavailable in India. Finally, imperial troops on duty in tribal territory were specifically warned to stay alert despite prolonged periods without contact with hostile tribesmen, and officers were encouraged to read histories of past campaigns to prevent the repetition of mistakes previously committed by imperial troops.[21]

The Search for Mobility

The Army in India quickly settled into the normal routine of peacetime service. Throughout the remainder of the inter-War period, Indian regiments served a two-year tour of duty in the Covering Troops' Districts, allowing them to accumulate steadily a cadre of trained and experienced officers and men. By comparison, British infantry battalions served only an infrequent one-year tour of duty in the area.[22] While stationed in the border cantonments, imperial units trained intensively in mountain warfare, based on the *Manual of Operations on the North West Frontier of* India, and supervised by the staff and senior officers of the formations to which they belonged. Standing Orders periodically issued by the formations permanently stationed in the NWFP provided a further source of guidance for both peacetime training and active service, amplifying points laid down in the official manual and taking into account local conditions and requirements at each station.[23] Those British and Indian units serving in the Field Army concentrated on conventional 'open' warfare against a 'second class enemy' during both the individual and collective training seasons into which each year was divided. The priority attached by the Army in India to training in mountain and open warfare was a subject of considerable professional controversy between officers whose attention was focused on a likely conventional conflict and those concerned with the day-to-day requirements of Indian defence. Many British service officers were highly critical of the specialized doctrine for 'savage warfare' employed on the frontier, believing that the lesser was by default contained in the greater.[24] Most Indian Army officers, for whom frontier service formed such a large part of normal military experience more readily appreciated its importance. As one pointed out in the *JUSII* in July 1930:

> There are two forms of warfare to be taught in India, *viz*, open warfare and mountain warfare. Except for those stationed on the frontier the former of course requires the most attention, but mountain warfare should never be entirely neglected in view of the fact that wherever the Army in India fights in the future it is almost certain to be in mountainous country. In addition, about a third of our Army in India is presently stationed on the frontier and practically every unit takes a turn of duty there sooner or later.[25]

The criticism levelled at the methods employed by British and Indian units on the North-West frontier redoubled during the summer of 1930, when civil disturbances in the NWFP sparked widespread unrest in tribal territory.[26] During the ensuing operations, it appeared to many outside observers that army units had grown ponderous and over-cautious, and their tactics too stereotypical, especially after large Afridi lashkars raided Peshawar District and then escaped largely unscathed. In comparison, the high mobility of the lightly equipped Scouts and Frontier Constabulary (elements of the Civil Armed Forces) enabled them to deal successfully with elusive tribal raiders, prompting accusations that the military was incapable of performing its allotted role in the watch and ward of tribal territory. The very fact that the garrison in Peshawar District had had to be reinforced with irregulars appeared to indicate that its effectiveness had declined, prompting several suggestions in the press for the re-establishment of a localized force organized, trained, and equipped exclusively for operations against the trans-border Pathans.[27]

Most of the lessons the Indian Army learnt from the 1930 operations were mixed and contradictory. The mobility conferred by the road network in Waziristan and within the NWFP, together with the provision of armoured cars and motor transport, had clearly altered the strategic, tactical, and administrative conduct of frontier warfare, enabling reinforcements to be rushed to the threatened points along the border. For example, two-and-a-half infantry battalions and a company of sappers were transported 42 miles by lorry from Bannu to reinforce Razmak between 7 and 9 July 1930. The speed of motor transport convoys also eased picketing and eased the task of the road protection troops in areas where light opposition was encountered. Perhaps more significantly, motor transport (hereafter MT) greatly simplified the logistical and administrative problems encountered by troops operating in tribal territory. The Indian columns utilizing MT were tied, however, to advancing along predictable routes, enabling hostile tribesmen to anticipate their lines of approach, and to concentrate and prepare defences as well as ambushes.[28]

The off-road mobility and tactical effectiveness of imperial columns in Waziristan, however, had sharply declined due to the large numbers of troops deployed and changes in their organization, equipment, and training. As a result, the pace of an advance and the distance a column could march in a single day were lower than fifty years earlier, as the number of mules on which they depended had dramatically increased due to the higher scales of arms, equipment, supplies, and maintenance services now required in the field. This growing 'tail' of pack animals compounded the administrative and tactical problems faced by Indian commanders and acted as a brake on mobility, reducing the circuit of action of columns and slowing down every stage of operation, lengthening the line of march and exacerbating the already difficult problem of ensuring all-round protection.[29] To complicate matters, in accordance with a new imperial establishment, a company of Vickers medium machine guns was formed in each British and Indian infantry battalion in 1929. This meant additional mules were now needed to carry these heavy weapons. This considerably reduced the rifle strength of Indian battalions, despite restrictions initially placed on the number of heavy weapons to maintain mobility in the hills.[30] An infantry battalion could not provide the same number of pickets as before, lowering the distance it could protect from 3 to 2 miles, which in turn limited the distance a column could march in a single day.[31] The additional machine guns dramatically increased the firepower, making lashkars wary of engaging Indian columns or following up rearguards, thereby limiting opportunities to inflict heavy casualties.[32] Further problems were caused by an obsession with security which overrode other operational requirements, slowed movement to a crawl, and tied Indian columns to cautious and unimaginative advances along the valley floors. It now took longer to picket a route as periodic halts were necessary, while covering machine gun and artillery fire was carefully arranged to support the placement and withdrawal of pickets. Fear of casualties, recovery of the dead and wounded, and efforts to prevent the theft of arms and ammunition also stultified efforts to bring hostile lashkars to battle or to achieve surprise. An inability to differentiate between the tactical requirements of conventional warfare and those on the frontier compounded the problem. On many occasions, Indian commanders mounted deliberate set-piece attacks backed with a full panoply of supporting arms, despite the fact that the lashkars seldom awaited the assault.[33]

These failings revealed in 1930–1 did not escape the attention of the civilian and military members of the Tribal Control and Defence Committee appointed to examine the entire system of tribal management. Its final report echoed earlier press criticisms, and suggested that the military authorities should consider lightening the arms and equipment of regular units and even the merits of forming a new PFF.[34] The latter view, however, was dismissed out of hand by the General Staff in India, which strongly opposed the idea given the inherent organizational difficulties involved and the fact that it ignored the other important roles the Covering Troops performed, such as aid to civil tasks in the plain, etc. Instead, senior officers argued that the organization, equipment, and training designed to fight the Afghan Army, supported by foreign troops and the frontier tribes, was by default automatically suited to fighting the tribesmen alone. Moreover, as long as the North-West frontier remained the most likely theatre of operations of the Indian Army, it strongly believed that all imperial troops required experience of the terrain, and tactics similar to those required in Afghanistan.[35] This view was also supported in the service press. Writing in response to calls for radical changes in the Indian Army's current organization, training, and equipment to make it more effective in operations in tribal territory, one anonymous officer observed in 1932:

> Surely no one wants an army trained on North West Frontier mountain warfare lines only. This would be truly retrograde. Then indeed would it become a second rate army. All the cost of higher military education, Staff College and modern equipment could be economized if we are to limit our horizon to the hills of the Frontier .... Any tendency for specialization for mountain warfare operations on the North West Frontier must be resisted .... The thinking soldier, if he is to be any value to his profession, must avoid parochialism. The 'khaki' of the Frontier is undoubtedly fascinating, but it is not the only topic of thought for the British officer.[36]

Rather than fundamentally changing current organization, the General Staff directed particular thought towards increasing the circuit of action of mechanized Indian columns and the cross-country mobility of Indian soldiers in the hills.

The strategic mobility and circuit of action of the columns in the Covering Troops Districts was comparatively easily increased by the General Staff during the 1930s by further road-building in the NWFP. Most work was carried out in Waziristan. But to pacify new areas, construction began on a further series of roads elsewhere in tribal territory in 1934, although it proved an expensive, time-consuming process and frequently provoked opposition.[37] Henceforth, punitive operations in tribal territory were normally combined with road construction to allow small, lightly-equipped columns to be supplied and to operate in the hills, as well as extending political control.[38] Hand in hand with road-building, went the slow introduction into service in India of motor transport, tractors, 'half tracks', and fully-tracked vehicles—Carden Lloyd Mark VI Armoured Machine Gun Carriers and Mark 1A Light Tanks—with much-improved cross-country performance.[39]

It proved far more difficult to improve the off-road mobility of imperial troops in mountainous terrain, although this was addressed by reducing or lightening personal clothing, arms, and equipment, decreasing the scale of supporting weapons and changes in training. Many Indian battalions replaced their heavy ammunition boots with *chappals* (grass sandals) and substituted lightweight clothing in place of the normal issue. Amounts of ammunition and equipment carried by each soldier were also reduced and from 1934, a considerably lighter and more reliable replacement for the cumbersome Lewis gun, with its attendant mule, began to be issued.[40] Yet, despite continued criticism of the new machine gun company, the number of Vickers medium machine guns in each battalion was increased during 1931 by two weapons, to maintain uniformity with the rest of the British Army.[41] Since it represented the main brake on the mobility of columns operating in tribal territory, the reduction or complete replacement of the large quantity of pack transport was carefully considered. This administrative tail was successfully 'docked' by cutting down superfluous animals and the number of troops required for their care and protection. However, despite being regarded as anachronistic by many officers, pack mules and camels still remained essential in all operations mounted beyond a road head in tribal territory.[42] Air supply was also carefully examined as an alternative means of maintaining troops and reinforcing isolated posts now that two bomber transport aircraft were available in India.[43] Despite the potential demonstrated by air supply on two occasions in 1930, the General Staff remained sceptical because of the limited number of aircraft available, the expense, and their inability to evacuate casualties.[44]

No radical changes were made by the General Staff in the system of periodic relief of units stationed in the NWFP or the training methods used by the Army in India apart from greater emphasis on light infantry training. By the mid-1930s, Indian Army regiments were highly proficient in frontier warfare. Most now contained a large cadre of officers, NCOs, and other ranks with both practical experience and training in frontier warfare, enabling them to quickly achieve a high standard of efficiency when they returned to a border station. In comparison, British regiments were the 'natural prey' of the tribesmen as most of their training was predicated on conventional 'open warfare' or internal security duties. An intermittent one-year tour of duty in the NWFP prevented them accumulating a cadre of 'frontier hands', placing even greater reliance on theoretical instruction, and 'on the job' training. To a large extent, the performance of British units depended upon their willingness to adapt. As Colonel Hugh Pettigrew later noted:

> How good or bad these regiments were on the frontier depended on just one thing, and that was how ready they were to learn .... If a British regiment

> arrived at Razmak, or better still at Bannu prior to its march up to Razmak, and said: 'We are new to this. You are not. Please teach us!' then it would soon be a regiment well able to look after itself and take a share of responsibility in mobile columns, picketing and so on. But let a regiment think that it knew, and that it was too famous to have to learn, to think that the Highlands of Scotland bore any real resemblance to the mountains of Waziristan, and that regiment might have trouble. And during its year in Waziristan it would be of little use to anyone, and often a liability.[45]

A combination of cap-badge rivalry between regiments, rapid changeovers in personnel, the comparative 'amateurism' of British officers, professional arrogance, and racism often militated against the assimilation of military skills required on the frontier from experienced Indian units.[46]

Training of British officers, NCOs, and men was facilitated by the publication of an important unofficial textbook in 1932 written by General Andrew Skeen, specifically directed at junior British Army officers as they were less likely in their wider range of service to be trained for the local problem which all officers in India have to keep in mind. *Passing it On: Short Talks on Tribal Fighting on the North-West Frontier of India* provided a detailed source of clear and comprehensive information in an easily readable form regarding the trans-border Pathan tribes, and tactics plus administration of hill warfare, being based on the author's extensive experience.[47] It assumed an authoritative position, running to three editions, and was widely read in Britain and India. Copies were specially issued to British Army officers' and sergeants' messes, and also to other British and Indian combatant units in India on the orders of Commander-in-Chief Philip Chetwode. The objective was to allow troops to benefit from the tactical and administrative guidance provided by probably the Indian Army's most experienced frontier soldier.[48]

The tactical handling of frontier operations remained a subject of controversy in the service press during the early 1930s.[49] For example, in the question set for the 1933 *JUSII* prize-essay competition, the growing complexity of modern weapons, mechanization, and the increasing dependence of Indian columns on maintenance services in the field were explicitly linked to the declining effectiveness and relative mobility of the Indian Army. 'Borderer' argued in the winning essay that military organization, equipment, and training devised for 'civilized' European warfare were inappropriate for operations against lightly armed tribesmen. In a telling critique, he identified a fundamental conflict between the requirements of tribal control and European warfare that had been made explicit, and the initial hesitant attempts of the Indian Army to modernize during the early 1930s. 'Borderer' believed that the growing divergence—in terms of training, organization, and equipment—between the military requirements of 'savage' and 'civilized' warfare could no longer be reconciled, and presented such an insuperable problem that he advocated a controversial scheme for the formation of a localized frontier force for service on the North-West frontier.[50] Writing in 1934, Major General Henry Rowan-Robinson summed up an opinion shared by a growing number of British officers:

> The normal methods employed in such operations are elaborately described in the training manuals and elsewhere. A considerable literature has in fact grown up around them. They are, however, recognized to be thoroughly unsatisfactory; and, with the multiplication of weapons, vast requirements in ammunition and insistence on luxuries, they are daily becoming more so.[51]

The Mohmand Campaign, August–September 1935

The Mohmand operations provided a practical test of the various organizational and tactical changes introduced during the early 1930s. A combination of lightened personal equipment and light infantry training speeded up picketing and improved cross-country mobility, but the Vickers machine gun company in each battalion remained a serious brake on mobility. Perhaps the most striking feature of the campaign was the willingness of Indian commanders to undertake large operations at night, enabling them to seize the initiative, upset tribal plans, and avoid the delay inherent in mounting deliberate attacks. As a result, columns penetrated deeper into tribal territory before they had to return to the security of a perimeter camp each night.[52] New equipment also made its debut. A single tractor-drawn battery of 18-pounders, whose longer ranged and more powerful guns supplemented mountain artillery batteries, was able to support several widely separated Indian columns. Perhaps of greater significance was the successful deployment of a single company of Mk II light tanks. Their invulnerability to rifle fire and cross-country mobility quickened the pace of operations as tanks could easily advance through tribal positions. Although cavalry was needed to reconnoitre the ground and engineers had to construct tank crossings over *nullah*s and improve the track across the Nahakki Pass, the terrain in Mohmand country did not present an appreciable obstacle nor did an attempt by the tribesmen to impede movement by digging pits and strewing the roads with rocks and boulders.[53]

'Mohforce' was heavily dependent on large numbers of non-combatant ancillary units throughout the fighting, which had both tactical and administrative implications for frontier warfare. A large number of signallers, field ambulances, engineer parks, ordnance depots, and motor vehicles accompanied 'Mohforce' and each day motor transport carried ammunition, supplies, and water to a roadhead from where pack transport carried it to the forward troops. To encompass the large number of vulnerable vehicles and non-combatant troops, perimeter camps grew in size and complexity. It often proved difficult to find a flat space large enough for all troops and equipment, and their construction was both time-consuming and required considerable labour. The amount of manpower required for their defence, moreover, was considerable; but as the proportion of infantry to other arms had fallen, it was often difficult to provide sufficient troops.[54] A heavy consumption of ammunition made it vital to maintain and protect a permanent line of communication along the Gandab Road to service growing logistical requirements, facilitate the movement of reinforcements, and evacuate casualties.[55] Armoured cars regularly patrolled the Gandab Road, but the burden of protection—as always—fell on the infantry. Permanent pickets were constructed in the Karappa Pass, but the intricate and relatively low-lying land between Kialgai and Karappa lacked terrain features that afforded a field of vision and fire. The Nowshera Brigade and 3rd (Jhelum) Brigade adopted a new system based on mobility and offensive defence, employing lightly-equipped fighting patrols who operated between strong posts constructed on either side of the road to deny tribal marksmen good positions.[56]

The lessons learnt in Mohmand country had clearly convinced the General Staff in India and many other British officers that both the tactical and administrative conduct of hill warfare had undergone major changes. A detailed section discussing this campaign was included in the *A.H.Q. India Training Memorandum* for the 1935–6 collective training season. It began:

> The recent Mohmand operations showed marked advance in the conduct of operations of this nature and the methods employed. Apart from the advantages of a L.[ine] of C.[ommunication] with a road for M.T. [Motor Transport], which was effectively maintained, and of efficient administrative arrangements, the rapid and complete success obtained in this campaign may be attributed to enterprising leadership, development of existing methods, and the introduction of innovations.[57]

Units throughout India were ordered by the Commander-in-Chief to follow guidelines laid down in this publication during the forthcoming training season,which incorporated various lessons learnt regarding the employment of night operations, light tanks, and armoured cars, and the protection of the lines of communication. Sufficient practical experience of the impact of changes in the tactics, training, organization and equipment on the conduct of hill warfare had now been gained to prompt the military authorities to begin preparation the long-awaited replacement for *The Manual of Operations on the North-West Frontier of India*.[58]

The greater cooperation and improving relations evident between the Air Staff and the General Staff, following the appointment of Air Marshal Edgar Ludlow-Hewitt as Air Officer Commanding in India, meant the RAF also took a far greater interest in tactical cooperation with the army in mountain warfare during 1936.[59] Under his command, in April 1935 the Air Staff in India had already issued instructions that RAF training in the Subcontinent should henceforth be directed solely towards efficiency in tribal warfare, although primarily employing independent bombing operations.[60] This decision had strengthened Wing-Commander John Slessor's growing conviction that a radical change should be made in the system of army co-operation used in India, as the existing 'Aldershot model'—devised for conventional European warfare—was largely ineffective in mountainous terrain.[61] Writing on 10 April 1936, he urged:

> The great cry now-a-days seems to be co-operation—the balanced use of all arms and Services in Frontier warfare .... I should have thought there could be no better way of ensuring that good co-operation than by having a combined manual on which we all work, containing the description of all methods of Frontier warfare.[62]

During the summer, 'Tactical Exercises Without Troops' were held near Rawalpindi to demonstrate the effectiveness of close air support and study the inherent problems from the viewpoint of ground troops, while the Vickers-Bomb-Lewis (VBL) ground attack method was developed at Peshawar. The 2nd (Rawalpindi) Brigade and aircraft from No. 3 (Indian) Wing took part in a large combined exercise at Kanpur, between 17 and 25 November 1936, to develop and test close air support tactics in mountain warfare, based on a provisional close-support manual written by Slessor and a draft of the new frontier warfare manual.[63] These manoeuvers, simulating tribal opposition to an Indian column engaged in road construction, conclusively demonstrated the practicalities of close support and indicated the importance of RAF liaison officers at column HQs to direct operations, as well as an effective means of inter-communication between the aircraft and forward troops, between columns and airfields.[64]

The Lessons of the 1936–7 Waziristan Campaign

The Waziristan Military District provided the RAF and the Army in India with an immediate opportunity to test the effectiveness of their new fighting methods when hostilities broke out in the Khaisora Valley in November 1936. This fighting, which ultimately involved 61,056 regular and irregular troops, dragged on during 1937 as imperial forces endeavoured to bring to battle an estimated 4000 hostile tribesmen. Most of the lessons learnt during the Mohmand operations were confirmed, indicating that there was no need for a major change in imperial tactics. It also provided further important practical experience regarding the use of light tanks, medium artillery, and aircraft in frontier warfare, although infantry—with mule first-line transport—remained the predominant arm during frontier fighting, which was now divided into two main categories: operations by columns operating in rugged, mountainous areas and those associated with road protection along Wazirforce's extended lines of communication.[65]

The infantryman and the pack mule still remained the mainstay of all operations in mountainous terrain impassable to wheeled transport and where limited scope existed for tracked vehicles. In November 1936, the Khaisora operations graphically demonstrated, however, that the maximum distance a fully equipped Indian column could march, taking full precautions and allowing sufficient time to establish a perimeter camp before nightfall, was now limited to 8–10 miles a day. Despite reductions in their number, the factor which above all dictated the speed of movement and circuit of action of a column remained the protection of the masses of pack transport still required to carry supplies. It was only possible to move further or faster by reducing picketing below an acceptable margin of safety, or by neglecting to provide sufficient supporting artillery and machine gun fire. To provide security, all commanding features upto 1500 yards had to be occupied by a full platoon to protect Indian columns on the move or troops halted at night from sniping. The perimeter camps were also justified when a massed assault was made on 2nd

(Rawalpindi) Brigade on the night of 27 April 1937. Night operations were once again thoroughly vindicated, reducing tribal resistance and increasing the Indian Army's mobility in the border hills; but they needed surprise and careful planning to prevent confusion. Two companies of Mk II and Mk IIb Light Tanks were employed in sections or sub-sections—when ground permitted—to carry out reconnaissance, protect flanks, cover withdrawals, and directly attack lashkars, adding to the strength and quickening the pace of movement.[66] Yet, while the weight of firepower provided by machine guns, artillery, light tanks, and aircraft proved highly effective against large concentrated lashkars in the opening phases of the operations, it exacerbated the problem of bringing the elusive tribesmen to battle. Moreover, the unrestricted employment of superior firepower was now a thing of the past, as the political restrictions associated with the 'hearts and minds' campaign in Waziristan exerted a powerful influence on the fighting.

It was clear that the Army in India was now more than ever dependent on roads which increased the mobility of units in Waziristan and facilitated the supply of imperial columns. Lorries were employed on an unprecedented scale, allowing a considerable reduction in the number of pack animals and non-combatants. The circular road allowed lightly equipped imperial troops to quickly concentrate and operate off a secure line of communication, greatly simplifying the whole problem of transport and supply, as well as reducing the size and unwieldiness of columns. The motor transport delivered troops, pack animals, and supplies to the point where columns left the roads; refilled supply aechelons; and dumped stores at roadheads—and were, to that extent, able to increase the radius of action of accordingly lightly equipped Indian troops. Roads also allowed heavy weapons to be deployed in Waziristan. Five batteries of mechanized field artillery, as well as a section of the 20/21st Medium Battery, equipped with a mixture of 18 pound, 4.5 inch, and 6 inch guns firing a heavier weight of shell than normally used in frontier warfare, supported columns within range and road protection troops.[67]

Road protection was the main task carried out by the imperial troops deployed in Waziristan as reliance on motor transport increased.[68] A full infantry brigade was normally required to picket 10–12 miles of road, with mobile reserves held ready in each sector to respond to tribal raids. The stereotypical tactics most units employed for 'Road Open Days'—normally held three days a week—allowed little opportunity for personal initiative or any variation in minor tactics when positions of tactical importance had to be repeatedly occupied. Most road protection schemes employed in Waziristan also surrendered the initiative and provided hostile tribesmen with an idea of the time, direction, method, and destination of each detachment as they picketed a road each day, making them vulnerable to attack. Armoured cars and, on occasion, light tanks proved an effective and economical means of patrolling roads, escorting convoys, and providing fire support to road protection troops. A clear lesson of the campaign following the ambush of a convoy in the Shahur Tangi, however, was that motor transport was still highly vulnerable to sniping and ambushes in hilly areas outside the security provided by static protective pickets.[69]

Perhaps the outstanding feature of the Waziristan operations was the close cooperation between the RAF and the Army in India at the tactical level, which dramatically improved combat effectiveness, although independent bombing operations were also carried out. Six squadrons equipped with Westland Wapiti, Hawker Audax, and Hawker Hart aircraft were used in the largest air operation ever undertaken in India, under detailed restrictions imposed by the Government of India in order to prevent the death of non-combatants and attacks on friendly tribal sections. Daily reconnaissance sorties located hostile lashkars, and enabled column commanders to determine the number and location of pickets and perimeter camps in advance, and to direct long-range artillery fire. The bomber transport aircraft frequently dropped supplies to imperial columns, maintained isolated posts, and evacuated casualties. This increased the administrative and hence the tactical mobility of columns to the extent that, following the Khaisora operations, it was proposed that supply drops of food, fodder, and ammunition should form a normal component of all military operations in tribal territory to reduce the amount of pack transport required, remove the need for a permanent line of communication, extend the circuit of action of ground columns, and increase their speed and mobility.[70] Throughout 1937, the close-support tactics developed at Kanpur formed an integral part of most operations in Waziristan, with aircraft engaging hostile tribesmen in contact with imperial troops and those advancing or retiring in 'proscribed' areas in advance or along the flanks of columns.[71] Writing in March 1937, General John Coleridge, GOC Northern Command, acknowledged that: 'These operations have definitely proved the great value which close support by aircraft in mountain warfare can afford.'[72] As had been anticipated, close communication between pilots and forward troops was essential. R/T between aircraft and mule-pack sets accompanying column head-quarters formed the basis of communication, while a simple 'XVT', 'Close Support Intercommunication Code' enabled forward troops to indicate their position and targets to supporting aircraft.[73]

The 1936–7 Waziristan campaign demonstrated once again the necessity of a high standard of specialized training in frontier warfare for units in the Covering Troops and elements of the Field Army detailed as immediate reinforcements. During 1937, the recent lessons learnt in tribal territory were included in reports issued by Northern Command, and the annual report on collective training distributed throughout India.[74] Training in frontier warfare was extended to form part of the individual and collective training period of every unit and brigade in India. The units of the 1st (Rawalpindi) Division and those stationed in Lahore District were also temporarily attached to the columns operating in tribal territory. The *Manual of Operations on the North West Frontier's* planned replacement was not immediately available to these troops, however, despite agreement between the General Staff, Air Staff in India, and the Foreign and Political Department regarding its contents. When the first draft was submitted for approval in February 1936, General William Bartholomew, the Chief of General Staff, observed: 'It is most comprehensive and much larger than the old manual, but I think that it is right that this should be so. It is intended primarily for the use of officers of both services at Home and in India who have no knowledge of the Frontier or of Frontier fighting.'[75]

Controversy over the politically sensitive sections dealing with aircraft, however, prevented publication when the Secretary of State for India decided they should be issued separately.[76] This decision bitterly disappointed Major General Claude Auchinleck, who had drafted the manual and secured agreement between the RAF, army, and political authorities in India. General Robert Cassels, the Commander-in-Chief in India, personally intervened in May 1937 to prevent the 'emasculation' of the manual, which he believed presented a comprehensive picture of frontier warfare under modern conditions.[77] As a result, the entire manual was finally reclassified as 'for official use only', although further differences over air operations meant it was not until November 1938 that it was approved for publication and not until March 1939 that it was issued.[78] During this period, a small section on frontier fighting was included in the

A.H.Q. India Training Memorandum, issued in July 1938, although the information it contained was deliberately kept limited pending the arrival of a new training manual.[79] Perhaps the most important means of disseminating information regarding the recent fighting was the service press. Many officers were eager to record their experiences and discern lessons from the recent operations, although not all expressed satisfaction with the current tactics or system of training employed in India.[80]

The 20,000 copies of *Frontier Warfare: Army and Royal Air Force* provided British and Indian units and RAF squadrons with a detailed and up-to-date formal written doctrine of frontier warfare. It formed the basis of training for companies and higher formations for the remainder of British rule. Despite growing criticism, the manual emphasized the continued importance of established orthodox methods of frontier warfare—columns, protective pickets, and perimeter camps. But it also warned officers against the dangers of operations becoming too stereotypical, and discussed the use of aircraft, light tanks, and heavy artillery in tribal territory. Officers were encouraged to read histories of military operations—the manual also included a bibliography of books dealing with both the frontier and frontier warfare—and the need for cooperation of land and air forces, and their dependence on each other, was stressed. It described in considerable detail air blockades, proscriptive air action, destructive air action, and ground/air cooperation in mountain warfare.[81] Other sources of unofficial guidance complemented the new manual during 1939. Perhaps the most significant addition to this literature was a fourth revised edition of *Passing it On: Short Talks on Tribal Fighting on the North-West Frontier of India of India*, which contained a new chapter written by several Indian Army officers discussing the 1936–7 Waziristan operations.[82]

CONCLUSION

The constant threat posed by the trans-border Pathan tribes prompted perhaps the most detailed official military response to the demands of colonial warfare in the British Empire. As the General Staff in India faced a definite, long-term military problem or 'threat', it adopted a far more pragmatic approach than the War Office (which directed military training elsewhere in the British Empire). It recognized the paramount importance of an officially sanctioned specialized doctrine and a system of training for frontier fighting.

Following the 1919–20 Waziristan Campaign, the General Staff again acknowledged that the inherent difficulties of frontier fighting—exacerbated by improving tribal military effectiveness—meant imperial troops could not be left to 'make it up as they went along' or rely on 'on the job training' without incurring significant casualties. As a result, it devoted considerable time and effort to collating, analysing, and disseminating lessons learnt by imperial troops fighting in tribal territory. These were passed on in new training manuals, annual training memoranda, and standing orders that incorporated new developments. Outside official channels, the service press, textbooks written by serving or retired officers, and a large cadre of experienced men within units also provided an important means of 'passing on' information. This was an important reflection of military professionalism directed towards colonial military requirements rather than imitation of European practice. The recurrence of so-called 'regrettable incidents' in tribal territory underscored the need for training and this need was further emphasized by the fact that imperial troops never really enjoyed a decisive technological advantage in weaponry over their Pathan opponents.

The effectiveness of the Army in India on the North-West frontier is open to question. Much criticism was directed by British officers at the so-called anachronistic methods employed in tribal warfare, and several historians have echoed their views. Yet the Indian Army officers were not dyed-in-the-wool conservatives clinging to long-outdated methods. The traditional approach to frontier warfare remained remarkably effective, as it was determined by such unchanging factors as the mountainous terrain and tribal military characteristics. It must also be remembered that frontier warfare was not the sole task performed by the Army in India and that training, organization, and equipment for its other roles directly affected both its tactical effectiveness during operations in tribal territory and its training approach. Both British and Indian units serving in India were always primarily organized, trained, and equipped for conventional military operations against a second-class opponent either in Asia or as part of an imperial expedition. Secondarily, the Army in India was also geared to conduct frontier warfare, and finally, internal security duties. As a result of these disparate tasks, it often proved difficult to achieve the correct balance between time devoted to training for conventional operations and that for frontier warfare or internal security duties, especially during peacetime, when local day-to-day military requirements always loomed larger in the minds of Indian Army officers.

Following World War I, the conflicting and often contradictory requirements of frontier fighting and conventional warfare became explicit as modern weapons and equipment intended for 'civilized warfare' were adopted, and dependence on supporting arms and services increased. As a result, the relative mobility of Indian columns operating in the hills progressively declined and they were tied to fixed lines of communication. While the construction of roads in tribal territory considerably eased supply and administrative difficulties, allowed heavy weapons to be used in their immediate vicinity, and facilitated the deployment of units with higher scales of equipment, they did not remove the essential problem encountered by imperial troops when they moved off-road. Apart from light tanks, the mountainous terrain afforded little scope for mechanization or heavy weapons and pack mules remained central to the army's logistical apparatus. So, infantry remained essential when columns operated in the hills. As it was impossible to reconcile the heavy scale of equipment carried by regular troops and the attendant first-line mule transport with rapid cross-country movement, the tactical flexibility and mobility evident in prior frontier campaigns progressively declined. In many respects, the Army in India's deployment on the frontier mirrored the paradox encountered by the US Army when it fought against American Indians during the nineteenth century.[83] While the commitment to tribal control reduced its effectiveness in conventional military operations, at the same time the army's normal preoccupation with conventional war made it less fit for its frontier mission. The various discussions regarding the relative merits of resuscitating the PFF in the 1920s and 1930s reflected widespread recognition that specially-trained and lightly-equipped localized troops would be much more efficient and mobile than regulars on periodic tours of duty. However, such proposals were unacceptable to the military authorities as long as Afghanistan remained the most likely theatre of operations for the Army in India, as tribal territory provided invaluable practical experience of the terrain and tactics likely to be encountered across the Durand Line. In any event, the Scouts and various militias performed the policing and, to a lesser degree, many of the military tasks previously carried out by the frontier force when it had been under civil control.

NOTES

1. For a comprehensive survey of the evolution of frontier fighting, see T. R. Moreman, *The Army in India and the Development of Frontier Warfare 1849–1947*, London: 1998.
2. *Frontier Warfare 1901*, Simla: 1901; *Frontier Warfare and Bush Fighting*, Calcutta: 1906.
3. See T. R. Moreman, 'Lord Kitchener, the General Staff and the Army in India, 1902–14', in David French and Brian Holden Reid (eds), *The British General Staff: Reform and Innovation 1890–1939*, London: 2002, pp. 57–74.
4. *Field Service Regulations, Part I, Operations, 1909*; reprinted with amendments, London: 1912.
5. *Report on the Principal Measures Taken in India During the War to Maintain Training at the Standard required in Modern War*, Calcutta: 1919, p. 2 and Appendix A.
6. *Report of a Conference of General Officers held at Delhi 22nd to 24th February 1917 under the Direction of His Excellency the Commander-in-Chief in India*, Delhi: 1917, pp. 21–6.
7. General Officer Commanding Northern Command to Chief of General Staff, 2 May 1917, L/P&S/10/373, Oriental and India Office Collections (hereafter OIOC), British Library, London.
8. See *The Third Afghan War 1919: Official History*, Calcutta: 1926.
9. See *Despatch by His Excellency General Sir Charles Carmichael Monro on the Operations in Waziristan 1919–1920*, Simla: 1920; *Operations in Waziristan 1919–1920*, Calcutta: 1921.
10. Waziristan Force Weekly Appreciation for week ending 13 January 1920, WO 106/56, Public Record Office.
11. Alan Warren, *Waziristan: The Faqir of Ipi and the Indian Army, The North West Frontier Revolt of 1936–7*, Karachi: 2000, pp. 50–1.
12. *Mountain Warfare School, Abbottabad, Synopsis of Lectures 1920*; revised, Rawalpindi: 1921.
13. See *Proceedings of the Military Requirements Committee 1921: Report (Lord Rawlinson's Committee)*, Simla: 1921, p. 6.
14. *Notes on Mountain Warfare*, Calcutta: 1920.
15. *Wazirforce Tactical Notes*, Dera Ismail Khan: 1921.
16. See S. H. C., *Mountain Warfare Notes*, Poona: 1921; 'Frontier', *Frontier Warfare*, Bombay: 1921.
17. Colonel D. E. Robertson, 'The Organization and Training of the Army in India', *Journal of the Royal United Service Institution* (henceforth *JRUSI*), vol. 69, 1924, pp. 327–8. For more about the service press, see T. R. Moreman, 'The Army in India and the Military Periodical Press 1830–98', in David Finkelstein and Douglas M. Peers (eds), *Negotiating India in the Nineteenth Century Media*, Basingstoke: 2000, pp. 210–32.

18. Colonel F. S. Keen, 'To What Extent Would the Use of the Latest Scientific and Mechanical Methods of Warfare Affect Operations on the North West Frontier of India?', *Journal of the United Service Institution of India* (hereafter *JUSII*), vol. 53, 1923, p. 415.
19. Captain M. C. Gompertz, 'The Application of Science to Indian Frontier Warfare', *Army Quarterly*, vol. 10, 1925, p. 133.
20. *Field Service Regulations:Operations*, vol. 2, London: 1924, p. 215.
21. *Manual of Operations on the North West Frontier of India*, Calcutta: 1925.
22. Lieutenant Colonel H. B. Hudson, 'Those Blue Remembered Hills', TS Memoir, 1980, p. 70, Photo.EUR.179, Hudson MSS., OIOC; Colonel H. R. Pettigrew, '"It Seemed Very Ordinary": Memoirs of Sixteen Years Service in the Indian Army 1932–47', TS Memoir, 1980, p. 65, Imperial War Museum, 84/29/1.
23. See *Kohat District Standing Orders for War and for Local Columns*, Lahore: 1927; and *Landi Kotal Standing Orders for War 1936*, Landi Kotal: 1936.
24. Lieutenant General Frederick Morgan, *Peace and War: A Soldier's Life*, London: 1961, pp. 90–1.
25. 'An Infantry Officer', 'Collective Training in a Battalion', *JUSII*, vol. 60, 1930, p. 128.
26. See *Despatch by H. E. Field Marshal Sir W. R. Birdwood on the Disturbances on the North West Frontier of India from 23rd April to 12th September, 1930*, Delhi: 1930, L/MIL/7/16956, OIOC (hereafter *Despatch on Disturbances*).
27. 'Editorial', *JUSII*, vol. 61, 1931, pp. 1–9; 'Mauser: A Forgotten Frontier Force', *English Review*, vol. 52, 1931, pp. 69–72.
28. Review of Important Military Events in India, no. 3 of 1930, 28 October 1930, L/MIL/7/12491, OIOC.
29. 'Editorial', *JUSII*, vol. 61, 1931, p. 8
30. Kirke to Bethell, 1 June 1928, Kirke MSS, MSS.Eur.E.396/7, OIOC; *Memorandum Explaining the Proposed Reorganization of Cavalry and Infantry Units in India*, L/MIL/7/13317, OIOC.
31. *Memorandum on Army Training (India) Collective Training Period 1929–30*, Simla: 1930, p. 4.
32. *Despatch on Disturbances*, p. 18; *Review of Important Military Events in India*, no. 3 of 1930, 28 October 1930, L/MIL/7/12491, OIOC.
33. 'Mouse', 'Babu Tactics', *JUSII*, vol. 61, 1931, pp. 60–5.
34. Report of the Tribal Control and Defence Committee 1931, Delhi: 1931, pp. 38–9, L/MIL/17/13/34, OIOC.
35. General Staff Criticism of the Tribal Control and Defence Committee, 19 May 1931, L/P&S/12/3171, OIOC; M. Jacobson, 'The Modernization of the Indian Army, 1925–39', PhD thesis, University of California, Irvine: 1979, p. 92.

36. 'Light Infantry', 'Mobility', *JUSII*, vol. 62, 1932, pp. 11, 17.
37. Field Marshal Philip Chetwode, 'The Army in India', *JRUSI*, vol. 82, 1937, pp. 7–8, 12.
38. General Kenneth Wigram, 'Defence in the North West Frontier Province', *Journal of the Royal Central Asian Society*, vol. 24, 1937, pp. 77–8.
39. *Review of Important Military Events in India*, no. 2 of 1930, 12 July 1930, and *Review of Important Military Events in India*, no. 4 of 1930, 26 January 1931, MIL/7/12491–2, OIOC.
40. *Review of Important Military Events in India*, no. 3 of 1932, 9 November 1932; *Review of Important Military Events in India*, no. 2 of 1934, 21 July 1934, L/MIL/7/12492, OIOC; Jacobson, 'Modernization', p. 320.
41. AHQ to Headquarters Northern Command, Southern Command, Eastern Command, Western Command, and Burma Independent District, 1 June 1931, L/MIL/7/5505, OIOC.
42. Field Marshal William Birdwood, 'Recent Indian Military Experience', *United Empire*, vol. 22, 1931, p. 246.
43. Field Marshal William Slim, *Defeat into Victory*, London: 1956, p. 544.
44. *General Staff Criticism of the Tribal Control and Defence Committee, 1931*, 9 May 1931, pp. 3–4, L/P&S/12/3171, OIOC.
45. H. R. Pettigrew, *Frontier Scouts*, Selsey: 1965, pp. 65, 88–9.
46. Major General Charles Gwynn, *Imperial Policing*, London: 1936, p. 7.
47. General Andrew Skeen, *Passing it On: Short Talks on Tribal Fighting on the North-West Frontier of India*, Aldershot: 1932.
48. Indian Army Order 80, Books, 'Passing it On' by General Andrew Skeen, 22 December 1932, L/MIL/17/5/274, OIOC.
49. See 'Auspex', 'A Matrimonial Tangle (or Mountains and Machine Guns)', *JUSII*, vol. 63, 1933, pp. 367–74; Lieutenant Colonel O. D. Bennett, 'Some Regrettable Incidents on the N.W.F.', *JUSII*, vol. 63, 1933, pp. 193–203.
50. 'Borderer', 'With the Tendency of Modern Military Organization towards Mechanization, the increasing complexity of modern weapons and the dependency of troops on the maintenance services, it is asserted by many that Regular troops are losing the degree of mobility necessary for the successful performance of their role on the North West Frontier. Discuss how this can be overcome so that freedom of action and tactical mobility are assured in the Army of India', *JUSII*, vol. 64, 1934, pp. 14–15.
51. Major General Henry Rowan-Robinson, *The Infantry Experiment*, London: 1934, p. 10.
52. *Official History of Operations on the N.W Frontier of India 1920–35*, Delhi: 1945, p. 240–1.
53. Lieutenant Colonel Lawrence Lawrence-Smith, 'Cavalry and Tanks with Mohforce, 1935', *Cavalry Journal*, vol. 26, 1936, pp. 552–61; *Official History 1920–1935*, pp. 243–4; Jacobson, 'Modernization', p. 80.

54. 'Shpagwishtama', 'The Changing Aspect of Operations on the North West Frontier', *JUSII*, vol. 66, 1936, pp. 102–10.
55. 'Commenger', 'Engineer Work in the Mohmand Operations', *Royal Engineers Journal*, vol. 51, 1937, pp. 507–22.
56. Major J. D. Shapland, 'North West Frontier Operations–Sept/Oct, 1935', *Journal of the Royal Artillery*, vol. 64, 1937–8, p. 208; *Official History, 1920–1935*, p. 244.
57. *A.H.Q. India Training Memorandum no. 12 Collective Training period 1935–36*, Delhi: 1936, p. 2.
58. Ibid., pp. 3–7.
59. D. J. Waldie, 'Relations between the Army and the Royal Air Force', PhD thesis, University of London, 1980, pp. 210–11.
60. See 'Air Staff (India) Memo no. 1 April 1935: Tactical Methods of Conducting Air Operations against Tribes on the North West Frontier of India', 17 May 1935, Bottomley MSS, B22, RAF Museum, Hendon.
61. Slessor to Sutton, 15 April 1935, Slessor MSS, AIR 75/29, PRO; Air Chief Marshal John Slessor, *The Central Blue: Recollections and Reflections*, London: 1956, pp. 121–3.
62. Slessor to Peck, 10 April 1936, Slessor MSS, AIR 75/31, PRO.
63. 'Close Support Tactics. Provisional', 1936, Slessor MSS.
64. 'Combined Report on Air Co-operation Training 2 (Rawalpindi) Infantry Brigade and 3 (Indian) Wing, RAF, Kanpur Area, 17–25 November 1936', Slessor MSS.
65. See *Official History of the Operations on the N.W. Frontier of India: 1936–7*, Delhi: 1943; Warren, *Waziristan: The Fakir of Ipi and the Indian Army*.
66. Gort to Inskip, 29 December 1937, Inskip MSS, INP 1/2, Imperial War Museum; Slessor, *Central Blue*, p. 131.
67. 'Chimariot','Mountain Artillery in Frontier Warfare', *Journal of the Royal Artillery*, vol. 65, 1938–9, pp. 90–5; C. A. L. Graham, *A History of the Indian Mountain Artillery*, Aldershot: 1957, p. 249.
68. Lieutenant Colonel F. C. Simpson, 'Review of Frontier Policy from 1849–1939', *JUSII*, vol. 74, 1944, p. 307.
69. C. G. Ogilvie, Secretary to Government of India, to Secretary Military Department, India Office, 4 February 1938, L/MIL/7/7235, OIOC; Jacobson, 'Modernization', pp. 81–2.
70. Captain A. V. Brooke-Webb, 'Relief by Air', *Journal of the Royal Artillery*, vol. 66, 1939–40, pp. 225–8; *Review of Important Military Events in India*, no. 4 of 1937, 30 October 1937, L/MIL/7/12492, OIOC.
71. Report on the Operations in the Khaisora-Shaktu area of Waziristan, 25 November 1936 to 25 January 1937, 25 February 1937, Bottomley MSS, B2300.
72. General John Coleridge to Chief of General Staff (CGS), 12 March 1937, Rees MSS, MSS.EUR.F.274/4. OIOC.

73. 'AILO', 'Close Support by Aircraft on the North West Frontier', *JUSII*, vol. 70, 1940, p. 16.
74. Comments and Deductions on the Khaisora Operations, Waziristan, 8 June 1937, Rees MSS; *A.H.Q. India Training Memorandum No. 14 Collective Training Period 1936–37*, Delhi: 1937, pp. 8–12.
75. Bartholomew to Major General R. C. Wilson, February 1937, L/WS/1/257, OIOC.
76. Wilson to Auchinleck, 18 May 1937; and Auchinleck to Wilson, 27 May 1937, L/WS/1/257, OIOC.
77. Commander-in-Chief to Wilson, 28 May 1937, L/WS/1/257, OIOC.
78. Wilson to Auchinleck, 2 July 1937, Under Secretary to the Government of India Defence Department, to Military Department, India Office, 28 June 1938, and Secretary of State for India to Government of India Army Department, 3 November 1938, L/WS/1/257, OIOC.
79. *A.H.Q. India Training Memorandum no. 16 Collective Training Period 1937–38*, Delhi: 1938, p. 1.
80. See 'Auspex', 'The Dream Sector, L. of C.', *JUSII*, vol. 68, 1938, pp. 201–10.
81. *Frontier Warfare: India (Army and Royal Air Force)*, Delhi: 1939.
82. General Andrew Skeen, *Passing it On: Short Talks on Tribal Fighting on the North-West Frontier of India*, 4th edn, London: 1939.
83. R. M. Utley, 'The Contribution of the Frontier to the American Military Tradition', in H. R. Borowski (ed.), The *Harmon Memorial Lectures in Military History, 1959–1987*, Washington: 1988, p. 58.

10

Were the 'Sepoy Generals' Any Good?

A Reappraisal of the British-Indian Army's High Command in the Second World War

Raymond Callahan

Generalship is a much-discussed, and yet an elusive art. There is no all-encompassing formula by which a good or great general can be determined. This is not merely because the weaponry and equipment of armies has changed with ever-greater rapidity for the last five hundred years, or even because the conditions—climate, terrain, equipment, quality of troops—are rarely the same from battle to battle. It is, above all, because generals—themselves fallible humans—must try to impose order, control, and design on inherently chaotic situations in which thousands (or tens or hundreds of thousands) of people, often tired and hungry, frequently scared, seldom aware of anything beyond their section, platoon, or company, struggle to accomplish tasks whose full significance they rarely understand. The wonder is not that there are so few good generals, but that there are any at all.

The problems and the essence of generalship have seldom been as pungently described as by the greatest army commander produced by that remarkable institution, Britain's Indian Army. Field Marshal Slim suggested that those who wrote military history 'in nice warm studies with all the time in the world at their disposal' should first consider:

> the poor general! He is short of sleep, he is tired .... Before him stand, in a rather forlorn group, some of his staff, a couple of subordinate commanders,

> convinced that whatever eventuates they will have the dirty work to do, and, most embarrassing of all, an ally or two, oozing suspicion. If the military situation is bad—and the odds are it will be—they will just stand looking at him, their eyes all asking the same mute question, 'What do we do now?'.... They want an answer and they want it now. The wretched man cannot say, 'Wait a few days until I've consulted with Generals X and Y'.... Nor can he mark time with 'In a week or two I'll get reports that will make everything much clearer' .... He knows and they know that unless something pretty brisk and decisive is done quickly neither he nor they will be there in a week's time.
>
> But the general realizes that at least half the information on which he must base his decision is either wrong or at best incomplete—worst of all he does not know which half .... He realizes that many and potent factors are in operation completely beyond his control but which can suddenly make nonsense of all his calculations .... The general has all these anxieties and uncertainties and in addition he feels on his shoulders the crushing weight of a responsibility he cannot share for the lives of his men, the success of a campaign, perhaps for the fate of his country.[1]

It was to reduce—for it could never be eliminated—this crushing burden, and to build a support system around the general as he made those lonely and risky decisions, that armies professionalized their officer corps during the nineteenth century, elaborating a system of selection, education, and promotion that—allied to the creation of general staffs and staff colleges—was supposed to give the general a body of staff officers and subordinate commanders who, on the basis of shared training grounded in a doctrine understood by all, would both help formulate the general's decisions and carry them smoothly into effect.[2] That was the ideal, sometimes fully realized, sometimes not quite. Nothing, however, could ultimately relieve a general of the final responsibility for answering that terrible question: 'What do we do now?' the test and vindication of generalship. What follows in this essay is a consideration of how the old Indian Army's British generals met that test in their army's last and greatest war.

An Army's Heritage

Arthur Wellington was dismissed by Napoleon as a mere 'sepoy general'. So he was, in a very important sense. His tutelage in the command of large units and the conduct of complex operations came during his years in India, in the series of wars that made Britain the paramount power in the Subcontinent. Waterloo may have been a 'close-run thing', but no closer than the ferocious action at Assaye in 1803 which, years later, Wellington remembered as the 'best thing' he had ever done on the battlefield.[3] The Iron Duke was not the last British commander to get his professional training in India. Throughout the century that separated Waterloo from Mons, the British-Indian Army saw far more large-scale combat than did the British regular army. When to the major campaigns against the Marathas, Pindaris,[4] and the two Sikh wars[5] are added two wars in Afghanistan; three in Burma; overseas expeditions to Abyssinia, China, and the Sudan; as well as counter-insurgency and pacification campaigns—not to mention the North-West frontier and the 1857 Mutiny—it is clear that the British officers of the Indian Army had abundant opportunities to hone their professional skills. It is not surprising that one of the two best-known imperial soldiers of the Victorian era was Frederick Sleigh Roberts, who began his career as an officer of the East India Company's Army and ended it as Field Marshal Lord Roberts, V.C. (with Rudyard Kipling as his publicity agent).[6]

After Roberts' retirement as Commander-in-Chief of India in 1893, however, the Indian Army began to lose its edge. The British Army, reorienting itself towards a future Continental commitment, started to modernize in a way the Indian Army had difficulty in matching. Certainly Indian Army officers had known for a generation that combat against European (or, at least, Europeanized) opponents was a possibility for their service. Tied to the North-West frontier, however, and trammelled by the Government of India's concern over expenditure levels, modernization was a more complicated issue—especially for a service that had been denied its own artillery units since the Mutiny.[7] Moreover, the Indian Army as a whole did not feel the jolt administered to the British service by the South African war, since a curious deference to Boer racism kept that service on the sidelines. One wonders what Spion Kop might have been like had the troops involved been Frontier Force units under officers with rather more tactical skill than Redvers Buller. By 1914, the Indian Army, although still formidable in its unit cohesion and tactical skills, was beginning to have an old-fashioned air. Its performance in 1914–15 confirmed this. The unit performance was good; that of the senior officers, from poor to lamentable.[8] Indeed, the Indian Army, whose war effort soon focused on the Middle East, won its greatest successes there under British Army officers—Stanley Maude in Mesopotamia (where both Claude Auchinleck and William Slim served)[9] and Edmund Allenby in Palestine. Only two Indian Army officers rose to real prominence during World War I. One was William Birdwood, who had the inestimable advantage of being a Kitchener protégé. The other was the tough frontier soldier Claude Jacob, the only Indian service officer to hold high command on the Western Front (and considered by Lloyd George at one point as a possible replacement for Haig). Both Birdwood and Jacob would end their careers as field marshals and commanders-in-chief in India.

The relative scarcity of Indian Army officers in senior positions outside India tells us something about not only the relative modernity of the British Empire's two major armies, but also about the deep social and professional cleavages between the two services. The Indian Army had always been a thing apart. From its origins as the private army of the East India Company, it had always been more 'middle class' than the British Army ever became during the age of empire.[10] Its promotion system never ran on purchase. It jealously guarded its corporate identity, autonomous existence, and professional traditions. It weathered even the great explosion of 1857 intact, merely substituting Crown for Company as its employer. Living in isolated cantonments, intermarrying, returning home seldom except to retire, the officer corps of the Indian Army became at an early date very much a family affair. Roberts was the son of an Indian Army officer; so was Claude Jacob, whose family sent 52 men into the Indian Army over a century and a quarter; so, in the last generation of its British officers, was John Masters, author of the classic *Bugles and a Tiger*. The insular, tribal characteristics of the British Army—the adjectives are Field Marshal Lord Carver's—are well known and usually ascribed to the power of the regimental system. The Indian Army was no less insular and tribal. Regimental loyalties were strong especially in the elite Gurkha units, the Indian Army's equivalent of the Brigade of Guards. Above all, however, the sense of difference was reinforced by differences in class background as well as by a nearly self-contained existence much farther from 'home' than we, in the days of jet travel and instantaneous global communication, can easily realize. After all, Americans are accustomed to accept, as a fact of US military history, the differences in professional outlook and attitude between officers of the United States Army and the United States Marine Corps both based for most of their careers in the same country and drawn from a society whose class distinctions are much less sharp than those of imperial Britain. The under-representation of Indian Army officers in senior posts in 1914–18 had other causes than the level of professionalism in the two services.

After the Armistice, the pre-1914 pattern reasserted itself. The Indian Army—whose wartime experience had in any case not been dominated by the Western Front—returned to its own concerns, albeit in a much altered India where political change was reflected in pressure to open the officer corps to Indians. There remained also the North-West frontier, a sort of national training centre with live fire, and the conundrums of modernization and mechanization, the latter especially pressing if the Indian Army was again to play a major role outside India something planners in London and Delhi (in something of a disconnect with political developments) expected it to do in the event of another major war.[11] Certainly there were strengthened professional contracts between the services. The Indian Staff College at Quetta, established by Kitchener, numbered among its interwar instructors two of the British Army's 'apostles of mobility', P. C. S. Hobart (one of whose pupils was Slim) and Bernard Montgomery. Conversely, Slim was on the Directing Staff at Camberly, and a pupil at the Imperial Defence College, among whose alumni Claude Auchinleck was also numbered. That redoubtable Indian cavalryman and consummate staff officer, Hastings Ismay, began his ascent of the Committee of Imperial Defence ladder in the 1930s. All this said, it nonetheless remains true that the Indian Army the young John Masters joined in 1934 was still very much a thing apart—and that must be kept in mind when assessing how its senior officers performed when, in September 1939, the Viceroy—speaking for the King-Emperor—sent Britain's Indian Army into its last great war.[12]

Frustration in the Desert

There was one very significant difference between the 1914–18 and 1939–45 eras as far as the British-Indian Army was concerned. In World War I, the only theatre in which it played a dominant role, Mesopotamia, was not one where Britain could lose the war. In World War II, the Indian Army played a crucial role in the Middle East during 1940–2, when London felt that the war could very well be lost there. It carried, throughout the conflict, the burden of Britain's war against Japan, a struggle that raised the issue not of whether Britain would win the war but of the nature and duration of its great Asian empire thereafter. The stakes were much higher, the interaction with the British Army (under circumstances of great stress) more significant, and the scrutiny from the top more intense—particularly for the former 4th Hussar in Downing Street, whose youthful complaints that there was no one interesting in India did not refer to Indians.

The British-Indian Army had suffered in 1914 from lack of a mechanism for rapid expansion. In 1939, there was a plan for a wartime doubling of the army (which then numbered about 2,00,000). That went out the window in June 1940, when the decision to hold on in the Middle East had as its corollary a breakneck rate of expansion in India: for 1940, five (then six) infantry divisions and an armoured division; for 1941, four more infantry divisions and another armoured division; and for 1942, another quartet of infantry divisions and a third armoured division. As the Indian Army ballooned—ultimately, nearly tenfold—and quality dipped sharply, Indian units poured into the Middle East, where they soon outnumbered British and Commonwealth formations. For the next two years, Indian Army officers played a major role in the theatre upon which Churchill came to feel Britain's fortunes—and his own—depended.[13]

As the best source of high-quality, combat-ready troops, India provided a high proportion of Archibald Wavell's forces in 1940–1. Playing key roles both in the defeat of Marshal Graziani's army in the Western Desert and in the destruction of Italy's East African Empire, the 4th and 5th Indian Divisions began their long record of martial achievement. When Churchill swapped Wavell for Auchinleck, the role of Indian Army officers became much more prominent. The occupation of Persia, the pacification of Iraq, and the Syrian campaign all depended heavily on the Indian Army. Here, the effect of the parallel worlds of the two services began to tell. Auchinleck had been at the Imperial Defence College—and home on leave at long intervals—but the British Army was largely unknown to him. He, therefore, drew heavily on his own service. In March 1942 Auchinleck brought an Indian Army officer, Lieutenant General T. W. Corbett, to Cairo as his chief of staff, and when he needed a commander for the newly arrived British 1st Armoured Division, chose an Indian cavalryman, Frank Messervy. Corbett has been judged—perhaps not entirely fairly—a failure. Churchill would later dismiss him as 'a very small, agreeable man, of no personality and little experience'.[14] Messervy had never commanded armoured units before. The pre-1939 Indian Army had none; and despite plans to raise three, there was not yet, in mid-1941, a single modern armoured fighting vehicle in India. Major General Herbert Lumsden, a British cavalry officer who succeeded Messervy at 1st Armoured, felt that the division had been mishandled during Rommel's successful

January 1942 offensive and resolved not to allow any of his units to operate under Messervy (who had moved on to 7th Armoured, the original 'Desert Rats'). When, therefore, Rommel launched the May 1942 attack that would carry him to El Alamein, the commanders of the two key British formations had, in addition to their other difficulties, a legacy of distrust between them. While no senior British commanders distinguished themselves in the May–June fighting, Indian Army officers certainly did no worse than their British service brethren. That, however, was not how matters appeared when, as was inevitable after such a defeat, it came time for heads to roll.

During the chaotic withdrawal into Egypt in June, the 13th Corps commander, Lieutenant General W. H. E. ('Strafer') Gott, a Rifle Brigade officer, ordered Major General T. W. ('Pete') Rees, an Indian Army officer, to hold an indefensible position—the 'Sollum Box' on the frontier between Libya and Egypt—against the Afrika Korps with his depleted 10th Indian Division, which was moreover supposed to do so without armoured support. Rees and Gott had a guarded conversation over a radiotelephone link during which Rees, for security reasons, used cricket terminology to make his points. As Rees subsequently described the conversation:

> What I attempted to point out to General Gott, in a necessarily disguised telephone conversation in the field, was that my Division, unsupported by adequate armour, would be unlikely to be able to hold the Sollum [sic] position against a prolonged full-scale enemy attack. I submit that we have ample evidence of this and of the fact that my appreciation of the situation was correct. Indeed, General Gott himself, less than six hours later, gave my successor instructions to evacuate the position because it was realized it was untenable.[15]

Rees's refusal to 'guarantee' to hold his position for 72 hours decided Gott to relieve him. Rees, who had told his brigade commanders prior to talking with Gott that 'it would now not be best to stand firm on Frontier Defences' but that 'if so ordered, we would put up as stubborn a defence as any troops could, and fight till water gave out'[16] was relieved because, in Gott's words, he 'lacks the self-confidence, vigour and robust outlook necessary'.[17] In a subsequent interview with Rees, Gott admitted to misunderstanding Rees' intent—and of course he had already ordered the new 10th Indian Division commander to retreat. Rees subsequently saw Lieutenant General Neil Ritchie, the Eighth Army commander, a British service officer and protégé of Alan Brooke (the Chief of the Imperial General

Staff, hereafter CIGS), and possibly Auchinleck's worst appointment. Ritchie defended Gott's action by telling Rees he was too prone to argue over orders. When Rees pressed him for an example, Ritchie cited an order to Rees to attack the German 90th Light Division, which was heavily supported by armour. Rees pointed out that he had not argued the order, only asked if he could be given some British armoured support. Ritchie had no rejoinder to this and the conversation came to an end. The impression left is that Gott and Ritchie were, at this point, rather more rattled than Rees.[18]

Auchinleck apparently thought so. Writing to the Commander-in-Chief of India, he noted of Gott and Ritchie: 'their acquaintance with General Rees was short and their personal knowledge of him limited ... .'[19] Auchinleck gave Rees the job of organizing the last-ditch defense of the Delta—hardly a job for the fainthearted—and in due course Rees returned to India and command of one of the most distinguished of Slim's 14th Army divisions. After the war, he would go on to command the Punjab Boundary Force at the time of Partition, a harrowingly difficult job. A few days after the Rees affair, Ritchie (who had been quite unable to control his own corps commanders, never mind Rommel) sacked Messervy and replaced him with Lumsden. Lumsden, whose record was certainly no better than Messervy's, remained until Montgomery got rid of him—but that happened only after Lumsden, by then a corps commander, had botched his part at El Alamein.[20]

What happened during the retreat into Egypt, however, was only a prelude to the great purge wrought by Churchill and Alan Brooke, in August—by which time Auchinleck had stabilized the situation. Auchinleck of course went, as did Corbett, summarily dismissed by Brooke in a conversation Corbett remembered as of only 'a few moments' duration.[21] (Lieutenant Colonel Ian Jacob, who carried Auchinleck's dismissal notice to him, was ironically, the son of an Indian Army field marshal, and the first of his family to elect the British over the Indian service.) What is sometimes not noticed is that the consolation prize offered to Auchinleck—the newly christened Persia and Iraq Command—was simply an upgraded version of a post that had always been held by a senior Indian Army officer. When Auchinleck refused, it became a convenient way to solve the problem of what to do with Lieutenant General Henry Maitland ('Jumbo') Wilson, the outsized Rifleman whose ultimate field marshal's baton was pronounced 'inexplicable' by one of the most perceptive students of British high command in World War II.[22] In effect, senior Indian Army generals were swept out of the Mediterranean theatre, although Indian Army units remained deployed from Italy to Persia for the balance of the war, and in Italy, Francis Tuker's 4th Indian Division compiled a fine record as did Dudley ('Pasha') Russell's 8th—indeed the Indian Army made up a substantial part of the Eighth Army in 1944–5. By that time, however, the Indian Army had its own war to manage.

Triumph in Burma

If the Indian Army's existence—and expansion—was crucial to the British Empire's war in the Middle East, it was absolutely indispensable in the war against Japan. Oddly, however, it did not dominate senior appointments in that war until 1943. An air chief marshal dug out of retirement filled the theater command created for the Far East in 1940. The Indian Army units comprised the bulk of the force building up in Malaya in 1940–1, but when the General Officer Commanding there, a British service officer, was replaced, it was by another British officer, Lieutenant General A. E. Percival. The corps commander under him was Lieutenant General Lewis Heath, an Indian Army officer. Percival, after distinguished World War I service, had been a staff officer for most of his career and indeed owed his appointment (and the promotion that vaulted him over Heath) to the impression he had made on John Dill, the CIGS, while serving at the War Office. Heath, on the other hand, was a frontier soldier, who had commanded the 5th Indian Division in the Western Desert and at Keren in Eritrea. Percival, with little experience of the Indian Army, nonetheless held the all-too-common British-service view that it was second rate. In a petulant and revealing note written years later for the official historians, Percival remarked:

> ... the greatest handicap from which General Heath suffered was what might be called the 'Indian Army complex'. He had not been to any of the Staff Colleges and had seldom, I think, came into contact with British troops. To him the Indian Army was everything and his loyalty to it was far stronger than it was to the 'Imperial Army' of Malaya.[23]

There are two interesting points about this complaint. Heath had had more British units under his command in action than Percival. His disloyalty, moreover, seems to have consisted of pointing out to Percival the flaws in his dispositions and plans, a point the Imperial Japanese Army quickly underscored.[24]

In Burma, the two weak divisions available to defend the country were both from the Indian Army. The Burmese units of 1st Burma Division largely melted away. As in Malaya, a senior British service officer was brought in as overall commander, with an Indian Army officer as corps commander under him. Here the resemblances with Malaya ceased. Lieutenant General Harold Alexander, in addition to courage, good looks, and abundant charm, was smart enough to know a capable subordinate when he saw one. In William ('Bill') Slim, rushed from the 10th Indian Division in Iraq to take over Burcorps, a hastily improvised corps headquarters in Burma, 'Alex' had the right man for an appallingly difficult job, the longest retreat in British (or Indian) military history. Slim came from the 6th Gurkha Rifles, so did his two divisional commanders, Major Generals D. C. T. ('Punch') Cowan and Bruce Scott. It was the first appearance of a sort of 'Gurkha Rifles mafia' that would come to dominate the war in Burma. In the aftermath of Burcorps' withdrawal into Assam in May 1942, Alexander returned to England; Cowan remained with the 17th Indian Division, which he would command for the rest of the war as it won more VCs than any other Indian Army division; and Slim began the relentless ascent that would take him to a field marshal's baton and a peerage.[25]

By spring 1943, Slim was a corps commander and the Indian Army was being committed to the war's worst-managed offensive effort under British command, the First Arakan campaign. Under intense pressure from Churchill, Commander-in-Chief of India Wavell drove the operational commander, Lieutenant General N. M. S. Irwin, who commanded the Eastern Army. Irwin in turn, ignoring the availability of Slim's corps headquarters, fed brigade after brigade of mostly raw troops into Major General W. T. Lloyd's 14th Indian Division, which was conducting the attack, until the unfortunate divisional commander had a corps' worth of infantry to manage. In Irwin's refusal to use Slim lay another story of inter-service tension. As a brigadier conducting his first offensive operation against Italian forces in August 1940, Slim had sacked a British battalion commander for inadequate performance. The battalion concerned was from the Essex Regiment. So was Irwin.

When the Japanese counter-attacked in the Arakan, tumbling Irwin's troops into precipitate retreat, Slim's XV Corps Headquarters was finally brought in. He stabilized the front but only by pulling it back further than authorized by Irwin, who thereupon decided to sack Slim. The 'revenge of the Essex' was, however, foiled by Irwin's own removal. No one ever had much luck trying to take a job away from Bill Slim.

The disastrous close of the first Arakan campaign brought with it a complete overhaul of the command structures for Britain's war against Japan. Driven by Churchill's belief that alliance politics required a better British showing against Japan, it had the consequence of opening the way for the Indian Army to take control of its own war. There was great irony in this, for Churchill neither admired nor trusted the Indian Army.[26] Wavell was kicked upstairs to viceroyalty and a new theatre command, Southeast Asia Command (SEAC), came into being. Louis Mountbatten, the SEAC 'Supremo'—like Alexander—had charm, photogenic qualities, and an eye for able subordinates. Slim went from the verge of dismissal to command of SEAC's principal operational formation, 14th Army. Between Mountbatten and Slim was the 11th Army Group, whose commander, the self-effacing British service officer George Giffard, worked very smoothly with Slim—largely by supporting rather than trying to direct him. Further afield, other major changes reinforced Slim's position.

Wavell's replacement as commander-in-chief was Auchinleck, who revitalized the whole structure that raised, trained, and supported the troops Slim would use. Major General Reginald Savory, brought back from divisional command on the Assam front, became inspector, and then director, of infantry at Army Headquarters in Delhi. Savory had a very clear picture of what he wanted to do. Complaining that the infantry that went forward with the rifle, the bomb, and the bayonet had been drained not only of its best men in quality but of large numbers in quantity. So that the hitting end of the battalion had become very weak, he laid down new priorities:

> If I were asked to state a general principle for the organization of Infantry, I would adopt the following slogan: 'Bayonets take precedence', by that I mean that in considering all Infantry organization it must be remembered that the real Infantry consists of Riflemen who must have precedence both in quality and quantity and that once their ranks have been filled to the number required the residue may be allotted to so-called specialists' duties.[27]

Savory's determination, backed by Auchinleck, gave not only a new orientation to manpower policy (and one very different from that prevailing in either the British or American armies), but ensured that Slim's Indian units met the standards of the pre-War Indian Army regulars, standards the Japanese had yet to encounter in Burma.

By early 1944, not only were veteran Indian Army units back from the Middle East, but the new training regimen and new troop welfare schemes were in place. Slim also had available a body of unusually competent divisional commanders. In the Arakan, where he met and broke the first stage of the sweeping Japanese U-GO offensive, he had the combat-tested 5th Indian Division from the Middle East and three excellent commanders in Harold Briggs, Geoffrey Evans, and Messervy. On the vital central front, at Imphal, the Gurkha Rifles' officers dominated the command structure. The corps commander (Geoffrey Scoones) and two of the three divisional commanders (Cowan and Douglas Gracey) were Gurkha officers, while the third (Ouvry Roberts) was a British service officer who had been on the staff of Slim's 10th Indian Division in 1941–2. The dramatic victories of 1944 were owing to many things—the DC-3 prominent among them—but a revitalized infantry and the cohesion and professionalism of Slim and his (mostly Indian Army) commanders were crucial.[28]

The inter-service tensions that were apparent in the Middle East in 1942 as well as in Malaysia and in the Slim–Irwin encounter were abundantly displayed during the 1944 battles as well. The charismatic—and highly eccentric—military visionary Orde Wingate had caught Churchill's eye at the end of the First Arakan Campaign as a result of his rather over-hyped Chindit raid into Burma. The result was his corps-sized Special Force, with its dedicated air component and 'hotline' to 10 Downing Street. Wingate, a British Army gunner, thought the Indian Army second rate and said so much more pungently than Percival ever had. Wingate had also deeply angered the tightly knit and highly influential Gurkha officers by his handling of a Gurkha unit during his first Chindit expedition. It is clear that Slim was irritated by the Chindit gospel. He later told the official historians of the war in Burma:

> If the experienced 70th British Division which I had trained in jungle fighting at Ranchi had been used as a division in main theatre, it would have been worth three times its number in Special Force. We are always inclined in the British Army to devise private armies and scratch forces for jobs which our ordinary formations with proper training could do and do better.[29]

Despite his reservations about both Wingate's concepts and his character—'he was not a reliable chap'[30]—Slim nonetheless got Wingate's massive operation 'Thursday' launched while simultaneously coping with the Arakan and Imphal campaigns. It may well, however, have been his reservations—compounded by the

Gurkha factor—that led him, when Wingate died in an air crash shortly after Thursday began, to appoint as his successor the Special Force brigadier least imbued with the Chindit gospel, Joe Lentaigne, another Gurkha officer. It was a not entirely successful appointment, even if comprehensible in the circumstances.[31]

When Slim, after breaking the Japanese 15th Army at Imphal and pursuing its remnants through the 1944 monsoon, began his 1944–5 dry weather campaign, a sharp change in the tempo of operations was apparent. The 1944 fighting, both in the Arakan and on the central front, had often been on a company or battalion level, intense, small-unit actions in some ways reminiscent of the North-West frontier fighting.[32] The 1944–5 sweep across the 'dry belt' of central Burma, the assault crossing of the mile-wide Irrawaddy, the crucial thrust to Meiktila, and finally the 300–mile drive to Rangoon depending on air supply alone, required very different qualities in both commanders and troops.[33] Slim switched Scoones for Messervy as his spearhead corps commander; the crucial assault across the Irrawaddy north of Mandalay, intended to distract the Japanese from the real focus of Slim's drive—the thrust to Meiktila—was ably handled by Rees, commanding the 19th Indian Division. It was almost as if Slim was answering Lumsden, Gott, and the whole chorus of British Army doubters. Cowan and the 17th Indian Division took Meiktila and were in the lead when Slim's drive finally was stopped—not by the Japanese, but by the 1945 monsoon. John Masters' famous description of the Indian Army going into action for the last time is well known and much quoted.[34] The degree to which Slim's victory was an Indian Army affair is, however, not fully apparent until one looks at the numbers. The British Army, never heavily employed in the war against Japan, was by 1944–5 a fading presence in the 14th Army, the result of Britain's increasingly desperate manpower situation. By 1945, Slim's 'British' army was only 13 per cent British. Over 60 per cent of his troops were Indian. The balance—roughly 25 per cent—was mostly African.[35] As the British Army faded from view in the 14th Army, it was busily installing itself at the theatre level.

In November 1944, the 11th Army Group was wound up, and in its place there appeared the Allied Land Forces, South East Asia (ALFSEA). The ALFSEA commander was Lieutenant General Oliver Leese, one of Monty's favourite subordinates and his successor in the 8th Army. His appearance—like that of Lieutenant General F. A. M. ('Boy') Browning as Mountbatten's chief of staff at about the same time—was part of a pattern, as the European war wound down, of recycling senior British officers to the eastern theatre. In this case, it was a disastrously bad appointment. Leese brought most of his staff with him, and from the beginning there were tensions between the mostly British-service ALFSEA and the largely Indian Army staff of the 14th Army. The strain was compounded by the close link between Mountbatten and Slim, which tended to sideline Leese (as it had Giffard before him).[36] It culminated in a bizarre episode shortly after the re-taking of Rangoon, when Leese tried to remove Slim and replace him with a British-service officer, Lieutenant General Philip Christison, who commanded Slim's old XV Corps in the Arakan. The whole episode is worth examining at some length, because it is one of the most illuminating and incompletely examined parts of this story.[37]

The background to this attempt to sideline Slim lies in the command changes of November 1944. When Leese arrived, he brought with him not only 8th Army staff officers, but a set of attitudes that verged on the condescending. Slim later wrote that ALFSEA 'had a good deal of desert sand in its shoes, and was rather inclined to thrust Eighth Army down our throats'.[38] Privately, he was much more pointed. He told Mountbatten that the ALFSEA's attitude was 'now the Eighth Army is here, things are going to be done very differently'.[39] Years later he candidly told a friend, 'the whole 14th Army was a bit looked at sideways. Only don't say I said so.'[40] Percival's reaction to Heath comes to mind.

The tension between Leese and Slim was intensified by the palpable fact that the war in Burma was being run, and run very well, by the 14th Army. Used to working with the accommodating Giffard, Slim made little effort to defer to Leese, as he later made plain to the official historians: 'I always went on the principle that my plans, as long as they carried out the general directions I had received from above and did not require more resources than I had under my control, were my business and did not require anybody's approval or sanction.'[41]

This attitude, of course, left ALFSEA with relatively little to do—perhaps fortunately, since Major General H. L. ('Taffy') Davies, who had been Slim's chief of staff during the retreat from Burma and later worked on the Cabinet Office official histories of the Mediterranean theatre, told Slim's biographer that, after an assessment of Leese, 'he reckoned he was never above the level of a Divisional Commander'.[42] Slim himself later told Brigadier Michael Roberts, one of the team working on the official history volume covering the great campaign that re-conquered Burma:

> Between ourselves, I had all this time the impression that ideas at ALFSEA were lagging behind Fourteenth Army .... While ALFSEA and still more SEAC produced many plans, the only ones, pedestrian as they may have been figuratively and literally, that were actually put into operation and carried through were those of Fourteenth Army.[43]

To this tension was added the ambiguous attitude of Mountbatten. Slim's official biographer, writing in the 1970s, certainly exonerated Mountbatten of any responsibility for Leese's actions in May 1945; but the situation may not have been quite so clear. Leese conferred with Mountbatten at the Supreme Commander's headquarters at Kandy in Ceylon (now Sri Lanka) on 5 May. One version of what happened is that Leese, arguing that Slim was tired, proposed removing Slim from the 14th Army and replacing him with Christison, who would plan and lead the impending invasion of Malaya (Operation Zipper) while Slim remained in Burma commanding a new 12th Army, essentially a mopping-up and occupation force. Mountbatten, in this version, authorized Leese only to discuss with Slim his future plans.[44] There is another version, however, based on Christison's diaries. After conferring with Mountbatten, Leese flew to Akyab to meet Christison at his Advanced Headquarters. Leese told him that the idea of removing Slim came from Mountbatten. Leese also referred to the rumours that 'Dickie' was jealous of Slim (using the Anglo-Indian slang phrase 'gup', meaning gossip). He added that he was uneasy with the whole business and had urged Mountbatten to break the news to Slim personally, which Mountbatten declined to do on the grounds that Leese was Slim's immediate superior. Leese then flew off to Slim's headquarters at Meiktila and told him of the decision to remove him from the 14th Army. Slim declined the consolation prize and asked to be retired (in his diary he noted for 7 May, 'Sack. 1530hrs.'[45]). There are some problems with Christison's account, which is based on his diaries but was written up at leisure after the war. He did however take the precaution of checking his diary notes and recollections with Leese: 'I went to see Oliver Leese at his home near Bridgnorth [*sic*] and he agreed that my notes were correct.'[46] A few weeks later, Leese would tell Christison: 'I gather I'm carrying the can for Dickie over this.'[47] A decade afterwards, Brigadier Michael Roberts, with the documentary access of an official historian, told Slim that there was a good possibility Mountbatten had indeed been behind Leese's action.[48] The origins of the affair may well be fated never to be completely resolved; but the explosive consequences, which resulted in Leese's 'carrying the can', are very plain on the record.[49]

Slim's staff were aghast, and as the news percolated through the 14th Army, the reactions were intense. One of Slim's staff officers, in a note written at the time, spelled out just how angry the 14th Army was at the prospect of Slim's departure:

> I'm pretty certain the whole HQ would strike, resign, mutiny or whatever the correct expression would be. I learned later that one Corps Commander and two Divisional Commanders would have resigned when it came; God knows what the troops would have done.[50]

One of the official historians later wrote to Slim that, according to Brigadier J. S. ('Tubby') Lethbridge, the 14th Army chief of staff, 'XIV Army HQ ... had apparently decided on a sit-down strike, if you were demoted, and to be court martialled if that were necessary to bring the matter into public notice .... '[51] Later historians have echoed these reactions: 'anger and revulsion' swept the 14th Army, in the words of Slim's official biographer.[52] 'Troops became near mutinous and officers threatened to resign' was the comment of a later writer.[53]

Leese had apparently warned the CIGS that some changes might be impending in the senior commands in Burma, but the command crisis Leese and Mountbatten precipitated clearly caught Brooke by surprise. Slim had sent Auchinleck a letter requesting immediate retirement. Auchinleck, in London for consultations, raised the whole business with the CIGS on 17 May. According to Brooke's diary for that day: 'interview with Auk about appointment of Slim to Burma Command. Leese is going quite wild and doing mad things, prepared a fair rap on the knuckles for him!'[54] It was not only Leese's knuckles that suffered. Brooke had never succumbed to Mountbatten's charm, and called the SEAC Supreme Commander as well as Leese to order. After spending a great deal of time and energy cleaning up Monty's broken crockery, he was not prepared to do similar duty for Leese and Mountbatten. Brooke's sharp reaction settled the matter, or rather, confirmed authoritatively what had already been made clear by the 14th Army's attitude. Mountbatten quickly told Leese to undo what he had done. Leese told Slim on 23 May that he would remain with the 14th Army and command Zipper. Brooke, however, had no intention of allowing matters to stop there. On 18 June, he recorded in his diary: 'Drafted letter to Mountbatten advising him to get rid of Oliver Leese who has proved to be a failure in South East Asia Command.'[55] Ten days later, he noted about a meeting with Churchill:

> After lunch I had to go to PM at 3 pm to tell him that we should have to withdraw Oliver Leese from South East Asia and replace him by Slim. He kept me for an hour but agreed to all I wanted. We are now ordering Oliver home, appointing Slim in his place, and sending out Dempsey as the additional Army Commander.[56]

The Churchill-Brooke exchange was recounted more colourfully by Leese to Christison. The latter was summoned to Calcutta to confer with Leese, who was in his bath when Christison arrived. Leese said: 'Christie ... I've been sacked .... Brookie went to Churchill and told him the Indian Army wouldn't fight without Slim. "Who sacked Slim?" said Churchill. "Leese," said Alanbrooke [*sic*]. "Well, sack Leese."'[57] Some weeks afterwards, Alanbrooke saw Leese in London: '... poor Oliver Leese came to see me .... Shall have a difficult job to find employment for him.'[58]

Conclusion

What was it all about? There was clearly jealously and resentment at ALFSEA about the 14th Army, and there is good circumstantial evidence that Mountbatten may not have wanted any bright stars to shine near his own. One of the official historians, himself a former Indian Army officer, put it bluntly to Slim many years later: 'I fear my thoughts on the subject night be called "mean." In common with many British Service Generals [Leese] disliked the Indian Army ....'[59] Another factor may have been at work as well, one that Slim put his finger on when writing to Major General Reginald Savory about his 'sacking': 'There are dozens of Lieutenant-Generals with the highest reputations in Europe elbowing one another for jobs in this theatre.'[60] The movement of British Army officers no longer needed in Europe into senior command positions in the eastern theatre had, in fact, begun late in 1944 with 'Boy' Browning and Leese himself. A natural result alike of the winding down of the European war and the professional ambitions of British Army officers, it would have had the effect, if the war with Japan continued into 1946 or 1947, as expected, of displacing Indian Army officers in 'their' theatre, as they had been pushed aside in the Middle East in 1942. Slim, however, as Leese might have noticed (had he remembered Irwin), was never pushed easily. Moreover, Slim had just won a great victory. But then,

Leese was a Guardsman (an 'affected silk-handkerchief-waving' one according to a member of Slim's staff[61]) and may have expected the Indian Army to defer to that.

Slim, after a brief period of home leave, returned to SEAC to take up Leese's job and preside over the anti-climactic end of the war against Japan in South-East Asia. While in England he met Churchill and, discussing the impending general elections, told the Prime Minister that none of the British troops in SEAC would be voting Conservative, another point he got right.[62] The tensions, born of differing backgrounds and professional orientations, between the officers of the British and Indian services were real and often took the form of the British Army's denigration of the Indian Army's competence. Nothing in the performance of the old Indian Army's senior officers in its last great war supports this. Indian Army officers sacked in the Middle East performed competently—in some cases, outstandingly—under Slim. It would seem that, as is so often the case in matters of this sort, circumstances—as opposed to some notional group characteristic—explain results.

The postscript to this story comes a year after the old Indian Army had ceased to exist. Montgomery was CIGS; Slim had retired and was heading the Railway Executive; Attlee was in Number 10. Monty, never happy in Whitehall, had decided that the chairmanship of the military committee of the new Western European Union was more appealing. His personally designated successor was Lieutenant General Richard Crocker, drawn (like Leese), from his stable of reliable subordinates—and notable for the skill he had shown in 1943–4 in antagonizing both Americans and Canadians. Attlee wanted Slim. Monty dismissed Slim as an Indian Army officer unknown by, and therefore unacceptable to, the British Army. Then, fatally, he added that he had already told Crocker that the job was his. 'Very well,' said the ever-laconic Attlee, 'untell him.' And thus the last, and greatest, of Britain's sepoy generals ended his career by routing the victor of El Alamein.

Notes

1. This is from a brief typescript on generalship (pp. 5–6) in Slim's papers, SLIM 5/2/2 in the Churchill Archive Centre, Churchill College, Cambridge (hereafter CAC).
2. For the British Army's attempt to create a general staff, see Brian Bond, *The Victorian Army and the Staff College: 1854–1914*, London: 1972.

3. For Wellesley's campaigns against Mysore and the Marathas see Antony Brett-James (ed.), *Wellington at War: 1794–1815, A Selection of his Wartime Letters*, London: 1961, pp. 17–130; Anthony S. Bennell (ed.), *The Maratha War Papers of Arthur Wellesley: January to December 1803*, Phoenix Mill, Thrupp: 1998.
4. B. K. Sinha, *The Pindaris: 1798–1818*, Calcutta: 1971.
5. For military operations of the two Sikh Wars see Donald Featherstone, *At Them with the Bayonet*, London: 1968; Hugh Cook, *The Sikh Wars: The British Army in the Punjab, 1845–49*, New Delhi: 1975.
6. For Frederick Robert's generalship in India, see Brian Robson (ed.), *Roberts in India: The Military Papers of Field Marshal Lord Roberts, 1876–93*, Phoenix Mill, Thrupp: 1993.
7. There were of course the mountain batteries, the famous 'screw guns'; but their existence does not affect the argument made above.
8. Refer to Gordon Corrigan, *Sepoys in the Trenches: The Indian Corps on the Western Front, 1914–15*, Staplehurst, Kent: 1999, pp. 51–124.
9. For the Indian Army's operations in Mesopotamia see Colonel R. Evans, *A Brief Outline of the Campaign in Mesopotamia: 1914–18*, 1926; reprint, London: 1935.
10. P. E. Razzell, 'Social Origins of Officers in the Indian and British Home Army: 1758–1962', *British Journal of Sociology*, vol. 14, 1963, pp. 248–59.
11. Mark Jacobsen, 'Learning From the Great War: The Modernization of the Indian Army, 1919–1931', a paper for the New Military History of South Asia Conference, Wolfson College, Cambridge: July 1997, is a careful recent study. A more impressionistic, broad-brush treatment of the inter-war Indian Army is Philip Mason's *A Matter of Honour: An Account of the Indian Army, Its Officers and Men*, London: 1974, pp. 444–70. See also T. R. Moreman, *The Army in India and the Development of Frontier Warfare, 1849–1947*, London: 1998, pp. 99–172; S. L. Menezes, *Fidelity and Honour: The Indian Army from the Seventeenth to the Twenty-first Century*, 1993; reprint, Oxford: 1999, pp. 306–39.
12. Master's autobiographical account of the Indian Army in the 1930s, *Bugles and a Tiger*, London: 1956, is a deservedly much-read minor classic. However, two cautions are in order: by the time he wrote it, Masters was a successful historical novelist; and Gurkha regiments were not necessarily typical of the Indian Army taken as a whole.
13. I have previously explored the issue of expansion of the Indian Army and its consequences in *The Worst Disaster: The Fall of Singapore*, (Newark, DE and London: 1977; reprint, Singapore: 2001) and in *Burma: 1942–1945*, London: 1978, as well as in 'The Jungle, the Japanese and the Sepoy,' unpublished paper presented at Wolfson College, July 1997; and 'The Indian Army, Total War and the Dog That Didn't Bark in the Night', in Jane Hathaway (ed.), *Rebellion, Repression,*

Reinvention: Mutiny in Comparative Perspective,Westport, CT/London: 2001, pp. 119–28.

14. Quoted in John Connell, *Auchinleck: A Critical Biography*, London: 1959, p. 701. Connell drew heavily on Auchinleck's papers.
15. Rees to Deputy Military Secretary, General Head Quarter, Middle East Forces, August 1942, Confidential, MSS. EUR. 274/17, f. 8, British Library, Oriental and Indian Office Collections (hereafter BL, OIOC). This collection, Rees's papers, is very detailed on this episode.
16. MSS. EUR 274/17, f. 56, BL, OIOC. This is an extract from the 10th Indian Division War Diary.
17. 'Special and Confidential Report' by Gott on Rees, 22 June 1942, MSS. EUR 274/17, f. 22, BL, OIOC.
18. Rees made this point at the time in a note, written in a mixture of English and Welsh: 'unbelievable that—without interview—cryptic tel. Conversation—that, in itself, should show the state of mind of C[orps] C[ommander] and ought we not to consider the implications' [*sic*], MSS. EUR. 274/17, f. 91, BL, OIOC.
19. Auchinleck to Wavell, 12 August 1942, MSS. EUR. 274/17, f. 47, BL, OIOC.
20. Field Marshal Lord Carver's *Dilemmas of the Desert War: A New Look at the Libyan Campaign 1940–42*, London: 1986, is very illuminating on these events.
21. Corbett has disappeared from history in a manner reminiscent of Stalin's victims vanishing from photographs. Retired in 1943, with remarkably few decorations for an officer of his rank, he later farmed in Kenya and died in 1982. The relevant volume of the official history, I. S. O. Playfair, *et al.*, *The Mediterranean and Middle East*, vol. 3, London: 1960, mentions him once, in passing. Ironically his papers ultimately came to rest in the Churchill Archives Centre (henceforth AC) through the efforts of his daughter, who had been an undergraduate at Churchill College, Cambridge. Perusing them, an interesting picture begins to emerge. Corbett had a good background as a staff officer and had been selected to command one of the armoured divisions being raised in India. He had made two extensive visits to Cairo to study 'lessons learned' in the Western Desert fighting. His notes indicate that he had a good grasp of the issues and an awareness of Eight Army's characteristic vices ('Comments on the Campaign Starting with Axis Attack on Cyrenaica, 25 May 1942'). This three-page typescript is enclosed in Corbett to Alan Brooke, 18 August 1942, CORB 4/16, CAC. The Corbett papers also demonstrate how close Corbett was to Auchinleck. His appointment was, in fact, a perfectly reasonable one in the circumstances and not proof that Auchinleck was, as often alleged, a bad picker of key subordinates. Corbett's bitter recollection of his dismissal is in Corbett to Brooke, 15 August 1942, CORB 4/16, CAC. This letter may never in fact have been sent, but it

clearly reflects Corbett's intense anger at his treatment: 'The principle of British justice is a fair hearing. This is one of the major causes for which we are fighting the war.'

22. A view put by the late Ronald Lewin to the author frequently in conversation.
23. Quoted, from the Percival Papers at the Imperial War Museum, in Callahan, *Worst Disaster*, p. 111. Heath had in fact been an instructor at the Senior Officers School at Belgaum in India.
24. For Arthur Percival's indifferent generalship at Singapore see Clifford Kinvig, 'General Percival and the Fall of Singapore', in Brian Farrell and Sandy Hunter (eds), *Sixty Years On: The Fall of Singapore Revisited*, 2002, reprint; Singapore, 2003, pp. 240–69.
25. Scott's health was broken by the campaign and he did not hold further high command–but he did chair a committee that began the process of readjusting Indian Army training and tactics to the challenge of Burma.
26. On this, see Callahan, *Burma*, pp. 94–6. This is the tip of an iceberg of evidence.
27. One of the insufficiently-explored dimensions of the Indian Army's war is the remarkable feat of rebuilding, re-training, and re-orienting undertaken by Auchinleck in 1943–4, which gave Slim the army he led to victory. The standard biography of Auchinleck, John Connell's *Auchinleck*, devoted one chapter in a book of over 900 pages to Auchinleck's second tour as Commander-in-Chief, India. With Auchinleck's papers available (at the John Rylands Library in Manchester), the subject badly needs to be revisited. Second only to Auchinleck's role was that of Savory, who ultimately became the last adjutant general of the old Indian Army. He wrote no memoirs and his role has yet to be fully studied. His papers are in the National Army Museum in London. The quotation in the text is from 'Changes in Infantry Organization', a four-page typescript of a 1945 broadcast in the Savory Papers, 7603/93/69. This is a summary of a longer document, 'Developments in Infantry Organization, 1939–44,' Savory Papers 7603/93/69. This 13-page typescript report is a very good overview of the multiple changes in structure that bedevilled the Indian Army during the rapid expansion of 1940–3.
28. Slim's own memoirs, *Defeat into Victory*, London: 1956, is a minor classic and a key source for the Burma campaign. Ronald Lewin's official biography, *Slim: The Standardbearer*, London: 1976, is an important commentary. The official history—S. W. Kirby *et al.*, *The War Against Japan*, vols 2–4 (Her Majesty's Stationary Office, 1958–65), is the foundation for critical appraisal, although of course totally silent on crucial issues like SIGINIT. There are surprisingly few good secondary accounts. Geoffrey Evans' *Slim as Military Commander*, London: 1969, is workmanlike but adds little. Callahan's *Burma* covers

theatre strategy rather than operations. It is interesting how few of the divisional and corps commanders who served in the 14th Army either wrote memoirs or had anything written about them. There is a rather worshipful biography of Frank Messervy—Henry Maule, *Spearhead General*, London: 1961, and Philip Christison left not entirely reliable typescript memoirs, now in the Churchill Archive Centre, Churchill College, Cambridge. A 'collective biography' approach to this group would be a very interesting undertaking, especially if contrasted to a similar group profile of those generals who held senior operational commands in the British 1st, 2nd, or 8th Armies in European and Mediterranean theatres.

29. Slim to Major General S. W. Kirby, 14 December 1959, Slim Papers 5/3, CAC. The 70th Division had been broken up to provide 'columns'—their basic tactical unit—for Special Force.
30. Slim to Brigadier Michael Roberts, 23 March 1954, Slim Papers 5/1, CAC. The emphasis is Slim's.
31. Wingate produced controversy during his life and it reverberates still. The official historians were critical. Wingate's loyalists responded with a paper by Robert Thompson and Brigadier P. W. Mead ('The Official History of the Second World War; The War Against Japan, vol. 3 by S. Woodburn Kirby and others. Judgement on Major General O. C. Wingate') which basically demanded a rewrite. A copy of this curious document is in the Imperial War Museum's Department of Documents. Shelford Bidwell's *The Chindit War*, New York: 1979 and Callahan, *Burma* both critical of Wingate were answered by Peter Mead, *Orde Wingate and the Historians*, Braunton, Devon: 1987, on behalf of Wingate's admirers. The argument is unlikely to die. One thing is clear, however: Wingate disliked and denigrated the Indian Army consistently, and this found a hearing at the highest levels in London.
32. Writing to Slim after the war, Brigadier Michael Roberts, a fellow Gurkha officer, remarked, 'The more I think of it the more sure I am that the NWF was the finest training for any sort of war that anyone ever had. The experienced frontier soldier never put a foot wrong once he got the hang of how to look after himself in the jungle ....' This appears in 'Comment on Chapter XIV: Irrawaddy Shore' n.d. (but 1954–5). Slim Papers, 5/1, CAC. Roberts did much of the research for Slim's *Defeat into Victory* and offered detailed comments on each draft chapter.
33. Not the least interesting aspect of the Burma campaign is its immensely complex, and ultimately remarkably successful, logistic infrastructure. There is no monographic study of the subject, but it can be tracked in Kirby, *The War Against Japan*, vols 2–4. It is interesting to compare the innovative, flexible (and under-resourced) logistic system that supported Slim in Assam, and then onwards to Rangoon, to the lavishly

supported advance in north-west Europe after D-day (which nonetheless stalled on the borders of Germany).

34. John Masters, *The Road Past Mandalay*, New York: 1961, pp. 306–7. The reference is to the US paper edition.
35. Louis Allen, *Burma: The Longest War, 1941–45*, 1984; reprint, London: 2002, Appendix 4, pp. 655–60. The considerable contribution of troops from east and west Africa to the Burma campaign has attracted little historical attention. This has now been (partially) rectified by John A. L. Hamilton, *War Bush: The 81st (West African) Division in Burma 1943–45*, Norwich: 2001. Hamilton, whose book is a model divisional history, is rather critical of the attitude of the 'sepoy generals' to the fighting qualities and services of the African troops, an attitude he sees as mirrored by subsequent writers on the Burma campaign.
36. Slim privately thought that Giffard had been sacrificed to American, i.e., Stilwell's dislike of him and regretted his departure. He would tell the official historian that his own success rested on 'Giffard's sound administrative foundations'. Slim to Kirby, 21 September 1959, Slim Papers 5/3, CAC.
37. Slim did not discuss the episode in *Defeat into Victory*, although in his papers there is a four-page typescript draft about it, which Slim ultimately decided to drop from the book. Leese emerges from these pages looking inept, while Mountbatten's role is downplayed. Slim Papers 2/3, CAC. In the official biography, titled *The Standardbearer*, Ronald Lewin devotes a chapter to it (pp. 237–46), pulling his punches a bit where Mountbatten's role was concerned. Mountbatten's official biographer, Philip Ziegler, in *Mountbatten: A Biography*, New York: 1985, pp. 293–5, explains Mountbatten's ambiguous behaviour by reference to the amoebic dysentery from which he was recovering at the time. In Ziegler's edition of Mountbatten's official diary, *The Personal Diary of Admiral the Lord Louis Mountbatten, 1943–1946*, London: 1988, only the editor's footnotes call the reader's attention to the episode.
38. Slim, *Defeat into Victory*, p. 385.
39. Mountbatten to CIGS, 7 June 1945 in Slim Papers 2/3, CAC.
40. Slim to H. R. K. Gibbs, 17 October 1963, Slim Papers 8/2, CAC. Gibbs was a lifelong friend and fellow 6th Gurkha officer.
41. Slim to Brigadier Michael Roberts, 22 October 1959, 5/3, CAC.
42. Note by Ronald Lewin on information provided by Davies, Slim Papers, 5/4, CAC. Montgomery had of course made him a corps commander, and Brooke had pushed him up to army and then army group. Why?
43. Slim to Roberts, 22 October 1959, Slim Papers 5/3, CAC. The volume Roberts was working on, *The War Against Japan: vol. 4: The Reconquest of Burma*, was published in 1965.
44. Lewin, *Slim*, pp. 237–8.
45. Slim diary entry, 7 May 1945, quoted in Lewin, *Slim*, p. 238.

46. 'The Life and Times of General Sir Philip Christison, Bt., G. B. E., C. B., D. S. O., M.C., B. A., D. L., An Autobiography', p. 165. This typescript memoir is in the CAC, CHIE1. Basing it on his diaries, Christison, who died in 1993, wrote it at intervals from 1947 until 1981. Hamilton, *War Bush, passim*, points out numerous inaccuracies in Christison's account of the 81st (W.A.) Division's action, and the memoir is quite self-serving. It remains, however, a very useful source if treated with caution.
47. Christison, 'Life and Times,' p. 166. Interestingly, the day after Mountbatten met with Leese, he sent a letter to the CIGS, Alan Brooke, indicating dissatisfaction with Leese. Lewin, *Slim*, p. 243.
48. Roberts to Slim, 8 December 1955, Slim Papers, 2/3, CAC.
49. In one of the most recent books on the war in Burma—Major General Julian Thompson's *The Imperial War Museum Book of the War in Burma 1942–1945*, London: 2002—Slim's removal is described as 'the attempted sacking of this great general by the lesser men placed in authority over him', adding that 'Leese, for all his faults, was straight, and readers must judge for themselves where the ultimate blame lies' (p. 388). It is clear where Thompson thinks it lies. In spite of Slim's circumspection in *Defeat into Victory* and his biographer's corresponding caution about Mountbatten's role—it is clear that Slim privately remained suspicious: 'Sometime during his tenure as CIGS I remember his saying to me that the original idea of change of command of 14th Army might have been suggested by Mountbatten, ...' Roberts to Ronald Lewin, 8 February 1973, Roberts Papers MRBS 1/4, CAC. A member of Slim's staff, writing to Ronald Lewin after the publication of the official biography, stated that Slim had told his staff that the change of command proposal had originated with Mountbatten. He then referred to 'a long conspiracy of silence in which the Field Marshall [sic] was undoubtedly involved' about the Supreme Commander's role. Colonel F. A. Sudbury to Lewin, 10 January 1977, Slim Papers 12/11, CAC.
50. 'Almost unbelievable yet true: HQ 14th Army, Meiktila, May 1945'. This four-page typescript by Colonel James Godwin is in Slim Papers 2/3, CAC.
51. Roberts to Slim, 8 June 1955, Slim Papers 5/1, CAC.
52. Lewin, *Slim*, p. 242.
53. Thompson, *War in Burma*, p. 388.
54. Alex Danchev and Daniel Todman (eds), *War Diaries 1939–1945: Field Marshal Lord Alanbrooke*, London, 2001, entry for 17 May 1945, p. 694.
55. Danchev and Todman (eds), *War Diaries*, p. 698.
56. Ibid., entry for 29 June 1945, pp. 700–1. Lieutenant General Miles Dempsey had commanded 2nd British Army in Monty's 21st Army

Group, 1944–5. Ultimately he would succeed Slim at in the 14th Army when Slim moved up to ALFSEA.

57. Christison, 'Life and Times ...,' p. 166, CAC. It was on this occasion—which Christison dated as about 5 June, which is surely too early—that Leese made his remark about 'carrying the can' for Mountbatten. While the claim that the Indian Army would not fight without Slim is clearly an exaggeration, it does point to a 'corporate' reaction to Leese's ousting of him at the moment of victory. Christison also anticipates Brooke's peerage—he was still Sir Alan Brooke in May 1945.
58. Danchev and Todman (eds), *War Diaries*, entry for 10 July 1945, p. 703. Leese's career thereafter was in the minor key.
59. Roberts to Slim, 8 June 1955, Slim Papers 5/1, CAC.
60. Slim to Savory, 16 May 1945, quoted in Lewin, *Slim*, p. 241.
61. Quoted in Ziegler, *Mountbatten*, p. 294.
62. Duncan Anderson, 'Slim', in John Keegan (ed.), *Churchill's Generals*, 1991; reprint, London: 1993, p. 300.

11

The Shiver of 1942*

Indivar Kamtekar

It is a truism that history is about what actually happened and why. This article will suggest that an interesting history can be written around an event which never happened. That event was a major Japanese invasion of India in 1942.

Beyond the insight that this invasion did not occur, there are good reasons why the theme has not been minutely examined under the microscopes of imperialist or nationalist history. These historiographies, obsessed with Independence, Partition, and the end of Empire, highlight the incidents which led to the unfurling of new national flags in August 1947. They tend to portray the occurrences of twentieth-century Indian history as the inevitable results of deliberate policies. The correct calculation of outcomes, and a sense of their necessity, is used to confer legitimacy on different actors—whether these actors were Indian, British, or Pakistani. But a possible Japanese invasion was not under the control of any of these actors. As far as it went, the intentions of British and Indian actors counted for nothing. The Cripps Mission fits into the grand narrative of British decolonization; the Quit India Movement fits into the grand narrative of the Indian freedom struggle. The prospect of a Japanese invasion is not easily slotted into either of them. Consequently, in history textbooks, monographs, and published collections of documents, it has been pushed into the margin.[1]

* First published in *Studies in History*, 18(1), n.s., 2002.

Acknowledgements: The lectures of Professor Sumit Sarkar to students at Delhi University gave me my first whiff of this theme, and Professor C. A. Bayly supervised a part of the research that followed. Any errors are mine alone.

Different events have been pushed to the centre of the stage. As the ideology of the state in India has changed from imperialism to nationalism, the representation of the past has changed accordingly. Before 1947, textbooks discussed in detail the Montagu-Chelmsford Reforms and the 1935 Government of India Act; now they discuss in detail Non-Cooperation, Civil Disobedience, and Quit India. Before 1947, the focus was on government initiatives; afterwards it has been on Congress mass movements. The Quit India Movement, in particular, has become a frequently invoked part of the autobiography of the independent Indian nation state.[2] Roads, public parks, and buildings are named after the 'August Kranti'. Such ideological appropriations carry some irony. Several post offices were attacked, and their records burnt, during August 1942; more than fifty years afterwards, the Government of India issued special postage stamps to commemorate the Quit India Movement. In the United Provinces alone, over one hundred railway stations were destroy, or severely damaged in 1942.[3] The uprooting of railway tracks was among the hallmarks of the Quit India Movement; half a century later, a major train between New Delhi and Bombay was named the 'August Kranti Express' by the Government of India.

The passage of time can make the incongruous look apposite. It changes grand narratives. In the meantime, one way of looking beyond imperialism and nationalism, or of quarrelling with their grand narratives, is to study a subject they gloss over.

The State's Loss of Credibility

World War II caught the colonial state looking the wrong way. Traditionally, India had been invaded from the north-west; during World War II it was threatened from the east. For decades, defence policy had assumed that the attackers would be Russian and that the attack would be from the north-west through Afghanistan; but when the attack occurred, the attackers were Japanese and they came from the east, through Burma. After its entry into World War II, with the bombing of Pearl Harbour on 7 December 1941, Japan conquered Hong Kong, Singapore, Malaya, and Burma in such quick succession that Rangoon surrendered on 8 March 1942.

This development altered the complexion of the war as far as India, was concerned. A police report commented on the newly-awakened perception of danger in the United Provinces:

> Although 1942 was the third of the war years, it was during this year that more direct reactions to the war became perceptible for the first time in the United Provinces. The disaster of Malaya, Singapore and Burma transformed the Japanese from a threat beyond the horizon to an enemy battering at the gates .... The vague feeling of insecurity, which had previously been the general response to war conditions, sharpened rapidly to a feeling much more acute which, in some instances, bordered on panic.[4]

News travelled swiftly. Through Indian emigration, parts of India were closely tied to the countries conquered by the Japanese. There were over one million Indians in Burma.[5] The capital city of Rangoon had an Indian majority.[6] Some of the emigrants nervously scribbled letters home, with news of the bombing of cities and the disasters they had suffered. The censor reports tell us that a letter in Bengali lamented the number of deaths during one day's air-raid on Rangoon.[7] Some letters which reached the United Provinces and Bihar were like warning bells for the local population.

Though the emigrants' relatives sympathized automatically, their grief was often influenced by a personal economic distress. Flipping through the records of the Indian Posts and Telegraphs Department, we learn that in the year 1940–1, the number of money orders exchanged with Burma, Ceylon, Malaya, and so forth was over 2 million, and that their value was over 72 million rupees.[8] Some regions in India were more closely tied to the East than others. In Azamgarh, a district in the United Provinces, no less than 30 lakhs of rupees were received annually through money orders despatched from abroad.[9] Similarly, as the commissioner of Gorakhpur remarked:

> the economic balance was seriously disturbed by the Japanese war, specially in Gorakhpur where much of the population depended on remittances from relations working in Hong Kong, Bangkok, Singapore and Rangoon. It is estimated that in a normal year, the amount received in money orders in one tahsil alone was equal to the land revenue of that tahsil.[10]

The contributions from the Far East counted heavily—and they dried up in 1942.

After a while, the emigrants returned, now transformed into refugees who could confirm their stories in person, with the added anger of recent experience. They had horrible tales to tell. These Indian refugees from the fall of Burma had plodded painfully home in 1942.[11] Some of them crossed a terrible terrain: the 600-mile long and 200-mile wide region between India and Burma was heavily forested, lacked proper roads, and suffered tremendous rainfall. Others came by sea.[12] Three hundred thousand refugees had arrived in Bengal by May 1942; in March 1942, between 2000 and 3000 were being sent daily from Chittagong to Calcutta.[13] Not all the refugees survived the journey back, but some did, and those who had fled early were lucky. Some of them flooded the Sealdah railway station. The police of the United Provinces estimated that 30,000 emigrants returned to Gorakhpur later in 1942.[14] The refugees who returned to India from Burma, Singapore, and Malaya 'included merchants, traders, doctors, and teachers, officials, clerks, farmers and labourers, and the flotsam and jetsam which drift with every refugee tide'. Even if they had once been rich, they were able to carry hardly any possessions back with them on their trek to India. Demoralized and bitter, they streamed in, by rail and foot to Imphal and Calcutta, and by sea to Bombay and Madras. 'Many had alarmist tales to tell of the prowess of the Japanese military machine, and in the then hothouse atmosphere of India their defeatism unleashed more panic and despondency', wrote the journalist Frank Moraes.[15] For the refugees the outcome of the war was not in doubt—a Japanese victory was certain. They had witnessed the Allied defeat; they knew the Empire was to end.

Within India, the sight of defeated soldiers returning from the Burma Front reinforced this impression. Trains full of defeated soldiers arrived in Bihar, making the plight of the state visible to the populace.[16] The army had been forced to retreat as the Japanese advanced, and the soldiers who reached Bihar were in a pathetic condition. Their clothes were in tatters. Many of them still had only the first field-dressings on their wounds. Their trains had sometimes taken weeks to reach. On the way to Bihar, a number of soldiers succumbed to their injuries, to be abruptly buried wherever the trains stopped. The living reached Bihar in the burning heat of summer, they overflowed from the hospitals, and had to be consigned to tents.[17] The movements of these defeated troops, together with the influx of refugees, had an immediate impact on the civilian population. The war looked dangerous and, more importantly, it looked like a lost cause. The weary, wounded, and demoralized soldiers and tired refugees may explain why the civilians believed a completely false ramour that the government intended to increase the bonus given to soldiers on enlistment, to attract new recruits who would replace those killed in the Far East.[18]

Rumours abounded at this time. In Orissa, the anthropologist Verrier Elwin found to his surprise that 'popular rumour had it that I myself was seeking to establish a place of refuge in the event of a Japanese invasion'.[19] In the coastal areas, there were false alarms of

Japanese landings. Deeper inland within India, some people said that the city of Calcutta had fallen into Japanese hands. The man who afterwards led the successful Burma Campaign, General Slim saw at this time 'developing in the civil population of Eastern India a restlessness, which, fanned by fantastic rumours and worked on by unscrupulous propaganda, might any time break out in violence'.[20] Enemy radio broadcasts added to the turmoil and confusion.

So rumours were rife; and currents of fear travelled through these rumours. Though always an important source of information, rumours now—in a context of wartime censorship of news—acquired a disproportionate influence, Perhaps this is why, in a book published in 1944 titled *India since Cripps,* Horace Alexander pronounced that 'no true history of India can be written that omits unsubstantiated rumour'.[21] The British had obviously distorted the story of the retreat from Burma, minimizing in their propaganda the hardships suffered by the refugees. Since they continued to alter the story even after the refugees had reached home, nothing the official channels said was easily believed; instead people listened to rumours more attentively, and gave them more credence. The records of military intelligence in India reveal to us what these rumours were. The rumours became so insistent that a military intelligence report in February 1942 carried the warning that 'rumours and stories of the wildest nature, which continue to circulate, are producing a degree of unrest which has serious possibilities'.[22]

What did these rumours say? They were horrifying not only because they magnified events, as rumours do, but because they carried an alarming assessment of the colonial state. They denied its competence and credibility. By examining the rumours which were rife, popular perceptions of state power are starkly revealed. Though many of the rumours have disappeared without trace, we can still recapture a few. They whispered:[23]

Assam and Chittagong have been captured by the Japanese.[24]

The Tatas have struck a deal with the Japanese to prevent the Jamshedpur steel-works from being bombed.[25]

The government has made arrangements for British residents to flee, Calcutta.[26]

British troops have already been evacuated in fear from Fort William, and are being replaced by Indian troops, because the British don't care if Indians are killed.[27]

Aeroplanes are standing by for the evacuation of Europeans. Port Blair has been captured by the Japanese, Colombo bombed, and General Wavell killed.[28]

Though only a few voices are audible, mentally we can hear the chorus: invasion is imminent; the Japanese are coming; the British are set to flee. A person convinced of all this would not have been difficult to find in India in 1942.[29] Once one found him, he might even ask how he could be sure that the Japanese were not deep in India already. Who were the Japanese, these men who could humble an empire that had seemed all-powerful? What awesome powers did they have? Was it true, as some people said, that a Japanese parachutist had landed in the middle of a *mela*, spoken to the crowds in their own language, and risen again into the heavens in his parachute?[30]

Of course the rumours cited must have been unevenly believed, frequently distrusted, often derided. Today we may smile at the advanced technology of the Japanese parachutist. But the military officer who made some of these reports, a man who stood high above all such nonsense, admitted that 'the credulity of large sections of the civil population is almost beyond belief, especially as regards the potentialities of our enemies'.[31] Over a decade later, an article in an armed forces journal looked back on this year, remembering how low civilian morale had been, and stressing the need for India to take steps to prevent similar panic and dismay in the future.[32] Clearly, in 1942, the rumours were believed by large sections of the civilian population.

Hearing such rumours, or observing the developments around them, many people packed their bags to move to safety. The city of Calcutta was in turmoil. Blackouts were strictly observed at night, sirens blared out many times as exercises to prepare for air raids, and volunteers in every locality were trained in air-raid precautions. A few bombs and leaflets did fall on Calcutta (one of the Japanese bombs, which did not explode, remains on display at the police museum). It seemed sensible to take no chances. As early as January 1942, Marwari businessmen in Calcutta were selling their stocks at reduced prices, closing down their businesses and moving in large numbers to central and north India.[33] It may have seemed to the population of Calcutta that the Marwaris were pulling down their shutters for the last time. Many Bengali middle-class men had links with the countryside: this helped them send their families there. Some colleges shifted parts of their teaching work to district towns. Children were evacuated from the city and school buildings were occupied by troops.[34] The worries of different people varied.[35] Jadunath Sarkar, the great historian of medieval India, worried about being driven out of Calcutta, and expressed his 'wish to cling to my library to the last moment possible—as migration elsewhere would enforce idleness on me'.[36]

The fear extended beyond the well-to-do. The working class shared the general fear, creating labour shortages. A powerful magnet, Calcutta had attracted labour to its factories from far away; but in the panic following the Japanese declaration of war, 'the flow of workers from adjoining states to Calcutta practically stopped and many preferred to return to their native places'.[37] Factories began to experience a loss of manpower because workers who had taken leave to evacuate their families to safe areas were too scared to return to work. The organization of Calcutta as a war base required that the docks be kept working, which was not easy 'when the smallest Japanese raid sent the dock labour streaming back to its villages'.[38] The district judge of Bankura, in western Bengal, recalled that people came to his area from Midnapur for fear of a Japanese invasion by sea, and from Calcutta because they feared bombing.[39] In her memoirs, written much later, a political activist reflected that 'perhaps the Japanese had just made some warlike faces at us and left. But that alone was enough to get the people of Calcutta to make a hysterical bid to escape. It made one think that if they didn't get seats on the train they'd perhaps kill themselves in order to escape the bombs.' It seemed to her that 'the lethal shadow of war lay everywhere'.[40]

Much further south from Calcutta, the inhabitants of Madras nervously scanned the sea for signs of the Japanese navy. A Japanese landing was feared on the beaches of Madras. There was no British fleet there for protection. People procured sandbags and set up shelters for their safety. The books of the Madras University Library were removed inland.[41] The leading business houses shifted elsewhere, Burma Shell moved to Salem, Standarad Vacuum to Bangalore. Some of the measures taken seem peculiar: 'All the potentially dangerous animals in the zoo were shot dead as a precautionary measure lest a bomb fall on the zoo and the animals run into the city.' The person who recorded this went on to note that:

> People fled from Madras in panic—the exodus was on an astonishing scale. Whole families left their homes, taking such belongings as they could in overcrowded trains, buses, cars and bullock carts that were piled to overflowing. Homes were almost completely deserted and most shops in the city closed.[42]

One of the favourite destinations chosen by men who sent their wives and children away was Mysore, because of its presumed inland safety. In Mysore, 'as a result, there was pressure on housing, and landlords generally tried to dislodge their existing tenants under various pretexts', said the novelist R. K. Narayan, who found his landlord dropping in on him frequently to urge him to vacate his house. Displaying no desire to move to his town of Malgudi, Narayan refused to do so.[43]

The other great colonial port city, Bombay, was also humming with rumours. One person stationed there found Bombay to be 'a city then rife with rumours of impending Japanese air attacks, nightly black-outs, short-lived friendships and sudden departures to destinations unknown or not to be disclosed'. As 'the bombing scare had sent hundreds of Bombayites scurrying to safer places inland', house rents had fallen, enabling him to get a two-bedroom flat in Mahim, within walking distance of the beach, for Rs 65 a month.[44] To people in Bombay, a place such as Baroda, further inland, seemed in the circumstances much safer to live in. Trains out of Bombay were more crowded than usual, as people continued to leave the city.[45] And while many people left, many others remained ready to flee at a moment's notice.[46]

Nor was the fear of the Japanese confined to the coastal areas. There was, for example, an exodus of unskilled labour from Jamshedpur in February, 'as a result partly of the bad war news'.[47] Members of the Delhi Gymkhana Club began asking, only half-jokingly, whether they ought to start learning Japanese.[48] A biography of the classical singer Bhimsen Joshi, who was then employed as a staff artiste by All India Radio at Lucknow on a salary of Rs 32 per month, records that 'sensing the Impending danger, and also in response to frantic pleadings from his father to rush back home' he wound up his Lucknow sojourn and left the city (for Bombay, it happens).[49] He may even have sung beautiful *bhajans* on his way.

Another, quite different vein of data can be tapped to depict the shiver of 1942. Rumours are elusive, and the evidence for migrations is anecdotal, but the picture that emerges from them is borne out by sources which are convincingly quantitative. The shadow that crept over the colonial state is also to be found in firm financial facts. So let us now explore some such indices.

One new activity was to attract money for the war effort. The air was full of government schemes: Defence Savings Certificates, National Savings Certificate, Post Office Cash Certificates, War Loans, Victory Loans, and Governors' War Purposes Funds. Publicly, officials said that funds were never formally requisitioned. Privately, they knew that arm-twisting was condoned. Bureaucrats applied intense pressure to compel reluctant donations and investments. With propaganda so formidable, the graphs of investment should leap upwards. But they do not. Instead, they plummet. The government's elaborate efforts seem to have been unheeded, brushed aside, or resisted vigorously. The statistics of the Posts and Telegraphs department, which tell us about small investments, point the same way as the rumours. Investments in Post Office Cash Certificates totalled less than half of those of the previous years. The private banking sector was relatively undeveloped in India at this time, so the post office bank was popular even among sections of society which would later turn to commercial banks. The number of active accounts in the Post Office Savings Bank fell dramatically, as did the amount on deposit. Over one million Indians closed their accounts in the early years of the war: 4.2 million accounts in 1938–9 fell to 2.8 million accounts in 1943–4.[50] Gandhi was widely (though as it happens incorrectly) said to have remarked that the Cripps Offer—which promised self-government after the war—was 'a post-dated cheque on a crashing bank'. This remark became the epitaph of the Cripps Mission. Ironically, in the assessment of many Indians about the colonial state; the picturesque phrase attributed to Gandhi was simply the literal truth. By 1942 the amount on deposit in the post office was the lowest since the Depression.[51]

The trend of disinvestment lasted only as long as the Allies looked likely to lose World War II. When the war swung in Britain's favour, deposits soared to record levels. Until 1942–3, the transactions in all forms of small savings resulted in net withdrawals by the public; in the latter months of 1943 and the early months of 1944, they yielded net deposits at the rate of over 25 million rupees a month.[52] The contrast is startling. Taken together with the government's efforts to attract investment and the relative prosperity of some sections of Indian society, which dusted off the remains of the 1930s Depression in this period, the heavy and swift withdrawals show a new political climate of insecurity, in which the state seemed brittle and untrustworthy. In other words, the economic facts make a political comment. If the queues outside the post offices grew longer and more impatient, it was not because of a boom in business, but because customers scrambled to close their accounts, to recover their money before it was too late. As they withdrew their funds, they withdrew their faith in the stability of the colonial state. In the judgement of many a small investor, the state could no longer be trusted with his savings.

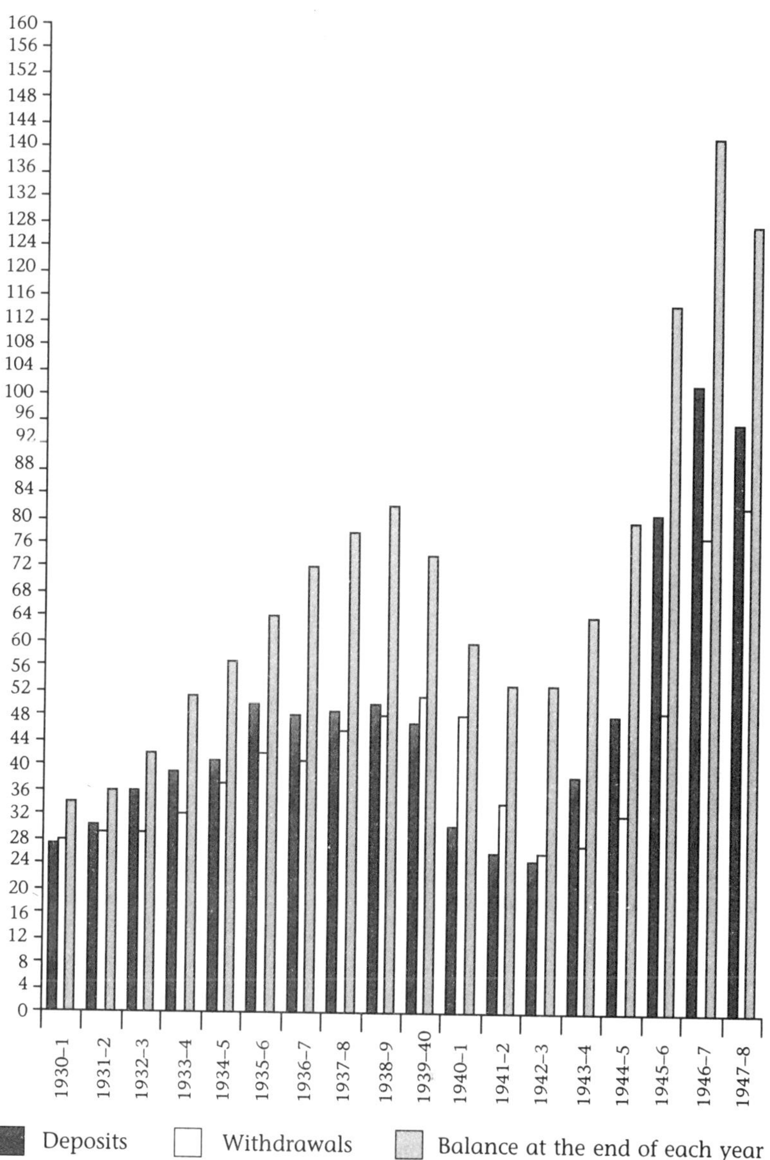

Figure 11.1: Total amount of deposits and withdrawls in the Post Office Savings Bank Accounts during each year and the total amount in deposit at end of each year

Source: Report on the Working of the Posts and Telegraphs Department 1947–48, IOL, V/24/3382.

More than in any other form, the state interacted with society through the issue of coins and currency notes. Much more often than in the form of government officials, the state came to the peasant in the form of money. But if the state was suspect, so was its paper currency.[53] The government's financial department could be heard to complain that large amounts of coins were being hoarded in preference to notes all over the country, and that the shortage of coins was consequently becoming acute. Matters became worse when the government started to withdraw standard rupee and half-rupee coins (which had a high silver content) from circulation, replacing them with coins of lower silver content, and by paper currency.[54] Whether they were legal tender or not, coins could be melted, while notes could not. Moreover, silver coinage had commanded confidence in India from the days of Akbar in the 1570s. The disappearance of silver from public view was obvious to the national press. The *Times of India* mentioned on 5 October 1942 that 'the Japanese onrush in the Far East precipitated a hoarding demand for silver in India itself, and before the Reserve Bank ceased its sales early this year a good deal of official silver must have been sold in the Bombay market'. What was the nature of the most common hoards? The sources divulge three things. The first is that these were new hoards, of a temporary character, formed during the war; they existed in addition to the usual semi-permanent, long-term hoards. Second, they were rural hoards, concentrated especially in the villages of the United Provinces and Bihar, though some hoarding occurred all over the country. Third, they were small hoards, since the big hoarder bought silver bars rather than coins. Together, these three things suggest a fairly broad social insecurity.[55]

Fears within the State

The fear of a Japanese landing lay not just in the popular imagination, but in the minds of the personnel, both British and Indian, of the colonial state. The fears floated outside the state, but lodged deep within it as well. Reputed to be brutal conquerors, the Japanese seemed to be winning irreversible victories. In February 1942, the provincial civil defence secretary in the Bihar secretariat told his colleagues that he expected Japanese bombs to be falling on Patna by the beginning of April.[56] On 13 April 1942, the Collector of Trichynopolly received news from Madras that a landing of Japanese troops was to be expected shortly on the coast of Thanjavur, from where the troops would infiltrate into the interior[57] Philip Mason, an ICS officer posted in Delhi in the Ministry of Defence, recalled in his autobiography how hopeless the situation seemed in April 1942. The Japanese navy had just sunk a hundred ships in the Bay of Bengal. The British had lost an army in Malaya, and another army in Burma. He felt they lacked real military resources, as 'there was not a division in India fit to fight'. If the Japanese army landed, it was not clear how it could be stopped. When he went to see his wife and children in Simla in May 1942, he returned to Delhi uncertain whether he would ever see them again.[58] Khub Chand, an ICS officer in the military finance department, recalled how in early 1942, 'among Indians, including some ICS officers, it was not unusual to lay bets on the exact date the Japanese would enter Singapore, Rangoon and what next'. In his view, Japanese successes were 'a terrific blow to Western prestige and authority'.[59]

Nearer the front, General Slim found 'a distinctly jumpy feel about the place' when he went to inspect military arrangements at the port of Chittagong. He felt that a couple of minor bombing raids had substantially damaged the morale of its Indian garrison. According to him, the most serious danger in Bengal, and the one they were least prepared to meet, was an invasion from the sea. The Japanese could send a battle fleet into the Bay of Bengal, secure in the knowledge that the British had no naval forces of any size nearer than East Africa, and that even these were incapable of challenging it. His calculations were that 'the most likely Japanese approaches were a landing at the mouth of the Hooghly with a direct thrust at Calcutta, or infiltration through the Sunderbans'. He and his men passed anxious days and nights 'when scares of invasion called us from our beds'. Though he later learnt that the Japanese never seriously contemplated a seaborne invasion of India, 'at that time it loomed constantly over us'.[60] This provided the context of what came to be known as the 'Denial Policy' in Bengal, which was designed to impede the progress of Japanese soldiers by the removal of food from coastal areas susceptible to invasion, as well as the removal of means of transport—which meant, in practice, thousands of country boats. The kinds of measures taken could not have reassured the coastal areas. Further down the coast, they could look very doubtful: for example, 'the coastline in Ganjam presented a picture of avid preparation with the setting up of dummy anti-aircraft guns all along'.[61]

At least some parts of India were expected to fall into Japanese hands. Even the fall of India's largest city, Calcutta, seemed a strong possibility. If Singapore could fall, so could Calcutta. A Deputy Inspector General of Police was commissioned to ensure a line of retreat for the inhabitants of Calcutta, at that time numbering about 2 million, in the event of an attack on the city. It was made clear to him that main roads would not be available, as these would be required for military purposes. 'I therefore had to improve the minor roads to make them passable', he said in his memoirs.[62] The irrepressible Nirad Chaudhuri, who said that the panic began as early as 9 December 1941, found that: 'Almost everyone I talked to in Calcutta, including high Bengali officials, believed that, by th end of February or at least by March, the whole of Bengal including Calcutta would be occupied by the Japanese.'[63] Various contingency plans were made. The Japanese were notorious for their brutality, but the inhabitants of Calcutta had good reason to fear the activities of the British if they were forced to abandon the city. 'So thin was our defence at this time that full arrangements were made to destroy, if necessary, the many installations in Calcutta that would have been invaluable to an invader had they fallen intact into his hands', recalled the military commander General Slim.[64]

Such scenarios raised a further question: how were the district officers to behave if the Japanese overran the territory? The imperial ideal was nonchalant courage. The officers of the ICS were meant to have imbibed certain standards, even without being told. They were meant to have learnt, automatically, that some things we never done. 'In all emergencies, it was one's duty to stand firm. However frightened one might feel, one did not show it.'[65] George Orwell, having 'already made up my mind that imperialism was an evil thing', went along with this view, describing in his essay 'Shooting an Elephant' how, for a White man, 'it is the condition of his rule that he shall spend his life in trying to impress the "natives"'. While serving in the imperial police in Burma, 'solely to avoid looking like a fool', Orwell had himself shot an elephant that had run amok. Musing on this, he wrote: 'A white man mustn't be frightened in front of "natives", and so, in general, he isn't frightened.'[66] In 1942, however, the image slipped. The Japanese soldier, though smaller than a Burmese elephant, evoked a bigger fear.

British officials in the coastal areas sent their families away to the hills; Indian officials sent their families away to relatives. The likelihood of invasion alarmed the district officers, who heard that the Japanese had murdered civilian officials in Burma, and were worried that they would share the same fate—they were sure as they said with some understatement, that international law would be violated in India too. Consequently there was a furore when, on 28 February 1942, the Home Department issued instructions that district officers were to remain at their posts in the event of a Japanese invasion. The furore made the government back down: on 9 April, fresh orders were issued. The new orders were a face-saving compromise: officials were told that they should stay as long as they felt they could help the civilian population.[67] The episode shows how tense and worried the officials were.

When tested, at least some of the officials were found wanting. Sections of the colonial state sent unmistakable signals of vulnerability. At about this time, there was a false alarm of a landing by the Japanese along the coast in the district of Balasore. A police officer remembered that 'the result was that the District Magistrate and the Superintendent of Police promptly scuttled their records and currency notes available in the treasury and rushed to areas at least a hundred miles away from the coast'.[68] Senior officials showed no great desire to remain at their posts either. When Japanese ships were sighted off the coast of Madras, most of the officials, including the British governor, evacuated the city. The governor went to Vellore, while his advisers went to the Nilgiris.[69]

A vivid account of the massive scare within officialdom has been left by Pulla Reddi, who was then commissioner of the Corporation of Madras. According to him, the government seemed to have received a false alarm that the Japanese were going to land early one morning on the beaches of Madras, 'so great commotion prevailed all the previous evening, hasty orders were issued for the Government to move out, judges ran helter-skelter, the Governor left for Vellore and the major Secretariat machinery left by the Blue Mountain Express for the Nilgiris'. When he asked for instructions about what he should do if the Japanese landed, Reddi was told by a superior to do what he liked, as there was no time for instructions—there was a train to catch. Almost all government officials dropped their work and fled, leaving behind Reddi and the Commissioner of Police, Sir Lionel Gasson, 'to maintain the city as best we could'. No street lighting was allowed, and no electric lights were allowed even inside houses, 'and finally and the worst of it all, I was asked to have all the lions, tigers, panthers, Polar bears and such dangerous animals in the zoo to be shot in a few minutes. Everybody seemed to have lost his head.' Reddi said that killing the animals in the zoo was 'too hasty and premature and we could wait'. He demurred, but the Police

Commissioner, insisting that the animals might break loose if Japanese bombs fell, refused to wait and sent a platoon of the Malabar Special Police to the zoo 'who to my great horror ruthlessly did their job in a few minutes'. A week of agony passed. As the Japanese showed no sign of arriving, people slowly began to return. Normal life took six weeks to be restored.[70] Evidently, official nervousness had reached bizarre proportions.[71]

As we saw, the populace took steps to keep its money safe. So did the state. Like the people over whom it ruled, the colonial state valued its gold, and so 'it was during this period when the Japanese navy made its appearance in the Indian Ocean, that the Reserve Bank considered it necessary to move its gold holdings from Bombay to a safe place and the operation was carried out with exemplary security and secrecy', revealed C. D. Deshmukh, who later became the governor of the Reserve Bank, before moving on to become finance minister in independent India.[72]

The attitude towards the state which has been sketched was a part of the atmosphere in 1942: it was inhaled by everybody. Japanese invasion seemed imminent. Moreover, by some of its behaviour, the Government of India seemed to be announcing its own impending demise.

How much actually happened? As we know, there was no Japanese invasion India in 1942; even in the remainder of the war, their army entered only north-eastern fringe of India, when the battles of Kohima and Imphal received much publicity. During 1942, there were some air raids: according to government figures, 484 people were killed and 615 were wounded in the whole country.[73] At this time, when wartime bombing was devastating cities elsewhere in the world, B. C. Roy—then Vice Chancellor of Calcutta University and later Chief Minister of West Bengal—in a speech on 2 January 1943, at the beginning of the Indian Science Congress session in Calcutta, commended the courage and determination which brought delegates 'to this much bombed city'.[74]

A Linkage with 'Quit India'

As we have shown, the Raj seemed on the run. While the shiver of 1942 is easily observed, its political implications must be suggested more tentatively.[75] Some political repercussions were bound to be there. In his book *The Discovery of India*, written while he was in prison after the Quit India Movement, Nehru commented:

While we were doubting and debating, the mood of the country changed, and from a sullen passivity it rose to a pitch of excitement and expectation. Events were not waiting for a Congress decision or resolution: they had been pushed forward by Gandhiji's utterances, and now they were moving onwards with their own momentum. It was clear that, whether Gandhiji was right or wrong, he had crystallized the prevailing mood of the people. There was a desperateness in it, an emotional urge which gave second place to logic and reason and a calm consideration of the consequences of action.[76]

It was common knowledge that Singapore, Malaya, and Burma had fallen to the Japanese in quick succession; India could fall too. Rajendra Prasad wrote in his autobiography that 'there was a feeling of inevitability in the air. It appeared as if, however determined the resistance to the enemy might be, the stage was set for a hurried retreat. The result of all this was confusion and fear in the country.'[77] Gandhi was reported to feel privately that the Axis would win the war.[78] He felt that the presence of the British was a provocation to the Japanese. He wrote in the *Harijan* that the presence of the British provided the Japanese with an incentive to attack India; British departure would lessen the likelihood of invasion, and India might be left alone, kept out of the war.[79] In this situation the British Cabinet, incarnated in Cripps, promised too little of significance in the present but much in the future. The Cripps proposals, said Congress, were 'too ridiculous to find acceptance anywhere'.[80] They belied the high hopes the announcement of the Cripps Mission had aroused. Disappointed by the Cripps fiasco, and faced with a sinking empire, the Congress—in this assessment—opted to set off Quit India.

The appraisal of British strength was differently articulated at different levels. For example, some Congressmen travelled around Bihar, saying that Britain had hitherto ruled large areas of the world by bluff, and that her essential weakness was at long last being exposed.[81] Also, for months before the Quit India Movement, some Congressmen 'had been preaching the doctrine that government were powerless to help the people ... and that the British Raj would soon be ended'.[82] Perhaps they were prisoners of such unexamined assumptions: at any rate, as propagandists they disseminated them and reinforced them.[83] A CID report of a Congressman's speech enables us to appreciate how persuasively they put the argument across. Speaking in Bihar in July 1942, this Congressman assured his audience that:

The crown is about to fall. Now we have to see who picks it up—we or the Germans or the Japanese .... Many people say that the British have big battalions ... (But) big battalions and police are limited in number. If you begin to estimate the strength of the police and the battalions it will prove to be quite worthless.[84]

It is another matter that soon after Quit India Movement began, the big battalions did move in, to crush, though only temporarily, such frail moments of hope.

Few participants in the Quit India Movement could have contemplated its brutal outcome. Many of them might have accepted that the crown was about to fall. The tottering colonial state was a mirage, but it was a mirage that mattered.[85] Now easily obscured by hindsight, perhaps it allowed the hostility to the state to find its dramatic expression. Men cannot rebel if there seems no prospect of success: in 1942, they may have rebelled because there seemed to be such a prospect.[86]

Conclusion

The British boasted of the Pax Britannica, of the sense of security engendered by imperialism, and of how visceral fears of anarchy had been allayed by their rule. To a lawless country, they claimed to have brought good government and stability. British rule in India strove hard to convey an impression of invincibility. In the late nineteenth century, this effort was successful enough to maintain, among the British in India, what has been called 'the Illusion of Permanence'.[87]

On the other hand, popular consciousness frequently contested the imperial image. The illusion of permanence was one side of the coin: the delusion of fragility was the other. If we listen with a stethoscope, rumours about the collapse of British rule, with a just social order to follow it, are quite audible in modern Indian history. They were audible during the Mutiny[88] (when the story of the greased cartridges underlined the role of rumour). In a fine article, Shahid Amin has demonstrated how, in the popular perceptions of Gandhi, rumours of the end of the Raj and of the Mahatma's miraculous powers upheld his halo.[89] It has been noticed that the onset of World War I inspired a rumour in Orissa that 'there would be no sahebs left in the country'.[90] A similar rumour about the imminent defeat of the British led to unrest among the Bhils in 1914.[91] 'A rumoured collapse of British authority during the war' led to violence against moneylenders in Punjab in 1915.[92] These rumours referred to battles far away. World War II was, as far as India was concerned, quite different from World War I: this time the front was closer. The Japanese were knocking at the gates of India. Conditions were ripe for the sounds to be amplified. Although murmurs can be discerned at other times, this article has suggested that, in the special circumstances of 1942, rumours about the breakdown of the Raj blared forth at a much higher volume.

By solving a jigsaw puzzle of rumours, migrations, speeches, and financial withdrawals, this article has reconstructed a situation which was totally unexpected and quite unplanned. It has shown that in 1942, as war-related activities made the state appear alarmingly aggressive and intrusive, a phantom crisis of the state occurred. The British Army had just suffered reverses: Hong Kong, Singapore, Malaya, and Burma had fallen in quick succession. The public in India was acutely aware of the progress of the war. Even schoolchildren were told war news when classes began. Stories were heard from the 4,50,000 Indian refugees who had painfully plodded back from Burma, having seen the British defeated with their own eyes. Trainloads of wounded and defeated soldiers were seen returning home from the Burma front. Consequently, the fear spread that the Japanese would invade and conquer India too. To the people, the state for once, due to the special circumstances of war, looked brittle.

The defeats in the war against Japan resulted in an optical illusion. At the very moment that the presence of its colonial masters seemed certain to provoke invasion, the state suddenly seemed fragile, indeed almost on the verge of collapse. The state sent signals of vulnerability. The tremendous awe which the British were held in rapidly disappeared. The British seemed set to flee, their government looked marked for oblivion. This impression was widespread. Port; and coastal areas felt very insecure, but the fear seeped deeper inland. People watched the state carefully. How strong or weak it looked was to them profoundly important. When the evidence is amalgamated, the pieces of the jigsaw fall into place, revealing that suddenly in 1942 the colonial state—that mighty pre-war machine—came to convey an impression of fragility.

Perhaps this helped some people to rebel in August 1942; it certainly led many people to take to their heels. In Indian historiography, the second aspect has received much less attention than the first. The Quit India Movement is part and parcel of our heroic fight for national freedom: the shiver of 1942 often involved, as we have seen, an ignominious flight for personal safety. Gandhi gave them the slogan 'Do or Die': but a common popular reaction in 1942 was to pack up and flee.[93] In due course, 'Do or Die' has become, in pictures on postage stamps and in the names of roads, trains, and buildings, a part of our national autobiography. The historic mirror must also reflect back to Indian society a less edifying image. In short, history requires remembering both courage and fear: Like all autobiography that of a nation requires honesty to retain its credibility and conviction.

This article began by suggesting that intentions loom larger in the historiography than in the history of modern India. Selectively recalled, the visions and calculations of leaders suggest wise statesmanship. In such perspectives, the British leaders were wise to train Indians and set them on the road to self-government, while Indians were wise in their choice of a non-violent strategy to challenge British rule. The historical record supplies, however, not just the ingredients for awestruck hero-worship, but its antidote. Alternative selections of leaders' thoughts provide examples of interesting errors, which dim their aura of omniscient wisdom. Gandhi spoke of 'Swaraj in One Year' in the early 1920s. In the late 1940s, Patel said Pakistan would desire reunification with India. Jinnah did not expect the partition of India to lead to mass migrations. Mountbatten expected independent India to be a part of the British imperial defence system. Before the Quit India Movement, the British had expected only familiar developments: a newspaper crusade, picketing, boycott, possibly attempts to start a no-rent campaign.[94] History as miscalculation would be a promising theme.[95] A systematic survey of the miscalculations of leaders could prove a salutary exercise, showing that their wishes matter less than we often suppose, and prompting us to look harder at the tidal forces over which these leaders had no control.

The tides caused by World War II swept not just through the politically active strata but through Indian society as a whole. Nationalist allegiance had an element of choice; wartime inflation was a given fact of life. An awareness of food shortages and high prices transcended social divisions. As human beings, we are agents; but we are victims as well. The passion of nationalism no doubt moved many of the Indian people; but the fear of Japanese invasion, or the effects of high prices, touched most of them. On the other hand, the Japanese frightened the British more than the Congress ever could. For British power in India, the Japanese army seemed to pose a much greater threat than the Indian national movement. Every official, in every department of government, was meant to respond to the needs of the war effort.[96] It bears repeating that war stretched the colonial state and convulsed Indian society to an extent which Indian nationalism never could. War affected everybody. Recognizing this, this article has tried to shift the emphasis, in the analysis of a period of Indian history, away from the political activity of a few, to the common predicament of the many.

This predicament, in 1942, encouraged national unity. Traditionally, nationalism proclaimed the Indian people to be one, while social divisions in India provided ammunition to the opponents of nationalism. But in 1942, the danger was that India would become a battlefield. This prospect was unwelcome to all. The Japanese army had a brutal reputation. The industrialists did not want their factories to be destroyed as a part of a 'scorched-earth' policy; the lowest social strata did not want their rice to be looted by Japanese soldiers either. Thus a common sentiment papered over, for a brief while, the cracks within Indian society. The unity nationalism frequently claimed, but never previously achieved, was induced in 1942 by the Japanese threat. The Quit India Movement aimed, by overthrowing British power, to remove any provocation for the Japanese to invade India, and thereby to keep India safely out of the war. This may account for the relative lack of a class or communal dimension to the Quit India Movement. Class-tensions were muted, communal incidents absent. As if to show unity, the Congress no longer asked for all sorts of concessions, but simply—a single demand—that the British leave immediately, that they Quit India. In its aversion to Japanese conquest, India was indeed unusually united. It is another matter that this unprecedented unity was short-lived. The Japanese threat soon receded, and the operations of the Indian war economy, from which the rich profited and the poor suffered, widened the divisions within Indian society.

The fear of Japanese invasion, once so widespread in India, left no enduring legacy. Panic generates no pride. But even if they do not materialize, our fears are history too.

* * *

History-writing is, of course, a part of man's battle against forgetting. Like the battle against our mortality, it is a losing battle, which produces nevertheless some heroic episodes. The publication, in 1932, of George Lefebvre's classic book, *The Great Fear of 1789* was one of these episodes.[97] With prodigious energy and virtuosity, Lefebvre tracked the progress, over hundreds of miles, of the rumour of an aristocratic conspiracy, involving marauding brigands and invading foreign troops, which swept the French countryside at the time of the French Revolution. No matter how mistaken they were, he focused unwaveringly on what the people thought was happening. He showed how the conviction that brigands were approaching travelled from place to place, identifying many of the people who unwittingly couriered it, giving the rumour dates of arrival in different places, and estimating the speed with which it travelled. The results of his labours were summarized by a profusion of arrows on a map of France: these displayed the progress of the rumour. Lefebvre gave the 'Great Fear' precise dates, showed which areas it reached, and where it did not. Thus, before it could escape and vanish, something as elusive and fleeting as a rumour was captured and trapped between the covers of a book. The historian triumphed: transient emotion was durably described. A rumour was impaled on a map. As they are by an Impressionist masterpiece, through human ingenuity and effort, the hands of the clock had been made to pause for a while. Lefebvre's feat, one of the peaks of twentieth century historical imagination and craftsmanship, still retains its ability to inspire.

This article has sketched, or scratched the surface, of one Indian fear. Quite obviously, Lefebvre's masterly precision has never been neared. Perhaps it emerges, however, that the building blocks are not lacking in the data on modern Indian history. Someone may yet use them.

Notes

1. For example, the *Transfer of Power* series of documents has two volumes on 1942: the first titled *The Cripps Mission,* and the second *Quit India.* Nicholas Mansergh (editor-in-chief). *Constitutional Relations Between Britain and India: The Transfer of Power 1942–47* (henceforth *TOP*), 12 vols, London: 1970–83.
2. A full page government advertisement in the *Times of India* on 9 August 1999 intoned: 'Fifty-seven years ago people from all over India woke up this day to hear two electrifying words. Quit India. On this day, Mahatma Gandhi, the father of the nation, asked the foreign ruler to quit our motherland. People lived for his words. People died for his words. And the foreign ruler was forced to leave.
3. In the United Provinces, 104 railway stations and 250 other government buildings were destroyed or severely damaged; and over 400 cases of the destruction of telegraph and telephone communications were reported. Government of the United Provinces, *The Congress*

Rebellion in the United Provinces 1942, p. 11, R/3/1/359. Archival reference numbers in this essay are, unless otherwise stated, to items in the India Office Library and Records, London.

4. *United Provinces Police Administration Report, 1942,* resolution dated 15 September 1943, p. 1, V/24/3177. Similarly, the report on the administration of the police in the province of Bihar for the year 1942 refers to the 'influx of refugees and the general unsettlement of the people due to the threat to India from Japan', V/24/3271, p. 1.
5. 'The Indian population in Burma according to the 1931 Census was 10,17,825, of whom 6,30,000 were born outside Burma. This formed 6.9 per cent of the total population. These Indians were deeply resented by the local population. Ma Mya Sein, *Burma,* London: 1943, pp. 24–5.
6. Rangoon is certainly a predominantly Indian town, and the Indian population (as much as 53 per cent of the total) here falls into three main categories, each of them unfortunately competing with Burmese labour: the unskilled port workers and stevedores, the semi-educated shop assistant and clerical employees, and the astute and prospering business man whose hold on the poorer Burmese, both in town and country, is too often a stranglehold. N. Gangulee, *Indians in the Empire Overseas,* London: 1947, p. 138. The number of Indians in Rangoon, about 2,80,000 in 1941, was drastically reduced by the events of the 1940s, so much so that by 1952 it was less than half the number recorded in 1941. Tin Maung Maung Than, 'Some aspects of Indians in Rangoon', in K. S. Sandhu and A. Mani (eds), *Indian Communities in Southeast* Asia, Singapore: 1993, pp. 586, 591.
7. L/WS/l/317, 4 March 1942.
8. The exact figures are 20,38,000 money orders and 725 lakhs of rupees. The largest amount received, 361.04 lakhs of rupees, was from Burma; next came Malaya with 197.53 lakhs. *Report on the Work of the Posts and Telegraphs Department, 1940–41,* p. 4, V/24/3381.
9. R. H. Niblett, *The Congress Rebellion in Azamgarh, August–September 1942.* Allahabad: 1957, p. 2.
10. *United Provinces Land Revenue Administration Report for the Year Ending 30 September 1942,* p. 3, V/24/2445.
11. For details, see H. Tinker's superb article, 'A Forgotten Long March: The Indian Exodus from Burma, 1942', *Journal of South-East Asian Studies,* vol. 6, 1975, pp. 1–15.
12. It was estimated that nearly 4,05,000 refugees passed through Calcutta, of whom 3,35,000 arrived by rail and 70,000 by steamer. The first shipload of 2,000 people arrived on 19 January 1942, after which ships laden with refugees landed almost daily. Marwari Relief Society, *Burma Evacuees Relief Works Report,* Calcutta: 1943. This pamphlet is available at the National Library, Kolkata.

13. Paul Greenoogh, *Prosperity and Misery in Modem Bengal,* New York: 1982, p. 88.
14. *United Provinces Police Administration Report, 1942,* p. 3, V/24/3177.
15. Frank Moraes, *Witness to an Era: India 1920 to the Present Day,* London: 1973, pp. 102–3.
16. Trains may be seen as symbols of the state. Racial discrimination on trains was a feature of colonial rule. The importance of racial incidents on trains in the lives of Nehru, and Gandhi in South Africa, is well known. Early in 1942, trains carrying wounded soldiers back from Burma gave the impression that the colonial state was being defeated. When the Quit India Movement began, rebels uprooted railway lines—manifestations of the hated state—all over the country. During the movement, trains were commandeered and these so-called 'Azad' trains went triumphantly through the countryside flying the Congress flag. Soon afterwards, when the government regained the upper hand, trains carried troops on internal security duty, stopping in the countryside to disgorge soldiers who put down the rebellion and punished the rebels. Throughout the subsequent years of war, trains would be seen heading eastwards taking supplies away from India, by then a country ridden with shortages and racked by famine. After the war, one of the signs of discontent within the state was a railway strike. Later, communal carnage occurred on trains carrying refugees, and these trains were symbols of the dividing state, as is evident in the title of Khushwant Singh's novel, *Train to Pakistan.*
17. Memoirs of J. W. Orr, a district officer in Bihar, MSS,Eur.F. 180/22, p. 20. In Ranchi, in the words of General Slim, who was appalled by what he saw: 'The hospital provision was inadequate. Inadequate in amount, in accommodation, staff, equipment, and in the barest amenities .... Schools and other large buildings were requisitioned, the medical staffs arriving barely ahead of, sometimes indeed after, a swarm of patients.' William Slim, *Defeat into Victory,* Dehra Dun: 1981, p. 129.
18. L/WS/1/317, 4 April 1942, p. 1.
19. Verrier Elwin, *The Tribal World of Verier Elwin: An Autobiography,* Delhi: 1988, p. 171.
20. Slim, *Defeat into Victory,* p. 131.
21. Cited in Partha Sarathi Gupta (ed.), *Towards Freedom: Documents on the Movement for Independence in India, 1943–1944,* part 3, Delhi: 1997, p. 2610.
22. L/WS/1/1433, 13 February 1942.
23. The rumours are in reported speech in the documents. They have been cited as they were recorded, apart from the change to direct speech.
24. Spread by workmen returning from Bengal to their homes in Bihar. L/WS/l/1433, report dated 6 March l942.
25. Memoirs of A. H. Kemp, MSS.Eur.F.180/18.

26. Reported in Bihar, L/WS/l/1433.
27. Reported in Gaya, L/WS/l/1433, 13 February 1942.
28. Reported in Madras, L/WS/l/l433, 6 March 1942.
29. Did the rumours resemble any echoes from the past? In 1670, the Marathas under Shivaji looted the port of Surat. Commenting on the period, Jadunath Sarkar wrote: 'For several years after Shivaji's withdrawal from it, the town used to throb with panic every now and then, whenever any Maratha force came within a few days' march of it, or even at false alarms of their coming'. Jadunath Sarkar, *A Short History of Aurangzib, 1618–1707,* second edition, Calcutta: 1954, p. 210.
30. 'One area reported public consternation' due to the activities of this extraordinary parachutist. Monthly military intelligence summary dated 4 May 1942, p. 1, L/WS/1/317.
31. Ibid.
32. Major R. P. Varma, 'Civil defence in India'. *Journal of the United Services Institution,* July-September 1955, pp. 232–3.
33. L/WS/1/317, 10 January 1942.
34. Renuka Ray, *My Reminiscences,* Delhi: 1982. pp. 104–5.
35. The concerns of the rich added to the worries of the poor. One of the submerged stories, which can only be guessed at, is of the beggars of Calcutta. 'Calcutta, under the threat of Japanese raids, attempted to remove its beggars outside the city limits and take charge of them. The attempt was admittedly a failure.' S. Natarajan, *Social Problems,* third edition, Bombay: 1944. p. 27.
36. Jadunath Sarkar to G. S. Sardesai, 28 December 1941, in H. R. Gupta (ed.), *Life and Letters of Jadunath Sarkar,* Hoshiarpur: 1957, pp. 229–30.
37. Arun Joshi, *Lala Shri Ram,* Delhi: 1975, p. 348.
38. Slim, *Defeat into Victory,* p. 136.
39. Interview with Ananda Shankar Roy, Calcutta, 3 January 1999.
40. Manikuntala Sen, *In Search of Freedom: An Unfinished Journey,* Kolkata: 2001, pp. 61, 69. Though data are unavailable, one may suspect, amid the prayers to the goddess Kali, a spurt in the sales of that soothing homeopathic remedy, *Kalium Phosphoricum.*
41. They were brought back to Madras in 1943, when the Japanese threat to the city had receded. Ranganathan Yogeshwar, *S. R. Ranganathan: Pragmatic Philosopher of Information Science,* Bombay: 2001, p. 66.
42. M. A. Sreenivasan, *Of the Raj, Maharajas and Me,* Delhi: 1991, p. 164.
43. R. K. Narayan, *My Days: An Autobiography,* Delhi: 1986, pp. 156–7.
44. Raj Chatterjee, 'The Boys Came Later', *Times of India,* 18 October 1997.
45. L/WS/1/1433, 20 February 1942.
46. In Britain, where there were official evacuation schemes, the whole process was, despite its imitations, much more under the control of the

state than in India. See Arthur Marwick, *Britain in the Century of Total War: War, Peace and Social Change 1900–1967,* London: 1968, pp. 264–5.

47. L/WS/l/1433, 20 February 1942.
48. Interview with Balbir Singh Grewal, Delhi, 20 October 1996.
49. Mohan Nadkarni, *Bhimsen Joshi: A Biography,* Delhi: 1994, p. 85
50. Government of India, *Proposals for the Post-War Development of the Indian Posts and Telegraphs Department,* Simla: December 1945, p. 8. Also see the *Report on the Work of the Indian Posts and Telegraphs Department for the Year 1945–46,* p. 47.
51. The bar chart in Figure 11.1 illustrates this strikingly.
52. 'News from India'. A cyclostyled sheet dated 6 November 1944, L/F/7/1166.
53. A history of the police in Bihar notes that 'In Bihar a number of persons were purchasing land and buildings as a precaution against devaluation of the currency and withdrawals from the banks during the first three weeks of February 1942 were nearly double of those in the corresponding weeks in the preceding years.' Sudhir Kumar Jha, *Raj to Swaraj: Changing Contours of Police,* Delhi: 1995, p. 376.
54. Victoria rupees ceased to be legal tender on 31 March 1941; Edward VII rupees on 31 March 1942, Finance department minute dated 22 September 1942, L/F/7/568.
55. Based on (a) L/F/7/568: telegram, Government of India Finance Department to Secretary of State for India, 20 September 1940; Baxter to Jones, 3 June 1942 (b) *Capital,* 15 October 1942 (c) *Times of India,* 4 October 1942 (d) L/I/1/1012: telegram, Government of India Finance Department to Secretary of State for India, 17 November 1943.
56. Memoirs of J. W. Orr, MSS.Eur.F.180/22.
57. S. K. Chettur, *Steel Frame and I,* Bombay: 1962, p. 89.
58. Philip Mason, *A Shaft of Sunlight: Memories of a Varied Life,* London: 1978, p. 166.
59. Khub Chand, 'Administration: Backbone of a Nation', in Raj K. Nigam (ed.), *Memoris of Old Mandarins of India,* Delhi: 1985, p. 143.
60. Slim, *Defeat into Victory,* pp. 132–4, 151.
61. Trilok Nath, *Forty Years of Indian Police,* Delhi: 198l, p . 56.
62. Memoirs of S. G. Taylor, MSS.Eur.F.161, 5/4, p. 4.
63. Never a man to mince words, he went on to say that 'this gave rise to the most abject and cowardly panic'. He was unusual in not being frightened, as 'those who could run away did so; those who could not, hoarded'. Nirad C. Chaudhuri, *Thy Hand, Great Anarch! India 1921–1952,* Delhi: 1987, pp. 592–3.
64. Slim, *Defeat into Victory,* p. 136.
65. A. D. Gorwala, *The Role of the Administrator: Past, Present and Future,* Poona: 1952, p. 8.
66. Written in 1936, this is reprinted in Sonia Orwell and Ian Angus (eds),

The Collected Essays, Journalism and Letters of George Orwell, vol. 1, London: 1968, pp. 235–42.

67. *Home Department War History,* pp. 33–34, L/R/5/289.
68. Nath, *Forty Years of Indian Police,* p. 54.
69. Frank Anthony, *Britain's Betrayal in India: The Story of the Anglo-Indian Community,* Delhi: 1969, p. 146; Sreenivasan, *Of the Raj, Maharajas and Me,* p. 164.
70. O. Pulla Reddi, *Autumn Leaves,* Bombay: 1978, pp. 55–6. Born in 1902, Pulla Reddi was an ICS officer who later became the first Indian Home Secretary of the Madras government, and eventually the Defence Secretary of the Government of India.
71. Consider this: 'Polar bears were killed in Madras by the Malabar Special Police because a British Police Commissioner feared a Japanese landing.' The facts of Indian history can sound stranger than fiction. I also derive pleasure from proving that, in the historiography of modern India, even Polar bears can find a place.
72. C. D. Deshmukh, *The Course of My Life,* Delhi: 1974, p. 113.
73. In 1943, 911 were killed and 1382 wounded. The total number of Indian civilians killed in air-raids during the war was 1429 and the number wounded was 2089. Government of India, *Statistics Relating to India's War Effort,* Delhi: 1947, p. 6. About 3 million deaths did occur, but these were due to famine, not bombing.
74. *Proceedings of the Thirteenth Indian Science Congress,* Calcutta: 1943, p. 18.
75. A useful collection of essays on the Quit India Movement is Gyanendra Pandey (ed.), *The Indian Nation in 1942,* Calcutta: 1988.
76. Jawaharlal Nehru, *The Discovery of India,* Bombay: 1961, p. 504.
77. Rajendra Prasad, *Autobiography,* New Delhi: 1994, p. 531. The first edition of this book was published in Bombay in 1957.
78. Hallett to Linlithgow, 31 May 1942, *TOP,* vol. 2: 113.
79. *Harijan,* 26 April and 3 May 1942. *The Collected Works of Mahatma Gandhi,* vol. 76, pp. 49, 67.
80. Ibid., p. 28.
81. L/WS/1/1433, military intelligence report dated 27 February 1942.
82. Government of the United Provinces. *The Congress Rebellion in the United Provinces,* 1942, p. 12, R/3/1/359.
83. The officials of the government also had many doubts. Later, an ICS officer wrote:

    > We had relied in peace on the active co-operation of about two or three million Indians and the passive tolerance of about four hundred million more: the active critics were about as many as the co-operators and so far less effective. But no one could suppose that the balance would be maintained if there was an enemy landing.

    Mason, *A Shaft of Sunlight,* p. 166.

84. The speech is quoted in Appendix A of Hallett to Linlithgow, 9 September 1942. Hallett Papers, MSS.Eur.E.251, item 38.
85. The governor of Madras felt that refugees from Burma may have been taking a prominent, part in the disturbances. *TOP*, vol. 2: 607.
86. This is more convincing than an economic explanation for the Quit India Movement. We may note in passing that many problems are sought to be solved by Poverty, the historian's *deus ex machina.* In this view, the misery of World War I precipitates the Non-Cooperation Movement; the misery of the Great Depression is responsible for the Civil Disobedience Movement; and the misery of the World War II permits Quit India. In the case of Quit India, there are only perfunctory genuflexions, as a general increase of poverty is difficult to prove. Yet the official historian of Indian nationalism does mumble (although mechanically): 'The rise in prices added to the miseries of the half-starved masses.' Tara Chand, *History of the Freedom Movement in India*, vol. 4, Delhi: 1972, p. 367.
87. Francis Hutchins, *The Illusion of Permanence: British Imperialism in India*, Princeton: 1967.
88. Gautam Bhadra, 'Four Rebels of Eighteen-fifty-seven', in Ranajit Guha (ed.), *Subaltern Studies,* vol. 4, Delhi: 1985, esp. pp. 238, 252, 260, 267.
89. Shahid Amin, 'Gandhi as Mahatma: Gorakhpur district, eastern UP, 1921–22. in Ranajit Guha (ed.), *Subaltern Studies,* vol. 3, Delhi: 1984, esp. pp. 6, 22–3, 26, 49, 52–3.
90. Sumit Sarkar, *Modern India,* Delhi: 1983, p. 154.
91. David Hardiman, 'Power in the Forest: The Dangs, 1820–1940', in David Arnold and David Hardiman (eds), *Subaltern Studies,* vol. 8, Delhi: 1994, p. 140.
92. David Gilmartin, *Empire and Islam: Punjab and the Making of Pakistan*, Delhi: p. 124.
93. In Sumit Sarkar's textbook, what I have here called 'The Shiver of 1942' is dealt with as one of the 'Roots of Rebellion': the events described in this article are swallowed and digested as a part of the 'Quit India' menu or rubric. *Modern India,* pp. 388–93. The contrast highlighted in this paragraph—between a heroic fight for freedom and a fearful flight to safety—is thereby clouded.
94. The governor of the United Provinces later confessed sheepishly: 'I anticipated a somewhat fatuous attempt at the forms of civil disobedience which have taken place during previous year.' Hallett to Linlithgow, 18 August 1942, Fortnightly reports, L/PJ/5/271. Later he wrote to the Viceroy: 'I admit that I only apprehended comparatively childish demonstrations, with which the movement indeed started.' Hallett to Linlithgow, 9 September 1942, Hallett Papers, MSS.Eur.E.251/38. See also *TOP,* vol. 2: 304, Linlilhgow to Amery, 22 July 1942.
95. In 1942, the grand aim of Reginald Maxwell of the state's home department was 'not merely to reduce the Congress to a condition in

which they will be prepared to make terms but to crush the Congress finally as a political organization'. G. Rizvi, 'The Congress Revolt of 1942: A Historical Revision', *Indo-British Review,* 11(1), December 1984, pp. 39–40. In the light of the misjudgements of better-known people. Maxwell's mistake seems less spectacular

96. 'Work as a Magistrate had to be almost completely abandoned in favour of new burdens,' recalled one officer, who found that 'touring had to be cut down to a series of lightning forays, often to track down and requisition stocks of hoarded rice.' Memoirs of R. S. Swann, MSS.Eur.F.180/25, p. 4.

97. George Lefebvre, *The Great Fear of 1789,* translated from French by Joan White, London: 1973. The most extraordinary chapter is 'The Currents of the Great Fear', pp. 169–97.

Annotated Bibliography

AUTOBIOGRAPHIES

Basu, Satyen, *A Doctor in the Army*, Calcutta: B. N. Bose, 1960.

Bristow, Brigadier R. C. B., *Memories of the British Raj: A Soldier in India*, London: Christopher Johnson, 1974.

Crasta, Richard, *Eaten by the Japanese: The Memoir of an Unknown Indian Prisoner of War John Baptist Crasta*, with an Introduction and two essays, 1998; reprint, Bangalore: Invisible Man Books, 1999.

Gourgey, Percy S., *The Indian Naval Revolt of 1946*, Hyderabad: Orient Longman, 1996.

Khan, Shah Nawaz, *My Memories of the INA and its Netaji*, New Delhi: Rajkamal Publications, 1946.

Kiani, M. Z., *India's Freedom Struggle and the Great INA*, New Delhi: Reliance Publishing, 1996.

Lunt, James (ed.) *From Sepoy to Subedar being the Life and Adventure of Subedar Sita Ram, a Native Officer of the Bengal Army, Written and Related by Himself*, [1873]; reprint, London: Macmillan, 1988.

Masters, John, *The Road Past Mandalay*, 1961; reprint, London: Four Square, 1967.

Molesworth, Lieutenant General G. N., *Curfew on Olympus*, Bombay: Asia Publishing House, 1965.

Pradip, Kalyan, *Kalyan Pradip, being the Memoir of Captain Kalyan Kumar Mukhopadhyay, IMS* [in Bengali], Calcutta: privately published, 1928.

Rao, K. V. Krishna, *In the Service of the Nation: Reminiscences*, New Delhi: Viking, 2001.

Rifleman to Colonel: Memoirs of Gajendra Malla 9th Gorkha Rifles, Compiled by Tony Mains and Elizabeth Talbot Rice, New Delhi: Reliance Publishing House, 1999.

Rikhye, Major General Indar Jit, *Trumpets and Tumults: The Memoirs of a Peacekeeper*, New Delhi: Manohar, 2002.

Roberts, Field Marshal, *Forty-One Years in India: From Subaltern to Commander-in-Chief in India*, vol. 1, London: Richard Bentley and Son, 1897.

Singh, Lieutenant General Harbakhsh, *In the Line of Duty: A Soldier Remembers*, New Delhi: Lancer, 2000.

Slim, Field Marshal William, *Defeat into Victory*, London: Cassell, 1956.

Biographies

Connell, John, *Auchinleck: A Critical Biography*, London: Cassell, 1959.

Evans, Geoffrey, *Slim as Military Commander*, 1969; reprint, New Delhi: Natraj, 1977.

Evans, Humphrey, *Thimayya of India: A Soldier's Life*, New York: Harcourt Bruce and Co., 1960.

Khanduri, C. B., *Field Marshal K. M. Cariappa: His Life and Times*, New Delhi: Lancer, 1995.

Lewin, Ronald, *Slim: The Standardbearer*, London: Leo Cooper, 1976.

Maclagan, Michael, *Clemency Canning*, London: Macmillan, 1962.

Palit, Major General D. K., *Major-General A. A. Rudra: His Service in Three Armies and Two World Wars*, New Delhi: Lancer, 1997.

Toye, Hugh, *Subhash Chandra Bose: The Springing Tiger*, 1959; reprint, Bombay: Jaico, 1966.

Warner, Philip, *Auchinleck: The Lonely Soldier*, 1981; reprint, London: Cassell, 2001.

Ziegler, Philip, *Mountbatten: A Biography*, London: Collins, 1985.

Coercion, Discipline, and Dissent in the Armies

Bandopadhyay, Premansu Kumar, *Tulsi Leaves and the Ganges Water: The Slogan of the First Sepoy Mutiny at Barrackpore, 1824*, Kolkata: K. P. Bagchi, 2003.

Barat, Amiya, *The Bengal Native Infantry: Its Organization and Discipline*, Calcutta: Firma K. L. M. 1962.

Bayly, C. A., 'Two Colonial Revolts: The Java War, 1825–30, and the Indian "Mutiny" of 1857–59', in C. A. Bayly and D. H. A. Kolff (eds), *Two Colonial Empires: Comparative Essays on the History of India and Indonesia in the Nineteenth Century*, Dordrecht/Lancaster: Martinus Nijhoff, 1986, pp. 111–35.

Cadell, Patrick, 'The Outbreak of the Indian Mutiny', *Journal of the Society for Army Historical Research*, vol. 33, 1955.

David, Saul, *The Indian Mutiny 1857*, London: Penguin, 2002.

Frykenberg, Robert Eric, 'Conflicting Norms and Political Integration in South India: The Case of Vellore Mutiny', *Indo-British Review*, 13(1), 1987, pp. 51–63.

Gregorian, Raffi, 'Unfit for Service: British Law and Looting in India in the Mid-Nineteenth Century', *South Asia*, 13(1), 1990, pp. 63–84.

Gupta, Maya, *Lord William Bentinck in Madras and the Vellore Mutiny, 1803–7*, New Delhi: Capital Publishers and Distributors, 1986.

Harrison, Mark, 'Disease, Discipline and Dissent: The Indian Army in France and England, 1914–15', in Mark Harrison, Roger Cooter, and Steve Sturdy (eds), *Medicine and Modern Warfare*, Amsterdam, Atlanta GA: Rodopi, 1999, pp. 185–203.

James, L., *Mutiny in the British and Commonwealth Forces, 1797–1856*, London: Buchan and Enright, 1987.

Kaminsky, Arnold P., 'Morality Legislation and British Troops in Late Nineteenth Century India', *Military Affairs*, XLIII(2), 1979, pp. 78–83.

MacMunn, Lieutenant General George, *The Indian Mutiny in Perspective*, London: Camelot Press, 1931.

Malleson, Colonel G. B., *The Indian Mutiny of 1857*, 1891; reprint, New Delhi: Sunita Publications, 1988.

Mead, Henry, *The Sepoy Revolt*, 1857; reprint, Delhi: Gian Publishing House, 1986.

Mukherjee, Rudrangshu, *Awadh in Revolt 1857–58: A Study of Popular Resistance*, New Delhi: Oxford University Press, 1984.

——, '"Satan let loose upon the Earth": The Kanpur Massacres in India in the Revolt of 1857', *Past and Present*, no. 128, 1990, pp. 92–117.

Norman, Henry W. and Keith Young, *Delhi 1857*, 1902; reprint, Delhi: Low Price Publications, 2001.

Palmer, J. A. B., *The Mutiny Outbreak at Meerut in 1857*, Cambridge: Cambridge University Press, 1966.

Parsons, Timothy, 'All *Askaris* are Family Men: Sex, Domesticity and Discipline in the King's African Rifles, 1902–1964', in David Killingray and David Omissi (eds), *Guardians of Empire: The Armed Forces of the Colonial Powers c. 1700–1964*, Manchester/New York: Manchester University Press, 1999, pp. 157–78.

Peers, Douglas M., 'Sepoys, Soldiers and the Lash: Race, Caste and Army Discipline in India, 1820–50', *Journal of Imperial and Commonwealth History*, 23(2), 1995., pp. 211–47.

Ray, Rajat Kanta, 'Race, Religion and Realm: The Political Theory of "The Reigning Indian Crusade", 1857', in Mushirul Hasan and Narayani Gupta (eds), *India's Colonial Encounter: Essays in Honour of Eric Stokes*, New Delhi: Manohar, 1993, pp. 205–54.

Roy, Kaushik, 'Coercion through Leniency: British Manipulation of the Courts-Martial System in the Post-Mutiny Indian Army, 1859–1913', *Journal of Military History*, 65(4), 2001, pp. 937–64.

——, 'Logistics and the Construction of Loyalty: The Welfare Mechanism in the Indian Army, 1859–1913', in P. S. Gupta and A. Deshpande (eds), *The British Raj and its Indian Armed Forces, 1857–1939*, New Delhi: Oxford University Press, 2002, pp. 98–124.

——, 'Spare the Rod, Spoil the Soldier? Crime and Punishment in the Army of India, 1860–1913', *Journal of the Society for Army Historical Research*, 84(337), 2006, pp. 9–33.

Roy, Tapti, 'Visions of the Rebels: A Study of 1857 in Bundelkhand', *Modern Asian Studies*, 27(1), 1993, pp. 205–28.

——, *The Politics of a Popular Uprising: Bundelkhand in 1857*, New Delhi: Oxford University Press, 1994.

Sen, Surendranath, *Eighteen Fifty-Seven*, 1957; reprint, New Delhi: Publications Division, 1995.

Spector, Ronald, 'The Royal Indian Navy Strike of 1946: A Study of Cohesion and Disintegration in Colonial Armed Forces', *Armed Forces and Society*, 7(2), 1981, pp. 271–83.

Stanley, Peter, '"Dear Comrades": Barrack Room Culture and the "White Mutiny" of 1859–60', *Indo-British Review*, 21(2), 1996, pp. 165–75.

Stokes, Eric, 'Rural Revolt in the Great Rebellion of 1857 in India: A Study of the Saharanpur and Muzaffarnagar Districts', *Historical Journal*, 12(4), 1969, pp. 606–26.

——, *The Peasant and the Raj: Studies in Agrarian Society and Peasant Rebellion in Colonial India*, Cambridge: Cambridge University Press, 1978.

——, *The Peasant Armed: The Indian Revolt of 1857*, edited by C. A. Bayly, Oxford: Clarendon Press, 1986.

Sundaram, Chandar S., 'Soldier Disaffection and the Creation of the Indian National Army', *Indo-British Review*, 18(1), 1990, pp. 155–62.

HISTORIOGRAPHY

Black, Jeremy, *Rethinking Military History*, London/New York: Routledge, 2004.

Clarke, Jeffrey J., 'World Military History, 1786–1945', in John E. Jessup, Jr. and Robert W. Coakley (eds), *A Guide to the Study and Use of Military History*, Washington D.C.: Center of Military History, 1982, pp. 117–50.

Foucault, Michel, *Politics, Philosophy, Culture: Interviews and Other Writings, 1977–84*, translated by Alan Sheridan and others, edited with an Introduction by Lawrence D. Kritzman, 1988; reprint, New York/London: Routledge, 1990.

Kaegi, Walter Emil, Jr., 'The Crisis in Military Historiography', *Armed Forces and Society*, 7(2), 1981, pp. 299–316.

Keegan, John, *The Face of Battle: A Study of Agincourt, Waterloo and the Somme*, 1976; reprint, Harmondsworth, Middlesex: Penguin, 1978.

Matloff, Maurice, 'The Nature of History', in John E. Jessup, Jr. and Robert W. Coakley (eds), *A Guide to the Study and Use of Military History*, Washington DC: Center of Military History, 1982, pp. 3–24.

Metcalf, Thomas R., 'Introduction', in *Forging the Raj: Essays on British India in the Heyday of Empire*, New Delhi: Oxford University Press, 2005, pp. 1–21.

Paret, Peter, *Understanding War: Essays on Clausewitz and the History of Military Power*, Princeton: Princeton University Press, 1992.

Roy, Kaushik, 'The Historiography of the Colonial Indian Army', *Studies in History*, New Series, 12(2), 1996, pp. 255–73.

——, 'Beyond the Martial Race Theory: A Historiographical Assessment of Recruitment in the British-Indian Army', *Calcutta Historical Review*, vols 21–2 combined, 1999–2000, pp. 139–54.

——, 'Mars in Indian History', *Studies in History*, New Series, 16(2), 2002, pp. 261–75.

Subrahmanyam, Sanjay, *Explorations in Connected History: Mughals and Franks*, New Delhi: Oxford University Press, 2005.

Votaw, Lieutenant Colonel John F., 'An Approach to the Study of Military History', in John E. Jessup, Jr. and Robert W. Coakley (eds), *A Guide to the Study and Use of Military History*, Washington DC: Center of Military History, 1982, pp. 41–56.

Military Culture and Society

Alavi, Seema, *The Sepoys and the Company: Tradition and Transition in Northern India*, New Delhi: Oxford University Press, 1995.

Andreski, Stanislav, *Military Organization and Society*, 1954; reprint, Berkeley: University of California Press, 1968.

Ashworth, Tony, *Trench Warfare 1914–18: The Live and Let Live System*, 1980; reprint, London: Pan, 2000.

Banskota, Purushottam, *The Gurkha Connection: A History of the Gurkha Recruitment in the British Indian Army*, New Delhi: Nirala, 1994.

Barkawi, Tarak, 'Peoples, Homelands, and Wars? Ethnicity, the Military, and Battle among British Imperial Forces in the War against Japan', *Comparative Studies in Society and History*, 46(1), 2004, pp. 134–63.

Barstow, A. E., *Recruiting Handbooks for the Indian Army: The Sikhs*, 1928; reprint, Delhi: Low Price Publications, 1993.

Barua, Pradeep P., 'Inventing Race: The British and India's Martial Races', *Historian*, 58(1), 1995, pp. 107–16.

Bingley, Captain A. H., *Handbook on Rajputs*, 1899; reprint, Delhi: Low Price Publications, 1999.

Cameron, Craig M., *American Samurai: Myth, Imagination and the Conduct of Battle in the First Marine Division, 1941–51*, Cambridge: Cambridge University Press, 1994.

Caplan, Lionel, '"Bravest of the Brave": Representations of "The Gurkhas" in British Military Writings', *Modern Asian Studies*, 25(3), 1991, pp. 571–97.

——, *Warrior Gentleman: 'Gurkhas' in Western Imagination*, Providence/Oxford: Berghahn Books, 1995.

Cohen, Stephen P., 'The Untouchable Soldier: Caste, Politics, and the Indian Army', *Journal of Asian Studies*, 28(3), 1969, pp. 453–68.

Constable, Philip, 'The Marginalization of a Dalit Martial Race in Late Nineteenth and Early Twentieth Century Western India', *Journal of Asian Studies*, 60(2), 2001, pp. 439–78.

Des Chene, Mary, 'Soldiers, Sovereignty and Silences: Gorkhas as Diplomatic Currency', *South Asia Bulletin*, 13(1-2), (1993), pp. 67–80.

——, 'Military Ethnology in British India', *South Asia Research*, 19(2), 1999, pp. 121–35.

Dodwell, Henry, *Sepoy Recruitment in the Old Madras Army*, Calcutta: Superintendent Government Printing, 1922.

Ellinwood, DeWitt C., 'A Rajput Aristocrat in Imperial Service: Ambiguous Relationships', *Indo-British Review*, 15(2), 1988, pp. 91–101.

——, *Between Two Worlds: A Rajput Officer in the Indian Army, 1905–21, Based on the Diary of Amar Singh of Jaipur*, Lanham, Boulder: Hamilton, 2005.

Enloe, Cynthia H., 'Ethnicity in the Evolution of Asia's Armed Bureaucracies', in DeWitt C. Ellinwood and Cynthia H. Enloe (eds), *Ethnicity and the Military in Asia*, New Brunswick/London: Transaction Books, 1981, pp. 1–14.

Fields, Lanny Bruce, 'Ethnicity in Tso Tsung-T'ang's Armies: The Campaigns in North West China, 1867–80', in DeWitt C. Ellinwood and Cynthia H. Enloe (eds), *Ethnicity and the Military in Asia*, New Brunswick/London: Transaction Books, 1981, pp. 53–88.

Gooch, John, 'Attitudes to War in Late Victorian and Edwardian England', in Brian Bond and Ian Roy (eds), *War and Society: A Yearbook of Military History*, New York: Croom Helm, 1975, pp. 88–102.

Guha, Sumit, 'Nutrition, Sanitation, Hygiene, and the Likelihood of Death: The British Army in India *c.* 1870–1920', *Population Studies*, vol. 47, 1993, pp. 385–401.

Hanson, Victor Davis, *Carnage and Culture: Landmark Battles in the Rise of Western Power*, New York: Doubleday, 2001.

Heaton, William R., 'The Chinese People's Liberation Army and Minority Nationalities', in DeWitt C. Ellinwood and Cynthia H. Enloe (eds), *Ethnicity and the Military in Asia*, New Brunswick/London: Transaction Books, 1981, pp. 176–92.

Hills, Carol and Daniel C. Silverman, 'Nationalism and Feminism in Late Colonial India: The Rani of Jhansi Regiment, 1943–45', *Modern Asian Studies*, 27(4), 1993, pp. 741–60.

Hobsbawm, Eric and Terence Ranger (eds), *The Invention of Tradition*, Cambridge: Cambridge University Press, 1983.

Holmes, Richard, *Sahib: The British Soldier in India, 1750–1914*, London: Harper Collins, 2005.

Hoover, James W., 'The Recruitment of the Bengal Army: Beyond the Myth of the Zemindar's Son', *Indo-British Review*, 21(2), 1996, pp. 144–56.

Kaul, Vivien A., 'Sepoys' Links with Society: A Study of the Bengal Army, 1858–95', in P. S. Gupta and A. Deshpande (eds), *The British Raj and its*

Indian Armed Forces: 1857–1939, New Delhi: Oxford University Press, 2002, pp. 125–78.

Keegan, John, 'Inventing Military Traditions', in Chris Wrigley (ed.), *Warfare, Diplomacy and Politics: Essays in Honour of A. J. P. Taylor*, London: Hamish Hamilton, 1986, pp. 58–79.

Killingray, David, 'Gender Issues and African Colonial Armies', in David Killingray and David Omissi (eds), *Guardians of Empire: The Armed Forces of the Colonial Powers c. 1700–1964*, Manchester/New York: Manchester University Press, 1999, pp. 221–48.

Kolff, Dirk H. A., *Naukar, Rajput and Sepoy: The Ethnohistory of the Military Labour Market in Hindustan, 1450–1850*, Cambridge: Cambridge University Press, 1990.

Lynn, John A., *Battle: A History of Combat and Culture from Ancient Greece to Modern America*, Boulder, Colorado: Westview, 2003.

MacMunn, G. F., *The Armies of India*, London: A&C Black, 1911.

——, *The Martial Races of India*, London: Sampson Low, 1935.

Mason, Philip, *A Matter of Honour: An Account of the Indian Army, Its Officers and Men*, 1974; reprint, Dehra Dun: EBD Publications, 1988.

Metcalf, Thomas R., 'Sikh Recruitment for Colonial Military and Police Forces, 1874–1914', in Thomas R. Metcalf, *Forging the Raj: Essays on British India in the Heyday of Empire*, New Delhi: Oxford University Press, 2005, pp. 250–81.

de Moor, Jaap, 'The Recruitment of Indonesian Soldiers for the Dutch Colonial Army, c. 1700–1950', in David Killingray and David Omissi (eds), *Guardians of Empire: The Armed Forces of the Colonial Powers c. 1700–1964*, Manchester/New York: Manchester University Press, 1999, pp. 53–69.

Morris, Major C. J., *The Gurkhas: An Ethnology*, 1933; reprint, New Delhi: Low Price Publications, 1993.

Omissi, David, '"Martial Races": Ethnicity and Security in Colonial India, 1858–1939', *War and Society*, 9(1), 1991, pp. 1–27.

——, *The Sepoy and the Raj: The Indian Army, 1860–1940*, Houndmills, Basingstoke: Macmillan, 1994.

Peers, Douglas M., 'Colonial Knowledge and the Military in India, 1780–1860', *Journal of Imperial and Commonwealth History*, 33(2), 2005, pp. 157–80.

Rosen, Stephen P., *Societies and Military Power: India and its Armies*, New Delhi: Oxford University Press, 1996.

Roy, Kaushik, 'Recruitment Doctrines of the Colonial Indian Army, 1859–1913', *Indian Economic and Social History Review*, 34(3), 1997, pp. 321–54.

——, 'The Construction of Regiments in the Indian Army: 1859–1913', *War in History*, 8(2), 2001, pp. 127–48.

——, 'Recruiting for the Leviathan: Regimental Recruitment in the British-Indian Army, 1859–1913', *Calcutta Historical Journal*, 23–4 (2001–4), pp. 59–81.

Rudolph, Susanne Hoeber and Lloyd I. Rudolph, 'Becoming a Diarist: Amar Singh's Construction of an Indian Personal Document', *Indian Economic and Social History Review*, 25(2), 1988, pp. 113–32.

Rudolph, Susanne Hoeber, and Lloyd I. Rudolph, with Mohan Singh Kanota, *Reversing the Gaze: Amar Singh's Diary as Narrative of Imperial India*, New Delhi: Oxford University Press, 2000.

Stanley, Peter, *The White Mutiny: British Military Culture in India*, London: C. Hurst & Co., 1998.

Streets, Heather, *Martial Races: The Military, Race and Masculinity in British Imperial Culture, 1857–1914*, Manchester/New York: Manchester University Press, 2004.

Sundaram, Chandar S., '"Martial" Indian Aristocrats and the Military System of the Raj: The Imperial Cadet Corps, 1900–1914', *Journal of Imperial and Commonwealth History*, 25(3), 1997, pp. 415–39.

——, 'Reviving a "Dead Letter": Military Indianization and the Ideology of Anglo-India, 1885–1891', in P. S. Gupta and A. Deshpande (eds), *The British Raj and its Indian Armed Forces, 1857–1939*, New Delhi: Oxford University Press, 2002, pp. 45–97.

Vansittart, Lieutenant Colonel Eden, *Gurkhas: Handbooks on the Indian Army Compiled under the Orders of the Government of India*, 1906; reprint, New Delhi: Asian Educational Service, 1991.

Wickremesekera, Channa, *'Best Black Troops in the World': British Perceptions and the Making of the Sepoy, 1746–1805*, New Delhi: Manohar, 2002.

Yong, Tan Tai, 'Sepoys and the Colonial State: Punjab and the Military Base of the Indian Army, 1849–1900', in P. S. Gupta and A. Deshpande (eds), *The British Raj and its Indian Armed Forces, 1857–1939*, New Delhi: Oxford University Press, 2002, pp. 7–44.

MILITARY TECHNOLOGY

Harding, David, 'Arming the East India Company's Forces', in Alan J. Guy and Peter B. Boyden (eds), *Soldiers of the Raj: The Indian Army, 1600–1947*, London: National Army Museum, 1997, pp. 138–47.

Headrick, Daniel R., *The Tools of Empire: Technology and European Imperialism in the Nineteenth Century*, New York: Oxford University Press, 1981.

Moreman, T. R., 'The Arms Trade and the North-West Frontier Pathan Tribes, 1890–1914', *Journal of Imperial and Commonwealth History*, 22(2), 1994, pp. 187–216.

Parry, V. J. and M. E. Yapp, 'Introduction', in V .J. Parry and M. E. Yapp (eds), *War, Technology and Society in the Middle East*, London: Oxford University Press, 1975, pp. 1–31.

Roy, Kaushik, 'Company Bahadur Against the Pandies: The Military Dimension of 1857 Revisited', *Jadavpur University Journal of History*, 19(2001–2), pp. 25–47.

——, 'Equipping Leviathan: Ordnance Factories of British India: 1859–1913', *War in History*, 10(4), 2003, pp. 398–423.

——, 'Firepower-centric Warfare in India and the Military Modernization of the Marathas: 1740–1818', *Indian Journal of History of Science*, 40(4), 2005, pp. 597–634.

Operational Studies

Allen, Charles, *Soldier Sahibs: The Men who made the North West Frontier*, London: John Murray, 2000.

Allen, Louis, *Burma: The Longest War, 1941–1945*, 1984; reprint, London: Phoenix, 2002.

Barua, Pradeep P., *The State at War in South Asia*, Lincoln/London: University of Nebraska Press, 2005.

Carver, Lord, *Dilemmas of the Desert War: A New Look at the Libyan Campaign 1940–42*, Bloomington, Indianapolis: Indiana University Press, 1986.

Corrigan, Gordon, *Sepoys in the Trenches: The Indian Corps on the Western Front, 1914–15*, Staplehurst, Kent: Spellmount, 1999.

Evans, Colonel R., *A Brief Outline of the Campaign in Mesopotamia: 1914–18*, 1926; reprint, London: Sifton Praed, 1935.

Greenhut, Jeffrey, 'The Imperial Reserve: The Indian Corps on the Western Front, 1914–15', *Journal of Imperial and Commonwealth History*, 12(1), 1983, pp. 54–73.

Kirby, S. W., *The War against Japan*, vol. 1, London: HMSO, 1957.

Latimer, John, *Burma: The Forgotten War*, 2004; reprint, London: Headline, 2005.

Latter, Edwin, 'The Indian Army in Mesopotamia, 1914–18', Part II, *Journal of the Society for Army Historical Research*, LXXII(291), 1994, pp. 160–79.

Linn, Brian McAllister, 'Cerebrus' Dilemma: The US Army and Internal Security in the Pacific, 1902–40', in David Killingray and David Omissi (eds), *Guardians of Empire: The Armed Forces of the Colonial Powers c. 1700–1964*, Manchester/New York: Manchester University Press, 1999, pp. 114–36.

Marston, Daniel P., *Phoenix from the Ashes: The Indian Army in Burma Campaign*, Westport, Connecticut/London: Praeger, 2003.

Menezes, Lieutenant General S. L., *Fidelity and Honour: The Indian Army from the Seventeenth to the Twenty-First Century*, New Delhi: Viking, 1993.

Moberly, Brigadier General F. J., *History of the Great War based on Official Documents: The Campaign in Mesopotamia, 1914–18*, vol. 1, London: HMSO, 1923.

Moreman, T. R., '"Small Wars" and "Imperial Policing": The British Army and the Theory and Practice of Colonial Warfare in the British Empire, 1919–39', *Journal of Strategic Studies*, 19(4), 1996, pp. 105–31.

——, *The Army in India and the Development of Frontier Warfare 1849–1947*, London: Macmillan, 1998.

——, '"Watch and Ward": The Army in India and the North West Frontier, 1920–39', in David Killingray and David Omissi (eds), *Guardians of Empire: The Armed Forces of the Colonial Powers c. 1700–1964*, Manchester/New York: Manchester University Press, 1999, pp. 137–56.

Pillai, E. K. K., *The Campaigns in the Western Theatre*, New Delhi: Combined Inter-Services Historical Section, 1958.

Skeen, Andrew, *Passing it On: Short Talks on Tribal Fighting on the North-West Frontier of India*, Aldershot: Gale and Polden, 1932.

Smith, Joseph, 'The Spanish-American War: Land Battles in Cuba, 1895–98', *Journal of Strategic Studies*, 19(4), 1996, pp. 37–58.

Warren, Alan, '"Bullocks Treading down Wasps"? The British Indian Army in Waziristan in the 1930s', *South Asia*, 19(2), 1996, pp. 35–56.

——, *Waziristan: The Faqir of Ipi and the Indian Army, The North West Frontier Revolt of 1936–7*, Karachi: Oxford University Press, 2000.

——, 'The Indian Army and the Fall of Singapore', in B. Farrell and S. Hunter (eds), *Sixty Years On: the Fall of Singapore Revisited*, 2002; reprint, Singapore: Eastern Universities Press, 2003, pp. 207–89.

Wilson, W. J., *History of the Madras Army*, vol. 3, Madras: Government Press, 1883.

Professionalism in the Armed Forces

Anderson, Duncan, 'Field-Marshal Lord Slim', in John Keegan (ed.), *Churchill's Generals*, 1991; reprint, London: Warner Books, 1993, pp. 298–322.

Barr, Ronald J., 'High Command in the United States: The Emergence of a Modern System, 1898–1920', in G. D. Sheffield (ed.), *Leadership and Command: The Anglo-American Military Experience Since 1861*, London/Washington: Brassey's, 1997, pp. 57–76.

Barua, Pradeep P., *The Army Officer Corps and Military Modernization in Later Colonial India*, Hull: The University of Hull Press, 1999.

Beckett, Ian F. W., 'Command in the Late Victorian Army', in G. D. Sheffield (ed.), *Leadership and Command: The Anglo-American Military Experience Since 1861*, London/Washington: Brassey's, 1997, pp. 37–56.

Bourne, J. M., 'British Generals in the First World War' in G. D. Sheffield (ed.), *Leadership and Command: The Anglo-American Military Experience Since 1861*, London/Washington: Brassey's, 1997, pp. 93–116.

Crowell, Lorenzo M., 'Military in a Colonial Context; The Madras Army, circa 1832', *Modern Asian Studies*, 24(2), 1990, pp. 249–72.

——, 'Logistics in the Madras Army *circa* 1830', *War and Society*, 10(2), 1992, pp. 1–33.

Dawson III, Joseph G., '"Zealous for Annexation": Volunteer Soldiering, Military Government, and the Service of Colonel Alexander Doniphan in the Mexican-American War', *Journal of Strategic Studies*, 19(4), 1996, pp. 10–36.

Gupta, Narayani, 'Military Security and Urban Development: A Case Study of Delhi, 1857–1912', *Modern Asian Studies*, 5(1), 1971, pp. 61–77.

Gupta, P. S., 'The Debate on Indianization, 1918–1939', in P. S. Gupta and A. Deshpande (eds), *The British Raj and its Indian Armed Forces: 1857–1947*, New Delhi: Oxford University Press, 2002, pp. 228–69.

Heathcote, T. A., *The Military in British India: The Development of British Land Forces in South Asia, 1600–1947*, Manchester: Manchester University Press, 1995.

Huntington, Samuel, *The Soldier and the State: The Theory and Politics of Civil-Military Relations*, Cambridge, Harvard University Press, 1957.

Kinvig, Clifford, 'General Percival and the Fall of Singapore', in Brian Farrell and Sandy Hunter (eds), *Sixty Years On: The Fall of Singapore Revisited*, 2002; reprint, Singapore: Eastern Universities Press, 2003, pp. 270–89.

Moreman, T. R., 'Lord Kitchener, the General Staff and the Army in India, 1902–14', in David French and Brian Holden Reid (eds), *The British General Staff: Reform and Innovation 1890–1939*, London: Frank Cass, 2002, pp. 57–74.

Peers, Douglas M., 'Between Mars and Mammon: The East India Company and Efforts to Reform its Army, 1796–1832', *The Historical Journal*, 33(2), 1990, pp. 385–401.

——, 'The Habitual Nobility of Being: British Officers and the Social Construction of the Bengal Army in the Early Nineteenth Century', *Modern Asian Studies*, 25(3), 1991, pp. 545–69.

——, *Between Mars and Mammon: Colonial Armies and the Garrison State in Early Nineteenth Century India, 1819–1835*, London: I. B. Tauris, 1995.

——, 'Imperial Vice: Sex, Drink and the Health of British Troops in North India Cantonments, 1800–1858', in David Killingray and David Omissi (eds), *Guardians of Empire: The Armed Forces of the Colonial Powers c. 1700–1964*, Manchester/New York: Manchester University Press, 1999, pp. 25–52.

Raugh, Harold E., Jr., 'Training Ground for a Future Field Marshall: Wavell in the Boer War and Edwardian India, 1900–1908', *Journal of the Society for Army Historical Research*, 72(289), 1994, pp. 8–18.

Razzell, P. E., 'Social Origins of Officers in the Indian and British Home Army: 1758–1962', *British Journal of Sociology*, vol. 14, 1963, pp. 248–60.

Roy, Kaushik, 'Feeding the Leviathan: Supplying the British-Indian Army, 1859–1913', *Journal of the Society for Army Historical Research*, 80(322), 2002, pp. 144–61.

Sundaram, C. S., 'Preventing Idleness: The Maharaja of Cooch Behar's Proposal for Officer Commissions in the British Army for the Sons of Indian Princes and Gentlemen, 1897–1898', *South Asia*, new series, 18(1), 1995, pp. 115–30.

——, 'Martial Indian Aristocrats and the Military System of the Raj: The Imperial Cadet Corps, 1900–14', *Journal of Imperial and Commonwealth History*, 25(3), 1997, pp. 415–39.

——, 'Reviving a Dead Letter: Military Indianization and the Ideology of Anglo-India, 1885–1891', in P. S. Gupta and A. Deshpande (eds), *The British Raj and its Indian Armed Forces: 1857–1947*, New Delhi: Oxford University Press, 2002, pp. 45–97.

Regimental Histories

Betham, Lieutenant Colonel Geoffrey and Major H. V. R. Geary, *The Golden Galley: The Story of the Second Punjab Regiment, 1761–1947*; reprint, New Delhi: Allied, 1975.

Cardew, Lieutenant F. G., *A Sketch of the Services of the Bengal Native Army to the Year 1895*, 1903; reprint, New Delhi: Today and Tomorrow's Printers & Publishers, 1971.

Gaylor, John, *Sons of John Company: The Indian and Pakistani Armies, 1903–91*, New Delhi: Lancer, 1993.

Khanduri, Brigadier Chandra B., *The History of the First Gorkha Rifles: The Malaun Regiment*, vol. 3, *1947–1990*, New Delhi: Vanity Press, 1992.

Pythian-Adams, G., *The Madras Regiment: 1758–1958*, Wellington: Defence Services Staff College, 1958.

Simon, Lieutenant Colonel Rufus, *Their Formative Years: History of the Corps of Electrical and Mechanical Engineers*, vol. 1, New Delhi: Vikas, 1977.

Total War and the Colonial State

Allen, Louis, 'The Campaigns in Asia and the Pacific', in John Gooch (ed.), *Decisive Campaigns of the Second World War*, London: Frank Cass, 1990, pp. 162–92.

Barua, Pradeep P., 'Strategies and Doctrines of Imperial Defence: Britain and India, 1919–45', *Journal of Imperial and Commonwealth History*, 25(2), 1997, pp. 240–66.

Bayly, Christopher and Tim Harper, *Forgotten Armies: The Fall of British Asia, 1941–45*, London: Allen Lane, 2004.

Bhattacharya, Sanjoy, 'British Military Information Management Techniques and the South Asian Soldier: Eastern India during the Second World War', *Modern Asian Studies*, 34(2), 2000, pp. 483–570.

——, *Propaganda and Information in Eastern India 1939–45: A Necessary Weapon of War*, Richmond, Surrey: Curzon, 2001.

Bond, Brian, *British Military Policy between the Two World Wars*, Oxford: Clarendon Press, 1980.

——, *War and Society in Europe: 1870–1970*, 1984; reprint, Phoenix Mill, Thrupp: Sutton, 1998.

Chickering, Roger and Stig Forster, 'Are We there Yet? World War II and the Theory of Total War', in Chickering, Forster and Bernd Greiner (eds), *A World at Total War: Global Conflict and the Politics of Destruction, 1937–45*, Cambridge: Cambridge University Press, 2005, pp. 1–16.

Cooter, Roger and Steve Sturdy, 'Introduction', in Roger Cooter, Steve Sturdy, and Mark Harrison (eds), *War, Medicine and Modernity*, Phoenix Mill, Thrupp: Sutton, 1998, pp. 1–21.

Corr, Gerrard H., *War of the Springing Tigers*, London: Osprey, 1975.

Deshpande, Anirudh, 'Hopes and Disillusionment: Recruitment, Demobilization and the Emergence of Discontent in the Indian Armed Forces after the Second World War', *Indian Economic and Social History Review*, 33(2), 1996, pp. 175–207.

Deshpande, Anirudh, *British Military Policy in India, 1900–1945: Colonial Constraints and Declining Power*, New Delhi: Manohar, 2005.

Dewey, Clive, 'Some Consequences of Military Expenditure in British India: The Case of Upper Sind Sagar Doab, 1849–1947', in Clive Dewey (ed.), *Arrested Development in India: The Historical Dimension*, New Delhi: Manohar, 1988, pp. 93–169.

Ellinwood, DeWitt C., 'An Historical Study of the Punjabi Soldier in World War I', in Harbans Singh and N. Gerald Barrier (eds), *Punjab Past and Present: Essays in Honour of Dr. Ganda Singh*, Patiala: Panjab University Press, 1976, pp. 337–62.

——, 'The Indian Soldier, the Indian Army, and Change, 1914–18', in DeWitt C. Ellinwood and S. D. Pradhan (eds), *India and World War I*, New Delhi: Manohar, 1978, pp. 177–211.

——, 'Ethnicity in a Colonial Asian Army: British Policy, War and the Indian Army, 1914–18', in DeWitt C. Ellinwood and Cynthia H. Enloe (eds), *Ethnicity and the Military in Asia*, New Brunswick/London: Transaction Books, 1981, pp. 89–143.

Fay, Peter Ward, *The Forgotten Army: India's Armed Struggle for Independence, 1942–1945*, New Delhi: Rupa, 1994.

Furedi, Frank, 'The Demobilized African Soldier and the Blow to White Prestige', in David Killingray and David Omissi (eds), *Guardians of Empire: The Armed Forces of the Colonial Powers c. 1700–1964*, Manchester/New York: Manchester University Press, 1999, pp. 179–97.

Gallagher, John and Anil Seal, 'Britain and India between the Wars', *Modern Asian Studies*, 15(3), 1981, pp. 387–414.

Ghosh, Kalyan Kumar, *The Indian National Army: Second Front of the Indian Independence Movement*, Meerut: Meenakshi Prakashan, 1969.

Gupta, P. S., 'The Army, Politics and Constitutional Change in India, 1919–39', in P. S. Gupta, *Power, Politics and the People: Studies in British Imperialism and Indian Nationalism*, New Delhi: Permanent Black, 2001, pp. 219–39.

——, 'Imperial Strategy and the Transfer of Power, 1939–51', in P. S. Gupta, *Power, Politics and the People: Studies in British Imperialism and Indian Nationalism*, New Delhi: Permanent Black, 2001, pp. 240–307.

——, 'India in Commonwealth Defence, 1947–56', in P. S. Gupta, *Power, Politics and the People: Studies in British Imperialism and Indian Nationalism*, New Delhi: Permanent Black, 2001, pp. 308–22.

Gutteridge, William, 'The Indianization of the Indian Army: 1918–45', *Race*, 4(2), 1963, pp. 39–48.

Harrison, Mark, 'Medicine and the Management of Modern Warfare', *History of Science*, part 4, 34(106), 1996, pp. 379–410.

——, *Medicine and Victory: British Military Medicine in the Second World War*, Oxford: Clarendon Press, 2004.

Howard, Michael, 'Total War in the Twentieth Century: Participation and Consensus in the Second World War', in Brian Bond and Ian Roy (eds), *War and Society: A Yearbook of Military History*, New York: Croom Helm, 1975, pp. 216–26.

Indian Voices of the Great War: Soldiers' Letters, 1914–18, Selected and Introduced by David Omissi, Houndmills, Basingstoke: Macmillan, 1999.

Jeffery, Keith, '"An English Barrack in the Oriental Seas"? India in the Aftermath of the First World War', *Modern Asian Studies*, 15(3), 1981, pp. 369–86.

——, 'The Eastern Arc of Empire: A Strategic View, 1850–1950', *Journal of Strategic Studies*, 5(4), 1982, pp. 531–45.

——, *The British Army and the Crisis of Empire, 1918–1922*, Manchester: Manchester University Press, 1984.

Jeffrey, Robin, 'The Punjab Boundary Force and the Problem of Order, August 1947', *Modern Asian Studies*, 8(4), 1974, pp. 491–520.

Kamtekar, Indivar, 'A Different War Dance: State and Class in India, 1939–45', *Past and Present*, no. 176, August 2002, pp. 187–221.

Kudaisya, Gyanesh, '"In Aid of Civil Power": The Colonial Army in Northern India, *c.* 1919–42', *Journal of Imperial and Commonwealth History*, 32(1), 2004, pp. 41–68.

Lebra, Joyce, *Jungle Alliance: Japan and the Indian National Army*, Singapore: Asia Pacific Press, 1971.

Mazumder, Rajit K., 'Military Imperatives and the Expansion of Agriculture in Colonial Punjab', *International Journal of Punjab Studies*, 8(2), 2001, pp. 157–85.

——, *The Indian Army and the Making of Punjab*, New Delhi: Permanent Black, 2003.

Modak, Captain G. V., *Indian Defence Problem*, Poona: Privately published, 1933.

Palit, Major General D. K., 'Indianization: A Personal Experience', *Indo-British Review*, 16(1), 1989, pp. 59–64.

Perry, F. W., *The Commonwealth Armies: Manpower and Organization in two World Wars*, Manchester: Manchester University Press, 1988.

Pradhan, S. D., 'Organization of the Indian Army on the Eve of the Outbreak of the First World War', *Journal of the United Service Institution of India*, 102(426), 1972, pp. 61–78.

——, 'The Indian Army and the First World War', in S. D. Pradhan and DeWitt Ellinwood (eds), *India and World War I*, New Delhi: Manohar, 1978, pp. 49–67.

Prasad, B. (ed.), *Official History of the Indian Armed Forces in the Second World War, 1939–1945: India and the War*, New Delhi: Combined Inter-Services Historical Section, 1966.

Prasad, S. N., *Expansion of the Armed Forces and Defence Organization: 1939–1945*, New Delhi: Combined Inter-Services Historical Section, 1956.

Reddy, K. N., 'Indian Defence Expenditure: 1872–1967', *Indian Economic and Social History Review*, vol. 7, 1970, pp. 467–88.

Sharma, Gautam, *Nationalization of the Indian Army: 1885–1947*, New Delhi: Allied, 1996.

Singh, Mohan, *Soldiers' Contribution to Indian Independence*, New Delhi: Army Educational Stores, 1974.

Sundaram, Chandar S., 'A Paper Tiger: The Indian National Army in Battle, 1944–1945', *War and Society*, 13(1), 1995, pp. 35–59.

Thorne, C., 'The British Cause and Indian Nationalism in 1940: An Officer's Rejection of Empire', *Journal of Imperial and Commonwealth History* 10(3), 1982.

——, *The Far Eastern War: States and Societies 1941–45*, 1986; reprint, London: Counterpoint, Unwin Paperbacks.

Towle, Philip, 'The Debate on Wartime Censorship in Britain', in Brian Bond and Ian Roy (eds), *War and Society: A Yearbook of Military History*, New York: Croom Helm, 1975, pp. 103–12.

Toye, Hugh, 'The Indian National Army, 1941–45', *Indo-British Review*, 16(1), 1989, pp. 73–88.

Vankosi, Susan, 'Letters Home, 1915–16: Punjabi Soldiers Reflect on War and Life in Europe and their Meanings for Home and Self', *International Journal of Punjab Studies*, 2, 1995, pp. 43–63.

Voigt, Johannes H., *India in the Second World War*, New Delhi: Arnold-Heinemann, 1987.

Woods, Philip, '"Chappatis by Parachute": The Use of Newsreels in British Propaganda in India in the Second World War', *South Asia*, 23(2), 2000, pp. 89–109.

Yong, Tan Tai, 'Maintaining the Military Districts: Civil-Military Integration and District Soldiers Boards in the Punjab, 1919–39', *Modern Asian Studies*, 28(4), 1994, pp. 833–74.

——, 'An Imperial Home Front: Punjab and the First World War', *Journal of Military History*, 64(2), 2000, pp. 371–410.

——, 'Mobilization, Militarization and "Mal-Contentment": Punjab and the Second World War', *South Asia: Journal of South Asian Studies*, new series, 25(2), 2002, pp. 137–51.

——, *The Garrison State: The Military, Government and Society in Colonial Punjab, 1849–1947*, New Delhi: Sage, 2005.

Contributors

RAYMOND CALLAHAN is Professor of History and Associate Dean of the College of Arts and Sciences, University of Delaware, Newark, USA. At present, he is working on the Army in India's leadership.

LIONEL CAPLAN is Emeritus Professor at the Department of Anthropology, School of Oriental and African Studies, London. His *Warrior Gentleman: 'Gurkhas' in Western Imagination* (1995) portrays the evolution of Gurkha concept under the colonial regime.

STEPHEN P. COHEN is a Senior Fellow in the Foreign Policy Studies Program, Brookings Institution, Washington DC. Besides writing on strategic affairs of South Asia, Cohen has also written numerous articles on the Pakistan Army and the post-independence Indian Army. His two recent books are *India: Emerging Power* (2001) and *The Idea of Pakistan* (2004).

SABYASACHI DASGUPTA is a Junior Fellow at the Centre for Contemporary Studies, Nehru Memorial Museum and Library, New Delhi.

SAUL DAVID is a prolific writer on British military history. He appears frequently on the historical programmes of the BBC.

ANIRUDH DESHPANDE was previously a Fellow at the Centre for Contemporary Studies, Nehru Memorial Museum and Library. His recent publication includes *British Military Policy in India, 1900-1945: Colonial Constraints and Declining Power* (2005).

DEWITT C. ELLINWOOD was Professor of History, State University of New York, Albany. He has written numerous articles on the Indian Army during World War I. Recently he has also published a monograph on the military aspects of Amar Singh's diary, titled *Between Two Worlds: A Rajput Officer in the Indian Army, 1905–21.*

INDIVAR KAMTEKAR is Associate Professor at the Centre for Historical Studies, Jawaharlal Nehru University, New Delhi. His 'Shiver of 1942' in *Studies in History* opens up a new dimension in studying Indian nationalism.

TIM MOREMAN is an independent researcher. His PhD thesis on frontier warfare was published as *The Army in India and the Development of Frontier Warfare* (1998). His recent work deals with armies in Burma during the World War II.

RUDRANGSHU MUKHERJEE is Editor of Editorial Pages of *The Telegraph.* He taught at the University of Calcutta and held visiting appointments at Princeton University, University of Manchester, and University of California. He is the author of *Mangal Panday: Brave Martyr or Accidental Hero?* (2005) and the co-author of *India Then and Now* (2005).

KAUSHIK ROY is Lecturer at the Department of History in Presidency College, Kolkata. He is currently working on the Indian Armed Forces during World War II. His recent publications include *From Hydaspes to Kargil* (2004) and *India's Historic Battles: From Alexander to Kargil* (2004). He is also associated with Peace Research Institute of Oslo and United Nations University.

CHANDAR S. SUNDARAM at present is teaching in Hong Kong University and engaged in writing a general history on South Asian warfare.